THE HABSBURG CHANCERY LANGUAGE IN PERSPECTIVE

Maximilian in the chancery "dictating personally in various languages to a number of his secretaries at the same time." (Caption
and illustration from Der Weißkunig; woodcut by Hans Burgkmair.)

The Habsburg Chancery Language in Perspective

by Elaine C. Tennant

UNIVERSITY OF CALIFORNIA PRESS
Berkeley · Los Angeles · London

FOR GRACE O'CONNELL

UNIVERSITY OF CALIFORNIA PUBLICATIONS IN MODERN PHILOLOGY

Editorial Board: Samuel G. Armistead, Jean-Pierre Barricelli, Gerd Hillen, Harold E. Toliver, Andrew Wright

Volume 114

UNIVERSITY OF CALIFORNIA PRESS
BERKELEY AND LOS ANGELES, CALIFORNIA

UNIVERSITY OF CALIFORNIA PRESS, LTD.
LONDON, ENGLAND

ISBN 0-520-09694-0
LIBRARY OF CONGRESS CATALOG CARD NUMBER: 85-16482

Library of Congress Cataloging in Publication Data

Tennant, Elaine C.
    The Habsburg chancery language in perspective.

    (University of California publications in modern
philology ; v. 114)
    Bibliography:
    Includes index.
    1. German language--Historiography. 2. German
language--Middle High German, 1050-1500. 3. German
language--Early modern, 1500-1700. 4. Diplomatics--Holy
Roman Empire--Terminology. 5. Holy Roman Empire.
Reichshofkanzlei. I. Title. II. Series.
PF3055.T46 1986   430'.9'024   85-16482
ISBN 0-520-09694-0 (alk. paper)

Contents

Contents

CONCLUSION   205

Preface

The Habsburg chancery language between 1440 and 1519 has been a part of traditional accounts of the emergence of the German common language since histories of the German language began to appear in the eighteenth century. The reasons for its continued inclusion in such works are complicated, the justification debatable. Until recently the absence of pertinent linguistic and extralinguistic data exempted the Habsburg chancery language from the sort of reconsideration other factors in the development of the German Hochsprache have undergone repeatedly during the past fifty years. The following study is an attempt to revise the image of the chancery language of Maximilian I that now appears in standard histories of the German language. It falls in the realm of the history of linguistics or the historiography of the German language, not paleography or historical linguistics. During the past decade considerable new material on the subject has become available. It not only clarifies the role of the chancery dialect in the development of the German language, but it also sheds interesting light on the state of linguistic thinking in Renaissance Germany and on a variety of related circumstances that appear to have affected the way in which the German language was evolving at the turn of the sixteenth century.

In 1977 Hans Moser and I each investigated aspects of the Habsburg chancery language. Moser's meticulous graphemic study was intended to explain the involved administrative relationships of

Maximilian's chancery organization, characterize the scribal practice of the chancery, and provide legitimate source material for other investigations of the chancery language. It is the first significant contribution to the linguistic scholarship on the Habsburg chanceries to have been published since Friedrich Kluge's Von Luther bis Lessing appeared in 1888, and for the most part it achieves each of its aims admirably. My 1977 Harvard dissertation focused on the Habsburg chancery language as a commonplace in the history of the German language. It attempted to account for and evaluate what have become traditional claims about the chancery dialect and those who wrote it. Like Moser I worked from original chancery manuscripts. My corpus of sample texts, which was considerably smaller than his, was selected specifically to substantiate or refute the assertions that had been put forward in the standard handbooks and banner articles on the history of the German language rather than to provide a general characterization of the language based on a large cross section of documents for use in future studies. My research was successful to the extent that it cleared away some scholarly debris that had distorted the role of Maximilian's chancery dialect in the development of the German common language. It fell short of answering several of the questions it raised, however, because of the lack of specific historical evidence.

Since 1977 several new studies have appeared and several earlier ones have come to my attention that provide some of this missing information. They include Christa Kohlweg's 1978 Graz dissertation on Niclas Ziegler, Martin Wierschin's 1976 research on Hans Ried, and Herrad Spilling's 1978 essay on late medieval German writing masters, as well as R. E. Keller's treatment of Gemeines Deutsch in his 1978 history of the German language, recent research by Erich Straßner and Robert Ebert on educational techniques in late medieval Germany, and more recently Klaus Mattheier's 1981 essay concerning trends in research on the Early New High German (ENHG) written languages. Although these investigations do not solve all the remaining problems associated with the Habsburg chancery language, they do permit a substantial reassessment of its role in the history of the German language and of the sociolinguistic environment in which it was written.

To date the results of this recent research have not been combined with Moser's analysis of the chancery language to provide a more balanced picture of Maximilian's chancery dialect in the context of its linguistic and political history. In doing so I hope to eliminate some of the questions that have produced confusion in earlier accounts of the Habsburg language and to point up broader issues in ENHG scholarship that remain to be resolved in other investigations. Portions of the text are adapted from my dissertation and some material is included from my 1981 essay on Niclas Ziegler. For the most part I have adopted Hans Moser's description of the chancery language as developed in his monograph, although I have occasionally offered explanations more in accordance with the results of my own research for phenomena he identifies. For the convenience of the reader I have at many places in the text translated into English run-in quotations from original German sources. These and the other translations in the study are my own unless otherwise noted. In most cases the original text either follows the translation in parentheses or it appears in a note.

I am most grateful to the Austrian-American Educational Commission (Fulbright Commission) and to the Marion and Jasper Whiting Foundation for awarding me the fellowships that supported my initial research on the chancery of Maximilian I, and to the University of California at Berkeley for the Career Development and annual research grants that have allowed me to complete this manuscript. I could not have begun the manuscript work for the project without the gracious and expert assistance of the Maximilian research group at the University of Graz and the staffs of the Österreichisches Staatsarchiv and of the manuscript collection of the Österreichische Nationalbibliothek in Vienna, as well as that of the Tiroler Landesregierungsarchiv in Innsbruck. Most particularly, however, I wish to thank those individuals who have given to me so generously of their advice, skills, and resources so that I might develop some sense of Maximilian's chancery and its language—Professor Hermann Wiesflecker and his associates Drs. Ingeborg Friedhuber and Peter Krendl of the University of Graz, and Hofrat Anna Benna of the Österreiches Staatsarchiv.

Abbreviations

AAWien	Anzeiger der Akademie der Wissenschaften in Wien
ADA	Anzeiger für deutsches Altertum und deutsche Literatur
ADB	Allgemeine deutsche Biographie
AÖG	Archiv für österreichische Geschichte
ArchZ	Archivalische Zeitschrift
BGDSL	Beiträge zur Geschichte der deutschen Sprache und Literatur (Tübingen)
BGDSL (Halle)	Beiträge zur Geschichte der deutschen Sprache und Literatur (Halle)
BNGÖst	Beiträge zur neueren Geschichte Österreichs
CUG	Central Upper German
DLZ	Deutsche Literaturzeitung
DU	Der Deutschunterricht
DVLG	Deutsche Vierteljahrsschrift für Literaturwissenschaft und Geistesgeschichte
EMG	East Middle German
ENHG	Early New High German
EUG	East Upper German
GRM	Germanisch-romanische Monatsschrift
HHSA	Österreichisches Staatsarchiv, Vienna
HJb	Historisches Jahrbuch
JbKhS	Jahrbuch der kunsthistorischen Sammlungen des allerhöchsten Kaiserhauses
LG	Low German

MG	Middle German
MGS	Michigan Germanic Studies
MHG	Middle High German
MIÖG	Mitteilungen des Instituts für österreichische Geschichtsforschung
NHG	New High German
NumZ	Numismatische Zeitschrift
OHG	Old High German
SB	South Bavarian
SEG	Southeast German
TLA	Tiroler Landesregierungsarchiv, Innsbruck
UG	Upper German
VL	Die deutsche Literatur des Mittelalters: Verfasserlexikon
WA	Weimarer Ausgabe (Luther)
WMG	West Middle German
WMR	Wiesflecker Maximilian Regesta
WUG	West Upper German
WW	Wirkendes Wort
WZUJ	Wissenschaftliche Zeitschrift der Friedrich-Schiller-Universität Jena
ZDA	Zeitschrift für deutsches Altertum und deutsche Literatur
ZDP	Zeitschrift für deutsche Philologie
ZGL	Zeitschrift für germanistische Linguistik
ZMF	Zeitschrift für Mundartforschung
ZHVSteierm	Zeitschrift des historischen Vereins für Steiermark
ZVThürG	Zeitschrift des Vereins für thüringische Geschichte und Altertumskunde

INTRODUCTION

Since the nineteenth century the late medieval chancery languages have been a traditional part of accounts of the emergence of
the German common language. While various chanceries have for a time
been considered particularly significant in this development, only to
recede in importance as the orientations in research changed, the
chanceries of the Wettin Elector Frederick the Wise and the Habsburg
Emperor Maximilian I were considered influential from the outset and
have withstood most of the intervening vicissitudes of scholarship.
The general interest of the first generations of Germanic philologists
in chancery languages as well as the continuing reputation of these
two particular chanceries can be attributed directly to this much-
discussed statement of Martin Luther's:

> 'Ich habe keine gewisse, sonderliche, eigene Sprache im
> Deutschen, sondern brauche der gemeinen deutschen Sprache,
> daß mich beide, Ober- und Niederländer verstehen mögen.
> Ich rede nach der sächsischen Canzeley, welcher nachfol-
> gen alle Fürsten und Könige in Deutschland; alle Reichs-
> städte, Fürsten-Höfe schreiben nach der sächsischen und
> unsers Fürsten Canzeley, darum ists auch die gemeinste
> deutsche Sprache. Kaiser Maximilian, und Kurf. Friedrich,
> H. zu Sachsen etc. haben im römischen Reich die deutschen
> Sprachen also in eine gewisse Sprache gezogen.'[1]

No matter how the debates have raged over spoken versus written language, the transmission routes of chancery practices, linguistic
standards versus customs, the linguistic climate of sixteenth-century
Germany, and, not least of all, Luther's personal role in shaping the

1

German common language, the fact that Luther claims a chancery language as the basis for his own German and that he credits Frederick
the Wise and Maximilian with the unification of that language is
inescapable.

That Luther himself provides the riddle of the roles of the
Wettin and Habsburg chancery languages in the evolution of the German
common language accounts for both the continuing pursuit of these
questions by historians of the German language and the uneven manner
in which these scholars have pursued them. The earliest histories of
the German language both romanticized and politicized Luther's extra-
ordinary individual contribution to the development of the modern
German language. This resulted in a less than critical view of
Luther's own pronouncements on language and a great enthusiasm for the
investigation of the language of Luther's own works and of the East
Middle German (EMG) chancery he held up for emulation. The first wave
of Germanic philologists, who are to a great extent responsible for
setting the perimeters of ensuing investigations of the late medieval
German chancery languages, were for the most part North German Protes-
tants. They associated the New High German (NHG) language directly
and emotionally with the Reformation and with Martin Luther himself.
The following statement from the preface to the first edition of Jakob
Grimm's Deutsche Grammatik (1819) is illustrative of this attitude:

> Man darf das neuhochdeutsche in der that als den protes-
> tantischen dialect bezeichnen, dessen freiheitathmende
> natur längst schon, ihnen unbewusst, dichter und schrift-
> steller des katholischen glaubens überwältigte. Unsere
> sprache ist, nach dem unaufhaltbaren laufe aller dinge,
> in lautverhältnissen und formen gesunken, meine schilderung
> neuhochdeutscher buchstaben und flexionen durfte es nicht
> verhehlen sondern hervorheben; was aber ihren geist und
> leib genährt, verjüngt, was endlich blüthen neuer poesie
> getrieben hat, verdanken wir keinem mehr, als Luthern.[2]

The nineteenth-century linguists did not develop a similar
enthusiasm for investigating the second half of Luther's statement,
in which he credits Maximilian equally with his patron, the Saxon
Elector, with having shaped the language in which he worked. This is
easy to explain. Not only were these early philologists interested

primarily in the language of Luther, whose personal role in the emergence of the modern German language they rather misinterpreted, but
they were also interested in what eventually became the stock of the
modern common language. Because they could construe this to be essentially EMG without reference to the Habsburg chancery dialect, investigation of the Imperial chancery language was long neglected. Also,
Maximilian was a generation older than Luther and was dead before the
Reformation had its impact; thus his chancery language could only be
tangential to discussions of the "Reformation dialect." Nevertheless,
reference to the southern language could not be omitted altogether,
because Maximilian had been acclaimed by Luther himself.

Nor is Luther's mention of Maximilian the sole reason why
early histories of the German language did make some reference to the
Imperial chancery or that later ones continued the practice, even if
the descriptions were cursory by comparison with those of the Saxon
chancery. In his own lifetime Maximilian deliberately set out to
create for himself a legendary reputation that would survive him, and
he was remarkably successful in this effort. Long before his death
Maximilian had become the stuff of legend and rumor, and immediately
after his death he was added to the semimythical cadre of Germanic
chivalric figures upon which writers of history and fiction continue
to draw.[3] The attraction of so colorful a personality for linguistic
historians is understandable. Further, the very conditions under
which Maximilian's literary and propagandistic projects were executed
made his chancery a tempting subject for Germanic philologists. Not
only did the Emperor write German literature, but he also had his chancery scribes embellish, rework, and in some cases actually ghostwrite
his autobiographical works in the chancery itself. Superficially
these circumstances would appear to parallel those under which the
cultural languages of France, England, and the Netherlands developed.[4]
For these and other reasons the chancery of Maximilian I has been
assured a place in histories of the German language, particularly in
those focusing on the intellectual historical, the sociological, or
the extralinguistic aspects of the development of German.

But until very recently the place reserved in ENHG studies for
the Upper German (UG) chancery dialects as a group,[5] and for the Habsburg chancery language in particular, has been small not only in
proportion to the emphasis Luther places on Maximilian, but also to
the volume of production and the geographic reach of the southern
chanceries, particularly the Imperial chancery of the Habsburgs. Many
older investigations also fail to take into account the literary and
linguistic significance of Upper Germany during the immediately preceding Middle High German (MHG) period. This has been due in part, as
suggested above, to the genuine preference of earlier researchers for
ENHG subjects that could be related more or less directly to the
person and production of Martin Luther.

The more critical reason for the postponement of research on
the UG antecedents of Luther's language, however, was a mechanical
one. Until Hermann Wiesflecker accepted the commission of the Austrian
Academy of Sciences in 1948 to prepare the Regesta Imperii for the
period of Maximilian's reign,[6] physical access to the manuscripts of
the Habsburg chanceries from this period was most difficult, particularly for researchers whose primary discipline was not history. The
documents from Maximilian's reign number in the tens of thousands and
are scattered, essentially unindexed, in archives throughout Europe.
Only with the preparation of the Wiesflecker regesta (WMR) has it
become possible to design and locate valid manuscript samples on which
to base investigations of Maximilian's chancery language. To date
only Hans Moser in his 1977 monograph Die Kanzlei Kaiser Maximilians I.:
Graphematik eines Schreibusus,[7] and I, to a lesser extent, in my
Harvard dissertation of the same year, "The Habsburg Chancery Language
(1440-1519),"[8] have made the original manuscript production of Maximilian's chanceries the basis for a linguistic description of the
written dialect of the Habsburg chanceries at the turn of the sixteenth century. This means that traditional handbook accounts of
Maximilian's Imperial chancery language are all based either on the
available external historical material, on the sixteenth-century
printed literary texts that can be vaguely associated with Maximilian's

chancery,[9] or on the few Habsburg <u>Urkunden</u> available in nineteenth-
century editions, which are of doubtful use for graphemic, phonological, or orthographic investigations because of the transcriptional
conventions of the day.[10]

In his 1951 essay on approaches to the history of the German
language, Friedrich Maurer cited three orientations that under optimum
conditions combine to present a genuine picture of the language's
history.[11] The first, the "external history of the language" ("die
äußere Sprachgeschichte"), concerns itself with the development of the
language in space and time; it deals with its distribution and divi-
sions, with linguistic movements, with leveling, and with the language's historical role. Each of these aspects is considered in the
more general context of German history. The second approach examines
"the internal history of the language" ("die innere Sprachgeschichte")
and includes "the intellectual growth of the language, its internal
change, the emergence of its worldview" ("das geistige Wachsen der
Sprache, ihre innere Veränderung, das Werden ihres Weltbildes").
This more or less intellectual historical approach treats the language's response to a new corpus of ideas. The third possibility is
"the history of language structure or language type" ("die Geschichte
der Sprachstruktur oder des Sprachtypus"); it examines the phonological, morphological, and syntactic development of the language,
although it need not be so comprehensive as an historical grammar.

The great majority of histories of the German language are in
these terms "external" histories, and only recently have linguistic
historians begun to attempt the synthesis of methodological orientations suggested by Maurer more than thirty years ago.[12] With respect
to accounts of the Habsburg chancery language, this combination of
orientations has still to take place. The existing handbook descriptions are for the most part "externally" historical and are not based
on internal linguistic evidence. Moser's synchronic graphemic
analysis of Maximilian's chancery language, on the other hand, may be
considered with the histories of language structure or language type.
While it is perhaps just the beginning of a total description of the

written dialect (which might also treat the morphological, syntactic, lexical, and phonological aspects of the language as such), the graphemic study as it stands is completely sufficient to answer most of the technically linguistic questions about the Habsburg chancery language implicit in the Luther statement above and in the handbook descriptions stemming from it.

A number of extralinguistic questions about Maximilian's chancery language remain unresolved, however. These arise from the historical lore that grew up around the written dialect before it had been described adequately; in standard histories of the German language they continue to distort the linguistic historical significance of the chancery language. For this reason and because of the discovery of pertinent new historical evidence during the past six years, it is necessary to turn once again to the external history of the Habsburg chancery, despite the attention it has received previously. This study is an attempt to adjust the external historical picture of the Habsburg chancery language and to reconcile the revised image with the internal graphemic data supplied by Moser's study. Its objective is to clarify the role of Maximilian's chancery language in the evolution of the German Gemeinsprache by considering it within the historical and linguistic context that produced it.

The conditions under which the Habsburg chancery dialect entered the historiography of the German language are different from those surrounding many other traditional subjects in the history of German. Whereas certain historical linguistic phenomena (e.g., umlaut, ablaut) were explained only in retrospect, centuries after their evolution in the language, the emergence of the German common language was a process that was discussed and documented as it was happening during the fifteenth and sixteenth centuries. Similarly, the linguistic activity of Kaiser Maximilian, his chanceries, and his scribes was noted by literati during the period when it is said to have had its historical impact on the German language. This Renaissance German linguistic self-consciousness is one of the most intellectually appealing aspects of the topic at hand, and it must be given special consideration in evaluating the external history of Maximilian's chancery language. Contemporary observations like the Luther statement above may or may not be accurate from a modern linguistic standpoint, but they cannot be overlooked. Their very existence substantiates the fact that German humanists themselves perceived the distinctive varieties of their written language that have been the subject of modern investigations. These perceptions alone would seem to justify the ongoing research.

Fifteenth- and sixteenth-century assertions about the German language must not, however, be taken at face value without allowing for the historical and linguistic context in which they were made. Until recently, much of the relevant Habsburg chancery manuscript material one may consult in this regard was all but inaccessible. And only recently has substantial background material on Maximilian's chancery, its operations, and its personnel come to light. For this reason one must suspect that the nineteenth-century scholars who introduced the Habsburg chancery as a theme in the histories of the German language adopted the sixteenth-century statements about it rather uncritically. This is at least in part true of the subsequent generations who have patterned their accounts after the nineteenth-century descriptions as well. To minimize this sort of historical distortion, the present investigation, in reviewing the traditional handbook material on the Habsburg chancery language, separates contemporary fifteenth- and sixteenth-century assertions from those portions of the accounts originating in the nineteenth century or later. It considers them individually against the expanded backdrop of historical material presented.

The first chapter of this study is essentially historiographic. It takes as its point of departure the image of the Habsburg chancery dialect that has evolved in the histories of the German language and uses this to establish the perimeters of the investigation. Various claims about the chancery language are examined, and specific semantic issues in the scholarship that have obscured the role of the Habsburg chancery language are clarified. The second chapter introduces

historical material not previously considered in examinations of the
chancery language, and it reassesses historical information presented
in earlier studies.   Here the chancery system of Maximilian I is
viewed in conjunction with the broader development of the Imperial
Chancery (Reichskanzlei) in late medieval Germany, with particular
attention paid to the internal procedures and personnel of Maximilian's
Court Chancery (Hofkanzlei).   The third chapter summarizes the linguistic descriptions of the written dialect now available and examines the
manuscript production of individual chancery members.   This material
is then related to the findings of the earlier chapters in order to
present a revised account of the Habsburg chancery language in its
historical context.

1

THE TRADITIONAL ASSESSMENTS OF THE HABSBURG CHANCERY LANGUAGE

The Assertions and the Lore

A new chapter in the development of the Imperial chancery
language begins with the election of Frederick Habsburg to the throne
of the Holy Roman Empire in 1440. Certain EMG features typical of
the production of Charles IV's Prague chancery gradually recede, and
over the next eighty years documents from the Habsburg chanceries
take on an increasingly UG tone. Although this is hardly surprising
in light of the fact that Frederick III's main chancery was at Graz[13]
and Maximilian I's at Innsbruck, both deep in the Austro-Bavarian
dialect region, some have seen this increase in UG features as a deliberate attempt by Frederick to reform the language of chancery communication within the Empire. Maximilian has also been credited with a
major reform of the Imperial chancery language. As a noted patron of
the arts and to some extent as an author in his own right, Maximilian
is said to have caused a standardization and streamlining in the
language of his chancery, which set the pace for chanceries and
printers throughout the Empire. The desirability of a written administrative or business language for the entire Empire (which during
Maximilian's reign included Burgundy, Carniola, and large holdings in
Italy, as well as the Habsburg ancestral territories in what are now
Switzerland and Austria) has caused some historians of the German
language to assume Maximilian deliberately created one.

There are nearly thirty handbooks and banner articles on the
history of the German language treating the Habsburg chancery dialect;[14]
more than eighty percent of them emphasize its external history. Taken
together, these descriptions, which are highly derivative and inter-
dependent, account for most of the material on the subject that has
become traditional in the history of the German language. The following is a pastiche of the ideas contained in these accounts. It does
not reflect the presentation of any single author, and it contains a
number of errors. It is, however, an accurate summary of the conven-
tional wisdom on Maximilian's chancery language offered by the handbooks, and it is a good point of departure for a review of the modern
scholarship.

> With the death of Albrecht II in 1439, the Imperial crown
> passed to Frederick III and the Leopoldine Habsburgs. The
> administrative center of the Empire shifted southward,
> and the chancery that had been in Vienna under Albrecht[15]
> functioned in Graz, Wiener Neustadt, and Linz as well as
> Vienna during the various phases of his successor's reign.
> Under Frederick, the Imperial chancery production showed
> the Austro-Bavarian linguistic features that have been
> associated with the Habsburgs, and it is during this
> period that a deliberate effort was made to eliminate dia-
> lectal idiosyncrasies from the official written language.
> During Maximilian's reign the reforms already in progress
> became a matter of personal concern both to the Emperor
> and to certain members of his court. Maximilian, an
> author himself, commissioned numerous German translations
> of classical works and had great monuments of MHG litera-
> ture collected and copied. UG grammars written by
> Maximilian's circle of literati reflect the linguistic
> awareness and the trend toward an UG common language that
> were developing in the Empire at the time. Two of these,
> lost to us now, are the "Opus grammaticale de lingua
> germanica certis adstricta legibus" by the distinguished
> humanist Protonotary Hans Krachenberger and the "Descrip-
> tio linguae vulgaris per superiorem Germaniam" by Hof-
> kaplan Ladislaus Sunthaym. More significant than either
> of these men in his role in shaping the Habsburg chancery
> language, however, was Chancellor Niclas Ziegler. He
> has been called the greatest linguistic authority of the
> period, and his regularized orthography is cited by Eck
> in the 1536 dedication of his Ingolstadt Bible as a model
> for emulation. By the end of Maximilian's reign in 1519,
> sufficient standardization had been achieved in the

chancery language so that all official documents proceeding directly from the Emperor, transmitted in his name,
or bearing his seal were written in the same language,
regardless of what part of the Empire they originated in—
whether Neustadt, Innsbruck, Ghent, Brussels, or Bruges.
The unified written language quickly began to make its
presence felt within the UG area; other chanceries
adopted it, and it became the language of the UG printing centers. The pre-Lutheran HG Bibles were printed
in this language. It is called "Gemeines Deutsch," that
is, "Common German."

How accurate is this presentation, and how valid from a modern
linguistic standpoint are the issues it raises? In the following
pages we will consider the individual components of the handbook
accounts and their sources and interdependence in order to suggest
initial answers to these questions. At the same time we will identify
areas in which additional historical evidence is needed to clarify the
context of the Habsburg chancery language and will outline the problems to be explored in the remainder of the study.

Terminology

Before proceeding to the traditional material, it is necessary
to consider briefly some semantic problems that blur the historical
image of the Habsburg chancery language. Most of the terminology
used in discussing its significance derives from studies conducted
over the past century and a half in which the Habsburg dialect is
only an ancillary issue in the investigation of some special topic or
relationship in the history of the German language. The titles of
but a few of these works suggest their emphases: Schriftsprache und
Dialekte im Deutschen (Adolf Socin, 1888); Geschichte der deutschen
Literatursprachen (Hans Naumann, 1926); "Die Entstehung der neuhochdeutschen Einheitssprache" (Hugo Moser, 1951); "Mundart, Urkundensprache und Schriftsprache" (Rudolf Schützeichel, 1960); Der Weg zur
deutschen Nationalsprache (Mirra Guchmann, [1955] 1964). These
studies are not primarily concerned with the Habsburg chancery language, but their orientations have had an important effect on thinking
about the chancery dialect. From these and similar investigations
come a group of designations that have often been used rather casually

in conjunction with the Habsburg chancery language. They fall into
two categories. The first are essentially descriptive and simply
identify the subject or area of investigation (e.g., "written language," "chancery language"). The second are essentially interpretive
and imply certain assumptions about the development of language that
are not explained by the terms themselves (e.g., "literary language,"
"national language," "standard language"). These interpretive designations have somewhat complicated research on the Habsburg chancery
language because scholars have occasionally used them differently from
the way in which their predecessors did without redefining them. Thus
the answers to seemingly simple questions like, Are "Gemeines Deutsch"
and "Maximilian's chancery language" synonymous? or, Was the language
of Maximilian's chancery a literary language? require rather careful
semantic footwork.

Certainly the issues raised by such interpretive terms are of
great interest in determining the historical significance of Maximilian's chancery language. They are better considered, however, after
the supplementary historical material and the recent descriptions of
the dialect itself have been examined. These questions are taken up
in the final section of this study.

In the meantime descriptive working definitions are necessary
for a survey of the extant scholarship on the subject and an examination of new data. I use the terms "Habsburg chancery language" and
"Habsburg chancery dialect" synonymously to mean the language of the
diplomatic and literary production of the Habsburg chanceries and
their scribes during the reigns of Frederick III and Maximilian I
(1440-1519). The Habsburg chancery dialect is a written language.
In this usage I overlook the objections of those linguists who insist
the English term "language" be applied only to oral utterance and the
German term "Mundart" be reserved for the spoken form of a regional
dialect; I acknowledge, however, the regional implications of the
term "dialect." The language under consideration is identifiably
regional, although it does not display all the possible dialectal
features of the region to which it is indigenous. The terms

"Maximilian's chancery language" and "Maximilian's chancery dialect"
mean the Habsburg chancery language as it was written during Maximilian's reign. I use the term "common language" to mean the dialect or
language of a region that through contact with other speech communities undergoes some leveling and ultimately becomes the standard language of a larger area; it covers the German terms "Gemeinsprache"
and "Einheitssprache" but not "Gemeines Deutsch." "Gemeindeutsch" is
a German regional written language that has not yet developed into a
common language; at the turn of the sixteenth century there were
several varieties of Gemeindeutsch (see "'Gemeindeutsch'" below).
The term "professional language" is used to indicate the language of
the members of a specific profession or the practitioners of a
particular art, for example, the language of the Habsburg chancery
scribes.

"Gemeines Deutsch"

As indicated above, most of the semantic issues that retard
research on the Habsburg chancery language are the product of modern
scholarship. One of the most troublesome terms associated with the
Habsburg dialect, however, has its roots in the German Renaissance
itself: "Gemeines Deutsch." In many ways the history of the Habsburg
chancery language has been the history of Gemeines Deutsch so far as
the handbooks are concerned. For various reasons the two issues have
been closely connected in the historiography of the German language
from its beginnings to the present. Thus it is useful to begin our
review of the handbook material on the Habsburg chancery language with
an examination of this term.

To this point I have avoided using the term "Gemeines Deutsch"
(or any of its orthographic variants such as "die gemeine Teutsch" or
"die gemeine theutsche") to refer to the chancery language under
investigation. This is because the term has several connotations
that have not always been kept distinct by the scholars who have used
it. To clarify the matter it is necessary to determine what the term
may have meant when it is first attested. As this is well before the
reigns of Frederick and Maximilian, one must then discover how the

term came to be associated with the Austrian chancery language and whether or not the association is valid. Finally one must determine how the term has been redefined de facto by historians of the German language, who have assigned it a meaning it did not originally have.

Of the many Germanic philologists who use the term "Gemeines Deutsch," four have addressed themselves particularly to the semantic aspects of the issue.[16] The following summary includes their major arguments.

The earliest attestation of "gemain teutsch" reported to date is contained in a statement cited by Stanley Werbow from the foreword of Leopold Stainreuter's translation of Bishop Wilhelm Durandus of Mende's "Rationale divinorum officiorum," dated 1384-85:

> Ich wil auch mein teusch nicht reimen vnd wil ez doch
> besliezzen so ich peste mag mit der chunste slozzen
> die da haizzent Rethorica vmb daz ich bei der schrifte
> worten beleibe vnd di selbe mazze behalte di in latein
> geschriben ist daz si deste minner verdriezze, di fürbaz
> werdent lesen daz teusche Racional. Dar vmb sol mich
> ewr lautterchait genedich versten ob ich etwenn an dem
> ersten secze ain wort oder ainen sinn der in gemainen
> teusche an daz leste gehoret oder an daz leste daz ze
> vor gehoret, wann daz tŭn ich nach der ordenung der
> schrifte die in latein mit rechter mazze geschriben ist.[17]

Werbow notes that Stainreuter uses the term to distinguish between two possible styles of translating Latin into German. The first and more ornate one attempts to reflect Latin style and syntax. The second is "gemain teusch" and from the indications of the passage above features simpler, non-Latinate syntax. Werbow explains that "gemain teusch" in this sense has nothing whatever to do with any sort of standardized language. In this context "gemain teusch" has only stylistic and syntactic implications.

Pursuing this line of stylistic interpretation, Werbow quotes Ulrich von Pottenstein (d. c.1420), Hofkaplan to Albrecht IV in Vienna. "Nu hab ich den gemainen lauf dewtscher sprach nach des lanndes gewonheit für mich genommen." Werbow distinguishes here between Pottenstein's term "gemain," referring to the simple vernacular that featured regular German syntax, and "aigne dewtsch," meaning German of the Latinate style:

> Darczu mag sich an allen steten aigne dewtsch nach der
> latein als sie lawtet vnd nach dem text liget, weder
> geschikchen noch gefügen; wann umbred bringen an maniger
> stat in der schrift mer nuczes vor dem gemainen volkch
> denn aignew deutsch, als es die gelehrten wissen; yedoch
> also daz die warheit des sinnes mit umbred icht verrucket
> werde.[18]

Werbow's argument here is completely convincing, and one must agree
that at the turn of the fifteenth century a possible reading of the
term "Gemeines Deutsch" was "stylistically simple German, featuring
regular, non-Latinate German syntax."

An Austro-Bavarian translation of the life of St. Jerome,[19]
recently shown to be the work of the Innsbruck Carthusian Heinrich
Haller,[20] contains another often-cited reference to "gemainen
theutsch":

> ich han auch das vorgenant puch verwandlet nach dem
> text und ettwen nach dem synne und das pracht zuo ainer
> schlechten gemainen theutsch die man wol versten mag,
> die vernunfft brauchen wöllen; das setz ich herzuo, und
> han das erleutret, als vil ich han mügen, und süllen.[21]

The phrase has been interpreted variously by the scholars who have
considered it since the passage was first published by Ernst Martin
in 1880. Relating it to later statements by Aventinus (Johann
Turmair) and Luther, Martin contends that this early reference is to
a supradialectal language that already existed in Tirol only three
years after the printing of the first German book. He says that the
term "aine schlechte gemaine theutsch" is in itself sufficient to
prove the existence of a common language. Because of the date and
location of the term's origin, Martin further asserts that the common
language developed independently of the influence of printing.

Paul Pietsch adopts and expands on the same argument.[22] He
asserts that the formulation "gemeines teutsch" itself indicates the
existence of a developed written German language prior to the time
when either the language of the chanceries or printing can be considered influential. Referring to the 1464 Haller translation, he says
that the language of the text already shows the character of NHG.
Pietsch does not further specify which aspects of the Haller

translation he considers to be modern. Later in his discussion he considers lexical changes in early editions of the German Bible and notes that these cannot be the result of the influence of the chancery language. The contribution of a chancery language toward the development of the common language must, according to Pietsch, be limited to phonology, orthography, and perhaps morphology; and even in these areas the chancery influence should not be overrated. A common language, on the other hand, has a different character:

> Sehen wir nun die Gemeinsprache mit einer syntaktischen und lexikalischen Physiognomie auftauchen, die gegenüber dem Durchschnitt der früheren Denkmäler des deutschen Schrifttums geändert erscheint, so muss sie diese anderswoher als aus der Kanzleisprache empfangen haben.[23]

If this sort of lexically and syntactically developed written language is what Pietsch intended in describing the "Schriftsprache" of Haller's 1464 translation, the evidence is rather insubstantial.[24] Similarly, Martin's assumption of the existence of a supradialectal written language on the basis of the phrase "aine schlechte gemaine theutsch" is unconvincing. Pietsch offers criteria for evaluating a written language but does not apply them to Haller's text. Martin does not specify in what sense Haller's "schlechte gemaine theutsch" was a supradialectal language. Although some gradual regularization of East Upper German (EUG) orthography was beginning to occur in the late fifteenth century, there is nothing in Haller's statement to suggest that this is what he meant. To the contrary, the sequence of adjectives "schlecht" and "gemain" modifying "theutsch" suggests instead that the translator in 1464 meant something like "plain simple German" and was not at all concerned with a common language.

Even so, "plain simple German" may be interpreted in two ways. Werbow offers a stylistic syntactic explanation. Hermann Paul (1887), on the other hand, suggests that the term is used to distinguish German from Latin. He further asserts that there is no reason to assume that the translator (Haller) is writing anything other than his native Bavarian and that there is thus no reason to see the text as an example of some sort of UG common language. This too is a

plausible reading of Haller's term. Martin argues correctly that the
1464 translator probably worked directly from a Latin text and not
from the earlier German translation by Johann, Bishop of Olmütz.[25]
This circumstance certainly permits Paul's interpretation.

"Gemeindeutsch"

Before turning to the handbook presentations of Gemeines
Deutsch let us consider briefly Arno Schirokauer's discussion of the
similar sixteenth-century term "Gemeindeutsch."[26] Where "common lan-
guage" is suggested as an alternative reading of the attestations of
"Gemeines Deutsch" cited above, it is the primary issue with the term
"Gemeindeutsch." "In seinem Mithridates (Zürich, 1555) schreibt er
[Conrad Gesner] das Vaterunser in seine Züricher Mundart um, wobei er
das von ihm angewandte Deutsch als lingua Germanica vel Helvetica
bezeichnet." Schirokauer translates Gesner's phrase: "im gemeinen
Deutsch [. . .] und zwar dem schweizerischen."[27] At first glance
Schirokauer's jump from the term "German language" ("lingua
Germanica") to "common German language" ("gemeine[s] Deutsch") appears
gratuitous. This is because the phrase is misquoted in the article.
The phrase in question appears above a Swiss version of the Lord's
Prayer in the Mithridates and reads "Oratio dominica in lingua Germanica communi, uel Heluetica" in both the first (1555) edition and in
the 1610 edition Schirokauer used.[28] This corrected statement taken
together with the following remark by Gesner from the preface to Josua
Maaler's German-Latin dictionary, Die Teütsch spraach (Zurich, 1561),
is the basis for his interpretation of the term "Gemeindeutsch." "A
nostra [lingua] quidem, id est, superioris Germanicae, & ueluti cōmuni
Germanica lingua, quantům & in quibus diuersae dialecti differant,
pluribus in Mithridate nostro ostendi [. . .]."[29]

On the basis of these statements he concludes that Gesner is
describing his own UG written dialect as one of several varieties of
common German ("Gemeindeutsch"). Gesner's Gemeindeutsch is distinguished from other varieties by dialectal features, although it should
not, according to Schirokauer, be confused with either the pure (one
infers spoken) dialect or the standard language.

> Was er sagen will ist also, daß sein eignes Oberdeutsch,
> sozusagen und beispielsweise ein Gemeindeutsch, von
> anderem Gemeindeutsch durch viele Dialekteigentümlich-
> keiten getrennt sei. Dabei hat das Wort <u>Oberdeutsch</u>
> regionale, <u>Gemeindeutsch</u> soziale Bedeutung. <u>Gemein-</u>
> <u>deutsch</u> ist weder die reine Mundart, noch aber die
> Hochsprache. Sein eigner Züricher (Schrift-) Dialekt
> ist ein Beispiel für Gemeindeutsch, er ist <u>sein</u> Gemein-
> deutsch gleichsam und sozusagen; aber da sind noch andere,
> und jeder hält seines für das beste.[30]

The concept of regional written languages was not first proposed by Schirokauer, although his explication of the Gesner passages
strengthens arguments for their existence. Konrad Burdach came to the
same conclusion in 1884,[31] only to be refuted by Hermann Paul in the
1887 article mentioned above. Recently, however, scholars have
returned to this line of thinking, and the results of their research
argue convincingly for the existence of several distinct regional
German written languages that evolved before the advent of printing.
The number of these languages and their precise descriptions vary
according to the investigative orientation of the individual
researcher.[32] Regardless of these differences, however, there is no
longer any doubt that by the fifteenth century regional written languages had developed in German-speaking Europe. One of these was
indisputably the language of the Southeast, the Austro-Bavarian region
in which the main chanceries of Frederick III and Maximilian functioned.[33]

Because our investigation is not concerned with the development of the German common language as such, these regional written
languages are of interest here only as they have direct bearing on our
understanding of the Habsburg chancery dialect and its significance.
In that connection two aspects of the phenomenon are pertinent. First,
one of these languages developed in the same geographic region as the
chancery dialect of Frederick and Maximilian. Second, as Schirokauer
has established, albeit on the basis of Latin texts, "common German
language" ("cōmuni Germanica lingua") in sixteenth-century usage may
refer to one or more regional written languages, but not to a single
written language used in all the dialectal regions, that is, not to a

Hochsprache or standard language. Thus it is possible that other
fifteenth- and sixteenth-century references in which "gemein" occurs
in combination with "deutsch" imply regional written languages. For
evaluating this aspect of both the contemporary and the modern statements about the Habsburg chancery language, the descriptive aspects of
Schirokauer's definition are as useful as any developed in more recent
studies. The various types of Gemeindeutsch are, according to him,
regional, written, not purely dialectal, and not equivalent to a
Hochsprache.

 Taken together, the above explanations of Gemeines Deutsch and
Gemeindeutsch suggest several possibilities that must be considered
in reviewing the handbook accounts of the Habsburg chancery language.
In fifteenth- and sixteenth-century statements where "gemein" occurs
in conjunction with "deutsch" it may refer to simple German that does
not imitate Latin style or syntax, German versus Latin, or one of
several varieties of regional written German. These terms do not on
the basis of the contemporary contexts that we have examined to this
point imply any deliberate linguistic standardization.

"Gemeines Deutsch" in the Handbook Accounts

 Karl Müllenhoff in the second (1864) edition of his Denkmäler
states that by the thirteenth century there already existed in Bohemia
a language that was a median between the dialects of Meissen and
Bavaria. Continuing this discussion, he cites the regular occurrence
of Imperial Diets as the main factor in the emergence of an Imperial
language in the fifteenth century.

> die hauptursache aber für die entstehung einer 'reichs-
> sprache' im XV jh. lag gewis in der häufigen, fast
> regelmäßigen wiederkehr der reichstage. man bedurfte
> eines 'gemeinen teutsch'. man fieng an sich nach der
> kaiserlichen kanzlei zu richten und diese sich wiederum
> in lauten und formen dem allgemeineren gebrauch anzube-
> quemen, wofür der umstand namentlich ins gewicht fallen
> muste, dass die mehrzahl der angesehensten und mächtig-
> sten reichsfürsten dem sprachgebiet des mittleren
> Deutschlands angehörte.[34]

In the very next sentence Müllenhoff begins his explication of the
Luther passage quoted in my introduction. The order of events as

Müllenhoff perceives them is: (1) a natural leveling of Bavarian and
EMG dialects beginning in the thirteenth century; (2) the development
of an Imperial language in response to the need for a common language;
(3) the deliberate adoption of the Imperial chancery language as a
model; (4) Luther.

   Müllenhoff does not explain his term "Reichssprache." Neither
does he substantiate the claim that other scriptoria (he implies a
written language) patterned their phonology and morphology after that
of the Imperial chancery. During the fifteenth century this was a
Habsburg chancery. The assumption that Middle German (MG) princes,
who were, as Müllenhoff notes, among the most powerful in the Empire,
should have deliberately affected the Habsburg chancery language
requires further investigation. On the basis of the limited information presented, it is probable that Müllenhoff derives his term
"gemeine[s] teutsch" from the Luther passage and construes it to mean
a written common language. He offers no evidence, however, that there
was any conscious attempt to develop such a common language during
the period of Maximilian's influence. Müllenhoff's statement is of
particular interest because it suggests a deliberate attempt to
create a common language, which he calls "gemeine[s] teutsch," and it
equates this with an Imperial language. It is also noteworthy because
of the emphasis it places on the Middle German princes. This is the
sort of interpretation that has contributed to the preponderance of
scholarship on the EMG dialects of the ENHG period.

   In 1875 Heinrich Rückert discusses the language of Berthold
Piestinger's "Teutsche Theologei" (1528). Although he notes somewhat
disparagingly that Piestinger continues to use some "ugly" ("häßlich")
Bavarian forms that have been replaced in the Gemeinsprache by MG
terms, his overall evaluation of the language is quite positive. "So
auch seine Sprache: sie ist klar, vielleicht das geläufigste und
sauberste Gemeindeutsch älteren Stils."[35] The adjective he uses in
this passage to describe the MG terms in the Gemeinsprache is "gemeindeutsch." Whatever meaning "gemeindeutsch" may have had in the sixteenth century, Rückert definitely uses the term to imply a common

language, and apparently one more MG than UG in character. There would
certainly be no objection to specific regionalisms, nor would there be
discussion of one set of regional forms replacing another, if Rückert
were concerned either with German as opposed to Latin or with stylistically simple, syntactically genuine German.

Burdach's 1884 formulation[36] is reminiscent of Müllenhoff's but
goes beyond it in describing the character of the common language
under discussion. Burdach defines a language applicable only to a
specific segment of the population and used only for specific purposes. His own suggestion that the language be called a "Staats-
sprache" (state or official language) indicates that he considers his
"Gemeinsprache" to be a professional language and not what one would
ordinarily consider to be a common language. Nevertheless he maintains the term "Gemeinsprache," de facto redefining it to mean a
professional language.

> Nach dieser Reichssprache der kaiserlichen Kanzlei
> hatten bald die mitteldeutschen Kanzleien—die öst-
> lichen zuerst—sich zu richten angefangen und gegen
> das Ende des 15. Jahrhunderts entstand so allmählich
> für ein 'gemeines Deutsch' [. . .] eine festere Grundlage.
> [. . .] Man könnte diese Gemeinsprache ganz gut eine
> Staatssprache heissen: sie galt jedesfalls zunächst und
> viel mehr im öffentlichen Verkehr des Staates und der
> Privatleute mit diesem, es war eine Sprache der Beamten
> und des Geschäfts, aber keine des Hauses, der Familie,
> des geselligen Umgangs.[37]

Since Burdach cites Gesner's statements from both the Mithridates (1610 edition) and the introduction to Josua Maaler's Wörter-
buch discussed above,[38] these are probably the source of his Gemeinsprache concept. He comes to much the same conclusion as Schirokauer,
positing the existence of three different common languages—Swiss,
Bavarian, and Swabian—in the UG area. He considers each of these to
be distinct "from the concept of a general UG language" ("von dem
Begriff einer allgemeinen oberdeutschen Sprache"). What Burdach means
by this last category is difficult to tell. Perhaps he is attempting
to distinguish between the regional common languages he describes and
a common language in the modern sense of the term. In any event there

is the same sort of tendency here to blend sixteenth-century terminology and modern linguistic principles as in the Müllenhoff and Rückert
passages above.

In his discussion of Maximilian and his chancery, Friedrich
Kluge (1888) cites Johann Eck's Ingolstadt Bible (1537)[39] as a particularly significant example of the influence of the Imperial
chancery and its linguistic standards.   "Ein Denkmal vergegenwärtigt
uns in besonders schlagender Weise die Bedeutung der Maximilianischen
Kanzlei und ihre Normen.   Es ist Ecks katholische Bibel (Ingolstadt
1537), der Luthers Übersetzung, zumeist in der Emserschen Über-
arbeitung, zu Grunde liegt."[40]   This statement is based on Eck's own
acknowledgment of the linguistic authority of Maximilian's chancellor
Niclas Ziegler.   The Bible is dedicated to the politically powerful
Archbishop of Salzburg, Matthäus Lang, who had during Maximilian's
reign been one of the most influential men in the chancery coterie
immediately surrounding the Emperor.   He served in the chancery
contemporaneously with Ziegler and was thus utterly familiar with
chancery business and procedures.   In the letter of dedication dated
1536, Eck writes to Lang that he has tried in his translation to
write German properly and with the standardized orthography instituted
by the estimable Niclas Ziegler.   He disclaims responsibility, however,
for the orthography of the printed text, saying that his own consistent orthography has not always been preserved in the printing.

For this investigation the Eck passage is second in importance
only to the remark from Luther's _Tischrede_ quoted above.   It is one
of very few sixteenth-century statements that traces a distinctive
manner of writing directly to Maximilian's chancery, and it is the
only surviving sixteenth-century reference to Ziegler's role in
crafting this written language:

> So auch etwas an rechter form zů schreiben vnd ortographei
> gelegen im teütschen: hab ich mich deren geflissen nach
> rechter art/ grund/ kunst/ vnd vrsach/ vnd mich die gmain
> Cantzler schreiber nit jrren lassen/ die lützel auf-
> merckens vnd Judici darauf haben/ wie dan treffenlich
> Herr Niclas Ziegler/ bei Kaiserlicher Maiestet hohlob-
> licher vnd vntödtlicher gedächtnuß Kaiser Maximilian/

    das teütsch nach rechter art vnd regulierter ortographi
    herfůr bracht hat: wie sollichs E.F.G. als do zemal
    fürnämsten K.M. Rat am hof/ baß bewißt/ dan ich anzaigen
    kan: So ist doch im truck die ortographei. Die ich für
    bestendig geacht/ nit allweg gehalten worden: deßhalb
    ich nit vil dar von disputieren will.[41]

In the phrase "die gmain Cantzler schreiber," Eck uses the
term "gmain" to distinguish the "'common' (ordinary, run-of-the-
mill)" chancery scribes and their writing habits from those of the
Emperor's chancery as exemplified by Niclas Ziegler. The common
scribes referred to here are presumably the public notaries, Schreibmeister, or Rechenmeister of the cities; the secretaries of the
lesser noble courts; or the scribes who served members of either of
these groups in the UG area (see "The Imperial Chancery Ordinance
[Reichskanzleiordnung] of 1494" and "The Training of Chancery Personnel," chapter 2). Apparently the language written in Maximilian's
chancery was perceptibly different to Eck from the German written
elsewhere in the region. In what ways he found it to be distinctive
is a moot point. The passage itself suggests that Eck may be speaking about nothing more than orthography. On the other hand, writing
"nach rechter art/ grund/ kunst/ vnd vrsach" may have implied something more than orthography in the modern sense of the word. To
speculate more accurately about what Eck may have meant requires a
broader look at the linguistic climate of Germany in the early sixteenth century. The discussion below of Luther's remarks on the
German language and of Fabian Frangk's Orthographia (see "Luther's
Tischreden WA I, 524 and WA V, 511" and "Fabian Frangk's Orthographia") suggests which features these contemporaries of Eck's
considered to be characteristic of the written German language they
describe. Their observations provide a basis for interpreting Eck's
statement.

    In considering Eck's text as a whole, Kluge finds that it shows
many phonological features that are common to the entire Austro-
Bavarian region of Upper Germany. "Für Eck ist der bayrisch-
österreichische Vokalismus maßgebend; er schreibt nach gemein ober-
deutscher Weise Brůder, gůt, thůn [. . .]." Similarly he notes, "Das

allgemeine oberdeutsche Gesetz, das die auslautenden e vernichtet,
hält Eck ein [. . .]." Kluge also observes that Eck's use of certain
verb forms, pronouns, lexical items, and orthographic conventions
makes the language of his Bible distinctively UG and readily distinguishable from Luther's MG.[42]   On the basis of this sort of analysis
he comes to somewhat hasty conclusions about "not only the regulation
but also the dissemination of a modern language" under Maximilian.[43]

Adolf Socin, writing in the same year as Kluge (1888), refers
to the (Haller) translation of the life of St. Jerome (1464) mentioned
in the section "'Gemeines Deutsch'" above and concludes, "Der Ausdruck
'das gemeine Deutsch' bezeugt allein schon das Vorhandensein einer
über den Dialekten stehenden Sprache."[44] How different this is from
Kluge's formulation of a "common UG manner" ("gemein oberdeutsche
Weise") of writing. Where Kluge speaks of "the common UG rule" ("das
allgemeine oberdeutsche Gesetz"), he does this apparently on the
basis of the phonological evidence he is able to extrapolate from the
texts; Socin, on the other hand, assumes this sort of evidence on the
basis of a fifteenth-century phrase, which had by the nineteenth
century come to connote something quite different. Socin continues
his discussion of this Gemeinsprache saying that it was taken over by
the printers of Augsburg and Nuremberg. Certainly the printers of the
Danube Basin did adapt the indigenous regional forms of written
German, but these were not the sort of unified common language Socin
suggests with his interpretation of the phrase "das gemeine Deutsch."

Virgil Moser in 1909 addresses himself not only to the issues
of the emergence of a relatively common written language in Upper
Germany, but also to the semantic problem that has arisen in trying
to describe it.

> Diese kurze skizzierung hat gezeigt, wie am ende des
> mittelalters die kanzleien Ober- und Mitteldeutsch-
> lands, während sie zuerst ihre eigenen wege gegangen,
> einer annäherung an die amtssprache des kaisers wenig-
> stens in grossen zügen zustreben und so zu einer
> grösseren einheitlichkeit untereinander gelangen.
> Diesen allerdings ziemlich relativen typus einer
> einheit bezeichnen wir heute [. . .] mit einem

gleichzeitigen, freilich etwas schief gebrauchten ausdruck
als G e m e i n d e u t s c h.[45]

It is not clear why Moser suggests that the outlying chanceries deliberately began patterning their written languages after that of the
Imperial chancery. This is a frequently proffered explanation of the
leveling perceptible in fifteenth-century written documents from
Upper and Middle Germany which continues through the time of Luther.
The solution is plausible, but to date there is little direct evidence
to indicate that other scriptoria consciously affected the writing
practices of the Habsburg chanceries. One must also ask which
general features ("grosse züge") of the Imperial chancery language
other chanceries are supposed to have imitated—orthography, diction,
format?

Having suggested that there are difficulties with the term
"Gemeindeutsch," Moser uses "gemeines Deutsch" in the remainder of
his discussion. As he uses it, there is little difference between the
two. Moser proceeds from an assumption rather like Werbow's discussed
in the section "'Gemeines Deutsch'" above; he acknowledges that the
term commonly connotes error, but he recognizes that it has become so
fundamental a part of the scholarship on the topic that he uses it
himself. When Moser says that the Strassburg printers adopted "das
gemeine Deutsch" earlier than the chanceries did (p. 32) and that the
local chanceries began to lose their individual characteristics in
part because of their adoption of "das gemeine Deutsch" (p. 53), it is
not altogether clear whether he means the gemeindeutsch based on the
Imperial chancery language that he describes in the passage quoted
above, one of the UG regional written languages, or a single UG
written language that, as Kluge suggests, may have been common to the
entire region at the time by virtue of its phonology.

Emil Gutjahr's 1910 definition of "die gemeindeutsche Sprache"
is similar to Müllenhoff's and Rückert's. He posits a common language
that was originally EMG in character and later took on UG features
as well. The language, he asserts, achieved its significance not
only as a business and chancery language, but also as a literary

language during the thirteenth and fourteenth centuries. It was not
only the language of the Imperial chanceries of Charles IV, Ludwig of
Bavaria, and Maximilian but, according to Luther, of all the German
princes and cities as well.[46] Although Gutjahr does at a later point
in his discussion go into more detail on the evolution of the
Imperial chancery language in this period (pp. 209-22), his explanation of the German common language remains so general that its only
particular contribution to the development of the concept "Gemeines
Deutsch" is the assertion that it was a literary language.

In his Geschichte der deutschen Literatursprachen (1926), Hans
Naumann's approach to the question of the German common language is a
little different from that of his predecessors. Using the terms
"gemeinsprachlich" and "das gemeine Deutsch," he emphasizes the
difference between the literary language and the common language.
The character of the NHG language is, he says, "first of all that of
a common language, of an official, practical [language], and only
secondarily that of a literary language."[47] This is similar to
Burdach's definition, which equated the "common language" with a professional language. Naumann sees the development of the "so-called
'Gemeine[s] Deutsch'" ("das [. . .] so genannte 'Gemeine Deutsch'")
to be the result of a movement within the specific speech community
that comprised offices and chanceries. Naumann also observes that
the presence of the Bavarian diphthongs alone would have been a sufficiently significant feature by which to characterize a language in
the sixteenth century. He implies that this may be the basis for
Luther's use of the term "gemein" in the Tischreden and notes that
the disparity between the Saxon and Habsburg chancery languages should
not be overemphasized (pp. 22-26).

The next significant presentation of the Gemeines Deutsch
material is that of Adolf Bach (1938).[48] Until the appearance of the
studies by Hans Eggers[49] and R. E. Keller,[50] discussed below, his was
the most exhaustive treatment of the subject in any of the histories
of the German language. Because most of the handbooks that have
appeared since are heavily indebted to Bach's work, his presentation

of the Gemeines Deutsch issue merits particular attention. The
virtue of Bach's comprehensive discussion is its attempt to relate the
many disparate strands of information offered by earlier authors. The
drawback is that the synthesis is uncritical.

As the following summary indicates, Bach presents a rather
muddled picture of the interrelationship of "das gemeine Deutsch,"
the Imperial chancery language during the reign of Maximilian I, the
German printers' languages at the turn of the sixteenth century, and
the German common language. Because of the occurrence of the term
"das gemeine Dt." in 1464, Bach assumes there was a Southeast German
(SEG) common language that had developed in Austria under the auspices of the Imperial chancery by that time. During the reign of
Maximilian I (1493-1519), the Emperor and his chancellor Niclas
Ziegler are supposed to have concerned themselves with the regulation
of orthography and the suppression of southern dialectal features in
the chancery language (p. 250). The language of Maximilian's chancery was emulated not only by chanceries in the Danube Basin, but by
the printers of the region as well (p. 251). In this "Gemeines Dt.,"
says Bach, Boner's "Edelstein," the "Ackermann aus Böhmen," Stein-
höwel's "Äsop," and the fourteen pre-Lutheran, High German Bibles
were printed between 1461 and 1518 (p. 254). He maintains that Hans
Sachs and Sebastian Franck also contributed to the promulgation of the
"obd. [UG] Gemeinsprache" by writing in the adapted form of the
Imperial chancery language developed by the printers (p. 251). It
was these printed versions of the Imperial chancery language that
caused it to have its historical impact on the German language. After
1550 there were five main varieties of printed Gemeines Deutsch: two
of these were UG; two were MG; and one was from a transitional zone
between the two regions (p. 255).

Bach's usage of the term "das gemeine Dt." undergoes several
transformations in the course of his presentation. At the outset it
is a regional written language developed under the auspices of the
Imperial chancery in Austria. In its 1464 state Bach declares it to
be a southeastern common language ("[eine] Gemeinsprache im dt.

S ü d o s t e n," p. 250). He then claims that it is the language in
which a number of UG printed texts appeared between 1461 and 1518.
The written professional language thus becomes the language of several
printers. Bach also speaks of "Maximilian's 'Gemeines Deutsch'"
("Das 'Gemeine Deutsch' Maximilians I.," p. 251), meaning the somewhat
regularized written language of the Imperial chancery as it evolved
through the efforts of Maximilian himself and Niclas Ziegler; and he
speaks of "Gemeines Deutsch" as it was written in the Saxon Electoral
chancery at the time of Luther (p. 259). This written language, like
that of the contemporary Habsburg chancery, was not yet a fully developed common language (p. 254); that development required the inter-
mediate stage of the printers' languages (p. 255). Bach begins then
with some variety of written SEG that he calls a common language and
after several developmental stages ends up with something that is
neither specific to the Southeast, nor a purely written language, nor
a common language. Both written and printed language, chancery and
literary texts, EUG and MG materials may in Bach's terms be called
"Gemeines Deutsch." The language of Maximilian's chancery was one
variety of "Gemeines Deutsch"; the language of the Wettin chancery
was another very similar one.

Bach's development of the concept "Gemeinsprache" is also
somewhat circuitous. Proceeding from the assumption that a southeastern Gemeinsprache existed by 1464, he adds that by the end of the
fifteenth century the concept of a common language, "Gemeines Deutsch,"
had become dominant in Germany although opposition to it persisted
through the second quarter of the sixteenth century. The chancery
languages contributed to the emergence of the common language but did
not represent the fully developed language themselves. The inter-
mediate transformation afforded by the printers' languages was necessary to produce the NHG common language. In speaking of the "Gemeinsprache" of 1464 and of the "obd. [UG] Gemeinsprache" of Sachs and
Franck, Bach is clearly describing something different from the "nhd.
[NHG] Gemeinsprache" he mentions later (p. 255). The first two terms
refer to written and printed varieties of what may be defined loosely

as an EUG regional language; the last is the pan-German common language in the modern sense of the term.

Bach's presentation does not permit much headway with the
terms "Gemeines Deutsch" and "Gemeinsprache." Like several of his
predecessors, he gives too much credence to the 1464 formulation "das
gemeine Deutsch." His subsequent use of the term is so imprecise as
to render it almost meaningless. Bach's innovation is the emphasis
he places on the role of Maximilian and his chancery in the development of "Gemeines Deutsch." For the first time in the histories of
the German language, Maximilian is said to have had a curatorial
interest ("pflegliches Interesse," p. 250) in the UG chancery language. Bach does not offer any hard evidence to support his redefini-
tion of Maximilian's role in shaping the Imperial chancery language,
however, and his summation suggests that the new image may be somewhat distorted:

> In Frankreich und England sind es staatl.-polit. Kräfte
> gewesen, die zu einer nationalen Gemeinsprache geführt
> haben. Wenn sich unter Maximilian stärkere Ansätze zu
> einer ähnlichen Entwicklung in Deutschland zeigten, so
> verhinderte doch die lockere Gliederung des Reichs wie
> der Umstand, daß der führende Staat der Habsburger am
> Rande des dt. Lebensraumes lag, eine nachdrücklichere
> Verwirklichung des Zieles, obwohl Maximilians Sprache
> zunächst eine große Zukunft zu haben schien. (p. 260)

One must ask what Bach means when he suggests that "Maximilian's
language appeared at first to have a great future." On the basis of
the information presented to this point, the only German language
that can be traced to a reasonable proximity of Maximilian is the
written dialect used in his chancery.[51] Only in a limited sense
could a professional language of this sort be considered "the strong
beginning" of a national language. At most its orthography, phonology, and perhaps morphology might contribute to the development of a
common language.

Fritz Tschirch, in his presentation, goes back to the assumptions that "Gemeines Deutsch" is synonymous with the language of the
Habsburgs' Vienna chancery, and that the linguistic rivalry that

emerged toward the beginning of the sixteenth century was between the
chancery languages of the Habsburgs (reaching its peak under Maximilian) and of the Luxemburgs (reaching its peak under Charles IV). The
Habsburg language spread in an east-west direction throughout Upper
Germany; the Luxemburg language similarly in southern Middle Germany.
Tschirch sees this linguistic development, coupled with attendant
political considerations, to have been in danger of splitting Germany
at the Main. He suggests that the rise of printing helped prevent
this.[52] The rise of printing and the complication of the printers'
languages, however, constitute a linguistic development separate from
and subsequent to the development of the Luxemburg chancery language.
That the two chancery languages under consideration were as politically significant in the mid-fifteenth century as Tschirch suggests
is doubtful; the chancery languages became somewhat politicized in
the wake of the Reformation, not in anticipation of it.[53] It is
unlikely that the two written languages, which had become quite
similar by that time, would have caused a linguistic rupture. One
must also question the continuing impact of the Luxemburg chancery
language as such in the fifteenth century. Even though Tschirch
speaks of the parallel development of the two chancery languages,
Luxemburg chancery personnel actually worked in the chancery of
Frederick III for the first decade or so of his reign. It would be
more accurate to speak of a sequential development—Luxemburg, and
then Habsburg—if one is really concerned with chancery dialects.
It should be mentioned here in passing that for the most part Germanic
linguists no longer assume that Luther's phonology derives directly
from that of the Bohemian chancery.[54]

John Waterman's account is not very different from the preceding ones: "Largely as a result of attempts to standardize the
principal _Kanzleisprachen_, two generalized and widely used varieties
of High German came into prominence during the ENHG era. Of these,
the so-called _Gemeines_ (=_allgemeines_) _Deutsch_, an essentially Upper
German dialect which had first been fashioned into a literary instrument in the imperial chancery of the Hapsburgs, came to serve as the

standard written language of Austria and southern Germany."[55]   He goes
on to say that this language did not ultimately give way to EMG until
the eighteenth century.

The interesting new aspect that Waterman presents is the idea
that Gemeines Deutsch evolved into a literary language in the Habsburg
chancery. Developing a literary language is not the ordinary business
of a chancery, but then neither was Maximilian's an ordinary chancery.
Its members had to concern themselves not only with the administrative
and diplomatic affairs of the Empire, but also with Maximilian's personal literary production. Maximilian's chancery scribes were sometimes entrusted with the completion of his literary undertakings. This
should have required a literary language. There is no indication that
Waterman investigated the literary production of Maximilian's chancery,
however, and he does not explain in what sense the chancery dialect
was "fashioned into a literary instrument" during Maximilian's reign.
These issues are considered in conjunction with the examination of
Maximilian's chancery language and the writing habits of individual
Habsburg scribes in chapter 3.

When Hans Eggers (1969) addresses himself specifically to the
issues of "das gemeine Deutsch" and the possible existence of a Gemeinsprache in sixteenth-century Germany, he focuses on Luther's celebrated statement and Fabian Frangk's observations about the German language recorded in the Orthographia of 1531 (discussed in "Luther's
Tischreden WA I, 524 and WA V, 511" and "Frangk's Orthographia" below).
He concludes that despite the verifiable tendencies toward unification
in the German written languages of the period, the observations of contemporary grammarians and literati, and the assumptions of modern
Germanists, a German common language as such could not possibly have
existed in the sixteenth century.[56]   The chancery language of Maximilian and Frederick the Wise is, as Eggers explains the Luther reference,
not the German common language, but the most common German language
of the time. Eggers' interpretation of the second occurrence of the
word "gemein" in the passage (where Luther claims not to use any
"gewisse, sonderliche, eigene Sprache im Deutschen" but rather to make

use of "der gemeinen deutschen Sprache") is in complete agreement with
Stanley Werbow's. He asserts that Luther means simple, non-Latinate
German (pp. 152-54). Elsewhere Eggers uses the term similarly in
describing the German of the rough burlesque literature of the second
half of the fifteenth century: "Die schlichte, allgemein verständ-
liche Sprache, die gemeine Teutsch, wie die Zeitgenossen sie nannten,
drohte in Banalität zu versinken" (p. 123). And in considering the
circumstances attendant on the Reformation, he observes that the
intellectual issues of the times required a gemeines Deutsch (p. 155).

In examining the linguistic consequences of the Reformation
for Germany, Eggers returns to the first meaning of "das gemeine
[gemeinste] Deutsch."

> Die nunmehr schroff betonte Glaubensspaltung zog auch
> einen scharfen Schnitt durch das große östlich-
> südöstliche Schreiblandschaft. Das 'Meißnische'—so
> bezeichnete man auch LUTHERS Schreibsprache—wurde als
> die Sprache der Protestanten abgestempelt. Für den
> bayrisch-österreichischen Südosten ergab sich daraus
> ein Rückfall in den sprachlichen Partikularismus. Zwar
> wollte man auch hier das gemeine Deutsch pflegen, aber
> Richtschnur sollte ganz allein die Sprache der kaiser-
> lichen Kanzlei sein, die 'Reichssprache', wie man damals
> zu sagen pflegte. Doch auch die großen Kanzleien, nun-
> mehr politisch und ideologisch verfeindet, begannen
> noch einmal, ihre eigenen Wege zu gehen. (p. 187)

The reference here to "das gemeine Deutsch" is somewhat curious. In
this context it does not refer to stylistically simple, non-Latinate
German but to the relatively unified chancery language of Maximilian
and Frederick the Wise. Eggers says that the Reformation caused the
written languages of East Middle Germany and East Upper Germany to
split, and that even the chanceries themselves began to develop in
different directions. This is accurate, but the sequence of events
he offers in explanation is not altogether clear. Eggers accounts for
the divergent development of the regional chancery languages by suggesting that the Southeast suffered a relapse of linguistic particularism and adopted as its sole standard the Imperial chancery language.
This occurred despite the desire (not attributed to anyone) to maintain "das gemeine Deutsch" in the region. In his earlier explanation,

however, Eggers has shown that "das gemeine Deutsch" is just what the
Imperial chancery was writing during the first decades of the sixteenth
century (pp. 152-54). Emulation of this chancery language would not
produce the more characteristically UG language he says was written in
the South as a political reaction to the Reformation. If the Imperial
chancery language was considered the only gauge for the writings of
the Catholic Southeast, one must ask, Which Imperial chancery? or, The
Imperial chancery in what period? In 1536, for example, so pronounced
an exponent of the Catholic point of view as Johann Eck writes in the
dedication of his Ingolstadt Bible that he has deliberately patterned
his German after that of Niclas Ziegler, the onetime chancellor of
Maximilian I. The German to which Eck refers here is the same German
that Luther described in his Tischrede. It is "das gemeinste Deutsch,"
the language as it had been written fifteen or more years earlier in
Maximilian's chancery, before the Reformation can be considered to
have been a factor.

Wilhelm Schmidt (1970) identifies "das Gemeine Deutsche" as
one of four late medieval German regional written business languages.
It evolved as the language of trade in the Danube Basin during the
fourteenth and fifteenth centuries and was influenced by the Imperial
chancery, which moved to Austria during this period. He asserts that
Maximilian and Niclas Ziegler were concerned with the development of
an UG common language that avoided dialectal features. The influence
of this Gemeines Deutsch spread throughout Southern Germany and as
far as Cologne in the sixteenth century.[57] In this presentation
Schmidt uses the term "Gemeines Deutsch" to describe both the
fifteenth-century regional written language of the South and the
altered form of this language that developed through contact with the
Imperial chancery and through the efforts of Maximilian and Ziegler.
It is apparently this second Gemeines Deutsch, the one he associates
directly with the Habsburg chancery, that is supposed to have exerted
influence beyond the dialectal region to which it was indigenous
during the sixteenth century.

R. E. Keller's recent (1978) explanation of <u>Gemeines Deutsch</u> is the most useful that has appeared to date.[58]   It takes into account most of the arguments on the subject that have been put forward during the past century and a half while eliminating much of the confusion they have produced.

> <u>Gemeines Deutsch</u> is a designation used by many authorities for Upper German, excluding in the early sixteenth century Swiss, i.e. South or High Alemannic. It is, however, doubtful whether the opposition ECGm. [EMG] <u>vs.</u> <u>Gemeines Deutsch</u> is really justified, and in light of Luther's and Frangk's comments made almost in the same year, it is unlikely that contemporaries saw their language situation in this way. Furthermore, although <u>gemein</u> could mean 'common' then as now, in most of the occurrences of <u>Gemeines Deutsch</u> at that time it meant 'simple, ordinary, straightforward German' as opposed to the involved, artificial, latinizing style of much contemporary writing. (pp. 373-74)

At this point Keller proceeds to specify exactly what Common German, as he uses the term, included during the early decades of the sixteenth century. He identifies five areas within the Common German region: (1) WCGm. [WMG]: Mainz, Worms; (2) ECGm. [EMG]: Erfurt, Wittenberg, Leipzig (Thuringian, Upper Saxon); (3) CUGm. [CUG]: Nuremberg, Bamberg, Würzburg (East Franc.); (4) WUGm. [WUG]: Strassburg, Basel (Low Alem.); and (5) EUGm. [EUG]: Augsburg, Ingolstadt, Vienna (Swabian, Bavarian, Austrian) (p. 374). By Keller's definition only three areas fell outside the Common German region at the time— Cologne, Switzerland, and Low Germany (p. 374).

This explanation agrees rather well with the concept of regional written languages suggested by Gesner's statements and adopted by Schirokauer and others mentioned above. It identifies five distinguishable varieties of Common German at the beginning of the sixteenth century, one of which (EUG) coincides geographically with the primary sphere of Habsburg influence at that time. Keller avoids equating EUG specifically with the Imperial chancery language, however, just as he avoids equating the Saxon Electoral chancery language with EMG. Neither does he associate the different varieties of Common German with specific printers' languages. He simply

delimits and subdivides a general geographic area in which a number of
more specific forms of written and printed German—all of which may be
called Common German—were produced. In keeping his definition of
Common German essentially dialectal, Keller avoids the issues of
deliberate language standardization, of the sixteenth-century German
impulse toward a common language, and of the association of Common
German with Luther, Maximilian, and the Wettin and Habsburg chanceries.
At the same time, however, his definition permits almost every other
interpretation of the term "Gemeines Deutsch" that has been proposed
by previous historians of the German language. Common German then
may mean simple non-Latinate German, or German instead of Latin. It
may refer to the entire group of German written languages at the turn
of the sixteenth century that excluded Swiss, Low German (LG), and the
written dialect of Cologne; or it may refer individually to any of the
five written languages in the group. Used in the latter way, it is
correct to say that both the Habsburg chancery of Maximilian I and
the Wettin chancery of Frederick the Wise wrote Common German. In
Keller's terms they wrote two different varieties of Common German.
In the terms of Eggers and others above who have not so subdivided
the Common German region, these two chanceries wrote the same Common
German.

      Keller's definition of Common German eliminates much of the
confusion about "Gemeines Deutsch" that has resulted from imprecise
use of the term. It also points up the areas, particularly with
reference to the Habsburg chancery language, where questions remain
to be answered. These are the aspects of the Gemeines Deutsch question that fall outside the limits of his definition. In the statement quoted above, Keller objects to the opposition of EMG and
"Gemeines Deutsch" for reasons that become apparent as he develops
his definition. When "Gemeines Deutsch," as we have seen in other
accounts above, is used in opposition to EMG, it connotes either
Southern German in general, SEG, or the Imperial chancery language of
the Habsburgs. Defined in any of these ways, "Gemeines Deutsch" is
simply a subset of the set Common German as defined by Keller and is

analogous to the subset EMG.   In Keller's terms the opposition <u>within</u>
the set Common German of the subsets UG versus MG, or EUG versus EMG,
is possible, but the comparison of one subset (EMG) to the whole
(<u>Gemeines Deutsch</u>) is rather pointless.

The preceding review of "Gemeines Deutsch" as it is explained
in the handbooks shows that the term, which thus far seems to have had
only stylistic or dialectal implications in the sixteenth century,
began to be associated with the emergence of the modern German common
language and with questions of deliberate language standardization
almost as soon as it entered the histories of the German language.
Later "Gemeines Deutsch" was also connected with Kaiser Maximilian
himself and with his literary interests and projects.   As the handbook accounts of the significance of the Habsburg chancery language
swelled, little new evidence was introduced to support the expanded
claims.   The questions that fall outside Keller's working definition
of Common German still remain to be answered in the following chapters, as do all the smaller issues raised in the composite account of
the Habsburg chancery language presented at the beginning of this
chapter.   Let us consider briefly these ancillary propositions, their
sources and accuracy, before considering the linguistic climate of
sixteenth-century Germany and finally the Habsburg chancery itself.

Frederick III and the Habsburg Chancery Language

Although most of the handbooks focus their attention on the
Habsburg chancery language as it was written during the reign of
Maximilian, some begin their accounts with the development of the
written dialect under Frederick III.   The first scholar to mention
Frederick in this connection is Ernst Wülcker in 1877.[59]   He acknowledges that the chancery language becomes decidedly UG under
Frederick III, but he in no way suggests that this is the result of
conscious effort on the part either of the Emperor or the chancery.
In his <u>Geschichte der deutschen Sprache</u> (1891), Otto Behaghel credits
the chancery itself with attempting to eliminate dialectal peculiari-
ties from its written language; Frederick's role in this attempt is
not clear.[60]   Sigmund Feist places Frederick along with Maximilian in

the elevated position of patron ("Förderer") of the German language,
and implies that Frederick participated actively in crafting the
chancery language: "Bekanntlich war dieser Kaiser [Maximilian]
neben seinem Vater Friedrich III. wie kein Anderer seit Karl dem
Großen und kein Späterer ein Förderer der deutschen Sprache und Dich-
tung, ja sogar selbst Schriftsteller."[61] Walter Henzen returns to the
more conservative viewpoint of Wülcker. He acknowledges a change in
the chancery language during Frederick's reign, but he connects this
with the fact that the axis of Frederick's activity was between
Vienna and Graz and that he was little interested in Imperial affairs.
Henzen implies no direct intervention by Frederick that might have
caused a change in the policies of his chancery.[62]

In his 1969 study of ENHG, Eggers has stressed the importance
of distinguishing between the Imperial chancery and the House chancery
of the Habsburgs during the reign of Frederick III. He sees the
former, which was based in Vienna, to have been the direct descendant
of the Luxemburg chancery, and the latter, which was located in Graz,
to have been a linguistically parochial office that handled only those
matters pertaining to the Habsburg ancestral holdings.

> Kaiser FRIEDRICH III. verfügt nicht nur über die Reichs-
> kanzlei, sondern gleichzeitig auch, für die Angelegen-
> heiten seiner habsburgischen Erblande, über eine in
> Graz beheimatete Hauskanzlei. Während nun diese in
> ihrer Schreibsprache die derb mundartlichen Züge niemals
> verleugnet, befleißigt sich die Reichskanzlei einer
> gezügelten übermundartlichen Schreibart, die alles Nur-
> Mundartliche zu meiden sucht. Diese überregionale
> Schreibsprache aber war, wie NOORDIJK nachweisen konnte,
> schon ausgeprägt, bevor die Reichskanzlei nach Wien
> verlegt wurde, nämlich in der Wiener Stadtkanzlei. (p. 141)

Continuing in this vein, Eggers concludes, "[. . .] es ist klar, daß
die Schreibsprache der Weltstadt Wien zum Vorbild auch der Reichskanzlei wird, und nicht etwa die provinzielle Rückständigkeit der
Grazer Hauskanzlei" (p. 141).

Eggers exaggerates the distinction between the orientations
and jurisdictions of the two chanceries. The chancery for the
Erblande was actually split off the Imperial chancery by Frederick

in 1442 and set up with its own staff. There continued, however, to
be regular cooperation between the staffs of the two chanceries.[63]
Eggers probably overstates the role of the written language of Vienna
in the development of the Habsburg chancery dialect in this period as
well. He suggests that the personnel Frederick took over from the
Prague chancery gradually adapted to the Viennese chancery style as
new local scribes began to replace the older Prague scribes who left
the chancery (pp. 140-41). The Prague chancery tradition itself is
sufficient to account for most of the features that distinguish the
early production of the Imperial chancery in Vienna from the "crudely
dialectal characteristics" ("die derb mundartlichen Züge") of the Graz
chancery. . The continued presence of Prague scribes writing the MG
they were accustomed to is a more plausible explanation for the continued presence of these features in the Imperial chancery language
during the first decade of Frederick's reign than Eggers' suggestion
that the Prague scribes over a ten-year period gradually learned the
Viennese written language. If the Prague scribes had wanted to
affect the Viennese style, it would hardly have taken them a decade
to do so. It is more likely that the similarity between Imperial
chancery documents and Vienna city documents increased over the first
decade of Frederick's reign because of the increased number of
Vienna-trained scribes in the Reichskanzlei.

These questions of emphasis are not critical to Eggers' interpretation of the Habsburg chancery language under Frederick. The
view of language and language standardization that he imputes to the
Imperial chancery of the late fifteenth century, however, is significant. He asserts that the Imperial chancery took great pains to write
a restrained, supradialectal language, which attempted to avoid all
specifically dialectal forms. Beyond this he says that the written
language of Vienna became the model for the Imperial chancery, and
that the older Prague scribes had to adapt to this written language.
All of these statements suggest that the Imperial chancery had a
highly self-conscious and specific view of the German it wrote.
Inherent to this view is a clear distinction between dialectal and

supradialectal language. Eggers indicates that the Imperial chancery
was sufficiently aware of the concept of a supradialectal language to
seek to write one. He implies that the chancery saw the written language of Vienna to be supradialectal and thus deliberately emulated
it. This would mean that the most important administrative office in
the Holy Roman Empire was concerned enough about language as such in
the fifteenth century to deliberately change its writing practices.
The claim for such linguistic awareness remains to be proven.

In 1970 Peter von Polenz presents the more conservative view of
Frederick as the monarch uninvolved with linguistic developments in
the chancery. He describes the linguistic changes that occurred
during Frederick's reign, but he does not make him the direct cause
of them.[64]

Maximilian I and Chancery Language Reform

Many historians of the German language have tried to explain
the development of the Habsburg chancery dialect during Maximilian's
reign in terms of the Emperor's personal interest in literature and
his direct contact with the chancery. In his 1879 article on the
Saxon chancery language, Ernst Wülcker explains that Maximilian's
chancery language was basically the same as that of his father's chancery.[65] His analysis of Maximilian's chancery dialect is based on a
volume of Urkunden that was edited and published by Joseph Chmel in
1845.[66] In this edition Wülcker discovered that certain Imperial
documents issued in Holland during Maximilian's reign were "written
just like Tirolean and Austrian ones" ("in ganz derselben Weise
geschrieben sind, wie die tirolischen und österreichischen," p. 366),
that is, in Austrian dialects. Because Wülcker writes from the assumption that the Emperor used local scribes to pen his diplomatic materials when he was traveling (p. 356), he suggests that Maximilian
introduced his own UG chancery language into Low Germany and that the
indigenous scribes adopted it. Although Wülcker presents Maximilian
not as the creator of the Habsburg chancery language, but rather as
its propagator, the following statement appears to have misled several

subsequent scholars who, like Wülcker, were insufficiently informed

about the internal procedures of the Habsburg chancery.

> Ueber die Sprache Maximilians kann man sich bei Chmel
> [. . .] unterrichten, aus seinem Buche ersieht man auch,
> dass Briefe, Erlasse u. s. w., welche in Holland aus-
> gestellt sind, in ganz derselben Weise geschrieben
> sind, wie die tirolischen und österreichischen. Und bei
> dieser Sprache ist es dann später in der kaiserlichen
> Kanzlei geblieben, alle nachfolgenden Herrscher fussen
> auf ihr. Maximilian aber, der dieser Schriftsprache
> zuerst in seinen niederländischen Provinzen mit klarem
> Bewusstsein und nothgedrungen Geltung verschaffen
> musste, dessen Kanzler also auch gewisse Instruktionen
> zu erlassen hatten—Maximilian galt später als ihr
> Begründer, obwohl sie vielleicht auch schon etwas früher
> für das eigentliche Deutschland nachgewiesen werden kann.
> (p. 366)

In 1888 Friedrich Kluge assumes that because Maximilian encour-

aged the translation of a number of works from the classical languages

into German, there is sufficient justification for attributing the

beginnings of the theoretical regulation of the language to him.[67]

To support this assumption he cites the following line from Theodor

Bibliander's 1548 treatise, De ratione communi omnium linguarum:

"ferunt et Maximilianum imperatorem in animo versavisse emendationem

sermonis Teutonici" (p. 31, n. 1). Kluge's reasoning here is uncon-

vincing; that Maximilian encouraged translation is no reason to assume

that he took a personally active role in linguistic reform. Bibliander

might have had personal knowledge of Maximilian to support his state-

ment, but this is unlikely since he was not born until about 1504.[68]

It is more likely that the statement derives from another contemporary

work on language. The passage from which Kluge quotes suggests its

source:

> Doctissimi autem uiri Ioan. Tritemij sentētiam paulô
> inferius reddā, quum de linguarū mutatione explicabitur.
> Non praeter mittere hic etiam sententiā grauem &
> sapientem, ut iudico, Fabiani Franki ciuis Boli-
> slauiensis, debeo. Cuius haec sunt uerba: Es wãr on
> schaden/ ja meins bedunckens hoch von nõten/ das ein
> gantze Grammatika hieriñ beschribē wurd/ recht
> regulierts Tütschen. Die sprach ist so lustig/ nutzlich
> vnd dapffer in jrer redmas/ als inndert ein andere
> befunden wirt.[69]

Although Bibliander does not quote Fabian Frangk exactly, these are
certainly close approximations of statements made by Frangk in the
Vorrede to the 1531 and later editions of his Orthographia.[70] Since
Bibliander knew Frangk's work, it is probable that his statement about
Maximilian is also based on Frangk's reference to Maximilian's chan-
cery (see "Frangk's Orthographia" below).[71] In 1888 Socin, like
Kluge, relates this statement of Bibliander's to Maximilian's sup-
posed attempts to produce a uniform written language.[72]

The first to question Maximilian's direct involvement with
linguistic reform is Virgil Moser in 1909. He says that since Maximilian "only builds a little further" on the language of Frederick III,
he can "hardly understand the praise awarded him and his chancellor
Ziegler because of his efforts at orthographic reform."[73] This point
is well taken. If the reform was simply orthographic, it is curious
that it should have received so much attention. The continuing
scholarly interest in this matter can only be explained when specific
details of the reform—if there was one—are produced. Henzen adopts
a similar line but with fewer specific objections; he simply questions
whether Maximilian was personally involved in the attempts at language
leveling that occurred during his reign.[74]

In 1925 Dirk Noordijk questions several aspects of Wülcker's
description of the activities and language of Maximilian's chancery.[75]
He objects particularly to Wülcker's suggestion that Imperial documents issued in the Lowlands by LG scribes were written in the same
variety of UG as those produced by the chancery in Austria; he notes
that the Habsburg documents from the Lowlands show numerous local
dialects and that some were actually written in French (p. 157). On
the basis of this evidence, he refutes Wülcker's contention that
Maximilian's chancery language enjoyed universal acclaim and was
written outside the UG region by scribes who were not from Upper
Germany. Unfortunately historians of the German language writing
since 1925 have for the most part overlooked Noordijk's sound objections and have adopted and elaborated on the mistaken conclusions of
Wülcker.

Hugo Moser, in his <u>Deutsche Sprachgeschichte</u> and in his 1951 article on the emergence of the NHG common language,[76] implies that Maximilian was personally involved in the reform. In the first he says, "Kaiser Maximilian und sein Kanzler Niclas Ziegler erstrebten eine einheitliche, von landschaftsprachlichen Zügen freie ober- deutsche Kanzleisprache" (p. 138); in the second, "Seine [der kaiser- lichen Kanzleisprache] innere Entwicklung und äußere Ausbreitung wurden vor allem durch die Tätigkeit Maximilians I. und seines Kanzlers Niclas Ziegler wesentlich gefördert" (p. 62).

Eggers adopts Kluge's view of Maximilian; he presents him as the author and literary patron who was, along with his chancellor Niclas Ziegler, concerned with the transformation of the chancery language. He attributes the renown of the Habsburg chancery dialect, "das 'Donauische'" or "die 'Donausprache,'" to its regularized orthog- raphy and claims contemporaries were aware "that strong impulses emanated from the Imperial chancery."[77] Later, however, Eggers sug- gests that the orthographic reform of Ziegler was short-lived: "Wenige Jahre nach Kaiser MAXIMILIANS Tod ist also ZIEGLERS Werk der Orthographiereform bereits verwässert. Landschaftliche Sonderbräuche und Schreibunarten zersetzen die auf Einheitlichkeit zielende Regelung" (p. 190). Polenz suggests a similar personal involvement on the part of Maximilian.[78]

The Grammars of Krachenberger and Sunthaym

Since the appearance of the first edition of Kluge's <u>Von Luther bis Lessing</u> in 1888, several historians of the German language have included references to the missing grammars of Hans Krachen- berger and Ladislaus Sunthaym as evidence of the deliberate linguistic activity Maximilian is supposed to have fostered in his chancery and elsewhere. Kluge cites the Bibliander statement discussed above and uses it as the basis for his assumption that Maximilian was concerned with normalizing the German language. Krachenberger, Sunthaym, and their respective grammars are mentioned to support this argument. Hans Krachenberger (Gracchus Pierius), Austrian Protonotary and <u>Land- schreiber,</u> is supposed to have begun but not completed an "<u>opus</u>

gramaticale de lingua germanica certis adstricta legibus," and Hofkaplan Ladislaus Sunthaym is said to have worked on a "Descriptio
linguae vulgaris per superiorem Germaniam," under the aegis of Maximilian. Socin, writing in the same year as Kluge, mentions only one
of the supposed grammarians. He states that Hans Krachenberger,
advisor and secretary at the courts of Frederick III and Maximilian I,
wrote a grammar of the chancery language entitled "Opus grammaticale
de lingua Germanica, certis adstricta legibus." Since then Henzen,
Bach, and Hans Rupprich have each mentioned Krachenberger and Sunthaym
in connection with Maximilian's putative linguistic activities. Each
of these accounts derives from Kluge's.[79]

The existence of these grammars would be extremely significant
for the present investigation and for other more general studies of
the development of the German vernacular at the beginning of the sixteenth century. The works would antedate by a generation other
sixteenth-century German linguistic treatises that invoke Maximilian's
chancery language as a model. This means they could not be seen as a
part of the wave of German grammatical works produced to teach the
unlettered to read (and secondarily to write) as a result of the
Reformation. Further the direct relationship of Krachenberger and
Sunthaym to Maximilian might allow one to establish more convincingly
than in previous studies Maximilian's own interest in the German
language. For these reasons it is necessary to attempt to trace the
grammars.

Neither Kluge nor Socin, both writing about the grammars in
1888, indicates his sources of information. Kluge, however, seems to
have taken his material on both Krachenberger and Sunthaym from
Johannes Müller's Quellenschriften.[80] His phraseology here is so
similar to Müller's that there is no reason to assume he consulted
the earlier sources Müller cites. Socin apparently used the following statement from Rudolf von Raumer's Geschichte der germanischen
Philologie (1870):

> Der erste, von dem uns berichtet wird, daß er eine
> Grammatik der deutschen Sprache unternommen habe, war
> Hans Krachenberger, kaiserlicher Rath und Secretarius

am Hofe Friedrich's III. und Maximilian's I. Das opus
grammaticale de lingua Germanica certis adstricta
legibus war seine letzte Arbeit. Er ist darüber hinge-
storben, ohne sie zu vollenden und zu veröffentlichen.[81]

Through these early modern works it is possible to trace
accounts of Krachenberger's grammar to 1553. Working backward from
Müller, one comes first to Aschbach and then to Klüpfel. The second
volume of Joseph von Aschbach's Geschichte der Wiener Universität
(1877)[82] offers good biographical material on Krachenberger, showing
his position in Celtis' literary entourage and mentioning his grammar
(pp. 421-22, n. 2). Engelbert Klüpfel's Latin biography of Celtis
written fifty years earlier (De Vita et Scriptis Conradi Celtis,
1827) seems to have given Krachenberger's missing grammatical
treatise the name by which it is still known. Klüpfel writes, "Operi
grammaticali de lingua germanica, certis adstricta legibus, est
immortuus."[83] A reference from Klüpfel can be traced through the
Kobolt-Gandershofer Baierisches Gelehrten-Lexikon (1824)[84] and Michael
Denis' Buchdruckergeschichte (1782)[85] to the first edition of
Cuspinianus' Austria (1553).[86] Cuspinianus mentions his longtime
colleague Krachenberger at the end of a passage comparing German
with the classical languages:

> Et olim Ioannes Gracchus Pierius, ni morte fuisset
> praeuentus, grammaticam pollicebatur in Germaniam
> linguam, sub certis regulis & inclinationibus sese
> scripturū, idq̄ multis doctis palàm testabatur: &
> si uixisset, proculdubio praestitisset. Erat enim
> acuti ingenij, & carmine & prosa probè doctus, ut
> eius syntagmata clarè ostendunt: Elegiae praesertim,
> quibus cum antiquis certat, in rebus praecipuè Ger-
> manicis Cuius utinam manes, ambrosia pascantur &
> nectare. (p. 593)

In the absence of the work itself, this evidence establishes
quite convincingly that there once was a partially completed Krachenberger grammar of the German language. Cuspinianus is writing here
about a man with whom he had been personally associated for decades.
(More than fifty years earlier, for example, Cuspinianus had dedicated one of his early publications to Krachenberger.)[87] Both were
principal members of the Danubian Sodality in Vienna.[88] Because

Cuspinianus knew the man he writes about and lived in the same city
as he, one may assume that he had more than hearsay knowledge of the
grammar's existence. Little more, however, can be said about the
grammar. From the sixteenth-century data, there is nothing to suggest
that Maximilian commissioned this work or that the German described
in it had anything to do with Maximilian's chancery language. Considered in the context of the linguistic climate of Germany at the turn
of the sixteenth century, the existence of Krachenberger's grammar may
be seen as evidence of the increasing humanist interest in the vernacular even before the Reformation. It cannot be used to support arguments for linguistic self-consciousness or standardization of any kind
in the chanceries of Maximilian I.

The association of Ladislaus Sunthaym with an UG grammar dates
from the mid-eighteenth century and the earliest stages of the historiography of the German language. In 1747 Elias Caspar Reichard
writes in his Versuch einer Historie der deutschen Sprachkunst: "Des
Ladislaus Suntheims descriptio linguae vulgaris per superiorem
Germaniam lässt sich nebst verschiedenen andern, deren Gesner und
Simler gedenken, nirgend antreffen."[89] This statement provides both
the title of the elusive grammar and Reichard's source: the published
catalog of the Conrad Gesner-Josia Simler library. Until now it has
generally been assumed that the reference in the 1583 edition of this
work was the earliest mention of the Sunthaym grammar. In his article
on Sunthaym in the Verfasserlexikon, Hermann Maschek writes: "Die
älteste Notiz darüber findet sich in dem Werk: 'Bibliotheca
instituta et collecta primum a Conrado Gesnero . . . aucta per Josiam
Simlerum . . . amplifiata [sic] per Joh. Jac. Frisium Tigurinum',
Zürich 1583, S. 531. Daraus ist sie in andere Nachschlagebücher
übergegangen."[90] The reference reads, "Ladislaus Suntheimus,
Germanus, scripsit de lingua vulgari per superiorem Germaniam. Item
historiarum collectanea."[91] This is not, however, from the first
edition of the catalog; the 1583 edition, which appeared after the
deaths of both of the collectors named in its title,[92] is actually
the third version of the work to have been printed. The second

appeared in 1574. The first edition was published under a different title in four volumes that appeared between 1545 and 1555.[93] All three editions were published in Zurich.

A different and earlier reference to a grammatical treatise by Sunthaym appears in the second volume of the first edition in 1548. In the chapter entitled "De Grammatica" we read that "Ladislaus Suntheim descripsit lingua uulgarem per Germaniā superiorē."[94] Although the content of this brief entry is very similar to the Sunthaym entries in the second and third editions, there is a major difference. Entries in the later editions are "in Epitomen redacta," that is, very briefly abstracted. In the last two editions the Sunthaym work is listed in this way: "Ladislaus, Suntheimus, Germanus, scripsit de lingua vulgari per superiorem Germaniā. Item historiarum collectanea."[95] This means that between 1548 and 1574, when the abstracts were being written for the second edition, someone must have discovered that the Sunthaym work had originally been misclassified; it was not a grammar at all but an historical treatise. Though the title continued to be misleading, the second and third editions of the catalog at least place Sunthaym's work in the proper category. The fact that no one has ever been able to produce a manuscript, a more detailed description of the supposed grammar, or corroborating contemporary evidence of its existence supports the theory of a cataloging error in 1548. The Sunthaym work appears to have been in the lingua vulgari and about Upper Germany rather than about the lingua vulgari in Upper Germany. If so, the Latin titles of the Sunthaym work are inaccurate in all three editions of the catalog.

In an interview with me on 18 May 1975, Dr. Friedrich Eheim of the Niederösterreichisches Landesarchiv[96] supported the assumption that Sunthaym had never written a grammatical treatise. Eheim's comments were based on a thorough acquaintance with the corpus of surviving Sunthaym manuscripts and on a detailed knowledge of the historian's biography, not on the catalog evidence just presented. He concluded that the work in question was undoubtedly about Upper Germany and not about UG. He described Sunthaym as more old-fashioned

than other members of the Celtis Sodality like Cuspinianus and
Krachenberger, who were closer to the mainstream of Viennese human-
ism. Sunthaym's great interest was history and his contribution a
new historical method; he never displayed any particular enthusiasm
for language as such. Despite his title "Hofkaplan," Sunthaym's
contact with the chancery was limited to collecting funds from it
occasionally. His title, like those supplied to various of Maximilian's diplomats (see "Chancery Activity under Maximilian I," chapter 2), does not necessarily mean that he actually served at Court.

Sunthaym's so-called UG grammar was probably never written;
Krachenberger's was partially written but has never been found. This
means that both of the putative grammatical treatises must be excluded
from the remainder of the present investigation. And because his
grammar has been lost, there is no reason to investigate Krachenberger further. Although he is the only early sixteenth-century
German grammarian known to have served in one of Maximilian's chanceries, the significance of the missing Krachenberger grammar for
determining the linguistic climate of the Habsburg chancery during
the period under consideration should not be overestimated. At the
time Raumer introduced the Krachenberger material into the historiography of the German language in 1870, he had not seen the grammar, nor
has anyone since. Thus Kluge's attempt to associate the work with
Maximilian's "theoretical regulation of the language"[97] is based on
nothing but speculation. In terms of the evidence currently available, neither of the "grammars" that has been associated with the
Habsburg chancery language can be shown to have had a direct connection with the written dialect, and neither can be used to support the
argument that any sort of deliberate regulation of the written language was practiced in Maximilian's chancery.

Ziegler and the Chancery Language of Maximilian I

It is also Friedrich Kluge who first mentions Imperial chancellor[98] Niclas Ziegler in conjunction with Habsburg chancery reform.[99]
Immediately after his statements concerning Sunthaym and Krachenberger, he continues:

Das höchste Ansehen aber in sprachlichen Dingen genoß
der kaiserliche Kanzler Niclaus Ziegler, dessen Namen
und Schreibart zahlreiche Urkunden weithin durch
Deutschland verbreiteten.

Bis auf Maximilian treffen wir eine consequente Schreibart
bezüglich der Consonantendoppelungen. Überall treten in
Urkunden Schreibungen wie Hellffershellffer, wie Czeytten
(Zeiten), weitter, Pottschafft u. s. w. auf [. . .] Aber
seit 1500 scheint eine strengere Orthographie durchzu-
dringen. Und besonders die von Niclas Ziegler gezeich-
neten Urkunden zeigen ein erfolgreiches Bestreben, die
unnötigen Consonantenhäufungen, zumal cz zu meiden. Er
schreibt Zeiten, Helfer; nur die unvermeidlichen nn (unns)
herrschen auch bei ihm. Sonst sehen wir in seiner Sprache
die Charakteristika des baierisch-östreichischen Dialekts:
das häufige kh im An- und Inlaut; sl, sw, sn für schl,
schw, schn (swebisch, Ratslag); anlautendes p (Pot 'Bote');
das Suffix -nuss; synkopirte Formen wie Glaub, Nam für
Glaube, Name. Nur in Bezug auf das baierische ai ist N.
Ziegler nicht so consequent wie die übrigen Kanzler des
Kaisers.

Wenn bald auf allen Gebieten das Lob der Maximilianischen
Kanzlei erschallt, so kann es sich kaum auf die Lautgebung
beziehen; denn diese deckte sich im wesentlichen mit der
Mundart der Donaulande. Jene Reformen in der Orthographie
scheinen den Kanzleiräten Maximilians sprachliche Anerken-
nung verschafft zu haben.[100]

Since this material first appeared, at least ten historians of
the German language have adopted it, most of them without alteration.
The first to question this presentation is Virgil Moser (1909) in the
statement cited above in which he expresses skepticism about the high
praise bestowed on Maximilian and Ziegler for what appears to have
been an orthographic reform.[101] The handbooks that have since come
to include mention of Niclas Ziegler all adopt Kluge's account more
or less at face value. Bach says that through Ziegler the striving
for a uniform language was promoted in orthography and Rechtschreibung,
and that in Southern Germany, provincial characteristics in the
written language were reduced. The examples he cites (Hellffershellffer and Czeytten) are apparently taken directly from Kluge.[102]

Henzen mentions Ziegler twice, once in conjunction with
members of Maximilian's literary entourage, and once in his role as
a contributor to the emergence of the new written language. "Es ist

behauptet worden, um 1500 sei Niclas Ziegler, der Kanzler Maximilians,
die höchste sprachliche Autorität gewesen." This can only be a para-
phrase of the Kluge statement that Ziegler enjoyed the highest esteem
in things pertaining to language. Waterman, Schmidt, Rupprich, Eggers,
and Polenz all include Ziegler in their presentations as Maximilian's
major language reformer. Each of their statements can easily be
derived from Kluge's and none of them offers more complete information
than he presents. Eggers and Schmidt, like Bach, take over Kluge's
example Hellffershellffer.[103]

This heavy dependence on Kluge in the matter of Ziegler was
first brought to light by Thomas P. Thornton in his article "Die
Schreibgewohnheiten Hans Rieds im Ambraser Heldenbuch."[104] In it he
says, "Trotz des vielen Suchens, habe ich nie Niclas Ziegler erwähnt
gefunden, außer bei Kluge und seinen Nachfolgern wie Henzen und Bach,
rein historischen Werken, und drittens in der berühmten Stelle am
Anfang der Eckbibel, wo Eck den 'trefflichen' Ziegler und Maximilian
wegen ihrer sprachvereinigenden Verdienste lobt" (p. 56). When
Thornton's article appeared in 1962 this statement was perfectly
accurate. Unlike Krachenberger and Sunthaym, whose association with
the language of Maximilian's chancery can be traced to post-sixteenth-
century works earlier than Kluge's, Ziegler appears first to have
been cast in the role of a linguistic reformer by Kluge himself.

In the last six years pertinent new information on Ziegler has
become available, making it possible now to assess his position in
both the linguistic and the political history of the early sixteenth
century. I consider this material in the following chapters in
examining the organization and dialect of the Habsburg chancery
during Maximilian's reign. Here, however, Kluge's sources are of
interest, for his account alone is responsible for the inclusion of
Niclas Ziegler in the standard histories of the German language. As
Thornton suggests, these materials are not easy to locate. In the
first (1888) edition of Von Luther bis Lessing, Kluge does not document the material on Ziegler, and in the last edition (the only one
to which documentation of this information was added), Kluge's

citation is incorrect.[105]   The most probable source of Kluge's account
is the first volume of Heinrich Ulmann's exhaustive biography, Kaiser
Maximilian I.,[106] which appeared in 1884, although the work contains
but four brief references to Ziegler.[107]   The Ulmann references lead
to manuscripts in the "Wiener Archiv" (the Österreichisches Staatsarchiv, which includes the former Haus-, Hof-, und Staatsarchiv
[HHSA]) or to the 1875 Victor von Kraus edition of certain of these
manuscripts.[108]   Although the manuscript holdings of the Staatsarchiv
and recent historical studies establish unequivocally Niclas Ziegler's
prominence in Maximilian's chancery hierarchy, the Wiesflecker
regesta indicate that there are far fewer surviving Ziegler manuscripts than Kluge's statement above might lead one to believe.[109]
It is unlikely that these documents, many of which are internal chancery communications, ever enjoyed any public circulation at all (see
"The Secretaries," "The Hofordnung of 1498," and "The Authentication
of Documents in Maximilian's Chancery," chapter 2).   Further, Kluge
never worked in or ordered materials from the Staatsarchiv.[110]

The question remains, then: Why did Kluge believe Niclas
Ziegler had an active interest in revising the language of Maximilian's
chancery? It is entirely possible that Kluge never saw a Ziegler
document. His original impetus for investigating Ziegler was certainly the reference from Eck's 1537 Bible, and it appears that this
statement plus the limited material from Ulmann's biography are the
major sources of Kluge's presentation. In speaking of Paul von
Liechtenstain, Ulmann makes a passing reference to Ziegler: "An ihn
[Liechtenstain] lehnte sich von den 'Geschriftweisen' vorzugsweise
der vielgeschmähte Niklas Ziegler an, ein entschiedener Widersacher
Langs und Sernteins."[111]   Here Kluge may have thought that the term
"Geschriftweisen" had something to do with language reform, when it
only refers to the so-called clique of scribes, ambitious educated
men who held high positions in the chancery and who were often criti-
cized for reaping private gains from their public positions. A misinterpretation of this word taken in combination with the Eck reference might have led Kluge to conclude that Ziegler had a prescriptive

interest in the UG written in Maximilian's chancery. This conclusion
would seem to take a great deal for granted, however, and it does not
account for the description of Ziegler's orthography included in
Kluge's statement above.

Further speculation about Kluge's sources is unnecessary. The
preceding review suggests that the Kluge account, on which many others
are based, is rather fanciful. On the basis of the data Kluge presents there is no reason to believe that an orthographic reform
occurred in Maximilian's chancery or that Ziegler was interested in
such issues. The high esteem Ziegler is supposed to have enjoyed in
matters of language appears to have been limited to the acclaim of
Johann Eck, and the reasons for this are not yet known. If any of
Kluge's assertions are accurate, they remain to be supported with more
substantial sixteenth-century evidence.

Chancery Procedures under Maximilian I

Some of the handbook accounts make reference to chancery procedures during Maximilian's reign that may have affected the complexion
of the language in which chancery documents were written. Although
these matters are considered in detail in the following chapter, the
assertions are mentioned here briefly to show how certain vaguely
understood chancery practices have been construed to have linguistic
significance.

Philologists, beginning with Wülcker in his 1883 article on
Luther's relationship to the Saxon chancery language, discuss the
uniform language in which official documents, issued "in the name of
the ruler" ("im Namen des Herrschers"), were written. Socin adopts
this phrase in his 1888 study. An alternative formulation was coined
by Behaghel in his Geschichte der deutschen Sprache; he speaks of
documents that proceed "directly from the Emperor" ("unmittelbar vom
Kaiser"). Bach has adopted this phraseology, and most recently
Waterman has written of chancery documents "bearing the emperor's
seal."[112]

What these phrases are meant to suggest is not clear. They
seem to imply that certain documents produced in the chancery, those

that went out in Maximilian's name or bore his seal, were scrutinized
for some sort of linguistic conformity. None of the scholars who
include these formulations, however, explain in what way the language
of these documents was uniform or what sort of approval the Emperor's
seal implied. Nor do they indicate whether the presence of the
Imperial seal meant that Maximilian had personally endorsed the document on which it appeared. To date no one has established that
chancery signatory practices reflect a control for linguistic conformity or regularity. The handbook accounts, however, suggest that this
may have been the case.

Expanding the idea that the Emperor's own communications displayed a degree of linguistic uniformity, some scholars have further
suggested that documents that proceeded "directly from the Emperor"
or documents from Imperial chanceries were written in the same standard language whether they were produced in Ghent, Brussels, Bruges,
Innsbruck, or Neustadt. In Die deutsche Sprache, for example,
Behaghel writes:

> [. . .] während früher die Urkunden mit der Unterschrift
> des Kaisers gar verschiedenen Charakter trugen, mannig-
> fache landschaftliche Färbung zeigten, geben schon seit
> Friedrich III. und mit voller, bewußter Entschiedenheit
> seit Maximilian die Schriften, die unmittelbar vom
> Kaiser ausgingen, die gleiche Sprache wieder, in welchem
> Teile von Deutschland sie entstanden sein mögen.[113]

It is again Wülcker who first suggests that the Austrian chancery
language was written in Low Germany as well as various other parts of
the Empire. In 1871 he mentions Holland,[114] and in the Luther
article[115] he lists Ghent, Neustadt, Innsbruck, and Bruges; Socin is
the first to add Brussels to the list. Bach adopts the catalog of
cities; Waterman chooses the Behaghel formulation.[116] So much for
influences and borrowings. To date historians of the German language
have presented these geographic details to imply that the regularized
language of Maximilian's chancery had an impact far beyond its own
Austro-Bavarian region.

Summary

The preceding review demonstrates that the handbooks as a group treat the Habsburg chancery language as a manifestation of the sixteenth-century German impulse toward a common language. The linguistic historians assume, as Eggers says, that this was "a time that had made Common German its goal."[117] They suppose the movement toward a supradialectal language was conscious and widespread during the period and imply that it motivated the Habsburg chancery under Frederick and Maximilian. From this premise they attempt to establish the supradialectal, deliberately regularized features of the chancery dialect. In many presentations this is done by combining (or confusing) the issues of the Habsburg chancery language and Gemeines Deutsch. This approach is explained in terms of the supposed linguistic concerns or climate of Germany at the turn of the sixteenth century. And indeed the unsubstantiated claims put forward in the handbook accounts of the Habsburg chancery language are meaningful only in the context of a deliberate movement toward a German common language: Were Maximilian's own official documents written in a kind of regularized, supradialectal German? Did all the chanceries of the Empire write regularized UG? Did Niclas Ziegler execute an orthographic reform? Were Habsburg chancery documents controlled for orthographic conformity? The significance of these questions depends on the actual linguistic concerns of Germany just prior to the Reformation.

It has been established thus far that the combination of "gemein" and "deutsch" in several late medieval German contexts could mean German versus Latin, stylistically simple German, or a regional German written language. None of the ENHG attestations examined above can be construed to mean a supradialectal common language in the modern sense of the term. With the semantic problem now somewhat simplified, it is time to consider the sixteenth-century references that are most responsible for the view of Maximilian's chancery dialect commonly held by historians of the German language. An examination of these texts may justify the present preoccupation with conscious sixteenth-century German efforts toward a common language. It may also establish a firm connection between this development and the chancery of Maximilian. In broadening our view of the sixteenth-century German linguistic climate, these texts may suggest which of the unsolved problems raised by the handbooks require further consideration. The texts are from two of Luther's Tischreden and from Fabian Frangk's Orthographia.

THE CONTEMPORARY ACCOUNTS

Luther's Tischreden WA I, 524 and WA V, 511

'Ich', sprach D. M. L., 'kann weder Griechisch noch
Ebräisch, ich will aber dennoch einem Ebräer und
Griechen ziemlich begegnen. Aber die Sprachen
machen fur sich selbs keinen Theologen, sondern sind
nur eine Hülfe. Denn, soll einer von einem Dinge
reden, so muß er die Sache zuvor wissen und verstehen.
Ich habe keine gewisse, sonderliche, eigene Sprache
im Deutschen, sondern brauche der gemeinen deutschen
Sprache, daß mich beide, Ober- und Niederländer verstehen mögen. Ich rede nach der sächsischen Canzeley,
welcher nachfolgen alle Fürsten und Könige in Deutschland; alle Reichsstädte, Fürsten-Höfe schreiben nach
der sächsischen und unsers Fürsten Canzeley, darum
ists auch die gemeinste deutsche Sprache. Kaiser
Maximilian, und Kurf. Friedrich, H. zu Sachsen etc.
haben im römischen Reich die deutschen Sprachen also
in eine gewisse Sprache gezogen. Die märkische Sprache
ist leichte; man merkt kaum, daß ein Märker die Lippen
reget, wenn er redet; sie ubertrifft die sächsische.'[118]

It is easy to see how this passage is responsible for most of the assertions about the German common language examined above. Luther's meaning is anything but self-evident. Linguistic historians have generally assumed that the passage refers to some variety of supradialectal German common language but have not always agreed on the definition of that term. Nineteenth-century linguists tended to see a fairly close correspondence between the common language suggested by Luther's statements and "common language" in the contemporary sense of the term. Thus Hermann Paul, for example, in the same passage in which he argues for a broader reading of the term "gemein

deutsch," asserts that Luther's phrase above can only imply a supradialectal language: "Wenn Luther in den tischreden von 'der gemeinen
deutschen sprache' spricht, so kann es nach dem zusammenhange nicht
zweifelhaft sein, dass dies im sinne einer für das gesamte reich
gültigen, über den mundarten stehenden sprache gemeint ist."[119] More
recently scholars have been somewhat skeptical of this kind of equa-
tion and have found different "common" aspects of the language Luther
describes. Werbow, for example, argues for a stylistic interpretation of the phrase "der gemeinen deutschen Sprache."[120] For the
present investigation, however, the problem the passage raises is not
whether Luther implies some sort of common language here. It is
rather what kind of common language he means and how it corresponds
to the modern conceptions of a German common language that have been
associated with Maximilian's chancery dialect on the basis of the
passage.

A comparison of the passage above to another of Luther's
pronouncements on the German language brings into sharper focus his
orientation toward the language he wrote and his sensitivity to
dialectal differences. The following statement is from another of
the Tischreden and seems to have been introduced to current ENHG
scholarship by Johannes Erben.[121]

> 'Ich glaub, Engeland sey ein Stück Deutschlandes, denn
> sie brauchen der sächsischen Sprache, wie in Westphalen
> und Niederlande; wiewol sie sehr corrumpirt ist. Ich
> halte, die Deutschen sind vor Zeiten hinein transferirt
> und gesetzt, wie noch heut zu Tage der Bischof zu Cöln
> schreibet sich Herzog zu Engern, da itzund Bremen,
> Hamburg liegt; etwa ists Britannia genannt, darnach
> Angera, vom Volk, das hineingefuhrt ist. Die dänische
> und englische Sprache ist sächsisch, welche recht deutsch
> ist. Die oberländische Sprache ist nicht die rechte
> deutsche Sprache, nimmt den Mund voll und weit, und
> lautet hart. Aber die sächsische Sprache gehet fein
> leise und leicht ab.'

> 'Deutschland hat mancherley Dialectos, Art zu reden,
> also, daß die Leute in 30 Meilen Weges einander nicht
> wol können verstehen. Die Oesterreicher und Bayern
> verstehen die Thüringer und Sachsen nicht, sonderlich
> die Niederländer. Ja, jutha, ju, ke, ha, solch verjahen

ist mancherley, und eines anders denn das ander.
Arnoldus, Ehrenhold; Arnolf, Ehrnhulf; Ulrich,
Huldenreich; Leudolf, Leuthülf, eben wie Alexander;
Ludwig, des Volks Zuflucht; denn Wigk heißt ein
Schloß, _Refugium_, Hort, _Asylum_.'[122]

Luther's remarks here comparing UG ("oberländisch") to Saxon
("sächsisch"), and Austrian and Bavarian to Thuringian, Saxon, and
LG, like those from the better-known _Tischrede_, WA I, 524 (in which
he compares Saxon to the language of the March), show clearly that
he knew the spoken languages of Austria and Saxony were considerably
different at the time he wrote. Luther perceives them as being so
different in fact that he categorizes Danish and English along with
Saxon as "real (proper) German" ("die rechte deutsche Sprache"),
while declaring UG not to be the real German language because it
"fills the mouth, stretches it wide, and sounds harsh." Beauty is
clearly in the ear of the hearer. Nevertheless there are limits to
Luther's regional chauvinism: though he declares Saxon to be
superior to UG, he finds the language of the March better than Saxon
because it is light and requires the speaker barely to move his lips.
However subjective his statement about the High and Low German
dialects may be, it is evident, when the two _Tischreden_ are considered together, that Luther is referring exclusively to a written
language in his remarks about the linguistic achievements of Frederick
the Wise and Maximilian. Thus the current tendency to read, "I write
in the manner of Saxon chancery," for "Ich rede nach der sächsischen
Canzeley," is perfectly correct. Bearing this in mind, let us return
to the first of the _Tischreden_ and see what it is that Luther says
about this written language.

When Luther delivered this _Tischrede_ in which he mentions the
chancery languages, sometime between 1530 and 1535, he had already
taught himself to write literary German and was fully aware of the
problems this entailed. Erben notes that in the period between 1516
and 1530 Luther had become familiar with the vocabularies of other
dialectal regions of Germany through his extensive reading of German
texts and his correspondence.[123] In saying that he writes the language

of the Saxon chancery, then, Luther is describing the language of his
own mature writings. As has often been noted, Luther cannot be referring to chancery style or syntax, for these were not appropriate to
the German texts he wrote. He is instead referring to features of the
chancery languages that need not be specific to either a single style
or dialectal region: orthography, graphemics, and perhaps morphology.
It is in these areas that one must look for a certain regularity in
the Habsburg chancery language at the turn of the sixteenth century,
and for a similarity between the chancery languages of Maximilian and
Frederick the Wise. If one limits the areas of comparison to these
features of the written languages, Luther's assertion that all the
cities and princely courts of Germany wrote the same language becomes
more plausible, although it is still not altogether accurate from a
modern standpoint. From an orthographic point of view, Luther may be
quite accurate in saying that he writes "die gemeinste deutsche
Sprache."

It is not this phrase, however, but the first conjunction of
"gemein" and "deutsch" in the Tischrede that has triggered the whole
common language debate with regard to the chancery languages: "Ich
habe keine gewisse, sonderliche, eigene Sprache im Deutschen, sondern
brauche der gemeinen deutschen Sprache, daß mich beide, Ober- und
Niederländer verstehen mögen." The interpretations of this statement
range from declaring "die gemeine deutsche Sprache" to be a full-
fledged common language in the modern sense of the expression, to
denying it any supradialectal features but stylistic simplicity.
That the professional language of the chanceries was not yet a supradialectal common language that altogether transcended specific dialectal regions and speech communities is quite certain.

The suggestion that the supradialectal aspect of language to
which Luther refers may be purely stylistic requires further consideration. Werbow assumes that the two combinations of "gemein" and
"deutsch" in Luther's Tischrede have different meanings. He suggests
Luther's first reference ("der gemeinen deutschen Sprache") is to the
simple non-Latinate style of his own writings, whereas the second

("die gemeinste deutsche Sprache") is to the phonology, orthography, and morphology he adopted from the chancery languages. Since first proposed by Werbow in 1963, this reading has been adopted by other historians of the German language:[124]

> Es gibt aber eine zweite Deutung des Satzes, die das
> Lautliche weniger schwer wiegen läßt, da es sich um
> die Schreibsprache handelt, und die Satzkonstruktion
> als das Gemeinsame anerkennt, was diese Sprache allen
> verständlich sein läßt. Luther wollte nicht nur, daß
> Ober- und Niederdeutsche ihn verstehen, sondern daß
> einfache Menschen aus allen Gegenden deutschen Landes
> ihn verstehen. [. . .] Kann er damals nicht gemeint
> haben, daß er sich der 'gemeinen deutschen Sprache'
> bedient habe im Gegensatz zu der auf gewisse Kanzleien
> beschränkten, an der lateinischen Rhetorik geübten
> Schreibsprache? 'Im Lautstande, der Schreibweise und
> der Wortbiegung hat er sich der hochdeutschen Kanzlei-
> sprache angeschlossen, und zwar besonders der
> Kursächsischen . . . Im Wortschatz, der Wortbildung,
> und im Satzbau hielt er aber in richtiger Erkenntnis
> des deutschen Sprachgeistes an die lebendige Sprache
> des Volkes.'[125]

There is no question that Luther wanted the common man to understand him and that to achieve this he used the stylistically simple, syntactically genuine German that Werbow describes in explaining the earlier attestations of "gemeines Deutsch" discussed at the beginning of this chapter. Werbow's definition is not convincing, however, in the context of the second Luther statement quoted earlier in this section. Although Latinate syntax is certainly not the feature of the chancery languages Luther adopted in his own writings, there is nothing in the larger context of the Tischrede to indicate that Luther is speaking of style and not dialect. If one reads "simple German" for "der gemeinen deutschen Sprache" in Luther's statement as Werbow suggests, it implies that no Upper or Lower Germans could understand the Latinate, chancery style of their own dialects, which is reading too much into Luther's statement. The opposition Werbow sets up in explaining his definition is troublesome. In saying that Luther wanted not only Upper and Lower Germans to understand him, but simple people from all regions of Germany, Werbow relates educational level to regional origin.

By interjecting the question of the common man into Luther's statement, Werbow creates an ambiguity not present in the original sentence; he confuses dialectal with stylistic or social aspects of language in a way that Luther does not. Presumably both regions of Germany produced both syntactically simple and syntactically complex varieties of German, as well as readers who could understand both styles. The regional chancery language represents the syntactically complex variety of German written in a given area. The common man Werbow mentions would have had difficulty understanding the chancery language of his own region because of its Latinate style even though it was written in his own dialect. The chancery language of another dialectal region would have presented two impediments to the untutored common man: its syntax would have been as difficult for him as that of the chancery language of his own region; its orthography and lexicon would have been unfamiliar. By abandoning the Latinate syntax of chancery communication, Luther would have overcome only one of these difficulties.

When Luther says he does not write any particular variety of German but uses the common German language so that both High and Low Germans can understand him, he is speaking loosely in dialectal terms. In asserting that he does not write any special German language, he means that he does not write a strictly dialectal form of German specific to a given locality. Instead he writes what in Gesner's terms might be called a "Gemeindeutsch," that is, a somewhat supra-dialectal regional written language that does not exactly correspond in its features to any one dialect of the region. The region indicated by Luther's description is the eastern portion of Keller's Common German Area (East Middle Germany and East Upper Germany), and his target audience was presumably the readership of the entire Common German area.

From a contemporary sixteenth-century point of view, Luther describes his written German quite accurately. It is a kind of common language, but not the sort that nineteenth-century philologists thought it to be. Günter Feudel's assessment of the statement is

most apt: "Es handelt sich dabei weder um eine Fiktion, die voraus-
nahm, was erst drei Jahrhunderte später Wirklichkeit werden konnte—
eine Vorwegnahme würde ja bedeuten, daß Luther unsere moderne Norm
gekannt hätte—noch um mangelndes Verständnis Luthers für sprachliche
Belange."[126]   If fiction has since crept into the interpretation of
the chancery languages, it did not enter the discussion at this point
in the sixteenth century. When Luther speaks of the chancery dialect
of Maximilian, he is referring to a common language in a rather
limited sense of the term. It seems to be a written language that
can be distinguished primarily in orthographic or graphemic terms from
other varieties of written German. Nothing in either of the statements from the _Tischreden_ considered above suggests that the language
Luther describes had come into being through deliberate efforts to
produce a supradialectal common language in the modern sense of the
expression. For this reason it is more logical to ask in what sense
Maximilian's chancery language was a variety of sixteenth-century
Gemeindeutsch than it is to ask how closely it resembles a modern
common language.

Frangk's _Orthographia_

Of all the sixteenth-century German grammarians, perhaps none
is so well remembered as the Silesian schoolmaster Fabian Frangk, who
was both the first to invoke Luther as a linguistic authority and the
first to prescribe a regularized supradialectal German common language. A native of Aslau and onetime tutor to Margrave Johann von
Brandenburg, Frangk wrote his _Orthographia_ in 1531 as a companion
piece to the much longer _Cantzley vnd Titel buchlin_ of the same year.
He intended that the works be used together.[127]   The _Titel buchlin_ is
essentially an etiquette book to teach the uninitiated to write their
Sendbriefe and other missives in the correct format and with the
proper forms of address. It reflects the author's complete familiarity with contemporary chancery usage. The _Orthographia_ teaches the
petitioners how to write their requests in correct German ("Recht
buchstäbig Deutsch"). In the introduction to the _Titel buchlin_ and

later in the Orthographia itself, Frangk notes that beyond the issues
of "Orthographia" and correct address, there are also stylistic
aspects of correct German. He does not treat these, however, because
they are matters of "redmas" (diction) and "Rethorik," subjects for
the schools of "Redkündiger" (stylists of language).[128] Frangk indicates that since there are already works on rhetoric available, his
buchlin will address the unmet needs in the areas of protocol and
grammar.

Frangk's Orthographia is written for German youngsters,
untutored laymen, and proponents of proper regularized German. Its
purpose is to school Germans in the proper use of their own language
lest they appear inept by comparison with other peoples ("andern
Nation," p. 93). Although Frangk points out the need for a complete
German grammar on the model of classical grammars, his own work is
more limited in scope. "Orthographia," he reminds the reader, is
simply the Latin and Greek term for what Germans call "Recht buchstäbig Deutsch schreiben" (p. 95), and this is the focus of his
buchlin. It is aimed primarily at teaching Germans to spell their own
language correctly. The Orthographia, however, like many sixteenth-
century German grammatical works, concerns itself with reading as well
as writing, and with spoken as well as written language. This
feature distinguishes Frangk's observations about German from those
that have been considered thus far.

Frangk asserts that the individual who wishes to write or speak
German properly must avoid the usage of any particular region and
"follow the good example of good German books and correspondence that
have been published in handwritten or printed form" ("das man gutter
exemplar warnehme/ das ist/ gutter deutscher bücher vnnd verbriefungen/
schriefftlich odder im druck verfast vnd ausgangen," p. 94). As
models worthy of emulation he cites the production of Maximilian's
chancery, the writings of Martin Luther, and the texts of the Augsburg
printer Johann Schönsperger. The context of this reference to Maximilian's chancery language is of particular interest:

Woraus man Recht

vnd rein Deutsch lerne.

WEr aber solche misbreuch meiden/ vnd rechtförmig deutsch
schreiben/ odder reden wil/ der mus deutscher sprachenn
auf eins lands art vnd brauch allenthalben nicht nachfolgen. Nützlich vnd gut ists einem jdlichen/ vieler
Landsprachen mit jren misbreuchen zuwissen/ da mit man
das vnrecht möge meiden/ Aber das fürnemlichst/ so zu
dieser sach förderlich vnd dienstlich/ ist/ das man gutter
exemplar warnehme/ das ist/ gutter deutscher bücher vnnd
verbriefungen/ schriefftlich odder im druck verfast vnd
ausgangen/ die mit vleisse lese/ vnd jnen jnn dem das
anzunehmen vnd recht ist/ nachfolge.

Vnder welchen mir etwan/ des tewern (hochlöblicher
gedechtnis) Keiser Maximilianus Cantzelej vnd dieser
zeit/ D. Luthers schreiben/ neben des Johan Schonsbergers
von Augsburg druck/ die emendirsten vnnd reinisten zuhan-
den komen sein/ Besondern/ wenn sie mit vleis jnngrossirt/
vbersehen vnd Corrigirt befunden werden/ Darzu/ aus jren
Cantzleyen odder wercksteten/ Erstlich new ausgangen/
Von andern vnuleissigen vnd vnuerstendigen nicht ander-
wert vmbgeschrieben odder nach gedruckt sein. [. . .]

Vnd ab denn auch/ dieser angezeigtenn deutsch/ einem
jdlichen jnn seinen ohren nicht klüng/ odder allenthalben
gnug thet/ wollen wir sie dennach (die wir der verbesserung
mangeln) nicht veracht nach jnn winckel werffen. Denn weil
wir sehen/ das sich viel jnn kurtzen jaren auff diese
sprache bevleissigen/ Bey vielen auch merglich gewachssen
vnd zugenohmen hat/ Wollen wirs die weil jnn dem es taug-
lich/ für lieb vnd danckbar annehmen/ Vnd gentzlich
darfür halten/ die werd nach von tag zu tage jhe schein-
barer/ auch endlich gantz rein balirt vnd ausgestrichen
werden etc. (pp. 94-95)

This passage is an unequivocal call for a supradialectal HG
written and spoken language. It differs from any of the statements
about Common German examined to this point in that it advocates the
creation of a common language instead of describing any sort of
regional language already in existence. The aspect of intentionality
is brand new here, as is the suggestion that this "rechtförmig
deutsch" should be spoken as well as written. From Frangk's statement we are led to believe that this program of linguistic regularization is already under way and that it is making considerable gains

in Germany. He says that even though the language may not sound right
to everyone or satisfy all, many have troubled themselves to learn it
in recent years and it is on the rise. He continues that the language
is becoming more noticeable every day and predicts that it will eventually be completely regularized.

According to Frangk, the best way to learn this correct German
is to read and imitate fine examples of written German. The models he
suggests are from two literary generations: the first is that of
Maximilian's chancery and Hans Schönsperger the Elder;[129] and the
second, Frangk's own, is the period of Luther. The examples include
both handwritten and printed texts. Although Frangk does not name
specific works from the sources mentioned, he does warn the student
particularly to seek engrossed or corrected texts (presumably in the
case of chancery manuscripts) and new texts directly from the print
shops, not yet paraphrased by the ignorant nor corrupted in pirated
editions. This comment reflects Frangk's awareness of chancery procedures (see "The Imperial Chancery Ordinance [Reichskanzleiordnung] of
1494," chapter 2) and suggests that the exemplary quality the models
share is orthographic. As indicated, we do not know precisely which
works of the Habsburg chancery, of Luther's, or of Schönsperger's
Frangk had in mind. He may have seen either literary or diplomatic
texts from the chancery, and these may have been written or printed.
He may have known any of a number of Luther texts. The 1538 edition
of the Orthographia suggests that Frangk had seen the splendid luxury
edition of Theuerdank that Schönsperger produced for Maximilian in
1517 (p. 94, n. 12); this may be the basis for his endorsement of the
Augsburg printer. Whatever the texts Frangk is referring to, however,
it is certain that from a modern linguistic standpoint they do not
represent a single standardized written language. But from a
sixteenth-century vantage point they may indeed.

It is to be expected that Frangk does not name similar models
of spoken German despite his contention that the new regularized language is gaining ground in Germany. In this period when the first of
the mass media was just beginning to have its impact, prescribing the

speech habits of select individuals would have been pointless.
Neither can Frangk extol the virtues of a regional dialect, having
categorically declared all dialects to be less than pure and unadulterated ("lauter vnd rein," p. 94) German. This does not mean, however, that Frangk is without a regional bias or that he does not
consider certain dialects to be closer to his theoretical standard
than others. In discussing the pronunciation of vowels, for example,
he declares specifically UG diphthongs substandard for correct German
(pp. 96-97), and his final tally of standard vowels represents an
essentially MG distribution. Frangk's treatment of pronunciation and
articulation is surprisingly scant throughout the Orthographia when
one considers that he is proposing a variety of spoken and written
German different from any of the spoken German dialects of his time.
One wonders how the untutored were to learn to pronounce the standard
spellings put forth in the Orthographia.

In several respects Frangk's phonetic and articulatory perceptions are less sophisticated than those of such contemporary
sixteenth-century grammarians as Ickelsamer and Kolroß.[130] This in
no way diminishes the significance of his farsighted call for a supradialectal German language, but it should be remembered in evaluating
his references to the Habsburg chancery language and to the common
language he thought he heard developing around him. What Frangk
interprets as the deliberate effort of individuals to learn the supradialectal language described in the passage above was probably nothing
more than the continuing natural evolution of the sorts of regional
languages suggested by the Gesner and Luther statements already discussed. If so, one must ask what sort of spoken German Frangk
considers to be evidence of the deliberate regularization of the
language, since the regional languages posited earlier were only
written languages. Frangk probably bases his statement on the speech
of educated persons who either come from dialectal interface areas,
travel widely, or come into regular contact with individuals from a
variety of dialectal regions. The homogenizing influences of education, travel, or heterogeneous association could easily account for

the kind of language Frangk both prescribes and believes his contemporaries deliberately to be adopting.

At the point in the _Orthographia_ (quoted above) where Frangk
calls for the artificial creation of a supradialectal language, he
mentions both Maximilian's chancery language and Luther's language as
models of fine German. Frangk does not claim that the chancery language is an example of the regularized German; he simply says it is
one of the best varieties of written German available to imitate.
Yet the statement can easily be misconstrued so that Maximilian's
chancery language is seen not as a means toward the standardized
language but as a product of the conscious regularizing process itself.
Read in this way, Frangk's statement, along with the reference from
Luther's _Tischrede_, has certainly contributed to the modern assumption
that the Habsburg chancery language was consciously standardized
during Maximilian's reign.[131]   This conclusion is no more justified
on the basis of Frangk's statement, however, than it is on the basis
of Luther's.

Frangk's contribution to the emergence of the German common
language is a theoretical, not a practical, one. The singular
feature of his work is that it is the first to prescribe the sort of
language that Luther and others only describe. Frangk misconstrues
his contemporary linguistic situation, however, when he interprets
the naturally evolving regional languages to be the result of deliberate attempts to regularize German. It has been suggested that
Frangk is neither an anomaly nor a solitary voice, but that he rather
points out the path that others follow.[132]   In the broader context of
the development of the German common language this is true. Frangk
is a transitional figure. He marks the beginning of a conscious
movement to regularize a regional language that has been developing
without prescription for some time. As an exponent of the early
sixteenth-century German linguistic scene, however, Frangk is rather
unusual. He is the only one prescribing a regularized supradialectal
written and spoken German language at a time when others are equally
articulate in their unabashed attempts to foster their own regional

dialects.[133]   The typical features of Frangk's <u>Orthographia</u> are its
indebtedness to the classical grammatical tradition, its amorphous
distinctions between sound and letter, its exuberant and imaginative
concern for the development of the German language. The call for a
standardized supradialectal German language, however, while characteristic of the experimental quality of the early German linguistic
treatises, is unique to Frangk. This fact is pertinent to our consideration of the Habsburg chancery language. It would be wrong to
impute a concern with linguistic regulation to Maximilian's chancery
on the assumption that Frangk's orientation toward language was typical either of his own generation or of the preceding generation represented by Maximilian's chancery.

                              SUMMARY

        The preceding review of scholarship changes the traditional
image of the Habsburg chancery language somewhat. It eliminates certain questions that have long been associated with the chancery
dialect and brings into sharper focus those that will be explored in
the remainder of this investigation.

        The discussion of "Gemeines Deutsch" shows that the term may
not simply be equated with the Habsburg chancery dialect. The modern
concept of a common language, which has been associated with <u>Gemeines</u>
<u>Deutsch</u> and hence with the Habsburg chancery language, does not have
its origins in pre-Reformation Germany; it is a nineteenth-century
interpolation. Three sixteenth-century German authors (Luther,
Frangk, and Eck) writing shortly after 1530 draw attention to the
language of Maximilian's chancery and establish its contemporary
reputation. Not one of these authors suggests that the dialect was
the sort of common language modern philologists assume it to have
been. Luther's description, from which the entire modern investigation of the subject arises, suggests a regional language on the order
of Gesner's <u>Gemeindeutsch</u>. But Frangk, who also proclaims the virtues
of Maximilian's chancery language, further calls for the creation of
a supradialectal German language and declares it already to be in

existence at the time of his writing. This isolated appeal for the
artificial development of a regularized, supradialectal written and
spoken German language to some extent legitimizes modern attempts to
discover a developed German common language in the early sixteenth
century. It does not justify the assumption that the written dialect
of Maximilian's chancery was such a language, however; nor does it
warrant attempts to establish this. The written professional language
of the chancery cannot have been the regularized spoken German to
which Frangk refers. But Maximilian's chancery dialect may have shown
features common to both EUG and EMG written languages of the period
and to both chancery and literary writing. In this case it could be
considered a kind of written common language, which is actually all
that the sixteenth-century sources suggest it was. The aspects of
Maximilian's chancery language that make it useful for literary as
well as business writing and render it somewhat supradialectal are in
sixteenth-century German terms "orthographic." These features of the
chancery dialect are considered in chapter 3.

     To support the argument that Maximilian's chancery was a
linguistically self-conscious agency that wrote a deliberately
standardized language, historians of the German language introduce
several ancillary issues. Some of these assumptions are based on
incomplete information; some merit further investigation. Frederick III's interest in language standardization appears to be a
nineteenth-century invention. Since there is no contemporary evidence to indicate such a concern, the following chapters concentrate
on Maximilian's chancery and its language, and consider the chancery
of his father only where it has bearing on the dialect or operations
of the Habsburg chancery during Maximilian's reign. The accuracy of
statements about Maximilian's role in the execution of chancery
documents and about the standardization and geographic range of the
chancery language can only be determined through a careful examination of the chancery, its production and procedures. This examination is also necessary to explain Eck's reference to Niclas Ziegler.
Since the sixteenth-century grammars that have been associated

traditionally with Maximilian's chancery language cannot be produced,
and because their relationship to the chancery dialect is much more
tenuous than histories of the language have suggested, one must dis-
count the linguistic awareness imputed to Maximilian's chancery unless
other materials are discovered that support the claim. The place to
look for such evidence is in the chancery itself.

2

THE HABSBURG CHANCERIES
UNDER MAXIMILIAN I

"Die kaiserliche Kanzlei" is the catchall phrase that historians of the German language have used to describe the administrative
network in which the Habsburg chancery dialect developed. In the
handbooks it is often an imprecise synonym for the actual Reichskanzlei and may also refer to any of several specifically Habsburg
chanceries. Although the kaiserliche Kanzlei is said to have been
the arena for both administrative and linguistic reform, histories of
the German language report little about the structure, operations,
and production of this bureaucratic system. To understand Maximilian's role in chancery affairs, speculate about the linguistic climate
in which Urkunden were produced, and determine the significance of
various forms of chancery endorsement, it is necessary to examine
several aspects of the history, structure, and procedures of Maximilian's chancery organization.

Three separate historical factors interweave to form the background against which the Habsburg chanceries and their language
emerge in the late fifteenth century. The first is the tradition of
the chancery as a conservative social institution that continued certain scribal practices from the late Roman Empire. The offices of
the chancery and the forms of its production are a part of this
tradition. The second is the development of the office of the
Imperial Archchancellor and its attendant powers and prerogatives.
The evolution of this office is directly related to the shifting

balance of power between church and state in Germany and between the
elected Emperor and the Stände to which he was responsible. The last
is the emergence of the House of Habsburg as a major dynastic power.
In this period its continuing claim to the Imperial throne was not
yet undisputed, and the Habsburg ancestral holdings were reorganized
in an attempt to strengthen the political position of the Emperor and
his line. One result of this reorganization was that a single chancery staff often handled both House and Imperial affairs.

These individual factors developed concurrently and interdepen-
dently. Which of them dominated conditions in the chanceries at any
given time depended primarily on where the weight of political power
rested at that moment. In years when the monarchy was weak, the
Imperial Archchancellor attempted to gain influence in the political
affairs of the Empire. At times when the power of the Emperor was
great enough to permit him to bypass the Archchancellor without fear
of interference from the Stände, the chancery activity at Court was
crucial. The checks and balances that theoretically existed between
the Emperor, the Estates, and the Electors in fact prevailed only when
the monarchy was too weak to do anything but comply with the other
standing authorities. Both Frederick and Maximilian favored the
medieval centralized monarchial administration of the Empire, although
Maximilian in his administrative reforms did take some steps toward
the delegation of authority.[134] Control of the chancery was one of
the stakes for which the monarch and the Estates contended; but even
though the chancery figured centrally in this political tug-of-war,
its internal everyday routines were not greatly affected by these
external events. Whereas the orthography of chancery production may
have changed somewhat between 1440 and 1519, the standardized formulae
of the professional language changed very little in Habsburg chancery
documents from the period.

Chanceries in the late Middle Ages were legal, business, and
diplomatic offices concerned with administration, official correspondence, and the production of documents that could serve as legal
records. Their activities ranged from routine clerical matters like

the recording of land transactions and wills to diplomatic and political issues of the highest order. Cities, wealthy nobles, and large clerical communities maintained chanceries to handle their correspondence, records, and bookkeeping. Itinerant and resident private notaries and Stuhlschreiber[135] wrote letters and made fair copies for the illiterate as well as for those who did not maintain their own chanceries. The routine activity of these offices was writing, and the legal and business documents they produced were highly standardized with respect to form. In general terms the internal operations of all the major German chanceries in this period were quite similar. This is certainly true of the Imperial chanceries.

By the late fifteenth century the Imperial chanceries had developed an organizational structure that divided chancery personnel into three broad strata.[136] At the lowest level were the simple copyists (schreyber) whose duties were basically confined to the penning, proofreading, and registration of chancery documents. Secretaries (secretarien) represented the middle level of the staff, and although their principal task was to draft, engross, and register chancery documents, they were also frequently used as diplomatic emissaries. It appears in fact that certain of Maximilian's secretaries functioned exclusively in the Emperor's private service and never wrote in the chanceries at all.[137] The highest level of chancery personnel included the Chancellor (kanzler), the advisors (räte), the senior secretaries (oberste secretarien), and the protonotaries. These positions were essentially political in nature, and although the individuals who occupied them were professional penmen and continued to discharge supervisory duties in the chancery, they were primarily concerned with the execution of Imperial policy.

The production of the chanceries can, according to Harry Bresslau, be divided into three general categories: (1) the written declarations (Urkunden) "that are intended to serve as depositions about events of a legal nature"; (2) the writings that arise from a ruler's intercourse with his subjects or employees; and (3) the intercourse of the latter with each other relating to the ordering,

preparation, introduction, or execution of a legal matter.[138]   The
issuance of a chancery document or Urkunde anywhere in Germany at this
time was the result of a fairly standardized procedure, reflected in
the chancery ordinances of 1494 and 1498 discussed below.

In very general terms the sequence of execution was as
follows.[139]   A matter might be referred to the chancery in either
oral or written form.   If brought orally, the text was dictated in
the chancery and written in draft.   The roughest form of a written
draft was called the "angabe"; the completed written draft from which
the final document was copied was variously called the "concept,"
"minute," "notel," "expeditio," or "copei."[140]   If a petitioner submitted his case to the chancery in writing, his statement is referred
to in modern diplomatics as an "Empfängerkonzept" because it was composed by the person (or his scribe) who would ultimately hold the
Urkunde as a legal document.[141]   The redrafting of such submissions
was often simply a matter of altering the diction or the formal
aspects of the texts to conform to chancery style.[142]   The completed
draft had to be presented to the head of the chancery for approval
and signature before it could be referred to a scribe for final copying.   This approval was called "expedition" and was often noted in
abbreviated form (e.g., exp., ex., E) on the draft itself.[143]   The
actual copying was known as "mundieren" or "ingrossieren," the latter
term deriving from the fact that the fair copies, or "originale,"
were normally written with larger strokes and in a more calligraphic
style than the drafts.   The fair copy was then proofread twice.
First the scribe who penned it compared it with the draft; then he
presented both draft and copy to a chancery secretary, who compared
them a second time.   In Maximilian's chanceries the secretary indicated his endorsement of the correct copy by his signature on the
lower right corner of the document.[144]

Registering outward-bound charters was a significant function
of the chanceries.   In an era when the forgery of documents was an
art practiced from the highest[145] to the lowest strata of society
and bribery an accepted if officially discouraged custom (see "The

Taxator" and "Chancery Activity under Maximilian I" below), the need
for a running record of official transactions was great. The chancery
register provided this sort of record as well as patterns for new
documents. Notarized copies of lost deeds, for example, might be
issued on the basis of an entry in the chancery register. In the
Habsburg chanceries at the turn of the sixteenth century, documents
to be issued with hanging seals were registered. A draft to be registered was marked "registranda" and turned over to the chancery registrar, who copied it into the register. The draft was then compared
with the register copy by a secretary. After the registered draft
had been engrossed, the fair copy was marked "registrata" and in the
Hofkanzlei was compared with the draft and the register entry by a
secretary.[146]

Although the practice of maintaining an official chancery
register continued in some form in the Empire from the time of the
Caesars through the period under investigation,[147] the haphazard
manner in which these records were kept casts doubt on the accuracy
of many register entries. As the Reichskanzleiordnung of 1494 confirms, it was the drafts of Urkunden that were submitted for registration. Corrections made in the fair copies were therefore not
recorded. Wilhelm Bauer, in his article on the practice of registration in Maximilian's Reichskanzlei, elaborates on the problems
inherent in using drafts for this purpose. He notes that as a rule
the dating of a draft was the final stage of its preparation and that
these concepte frequently remained undated. They were then entered
in the register with comments like "datum non reperitur in copia"
and in some cases with the name of the scribe who had failed to
supply the information, so that responsibility for the omission
would not be fixed on the registrar.[148]

THE IMPERIAL CHANCERY ORDINANCE
(REICHSKANZLEIORDNUNG) OF 1494

The Reichskanzleiordnung of 1494[149] provides a unique view of
the routine internal operations of one of Maximilian's most important

chanceries. This document, issued by Berthold von Henneberg, Archbishop of Mainz and Imperial Chancellor, is the oldest surviving ordinance for the disposition of the German Imperial Chancery. Although
the Reichskanzlei (Imperial Chancery)[150] is not the chancery with
which Maximilian was most closely associated, its internal procedures
and hierarchy should be considered typical of any of the major Habsburg chanceries during Maximilian's reign. Ferdinand Jančar argues
convincingly that it is because internal chancery procedures are outlined in such detail in the Reichskanzleiordnung that they are
omitted from the later chancery ordinances, which are discussed
below.[151] Although the 1494 Ordinance was not implemented exactly as
written, it provides excellent general information on the activities
of one of the Habsburg chanceries while introducing offices, procedures, and terminology that apply to them all.

If an UG Gemeindeutsch was fostered in the Habsburg chanceries,
the Reichskanzleiordnung of 1494 should show some evidence of this
linguistic interest. It is the most complete of the great chancery
ordinances from Maximilian's reign, and it describes in detail the
responsibilities of chancery personnel in executing official documents. When the Ordinance was issued, the Reichskanzlei was emerging
as a distinct agency under the personal leadership of Berthold von
Mainz. Both he and the Chancery were at Court during this period.
Thus Maximilian was also to some extent directly involved with
Imperial Chancery operations at this point. This may be significant
in attempting to identify the chancery dialect with the person of the
Emperor. The main reason for examining the Ordinance here, however,
is to gain a detailed picture of the medieval German chancery tradition as it is preserved in Maximilian's administrative system. The
document is divided into six sections, each outlining the duties of
an officer or a group of officers of the Reichskanzlei. It is
written from the standpoint of Archchancellor Berthold von Mainz. In
paraphrasing this text and the other documents pertinent to Maximilian's chancery organization that are discussed later in the chapter,

I have attempted to replicate in English the archaic administrative diction of the ENHG originals.

The Secretaries

The descriptions of chancery posts in the Ordinance of 1494 appear in descending order of importance. The first duties listed are those of the secretaries. According to the Ordinance, the secretaries' first obligation (I,1) was to swear both to His Royal Highness (Maximilian) and to the Archchancellor (Berthold) fidelity, obedience, and presence (presumably in the chancery chambers to execute their duties). They were further to defend from harm, be of use to, and do their best for Emperor, Empire, and Archchancellor.

More specifically the secretaries were to devote their best understanding and industry to all drafts ("concepten oder minutten") they were instructed to take. Before the secretaries engrossed fair copies, the drafts were to be read to the Archchancellor or his appointed underkanzler, who then signed the drafts (I,2). Once the copy was prepared, the secretary who had written the draft was to sit with the copyist, proofread the copy and correct any sort of error ("einichen mangel") he should discover, and sign it before it was taken to be sealed (I,3). Documents requiring registration were to be turned over to the registrar ("registrator") after they had been processed in the prescribed manner. The secretaries were to retain those documents that were exempt from registration. At the time of Maximilian such chancery materials often became the personal property of the senior secretaries. Although some efforts were made during his reign to establish a comprehensive Reichsarchiv, many state papers continued to remain in the hands of members and former members of the chancery through at least the first quarter of the sixteenth century.[152]

The Registrar

The second section of Berthold's chancery ordinance deals specifically with the process of registering documents and the duties of the registrator. The registrar was to record neatly in a book all

documents issued under hanging seals ("alle brief, so under anhangen-
den sigeln ausgeen"). He was either to do this himself or pay to
have it done. The register entries were to be compared with or
checked against ("collacionirt") the drafts to ensure that no error
was written into the register (II,1). The registrar was further to
write the word "registrata" on the outside of all letters,[153] especially of those with hanging seals; and beside that, his first and
last names (II,2). He was to require appropriate payment ("zimlich
leydlich belonung") of those bringing documents to be registered
(this applied only to those bringing documents that did not originate
in the Chancery) and was to do this in accordance with common practice ("wie in ubung herkomen unnd gewonnheit ist," II,3). (The
specific injunction to keep the registration fee within normal bounds
suggests that there may indeed have been a tendency to do otherwise.)

This procedure indicates that a registered document from the
Imperial Chancery during Maximilian's reign passed two screening
checks after it was engrossed before it left the Chancery. These
were apparently controls for accuracy of content. The fair copy was
to be compared with the register entry "so that nothing incorrect
would be found in the register" ("damit in dem register nichts unge-
rechts erfunden [werde]," II,1). Registered documents were the most
carefully scrutinized products of the Chancery. There is nothing in
the instructions to the secretaries or the registrar, however, to
suggest that they were checked for conformity to a chancery orthographic standard.

The Scribes and Secretaries

The third section of the Ordinance pertains exclusively to the
scribes (schreyber). Their oath of allegiance began exactly like
that taken by the secretaries, but it also required them to write and
execute to the best of their abilities anything the Archbishop, his
designated chancellors, or the secretaries commanded at any time
(III,1). The scribes were also to obey the chancellors and secretaries, quickly do the work assigned them, and proofread it against

the drafts before submitting the fair copies to the person who
ordered them prepared (III,2).

The long fourth section lists regulations that applied to both
the secretaries and scribes, the group constituting the bulk of the
Chancery staff and responsible for most of its manuscript production.
These provisions offer the greatest detail about the day-to-day concerns and operations of the Reichskanzlei. The first three items
deal with allegiance to the Empire, Emperor, Archbishop, and the
Chancery itself: secretaries and scribes were forbidden to serve,
attend, or receive payment from any other sovereign, lord, or free
state without the explicit knowledge and consent of the Archchancellor
(IV,1). They were instructed never to reveal but rather to keep to
themselves His Royal Majesty's or the Empire's secrets, regardless
of whether these members of the Chancery saw, heard, wrote, or read
such information in the Council of the Chancery ("im rate der
cantzley") or elsewhere (IV,2). Neither were they to take other
matters outside the Chancery nor in any way reveal its secrets to
outside parties. They were expressly forbidden to give out copies of
legal decisions ("urteylen") or of other business. Persons not connected with the Chancery were not to be permitted in the chambers of
the Chancery or in the actual scriptorium where the writing was done.
Strangers were not to be allowed to see, read, or search through
Chancery drafts, registers, or other secret Chancery materials; and
messengers were to be received and dealt with only outside of the
Chancery chambers (IV,3).

Items 4, 5, 8, 14, and 15 specify how Maximilian's personal
instructions and affairs are to be treated by members of the Reichskanzlei. These provisions are of particular interest because of the
overt competition that existed between the Court and Imperial Chanceries in this period. The former was directly responsible to the
Emperor; the latter was ostensibly under the direction of the
Erzkanzler, Berthold von Mainz. In many areas the jurisdictions of
the two agencies overlapped because Maximilian was reluctant to
relinquish authority in chancery matters. With this in mind it is

interesting to note how Berthold dealt with Maximilian's intrusion
into his sphere of influence in 1494, and how the internal priorities
of the Chanceries changed in the Hofordnung and the Instruktion für
die Hofkanzlei that Berthold exacted from Maximilian four years later.
In 1494 the Emperor's affairs were still to receive priority.

"Unnd was auß der ku. mt. unß oder unnser cantzler oder auß
beschlus des raths angeschaffen wurdet, furderlich verfertigen und
sunderlich wes die ku. mt. selbs anschafft" (IV,4). That is, all
matters ordered by His Royal Highness, Berthold, Berthold's chancellor, or by decision of the Council (i.e., der rat der cantzley, IV,2)
were to be expedited, but Maximilian's own affairs were to be given
particular attention. Item 5 further emphasizes this obligation of
the Reichskanzlei: "Auch vleyssige aufsehens haben auf unnsers herrn
des Romischen kunigs eigen sachen und darnach uf andere nottige sachen,
damit dieselben der gepure nach furderlich gefertigt werden." The
term "eigen" here refers not only to Maximilian's personal business,
but also to the affairs of the House of Habsburg, which were in many
cases distinct from his concerns as King of the Romans (Emperor
elect) and later Emperor. The Chancery was obliged to perform any
services Maximilian required of it—Imperial, monarchial, or personal.

Item 8 also singles out Maximilian's affairs for special attention: "Der ku. mt. unnd alle andere nottige sachen, der man gedechtnus haben muß, sonderlich die versigelt verschreybung, [. . .] so auß
seiner mt. selbs person unnd bevelh vlissen, [. . .] vleissiglich und
trewlich zu verwaren und was not ist dem registrator zu uberantwurten
solchs zu registriern." In Item 15, chancellors, secretaries, and
scribes are instructed to treat Maximilian's affairs with industry and
before their other Chancery duties. The care and frequency with which
Maximilian's requirements of the Chancery are mentioned in the 1494
Ordinance suggest that Berthold's authority as Erzkanzler was not absolute. It is also a reminder that between 1494 and 1498 the Imperial
Chancery was at Court, where it could be directly influenced by Maximilian.

The scribes and secretaries were also given specific instructions about correcting fair copies. They were to proofread their

copies, taking particular care to avoid misspellings and improper usage ("verhuten, damit nit misschriben oder falsch gebraucht werde," IV,6). No letters, particularly letters patent or those written on velum, were to be erased or altered "in sensitive areas" ("an argwonigen stetten"). Any emendation or correction that might cause the authenticity of the document to be questioned was forbidden. Thus changes in names, dates, and amounts necessitated recopying the document. Other corrections where possible were permitted, provided they were done with the knowledge of the underkanzler or secretary and by the scribe who had originally penned the document:

> Auch keinen brieff sonnderlich pergamen- oder offenbrieff
> an argwonigen stetten, als im namen oder zunamen in der
> suma der zall im datum tags oder iars und dergleichen
> sachen, radieren oder endern. ob aber an andern enden,
> die nit argwon auf im trugen, mißschryben were, so man
> dan solchs wol radiern mocht, sol alwegen mit unserm oder
> unnser cantzler oder secretarien wissen geschehen unnd
> mit des hant, der solchen brief geschryben heth, und keins
> andern handt widerumb geschryben werden. (IV,7)

This passage is of particular interest for our investigation of the linguistic climate of Maximilian's chanceries because it indicates that internal checks were intended primarily to guarantee the accuracy and authenticity of Reichskanzlei documents.

The Ordinance of 1494 prescribes the use of several seals in the execution of official documents.

> Doch sollen der ko. mt. angeschaffen sachen vor andern
> alweg verfertigt secretirt oder gesigelt und nach
> gestallt der sachen hinweg geordent werden. Unnd was
> mit dem grossen sigel zu siglen ist sol unns und das
> ander unserm cantzler oder dem, der das kleyn sigel
> oder secreth auß unsern bevelh zu yeder zeith haben
> wurde, zu underschreyben furpracht werden. (IV,17-18)

Berthold refers here to at least two and possibly three seals: the "great seal" ("gross sigel"), or Majestätssiegel; the "secreth," a smaller seal roughly half the size of the great seal and used in its place;[154] and the "small seal" ("kleyn sigel"), which may have been the same as the secreth. Berthold apparently reserved the use of the great seal primarily to himself, whereas the secreth, or smaller

seal, was entrusted to his Chancellor and possibly to others. Histories of the German language imply that Maximilian personally influenced the language of documents under seal that proceeded "directly
from the Emperor." Items 17 and 18 show, however, that officially
sealed documents were regularly issued without the Emperor's participation and that the presence of the Majestätssiegel on a chancery
document does not imply Maximilian's personal approval of the text.

> Ein ieder soll dem stilum der cantzley nach allem
> vermogen halten und sich umb kein sach davon dringen
> lassen. wes er aber nit wissen heth, sollen allwege
> die jungen die eltern fragen, dieselben dan inen
> darinn gutlich underrichtung geben soll. Was auch
> einem yeden zustellt in der cantzley notturfftig zu
> sein, dardurch der ku. mt. ere nutz gefurdert auch
> der stilus gehalten werde, das soll er treulich
> anzeigen und ermanen. (IV,19-20)

This passage indicates clearly that there was an acknowledged
manner of writing in the Reichskanzlei and that conformity to this
norm was considered important. Although it is conceivable on the
basis of Johann Eck's remarks in the dedication of his Ingolstadt
Bible that the distinctive features of Maximilian's chancery language
were orthographic, the context of the reference to chancery style
("stilus der cantzley") in the Reichskanzleiordnung of 1494 emphasizes the content and accuracy of Urkunden. This emphasis indicates
that Berthold was concerned primarily with diction and syntax, which
two examples cited by Bauer confirm:

> [Wir wissen] doch, dass Bertold streng darauf sah dass
> der 'stilus der cantzley' eingehalten werde. So verbes-
> serte man in einem für Trier eingelaufenem Konzepte
> reverendus pater in venerabilis pater, consanguinei
> in nepotis u. s. w. oder in einem anderen, das der
> Kanzlei des Markgrafen von Montferrat entstammte, die
> Poenformel, die mit Si quis autem begann in die mit
> Nulli ergo omnino etc.[155]

The final part of this section (IV,21-28) offers a picture of
the life of the lower ranks of the Chancery. As presented here the
Reichskanzlei was not only a working unit but also a social entity.
All secretaries and scribes were enjoined to live together in pleasant
harmony ("gutter einickeit"), without defaming, bothering, or

injuring each other in word or deed, and with the younger members
deferring to the older in all matters. Senior members were, however,
supposed to instruct their juniors well (see IV,19-20 quoted above).
Provision was made for discord in the company. In the event of
difficulty, the problem was to be brought before the Chancellor without ado, and if he was unable to settle the matter, before the Archchancellor himself. Any who disregarded or made light of this
injunction were subject to punishment or dismissal. Each member of
the Chancery was expected to be in the chambers every morning after
breakfast before seven in the summer and at around seven in the
winter. Half the members had to be present at all times, but apart
from this those who had finished their work might leave. When the
Chancery was on the road (literally "wo wir unsern leger in stetten
haben"), its members were expected to attend the Archchancellor wherever he went. Two of the youngest members were expected to wait the
Chancery table.

The Taxator

The last major office described in the 1494 ordinance is that
of the taxator, who collected fees for documents prepared in the
Chancery. He was to swear the same oath as the scribes (V,1) and
take charge of all documents completed in the Chancery, have them
sealed without delay, and put them safely out of sight (V,2). He
was not to give out any documents without payment except at the
instruction of the Archchancellor, and he was to consult the Archchancellor if in doubt about the amount of a fee. He was not to
change a standard fee or use his job to his own advantage; neither
was he to accept bribes of any kind (V,3). The taxator was not to
delay work because of a fee or the lack thereof, but was to do his
work speedily (V,4). No document that had been taxed was to be
released until the fee had been recorded in his register (V,5).[156] He
was to record the income and expenditures of the Chancery and submit
these accounts quarterly for an audit (V,7). Tips paid to Chancery
gesellen were to be recorded, pooled, and at an appointed time divided
among them according to their station and performance (V,8).

The Canntzleyknecht

The lowliest member of the Chancery community was the
canntzleyknecht; his task was to provide for the physical comforts of
the rest of the group. Although he was required to swear a modified
oath of allegiance to the Archbishop and the Emperor, its emphasis
was on obedience and his duties were quite simple. He had to clean
the Chancery chambers, make the fires in winter, and watch the door,
making sure that no unauthorized persons gained entrance to the Chancery itself or access to Chancery materials. The knecht was also
responsible for food. He was to order only enough to feed the
members, save any leftovers after meals, and prevent nonmembers from
cadging a free dinner (VI).

Summary

One might infer from the Reichskanzleiordnung of 1494 that
the Imperial Chancery of the late fifteenth century was an efficient
and highly organized agency in which industrious scribes worked
together congenially for the good of the Emperor and for their own
advancement. The provisions concerning the ordering of food, the
allotment of leisure time, the pooling of tips, and the instruction
of younger scribes suggest a closely knit group that placed great
emphasis on the common good. In fact nothing could be farther from
the conditions actually prevailing in the chancery system at this
time. During the fifteenth and early sixteenth centuries these
offices were rife with corruption and petty intrigues, and Maximilian's own chancery was no exception.[157] Thus the more pertinent
stipulations of the Ordinance are not those providing for group unity
but those prohibiting various sorts of corruption. That chancery
members had to be specifically forbidden to accept bribes, delay the
execution of documents for gain, and disrupt the harmony of the
little community attests to the dissension and subornation common in
the chanceries of the time. Accounts of the operation of the Imperial
Chancery from both before and after the period of Berthold's tenure

indicate that these conditions persisted throughout the reigns of Frederick and Maximilian.

In his biography of Aeneas Silvius (later Pope Pius II), Georg Voigt offers a description of the Italian's experiences in the Reichskanzlei at the beginning of the reign of Frederick III. According to this account based on Aeneas Silvius' own statements, the talented humanist secretary found life in the Chancery anything but harmonious in the early 1440s. The Imperial Chancellor delegated his duties to a vice chancellor, who had absolute control of all subordinate Chancery personnel. Only a few secretaries were salaried; the lesser copyists only received room and board and whatever payment their superiors saw fit to give them for specific tasks, plus an occasional gift or tip. The regular fee charged for the execution of a chancery charter went to the Chancellor, and giving the copyist a gratuity ("bibalia") was left to the discretion of the client. Scribes were not permitted to ask for tips when they prepared documents for which the Chancery did not charge a fee. All letters for the King and the Royal Court were prepared free of charge. The Chancellor could dismiss staff members at any time.[158]

In light of these circumstances, it is hardly surprising that half a century later Berthold still had to specify that the Emperor's affairs would be given highest priority in the Reichskanzlei. Otherwise Maximilian's business would have come after assignments from the Chancery's paying clientele. It also becomes apparent why the copyists' tips were withheld and then divided evenly among all the lesser members of the Chancery. In the absence of such an arrangement, some of the scribes would have been utterly without income.

The living arrangements of the Chancery staff were rather bleak. Scribes ate at a common table and slept in the same room. Except for those who rose to positions of political prominence and availed themselves of the opportunities for social and financial gain, life in the Reichskanzlei was trying. Aeneas Silvius' indictment of the Chancery is quite bitter:

> Es giebt, glaube mir, [. . .] kein härteres Heerlager
> als Fürstenhöfe, wo Neid, Eifersucht, Verleumdung, Haß,
> Feindschaft, Schande, Beleidigungen und unendliche Pein
> zu Hause sind, Dinge, die nur durch Geduld überwunden
> werden können.[159]

The Imperial Chancery Ordinance of 1494 is the most detailed
picture of the internal organization and routine operation of a Habsburg chancery that is available for the period from 1440 to 1519.
For this reason additional answers to the questions of chancery
procedures, policies, and orientation must be sought elsewhere. Some
answers are suggested by later chancery ordinances that offer information about the larger political concerns of the Habsburg administrative agencies, some by the historical circumstances of the Habsburg
chanceries, and others by the contemporary production of the chanceries themselves.

THE OFFICE OF THE IMPERIAL ARCHCHANCELLOR

During the reigns of Frederick and Maximilian, the Archbishop
of Mainz played a significant role in the course of chancery activities within the Empire. This was due not only to the implicit powers
of the Imperial and Archiepiscopal thrones, but also to the individuals occupying each at a time when the center of power oscillated
between the monarch and the Stände (often joined by the Archbishop
of Mainz). The personalities holding these key political positions
were crucial in determining how each office developed and how much
influence it retained. The offices that exerted the greatest influence over the Imperial chancery system and could thus have affected
the language it wrote were those of the Imperial Chancellor and of
the Emperor himself. The rivalry for control of the Imperial Chancery that had been evolving between these offices for centuries
became acute in the late fifteenth century, when the contenders were
Maximilian I and Berthold von Henneberg. The following summary of
this development is based primarily on the research of Gerhard
Seeliger and of Ferdinand Jančar.

The Imperial Archchancellor before 1440

By the time of Frederick Barbarossa, the Holy Roman Empire was divided into three major parts (Germany, Italy, and Burgundy), and the same Court staff was headed by a different prince of the Church when it traveled into each of these areas. Hence the Court Chancery of the Emperor functioned as an Italian authority when in Italy and as a Burgundian authority when in Burgundy. The lesser personnel was the same in both cases and only the director of the staff, the arch- chancellor, changed. Although largely a matter of form during this early period, there were three separate archchancellors, one for each of the regions, and documents issuing from the individual areas were executed under the auspices of the individual archchancellors. The twelfth century already saw each of these archchancellorships in the firm grasp of a specific archbishopric: the Archbishop of Mainz was automatically Archchancellor of Germany, that of Cologne was Archchan- cellor of Italy, and that of Vienne was Archchancellor of Burgundy. The archchancellors were among the most prominent officials in the Empire and enjoyed extensive privileges outside the jurisdiction of the Chancery itself. In 1147 there was even some thought of authoriz- ing the Archbishop of Mainz to supervise the administration of the Empire at times when the monarch was absent.[160]

Although the three archbishops bore the same title within the hierarchy of the Empire, the powers attending their individual offices were far from equal. As the circumstances of the Empire changed, the Italian and Burgundian chancellors dwindled in stature. The Burgun- dian chancellorship, for example, had to be transferred from the Archbishopric of Vienne to that of Trier as Imperial power receded in the face of French pressure.[161] The significance of the Archchan- cellorship of Germany, however, which had been controlled by Mainz since 965, continued to grow. The first major step in this develop- ment after the Hohenstaufen period occurred in 1298.

In a _Privileg_ issued on 13 September 1298, King Albrecht clari- fied general concessions that had been made to Mainz during the reign

of King Adolf, and he guaranteed the Archchancellor of Germany not
only a tenth of the annual Jews' Tax but also the right to name the
Hofkanzler (Court Chancellor).[162] Theoretically this concession is
of tremendous importance because it takes the direction of the highest
magistracy in the Empire out of the hands of the monarch and places
it under the complete control of Mainz. Having once acquired this
right to influence the direction of the Hofkanzlei, the Archiepiscopal throne never totally surrendered it or ceased to maintain its
claim to the privilege, although there were periods when it was unable
to exercise its authority. Indeed the influence of Mainz on the Court
Chancery increased over the next two hundred years and, despite
several major setbacks, reached its high-water mark during the reign
of Maximilian I.

On the other hand, the very fact that the German Archchancellor's power was greater than that of his counterparts for Italy and
Burgundy prevented Mainz's being accorded certain privileges enjoyed
by the other Chancellors. The Archbishop of Cologne was formally
obliged to supervise Chancery activities in Italy, for example, and
the Archbishop of Trier was to receive an income from his chancery
that in no way depended on his presence in or direction of the office
itself. Despite concessions made to the German Archchancellor, however, there was never any thought of allowing him to administer his
agency personally. Seeliger explains this quite simply:

> Ihm [dem Trierer] wurden Rechte zugesprochen, welche
> der König ohne große Schädigung seines Ansehens dem
> Mainzer nimmer gewähren durfte. Denn was für den
> einen ohne thatsächlichen Wert bleiben mußte, das
> bedeutete für den anderen eine dauernde Uebernahme
> der Reichskanzlei mit allen finanziellen und
> politischen Rechten der selbständigen Verwaltung.[163]

He adds, however, that despite the Privilegien giving the Italian and
Burgundian Chancellors the powers described above, neither of them
ever assumed the personal direction of the Chancery when the Emperor
was in his territory, and the same Chancery personnel from the German
magistracy worked in Italy or Burgundy on these trips.[164] This

pattern of a single chancery accompanying the monarch on his journeys
continued through the reign of Maximilian.

Though Mainz was not yet to be allowed to direct the German
Chancery personally, the Elector won new concessions during the reign
of Henry VII. At this time the Archchancellor gained the right to
name the Chancery protonotary and notaries as well as the Chancellor
himself.[165] For the German portion of the Empire ("deutsche Nation")
there does not appear to have been a dual chancery system at this
time, one staff concerned exclusively with Imperial matters and one
concerned with the House and Court affairs of the elected monarch.
As Seeliger presents the situation, there was a single German Chancery
that followed the itinerary of the Emperor, and it apparently handled
matters in both spheres of activity. This further underscores the
import of the privileges granted to Mainz in 1498. The Archbishop
received the right to appoint the chief members of the administrative
staff that handled not only the affairs of the Empire, but also the
personal and dynastic matters of the sovereign. The right to appoint
the protonotary and notaries should have further increased Mainz's
influence in what was essentially the Emperor's own chancery.
Bresslau, however, tempers this view somewhat. He notes that though
the Archchancellor had the right to fill these positions, he exercised it very little, particularly in the case of the lesser chancery
offices. Rather, the recommendation of the appointed Chancellor was
most important in filling the protonotary position, though the actual
naming and removal of protonotaries lay totally in the hands of the
King.[166]

The Golden Bull of Charles IV (10 January 1356) reversed what
had become the Emperor's official attitude toward the Archchancellors;
the Archbishops were now deprived de jure of the rights the Emperor
had long since reclaimed de facto. The 1356 declaration makes no
mention of the Archbishops' right to name chancery personnel, and its
stipulations about their personal direction of the Chancery effectively revoke the concessions made in earlier Privilegien. The Hofkanzler alone was given the supervision of the Chancery and the

custody of the great Imperial seal, which was to be turned over to the
Archchancellors for ceremonial occasions only and returned immediately
thereafter to the Hofkanzler. This action effectively pulled the
Imperial Chancery back totally into the Emperor's sphere of influence.
Under the Emperor-appointed Hofkanzler, the magistracy became an
administrative agency of the Court. The Archbishop did not accept
this situation without protest, but despite repeated demands from
Mainz that the Elector be allowed to exercise his traditional rights
in naming Imperial Chancery personnel, the claims went essentially
unheeded during the reigns of Ruprecht, Jobst, Sigmund, and
Albrecht II.[167]

The Imperial Archchancellor under Frederick III

When Frederick III's reign began in 1440 the situation was as
follows: for nearly a century Mainz had been deprived of direct
influence at the Imperial Court, but the successive Electors had continued to badger the throne for a restoration of the old privileges.
In 1440 Archbishop Dietrich tried again. He appointed Bishop Leonhard
of Passau to lead the Court Chancery. Frederick ignored the matter
and had Konrad, Provost of St. Stefan, who had served him as Austrian
Chancellor before his election to the Imperial throne, continue to
direct his Hofkanzlei. The next year Mainz tried the same ploy, this
time appointing Jakob, Archbishop of Trier, to the post. Dietrich
sent his appointee to Austria, and though Frederick did not acknowledge in writing the privileges of the Archchancellor for Germany, he
did turn the seals over to Jakob. Jakob was sworn in as Hofkanzler
in Wiener Neustadt on 31 July 1441.[168] This is an interesting rever-
sal of the pattern that emerged between 1298 and 1356. In that
period the occupants of the Imperial throne retained sufficient power
to be able to make the Archchancellors official concessions that they
in practice were prevented from enjoying. Here a weaker monarch
makes actual concessions to Mainz while refusing official acknowledgment of the Elector's claims.

Jakob's tour of duty was rather short. He left Frederick's
Court in 1441 and had returned to his archiepiscopal holdings by
December of the same year. Though away from Court, Jakob still
retained his title and functioned as the head of Frederick's Chancery
during the Emperor's visits to Nuremberg, Frankfurt, and Aachen in
the late spring of 1442. After this time, however, the remarkable
Kaspar Schlick (see "Chancery Activity under Maximilian I" below),
who had also served as Chancellor to Sigmund and Albrecht II, became
Frederick's _Hofkanzler_. From this point and for the duration of
Frederick's reign, the influence of the Archchancellor on the activity
of the Imperial Chancery was eclipsed. The only time during his entire
reign when Frederick seems to have felt obliged to acknowledge Mainz's
claim was the year following his election. After that he promptly
reclaimed his right to run the Chancery in his own way, as an administrative office at Court and with his own Chancellors.[169]

Jančar shows that Frederick III, whether for logistical or
political reasons, limited the independence of the _Reichskanzlei_
during his reign by assigning important matters of Imperial business
to members of his personal staff. This staff, on the other hand,
seems at least in part to have been detailed from the Imperial Chancery; so the issue is one of executive authority, not of scribal
personnel or usage. When Frederick came to the throne there was a
single chancery, the Imperial Chancery, that handled both the
Emperor's affairs and those pertaining to his ancestral holdings.[170]
Although Frederick did create an Austrian (House) Chancery from this
body in 1442 to treat matters concerning the _Erblande_, the jurisdictions of the two staffs continued to overlap. Specific scribes were
assigned to one or the other of the chanceries, and distinctive closing formulae (see "Commissions" below) were developed to distinguish
Imperial documents from House documents. Nevertheless the two groups
continued to share responsibilities and personnel. By assigning
important Imperial business to his own secretaries, Frederick effectively nullified the political significance of the Imperial Chancellor as a check to monarchial power. These circumstances reduce the

importance of the difference between the written languages of the Imperial and House chanceries during Frederick's reign, since many Imperial documents were actually written by Frederick's Austrian, or House, staff.[171]

Although an Imperial reform drafted in 1460 called for an expansion of Mainz's power, increasing the Archchancellor's political and financial stature, nothing came of this during Frederick's reign. The Archiepiscopal position, which had already been too weak in 1441 to maintain its appointees in their posts in the Hofkanzlei, was further reduced by an internecine struggle in the Electorate. In 1463 Adolf of Nassau challenged Dietrich for the Archiepiscopal throne. Dietrich withdrew, but Adolf's position was still so tenuous that it required Frederick's support. In return for the Emperor's assistance Adolf issued a statement on 31 October 1463 renouncing all claim to the right to direct the Imperial Chancery or to enjoy income from it during Frederick's lifetime.[172]

> Wirklich hat sich unter Friedrich das Verhältnis des
> Erzkanzlers zu der Reichskanzlei nicht mehr verändert.
> Auch die Verwaltung derselben durch Erzbischof Adolf
> [. . .] hat den staatsrechtlichen Zustand, welchen die
> Versprechungen des Jahres 1463 geschaffen, in keiner
> Weise beeinträchtigt. Denn als ein Beamter des
> Kaisers versah der Mainzer gleich seinen Vorgängern im
> Kanzleramte unter nicht außergewöhnlichen Bedingungen
> am wandernden Kaiserhofe den Dienst eines Kanzleivor-
> standes.[173]

Seeliger's statement makes plain the extent of the interdependence of the Habsburg House and Imperial Chanceries during the reign of Frederick III. Under Adolf the Imperial Chancery is with the House Chancery at Court. Together they form a single administrative staff, that group of itinerant scribes, nobles, and diplomats that followed the movements of the Emperor. Thus, at the end of Frederick's reign as at its beginning, there was for all practical purposes a single major chancery. The Imperial Chancellor, Adolf of Nassau, was the executive head of this office, and he served more or less in the capacity of the undercantzler described in the 1494 Reichs-kanzleiordnung. He was not an autonomous figure empowered to make

policy, and he was the agent of the Emperor, not of the Stände. This
pattern, which continued the medieval tradition of Frederick's predecessors, changed dramatically for a time under Maximilian.

The Imperial Archchancellor under Maximilian I

In order to be elected German King in 1486, Maximilian needed
the vote of Berthold von Henneberg, the Archbishop and Elector of
Mainz. He bought this at a high price that for a time considerably
changed the role of the German Archchancellor in the administrative
affairs of the Empire. In return for Berthold's vote, Maximilian
granted Mainz the right to direct the Imperial Chancery personally
and to enjoy certain prerogatives of the archchancellorship even when
he was not present at Court. These included the rights to issue documents under seal and to receive a portion of the Chancery revenues.[174]
The concessions are considerable. In them Mainz achieved the goal
toward which it had been striving for two hundred years: the right
to direct the highest magistracy in the Empire.

The political potential of the Imperial Chancery made it a
plum worth vying for. Until Maximilian's reign Mainz had basically
led an administrative office at Court under the supervision of the
Emperor. The terms of Maximilian's concessions, however, made possible, at least in theory, the development of an entirely new chancery
structure. If all Imperial Chancery documents were to be executed
under the Archbishop's supervision and he was not required to be at
Court, the administration of the Reichskanzlei might develop in any of
several ways. If the Archbishop remained at Court (the situation
delineated in the 1494 Ordinance), he would function as the administrative head of the Imperial Chancery, enjoying a degree of autonomy
within the Chancery itself, but remaining subordinate to the Emperor,
who could intervene at any moment. In this case he would act as an
undercantzler, and the power of policy would rest with the monarch.
If the Archbishop left Court, the physical distance between the party
wishing to issue edicts, etc. (the Emperor) and the party empowered
to authorize their execution (the Archbishop) would either cause both

to issue legal documents independently of each other (effectively creating two chanceries) or it would cause one to wrest power from the other (again focusing chancery activity in one place). Each of these eventualities occurred during Maximilian's reign.

Although Berthold was promised these concessions in 1486, they were not reaffirmed to him officially until May of 1494, after the death of Frederick III.[175] Berthold seems to have arrived at Court late in June of that year and by October, as indicated by the Reichs-kanzleiordnung examined above, had assumed control of the Chancery. During the years between 1486, when he was elected King, and 1494, when he actually took over the governance of the Empire, Maximilian began to make the institutional reforms associated with his reign. The basic impulse behind many of them appears to have been Maximil-ian's desire to decentralize administrative responsibility in order to allow the various regional agencies to function efficiently in his absence. Jančar has even speculated that the Chancery as an indepen-dent institution would have ceased to exist as a result of the admin-istrative reforms if the newly created agencies had been better organ-ized.[176] Many of Maximilian's experiments in administrative organi-zation were short-lived, however, and several of the offices he created, particularly those concerned with the financial administra-tion of the Erblande, went through a variety of changes during his reign. For the present investigation of the Habsburg chancery dialect, we need only be concerned with those changes that directly affected Maximilian's chancery system and may have influenced the German it wrote.

In 1490 Maximilian began reorganizing the Lower Austrian terri-tories. These included Austria Above and Below the Enns, Styria, Carinthia, and Carniola. The following year he authorized a govern-ing council (die Statthalter und Räthe zu Wien) to administer all five territories in his absence. After Frederick's death this ad hoc group became a standing administrative body and was known as the "Regiment zu Wien." It had its own Hofrat, Hofkammer, and Chancery. The chancery requirements of all the Vienna agencies were met by the

Austrian Chancery (österreichische Kanzlei); this was directed by the
Austrian Chancellor (österreichischer Kanzler), who was a member of
most of the agencies his chancery staff served.[177] When the Vienna
Hofrat was dissolved in 1502, the Austrian Chancellor assumed its
functions.[178]

Similarly, Maximilian established a Tirolean Regiment and
Chancery in 1490 to administer the Upper Austrian region. This
reorganization was simpler to implement than the Lower Austrian
reform. The Tirolean administrative system was already relatively
advanced by comparison with other contemporary systems, particularly
in the areas of finance and accounting. In addition to this, Maximilian became the independent ruler of Tirol when Archduke Sigmund
abdicated in 1490; thus he was able to regularize the institutional
changes he made from the outset here, where he did not rule at his
father's pleasure. The Tirolean Chancellor headed the Ländergruppen-
kanzlei in Innsbruck and was a member of the Regiment.[179]

As a result of this regional reorganization, Maximilian had
four major chanceries by the beginning of his Imperial reign in 1493:
the Austrian and Tirolean Ländergruppenkanzleien in Vienna and Innsbruck, and the Reichskanzlei and the Hofkanzlei at Court. The latter
two were separated only when Berthold assumed the direction of the
Imperial Chancery in 1494. When this occurred, Conrad Stürtzel, the
former head of Maximilian's Reichskanzlei, became the leader of his
Hofkanzlei; and Hans Waldner, who had handled the affairs of the
Court Chancery, was made Austrian Chancellor; the other personnel
remained the same.[180] This transfer of personnel within Maximilian's
administrative service is rather typical. His agencies often overlapped not only in jurisdiction but also in personnel. Authority was
loosely defined and there was little central coordination. Maximilian's individual retainers frequently served him in more than one
capacity and in more than one of his agencies. In seeking the Habsburg chancery with which Maximilian was personally associated and in
which an UG Gemeindeutsch may have been fostered, then, we are con-
fronted not with a chancery but with chanceries, not with one seal

but with many, and not with a single body empowered to act in Maximilian's name but with several that functioned relatively independently.

Only the chanceries that accompanied Maximilian's peripatetic
court (the Reichskanzlei for a brief time after 1494 and the Hofkanzlei) are of concern for this investigation, since these are the
only chanceries with which Maximilian was in regular personal contact.
If Maximilian affected chancery practice, the production of these
chanceries should show that influence. These are also the chanceries
in which Niclas Ziegler served. If Ziegler instituted an orthographic
reform, his own diplomatic production and the fair copies penned in
his chancery should reflect it. Furthermore, the regional authorities
were authorized to issue Urkunden independently,[181] thus the production of the Ländergruppenkanzleien does not imply the supervision of
Maximilian or of Reichs- or Hofkanzlei personnel. Of the two chanceries at Court the Hofkanzlei merits closest attention because it
was Maximilian's own chancery and it worked with his personal staff.
It treated matters of particular significance to the Emperor throughout Maximilian's reign, including the period between 1494 and 1502
when the Reichskanzlei functioned under the separate leadership of
Berthold von Mainz.

Until 1494 Maximilian conducted the business of the Empire
through his personal and court staffs. His Hofkanzlei together with
the Tirolean Chancery at Innsbruck handled the ongoing daily affairs
of the Empire between Frederick's death and Maximilian's return to
Germany in 1494.[182] Berthold's arrival at Court and his assumption
of the leadership of the Reichskanzlei in the same year were in themselves milestones in Mainz's continuing attempt to gain control of
the Imperial Chancery. The titular change of leadership did not mean,
however, that Maximilian had conceded to Berthold unequivocal control
of the Reichskanzlei. It was evident that Berthold intended to break
with the precedent of other Archchancellors by attempting to turn his
office into an independent agency from which he could conduct his
political opposition to the throne in Imperial affairs.[183] For this
reason Maximilian and prominent members of the Hofkanzlei resisted

Berthold, relinquishing to him as little authority as possible. If
Berthold were allowed to become a powerful force in the Imperial Chancery he could exert greater influence on the Reichsregiment. Maximilian worked with members of his Hofkanzlei and Hofrat (Court Council)
to prevent this.[184] They were in part able to do this because of the
overlapping jurisdictions of the Imperial and Court Chanceries and
the interface of personnel between the chancery staffs.

Berthold seems to have taken over the direction of the Reichskanzlei late in June 1494. He accompanied Maximilian to the Lowlands
that year, spent part of the winter there, and in February went south
with the Court to the Diet of Worms (1495), where both remained for
nearly a year.[185] The great Reichskanzleiordnung issued at Mecheln
in October 1494 is evidence of Berthold's efforts to strengthen the
position of the Imperial Chancery at the outset of his tenure in
office. By the end of 1495, however, Berthold complained officially
to Maximilian about Hofkanzler Stürtzel's failure to cooperate with
him:

> Allergnedigster herr. unser gnediger herr der ercz-
> bischoff zu Menncz hat uns an hewt muntlichen ersucht,
> ob wir von ewr ku. mt. dheinen bevelch haben, mit ewr
> ku. mt. canczler doctor Cunraten Stürczl zuschaffen,
> das sigl, so er hat, seinen furstlichen gnaden zuant-
> wurten, so hat uns derselb canczler doctor Cunrat
> zuerkennen geben, wie ewr ku. mt. im dasselb sigl
> bevolhen und zugesagt hab, im das bey seinen handen
> zelassen. des er sich also halten welle. solchs
> wolten wir ewr ku. mt. unverkunt nit lassen.[186]

This squabble over the seal is one of the first documented
skirmishes between the two chanceries, and it takes place while they
are both still at Court. Appeal is made here to an anything but
impartial arbiter. If Maximilian had wanted Berthold to have the
seal, one assumes he would have given it to him; Stürtzel's reaction
was probably not due to a misunderstanding. Although Maximilian was
obliged both through his 1494 affirmation of the Archchancellor's
rights and the Worms Resolutions (Wormser Beschlüsse) of 1495 to
grant Mainz considerable autonomy in the Imperial Chancery, he tended
to overlook Berthold's claim except when he was in difficulty with

the Stände. A part of Maximilian's strategy to prevent the Stände
from dominating the government was to organize, staff, and retain
control of the key Court and Imperial offices. Thus his supporters
in the Hofkanzlei, Stürtzel, Serntein, and Lang, conceded as little
authority as possible to the Reichskanzlei.[187] Predictably this
pattern continues in 1496, when the two chanceries go in different
directions.

The reasons for Maximilian's frequent circumvention of the
Reichskanzlei after this physical separation in 1496 were practical
as well as political. If more than one revision of a document had to
be agreed to by both chanceries or by Maximilian himself, the delay
involved in shuttling the text back and forth between staffs was considerable. Though some attempts were made to refer concepte from one
chancery to the other for approval,[188] the Reichskanzlei and Hofkanzlei began to function quite independently of each other.

In February of 1498 Maximilian proclaimed officially in a
detailed Hofordnung that the Hofrat and Hofkanzlei were authorized to
act in matters pertaining to both the Empire and the Erblande, a
jurisdiction these agencies had long since claimed in practice.
Berthold did not, however, abandon his attempt to see certain rights
guaranteed exclusively to the Reichskanzlei. During the summer of
1498 while he was once again at Court, Berthold had the opportunity
to buttress the position of his chancery. Maximilian was in financial
straits; he sought Imperial funds to solve his difficulties and
needed Berthold's support to secure these. This enabled the Archbishop to force Maximilian to execute two further ordinances that
spelled out the specific prerogatives and duties of the Reichskanzlei
and the Hofkanzlei.[189] Parts of the three ordinances are pertinent
to our investigation of the environment in which the Habsburg chancery
language was written during Maximilian's reign; we will return to
these after pursuing the contest for control of the Reichskanzlei to
its conclusion. The 1498 ordinances plainly separate the chanceries'
spheres of activity. Nevertheless the competition between the two

increased, and the Hofkanzlei continued to issue documents which
should clearly have been in the domain of the Reichskanzlei.

In 1500 at the Diet of Augsburg a new constitution was adopted
giving the government of the Stände (the Reichsregiment) the highest
powers in the Empire and the Archbishop of Mainz the responsibility
for staffing and directing its chancery.[190] Although this streng-
thened Berthold's legal claim to the right to operate the Reichskanzlei as an independent agency, it also put his position in greater
jeopardy because the constitutional recognition made him a greater
threat to Maximilian's sovereign authority. The new constitution
made the Archchancellor a privileged official of the Stände, with
which Maximilian was always at odds. As an organ of the Reichsregiment, completely independent of the Court Chancery, the Reichskanzlei
under Berthold's direction was no longer acceptable to Maximilian.
When the Stände entered into diplomatic negotiations with foreign
powers without consulting the Emperor, Maximilian caused the dissolu-
tion of the Nuremberg Reichsregiment.[191] On 21 March 1502, Maximilian
demanded that Berthold surrender the royal seal.[192] This marked the
end of the separate Reichskanzlei, which had come into being only
eight years earlier. At this point the Hofkanzlei resumed the functions that had temporarily been taken over by Berthold's chancery
(functions it had in many cases continued to perform throughout this
period anyway), and it assumed again its old role as the chief administrative office of the Empire. It is on this Hofkanzlei, its tenor,
personalities, and production that our investigation of Maximilian's
chancery language must focus.

THE CHANCERY ORDINANCES OF 1498

The ordinances[193] Maximilian drafted in 1498 concerning the
administrative organization of his government merit special attention
because they present, when taken together, a picture of the interrelationship between the Imperial and Court Chanceries, the Court
Council, and the governments of the Ländergruppen (of which
Niederösterreich and Oberösterreich were the most significant).

One of them also names some of the personalities who have been associated with the emergence of the Habsburg language. It describes their
regular offices, thus allowing us to see what their proximity to
Maximilian and his clerical staff was and to consider whether their
duties would have permitted them to effect the linguistic changes
attributed to them. The 1498 ordinances also offer a detailed picture
of the keeping of the chancery seals and indicate who was supposed to
have had access to them. Of the various 1498 decrees describing Habsburg administrative agencies,[194] the three that are of primary concern
for the development of the chancery language under Maximilian are the
Hofordnung of 13 February, the Reichskanzleiordnung of 12 September,
and the fragment of an Instruktion für die Hofkanzlei, which Thomas
Fellner dates 12 September 1498 as well.[195] Having already examined
the internal procedures of one contemporary Habsburg chancery in discussing the Reichskanzleiordnung of 1494 above, we will consider here
only those portions of the more recent directives that offer additional information on pertinent chancery subjects: chancery style
and personnel; the control, endorsement, and certification of chancery
documents; the role of the Emperor in chancery affairs.

The Hofordnung

The first portion of the Hofordnung[196] is concerned with the
legitimation and jurisdiction of the Hofrat. Because of its membership and the immense authority that it exercised, this agency is
particularly important in an investigation of the circumstances under
which Maximilian's chancery language developed.

> Zum ersten so verordnen wir hiemit unser hofrete, so
> jczo ungeverlich bei uns seien und die wir bisher in
> unsern eignen gescheften gepraucht haben, zu unsern
> obristen regenten, also das si alle und jeglich hendel
> sachen und gescheften, so künfticlich von dem heiligen
> reiche deutscher nacion gemainer cristenheit oder
> unsern erblichen fürstenthumben und landen herfliessen,
> desgleichen auch was unsern kuniclichen hofe und
> desselben verwandten betreffen wirdet ganz nichts aus-
> genommen hören, die eigentlichen und nach allen notdurf-
> ten und fleis erwegen und ermessen und darauf dieselben
> hendel und sachen nach irem maisten rate durch unser
> gewönlich hofsinsigel titel und secret, inmassen wir

> bisher gepraucht haben, verfertigen mögen; doch was
> gros und swere hendel seien, sollen si zuvor uns
> anbringen, unsern besluss und willen darauf zu empfahen,
> des wir inen dann hiemit unser ganz volkomen gewalt und
> macht geben.[197]

From a legal standpoint this is a remarkable statement when one remem-
bers that the Reichskanzlei, though not at Court when this ordinance
was issued, was still very much in existence under Berthold's direction at the time and was still the chancery through which Imperial
matters were supposed to be channeled. The Hofordnung demonstrates
Maximilian's refusal to concede this authority to the Archbishop of
Mainz.

In this document Maximilian regularizes his council of hand-
picked advisors (hofrete) by officially making them his highest
regents; he then gives them authority in affairs pertaining not only
to the Court and the Erblande, but also to all matters concerning the
Empire. He gives them three seals, the hofsinsigel, the titel, and
the secreth, and requires that they consult him only in great and
difficult matters.[198] This statement attests to Maximilian's unwill-
ingness to withdraw from Imperial affairs.

The newly recognized Council was to meet daily, as need
required, in morning and afternoon session. At these meetings two
secretaries were to be present, one to read aloud the matter under
consideration and the other to note the Council's recommendation concerning it. This recommendation was to be written with the knowledge
of the Chancellor, or in his absence with the approval of his Senior
Secretary (obrister secretari). The Chancellor or Senior Secretary
was then to take the recommendations written in the preceding Council
session, read them again, inquire personally whether they recorded
accurately the majority opinion of the Council, and if so, return
them to the two Council secretaries to be engrossed. The fair copies
were then to be read once more in the next session of the Council
and signed immediately by Elector Frederick of Saxony (in Maximilian's
stead) and by the Chancellor or Senior Secretary. No document was to
be signed except at the Council's direction. The approved recommendations were to be sealed in the Council by the two secretaries.

MS. C of the Hofordnung names several of the individuals besides the Saxon Elector who held the positions on Maximilian's Court Council just described. Conrad Stürtzel, who had been Berthold's opponent in the dispute over the surrender of the seal in 1495, was still Hofkanzler in 1498 and became a member of the Hofrat through this ordinance. Cyprian Serntein is named as the Senior Secretary, and Mathis Wurm and Niclas Ziegler are listed as the two Council secretaries.

The Hofrat was explicitly empowered to act in Imperial matters. Its select membership (which included the Hofkanzler, Hofmarschall, and Hofmeister, the Senior Secretary and the Council secretaries, but not the Imperial Archchancellor) guaranteed that it would conduct its affairs in a manner pleasing to the Emperor. The appointment of Frederick the Wise to oversee the Hofrat[199] should be seen in conjunction with the exclusion of Berthold von Mainz from the Council. It was certainly another of Maximilian's attempts to bring all the affairs of the Reichskanzlei back under the control of his own chancery and advisors. As Wiesflecker notes, the Emperor seems to have overreached himself by snubbing Berthold and bringing the Saxon Elector into the Hofrat,[200] however, and the ill-considered arrangement was short-lived. Naming Frederick to the Council not only deepened the existing antagonism between Mainz and the Emperor, but it also worried some of Maximilian's Upper German confidants. Probably sensing the precariousness of his position, Frederick quickly left both the Court and the new Court Council.[201] Thus the circumstances that placed one of the two princes Luther associated with the unification of the German language at the head of the other's chancery council lasted but a few months. Frederick's brief tenure as Maximilian's representative in the Hofrat between 1498 and 1499 seems to be the only time he, Maximilian, and Niclas Ziegler were ever personally involved with the same (Habsburg) chancery.

Like Berthold's 1494 ordinance, the Hofordnung prohibits bribery and requires each Council member to keep all Council secrets "till death" ("bis in seinen tod"). The Hofordnung also includes an exhaustive description of the Ratstruhe, a great chest containing many smaller chests or drawers ("kestlin"), in which all the valuables of the Council, from the Imperial seals and the petitions of supplicants, to writing materials and the tablecloth, were stored.[202] Of these provisions only those concerning access to the seals are of particular interest. The eleventh kestel[203] was to contain both the seal (the Majestätssiegel) and the secreth.[204] It was to have a lock to which the Chancellor or the Senior Secretary had the key. The great chest itself was to have four different locks. Frederick of Saxony as Maximilian's representative, the Hofmeister, the Hofmarschall, and the Chancellor or Senior Secretary each had a key to one of the locks. Theoretically all four would have to have been present to get the seals out of the chest at any given time. Jančar interprets this cumbersome, multi-lock arrangement to have been a deliberate if vain attempt by Maximilian to keep Berthold and his Imperial Chancery at Court.[205]

Beyond this the provisions of the Ordinance are much like those of the 1494 Reichskanzleiordnung with regard to the preparation, correction, and registration of documents, and concerning the conduct of Council personnel. A minor difference in the procedure is that the Hofordnung calls for one additional control not required in the Reichskanzlei: fair copies were to be rechecked against the register entries that had been penned from expedited drafts.[206] The duties of the Council secretaries are of interest because some were assigned specifically to Niclas Ziegler. Of the two secretaries mentioned above, Ziegler was the one who read the statements in the Council sessions. As in the Imperial Chancery, it was the Senior Secretary—not Ziegler or Wurm—who checked to see whether recommendations were written in the style of the chancery, and it was he who approved them before they were engrossed. The two Council secretaries (again as in the Reichskanzlei) were authorized to correct scribal errors in the fair copy. Ziegler and Wurm were to have the key to a chest with many drawers (apparently not the Ratstruhe) in which they were to store all the legal acts and orders they worked on. Aside from them,

only the Chancellor and Senior Secretary were to have keys to the
chest.   Ziegler and Wurm were also responsible for sealing any documents in the Council that required a seal.   They were specifically
instructed to give priority to matters concerning the Empire and the
Erblande.   From this we can conclude that by 1498 Ziegler had
achieved a position of sufficient trust on Maximilian's staff to be
given access to the Chancery seals.   This places him high in the
middle stratum of chancery employees, only two ranks below the Hofkanzler himself.   Nevertheless, there is nothing in the Hofordnung to
suggest that Ziegler was a language reformer.

The Reichskanzleiordnung

> Wir Maximilian von gottes gnaden römischer künig zu
> allen zeiten merer des reichs . . . etc. bekennen offent-
> lich mit disen brieve und thun kund allermeniglich: als
> bisher in unsern canzleien beide römisch und auch öster-
> reichisch hendel und sachen under einander vermischt und
> ausgegangen und deshalben die sachen als die notturft
> erhaischt, nit registrirt und eingeschrieben sein,
> dardurch (wo nit darein gesehen) uns, dem heiligen reich
> und unsern erblichen landen merklich irrung schade und
> nachteil erwachsen werde, als wir demnach aus denselben
> und andern ursachen mit wolbedachtem mut [. . .] ein
> ordenung [. . .] wie es hinfur mit unsern canzleien soll
> gehalten und alle sachen und hendel das hailig reich
> unser küniglich chamergericht und unser erbland berurnde
> ausgeen und gefertigt werden, gemacht und beslossen haben,
> inmassen wie hernach volgt.[207]

In this ordinance Maximilian guarantees Berthold and the
Reichskanzlei sole authority in the Imperial affairs over which he
had given the Court Council jurisdiction just a short time before.
As the introduction states, this clarification of administrative procedures was intended to improve the accuracy of the register, which
had suffered during the period when Imperial and dynastic affairs had
become confused, to the detriment of the Emperor, the Empire, and the
ancestral lands.   The first section of the new ordinance spells out
the specific prerogatives Maximilian granted the Imperial Chancery:
"no missive shall be written at our behest in our capacity as Roman
King to the Holy [Roman] Empire except that it be written in our

Roman [i.e., Imperial] Chancery, which the honorable Berthold, Archbishop of Mainz, Archchancellor of the Holy Roman Empire in Germany,
and our dear cousin and Elector is now administering [. . .]."[208]
There is no provision for handling incoming matters concerning the
Empire, no indication that this edict supersedes the earlier Hofordnung, and no specific provision for interaction between the Chanceries.

To expedite this new separation of responsibilities, Maximilian
planned to give Berthold the exclusive use of two seals: the great
seal ("unser gross sigl"), which Hofkanzler Stürtzel had refused to
surrender in 1495, and a new missifsigl the Emperor intended to have
made especially for the purpose. These Imperial seals ("reichs-
sigel") were to be kept in the great Ratstruhe, in the drawer next to
the one reserved for the other two seals and the secreth (the seals
that the Hofordnung had assigned to the Hofrat). Two of the Hofrat
seals, the secreth and one of the others, were to be used exclusively
for matters pertaining to Austria and Burgundy. The Archbishop alone
was to have a key to the drawer containing the Imperial seals; the
four locks to the chest itself, however, were to remain unchanged.[209]
Thus the Archchancellor, the Hofrat, and the Ratstruhe all had to be
in one place for an Imperial document to be sealed; or procedures
different from those outlined were used in the execution of official
chancery documents. In practice the prescribed procedures were sometimes disregarded. The fact that Maximilian had to send for Berthold's seals in 1502 confirms that the secure design of the Ratstruhe
was not sufficiently compelling to keep either the two chanceries or
their seals together in one place.

The Instruktion für die Hofkanzlei

The last of the 1498 ordinances that may have particular bearing on the development of the Habsburg chancery language is Maximilian's fragmentary Instruktion für die Hofkanzlei. This document is
thought to have been drafted in conjunction with the Reichskanzleiordnung just discussed.[210] It treats the interaction between the

Hofkanzlei and the Hofrat and the cooperation of the Hofkanzlei with
the Ländergruppenkanzleien in specific cases. The first section
deals with the duties of the Hofkanzler. In many ways they are reminiscent of duties Berthold outlined for his undercantzler in the
Reichskanzleiordnung of 1494. The Hofkanzler was to make sure that
the fees charged for Chancery services were standard and that no
business was delayed by obstructive copyists angling for higher fees.
He was to see that a register was maintained of all documents under
seal leaving the Chancery. The Chancellor also had proofreading
responsibilities:

> Item alle brief gescheft und verschreibungen umb clain
> und groß sachen sol der canzler selbst von wort zu
> wort mit vleis uberlesen und alsdann mit aigner hand
> underschreiben und solhs kainen secretarien bevelen
> noch zu tun gestatten.[211]

If one compares this statement with the passage from the more
detailed 1494 Reichskanzleiordnung, which specifies the portions of
fair copies that may be corrected without their being recopied, the
implication of this passage becomes clear. The Hofkanzler is to read
for accuracy and correctness of content because the documents proceeding from the Chancery are legally binding. There is no indication
that he was also to check for orthographic conformity or that this
was a contemporary chancery concern.

Beyond these internal matters the Hofkanzler was also to
coordinate the activities of his office with those of the Council and
the regional chanceries. The Chancellor was to bring all Chancery
business requiring a written response to the Council, read it aloud,
and with his own hand write on the petitions the recommendations of
the Council. These procedures are similar to certain of those outlined in the Hofordnung. In the Instruktion, the Hofkanzlei emerges
as the administrative and clerical staff of the Hofrat and the
Emperor himself. It also functioned as a clearinghouse for matters
concerning the Regiments that administered the Habsburg ancestral
territories. Either by direct royal order or at the recommendation
of the Council, the Hofkanzler was to forward matters pertaining to

the government or organization of the _Erblande_ to the governors
(_Stathalter_) and regents of Lower Austria, Upper Austria, High
Austria, and Burgundy.[212]

The duties of the _Hofkanzlei_ secretaries do not differ significantly from those outlined for the same positions in the _Reichs-
kanzleiordnung_ of 1494. These officials were to obey the Chancellor
and keep His Majesty's secrets until death. They were not to present
fair copies for sealing and dispatch that had not been proofread.
They were not to engross materials that had not been approved by the
Chancellor. Neither were they to undertake any private commissions;
they were forbidden to accept bribes or gifts. As in the case of
Reichskanzlei personnel, they were not to approach the Court without
the explicit consent of the Chancellor.[213]

THE AUTHENTICATION OF DOCUMENTS IN
THE CHANCERY OF MAXIMILIAN I

The chancery ordinances of 1494 and 1498 indicate that each
document originating in the Court and Imperial Chanceries during
Maximilian's reign was to be controlled and counterchecked several
times by more than one person before it was issued.[214] Though certain aspects of the ordinances were not implemented as written, the
surviving manuscripts from the Chanceries indicate that the rules
governing the control and endorsement of official documents were
generally observed. Where an official chancery document reflects
deviation from the normal routine, the irregularity is more often the
result of an external circumstance than of a casual attitude within
the chancery toward the prescribed system of controls. A frequent
variation in the standard pattern of checks is the issuance of an
official document under some seal other than the one required in the
ordinances because the correct seal was unavailable for either
political or logistical reasons. Documents also sometimes lack the
requisite number of signatures; some are issued with no visa at all.
Aside from these sorts of irregularity, however, the chancery documents were normally checked as rough drafts, checked against the

register, proofread in the fair copy, and in the <u>Hofkanzlei</u> checked
against the register a second time. These controls are recorded on
the documents with enough regularity so that one is usually able to
tell from the endorsements and other chancery notation exactly which
phase of the production process an individual manuscript represents
(draft, revised draft, fair copy, etc.).

Ordinarily questions regarding chancery notation fall in the
realm of diplomatics, where chancery endorsements, seals, and the
like are considered to be indications of a document's genuineness or
authenticity from a legal standpoint. In this context they imply
that the texts on which they appear are sufficiently accurate in content and correct in style to be considered legally binding documents.
Because historians of the German language suggest that the Habsburg
chancery dialect was consciously standardized, however, and because
they relate their claims to the Emperor's seal and to documents issuing directly from the Emperor, it is necessary to examine briefly the
forms of endorsement used in Maximilian's chancery, determine what
sort of check each endorsement represented, and establish whether any
of them implied the personal participation of Maximilian in the execution of a given document. A cursory survey of these endorsements
will also permit us to interpret more accurately the significance of
individual documents considered in chapter 3. Having already traced
the basic route of a document through a chancery in examining the
ordinances above, we will only be concerned here with the commissioning, signing, and sealing of documents.

Commissions

Fair copies from Maximilian's chancery normally show a notation at the upper right corner of the plica that tells who commissioned the text or under what circumstances it was assigned to the
chancery. These chancery notations serve primarily to indicate
whether the matter treated in the text pertains to the Empire or to
the House of Habsburg. Beginning early in the reign of Frederick III,
two such formulae were developed to distinguish the two realms of

chancery business. Although Frederick's two chancery staffs worked
together closely, they used the notation "commissio domini regis
(imperatoris)" on documents under the jurisdiction of the Austrian
Chancery, and the notation "ad mandatum domini regis" on Reichskanzlei
documents.[215] During the period between 1491 and 1492 the ad
mandatum formula was also used on documents pertaining to the
Erblande. Early in Maximilian's reign, however, the former usage was
reestablished; the commissio formula was again reserved for House
matters and the ad mandatum formula for Imperial ones.[216]

The Instruktion für die Hofkanzlei (1498) explains how these
notations were to be extended to indicate the circumstances under
which the Chancery was charged to draft a text. The addition of the
phrase "in consilio" to either of the preceding formulae meant that
the text represented a decision of the Hofrat. The addition of the
phrase "regis propria per dominum n.," a form rarely occurring in the
documents from Maximilian's reign,[217] indicated that the King's command to have the document executed was communicated to the person
whose name appears in the formula (that is, "n.").[218]

From the standpoint of our investigation, documents bearing
any of these notations may be of interest. Since the Hofkanzlei produced documents concerning Imperial matters throughout Maximilian's
reign, the ad mandatum formula does not necessarily mean the text was
produced under Berthold's direction. By the same token Maximilian's
commissioning of a text does not mean that he was personally involved
with its execution beyond that point. Not all the commissio regis
propria documents are signed by Maximilian or sealed with his seal.
In fact the Hofordnung of 1498 states explicitly in the passage
quoted above that Maximilian only wished to be consulted by the
Council in "great and difficult" matters. The commissioning notations, then, are not sufficient grounds to assume that the Emperor
himself endorsed the manuscripts on which they appear.

Signatures

By the reign of Frederick III, handwritten signatures,
initials, visas, and other formalized handwritten phrases of endorsement were frequently used by the monarch and by chancery personnel in
place of or in addition to seals in validating documents. Registered
fair copies from Maximilian's chanceries may show as many as three
different handwritten visas in addition to the commissioning notation
discussed above. Some documents, however, particularly those issued
under hanging seals, were executed without any written endorsement
at all.[219]

When written visas occur on documents from Maximilian's chanceries, they are usually of two types. If a document was approved
personally by the Chancellor or his agent (usually one of the Senior
Secretaries), that individual wrote his full formal signature (see
below) beneath the commissioning notation in the lower right corner
of the plica.[220] Below his name he typically wrote "m p" or "p m p"
("manu propria" or "per manum propriam"), indicating that the endorsement was by his own hand and that the document was an original rather
than a simultaneous copy prepared for record. This single signature
may be the only handwritten signature on a chancery document. If so,
it represents both a final proofreading check and an endorsement of
content. Many of the documents from Maximilian's chanceries show a
second form of visa. It is a notation at the upper left corner of
the plica that represents the countersignature of the monarch or his
agent. When the notation occurs in conjunction with a secretary's
visa at the lower right, the secretary's signature is essentially a
proofreading acknowledgment and the monarch's visa is the authorization of content.[221] This second endorsement is the formula "p reg
p s," that is, "per regem pro se";[222] it usually occurs on Urkunden
showing the Proprialvermerk, "commissio regis propria," and appears
much more frequently as an endorsement than any of the forms of Maximilian's signature or initials. Despite the literal meaning of the
phrase, however, and the fact that it appears on documents the

Emperor himself commissioned, the presence of the visa does not mean
that Maximilian personally endorsed the fair copies on which it
appears. Burkhard Seuffert notes that the regional chanceries were
not only given the right to seal documents in Maximilian's stead, but
that they were also permitted to use the per regem formulae after the
new Hofordnung came into effect in 1498. He cites examples in which
Frederick the Wise and Hans von Landau sign "Per Regem Fridericus
Saxonie D. Elector" and "Per Regem H. v. landaw," respectively. More
significantly, however, he mentions that Paul von Liechtenstain was
actually authorized to sign "per regem per se" for the Emperor.[223]
This means that even the documents that indicate they have been
approved by Maximilian himself (se) may not have been.

Some chancery documents show Maximilian's handwritten initials
or signature in the place of this monarchial visa. On these texts,
which actually passed through Maximilian's hands, his countersignature may represent the final endorsement or an agreement with other
signatories mentioned in the text, or it may be the sole authorization
of the document.[224] Maximilian used a variety of handwritten endorsements. The so-called großes Namenshandzeichen is a calligraphic signature in which Maximilian actually spells out his name. It was
reserved for extremely formal documents such as treaties[225] and royal
marriage contracts. Several versions of this signature are shown in
Peter Anton von Franck's Von dem großen Namenshandzeichen Maximilians I.[226] On less ceremonial occasions, Maximilian sometimes wrote
only his initial and a highly abbreviated form of his royal title:
"M. R. Kunig."[227] Maximilian also had an Imperial monogram that he
rarely used, although the use of monograms had been popular through
the reign of Sigismund and had continued during Frederick's reign.[228]

The matter of determining which documents Maximilian approved
personally is complicated further by the fact that he had three
silver stamps made of his Handzeichen in 1507 by Benedikt Burkhart in
Hall.[229] He announced to the Stände in July of the same year that he
had had a stamp made of his Imperial signature and that he intended
for it to be used by trusted individuals in executing royal documents.

Seuffert mentions references from 1510 and 1511 that indicate this
signature stamp, the Katschet, was actually lent to Konrad Peutinger
and Hans Paumgartner; in 1511 it was also lent to Serntein.[230]   In
addition to the Katschet Seuffert lists six other stamps. They are
not stamps of Maximilian's initials or signature, but of standard
diplomatic validation formulae. Three of these have the text "per
regem per," two the text "per Cesarem," and one the text "ũ per
Cesarem."[231]   The final word of each formula was written in by hand
on the documents. Seuffert notes that Serntein and Ziegler had similar stamps, but he does not describe them.[232]

The pattern one observes in Maximilian's own endorsements, if
more elaborate than some, appears to have been typical of the chancery practices of his day. Many of the Habsburg chancery officials
used at least two totally different signatures—one quite plain, and
one or more highly calligraphic—in validating chancery documents.
The type of signature used depended on the kind of document and its
function on the document.[233]   The calligraphic signatures appear on
fair copies, particularly on those where they endorse a text penned
by another writer. They are often, but not always, used on documents
for the public record[234] and on those requiring the countersignature
of the Emperor. The unembellished signatures usually appear on chancery drafts, reports written from chancery members on assignment, and
documents intended only for circulation within the chancery.

Seals

When the sealing of diplomatic documents is mentioned in discussions of the Habsburg chancery language, some scholars imply that
there was but a single seal used in executing official chancery
communications. The Court and Chancery Ordinances of 1494 and 1498
expand this number somewhat, but they still suggest a highly centralized and closely controlled system for authenticating documents in
the Habsburg chanceries. In his essay on Maximilian's seals and
their historical significance, however, Franz-Heinz Hye has identified fifty-two separate seals of various sizes and descriptions,

which were used on Habsburg diplomatic documents between 1486 and
1519.[235] Of these, more than a dozen were Court seals and the
Emperor's personal seals. This group included two ring seals and a
number of secreth seals.[236] Several were used only on documents that
bore the Emperor's own signature or that showed chancery notations
indicating the text had been written at the direct command of Maximilian.

Most of the separate Habsburg administrative authorities, such
as the Hofregiment, the Hofkammer, and the Kriegskammer, had separate
seals. The main Imperial seal was Maximilian's great royal seal,
over which the controversy between Stürtzel and Berthold von Mainz
developed. With the end of the Reichskanzlei in 1502, this seal
reverted to the Hofkanzlei. The seals used by the various Habsburg
agencies were not always their own. The großes secreth that Matthäus
Lang used in the Hofkanzlei, for example, was turned over unaltered
for use in the Hofkammer. Similarly the Lehenssiegel from the Land-
gravate of Nellenburg became a Court seal that was used on documents
signed by Ziegler, Serntein, and Maximilian himself. Generally
speaking, Court seals were used on documents with which Maximilian
was closely involved, whereas the seals of the regional authorities
were used quite independently of the Emperor.[237]

Even with the great number of official seals in use during
Maximilian's reign, many Habsburg diplomatic documents went out under
personal seals (which were often signets or petschaften), under
formal and informal signatures, and under borrowed seals. Hye's
research shows, particularly in the case of the Court, that certain
seals were often reserved for use on documents showing specific chancery notations. Documents bearing Maximilian's signature or the
notation that he himself had commissioned the text (the Proprialvermerk), for example, usually show seals different from those used
on texts that were otherwise commissioned and endorsed in the Chancery.
Members of the Hofkanzlei traveling on official missions were frequently obliged to borrow seals that were not official Habsburg seals
in order to conduct the Emperor's business,[238] and sometimes the lack

of a seal caused considerable inconvenience. In a letter to Cyprian
Serntein, for example, Niclas Ziegler complains bitterly that he has
been denied the use of the Chancery seal and for this reason put in
the embarrassing position of having to refer official business to
others:

> Wo Ich dz sigl gehept. het Ich etwas mugen fertigen.
> Also hab Ich es andern leuten muessen Zu schickhen
> das ist mir spotlich. auch lenger vnleidlich [. . .]
> darzu auch Ewr nachteil. Ewre zwen schreiben haben
> mir Zu fryburg nichts hellffen wellen/ Wo Ir ein
> vertrawen In mich setzen. als mit dem sigl. der Kunig.
> vnd hertzog fridrich getan haben/ welt Ich mich der-
> massen gegen Euch halten/ dz Ir darab ein gefallen
> hetten/[239]

The custody of chancery seals was both an administrative and a
political matter, since documents bearing official seals were considered genuine whether or not they showed other forms of endorsement.[240]
Ziegler's statement above indicates that he has been unable to conduct
chancery affairs without the seal in Freiburg even on the strength of
Serntein's official letters of introduction. That Serntein sent
Ziegler on this assignment without the Chancery seal was surely not
an oversight. He apparently did not altogether trust his subordinate,
and possession of the seal would have given Ziegler more authority
than Serntein intended him to have. This episode points up both the
competitive political climate of Maximilian's Hofkanzlei and the
significance of seals as a means of authenticating official documents.

Summary

The authentication of documents executed in Maximilian's chanceries guaranteed the scribal accuracy of the fair copy. The provisions of the chancery ordinances of 1494 and 1498 suggest that this
was the main objective of the series of controls prescribed. The
"chancery style" was a matter of diction. The impetus for producing
documents in consistent formulaic style was to make them legally
unimpeachable. Neither the chancery ordinances nor the authenticated
documents produced in accordance with them indicate that the internal
chancery checks were for compliance with any orthographic standard.

The chancery endorsements often make it possible to trace the route of a given text through the chancery from commission to issuance—to tell how it was assigned, who proofread it, and who approved its execution. In some cases the proofreader and the authorizer can both be established, in some cases neither is identifiable, sometimes they are one and the same. Practically speaking, the different forms of endorsement are not of equal significance. Chancery seals and Maximilian's handwritten visas outweighed the signatures of the Chancellor and Senior Secretaries. The presence of either of the former obviated the need for the latter.

The internal controls that actually prevailed in the Habsburg administrative network during the reign of Maximilian I permitted many more agencies and individuals to issue official chancery documents than the offhand references from the histories of the German language suggest. In associating the putative standardization of the Habsburg chancery language with Maximilian personally, Germanic philologists seem to have become the victims of some of the Emperor's own propaganda. In his self-aggrandizing autobiography, Der Weißkunig, Maximilian claims that not a single missive left the chancery without his personal endorsement:

> Er [Maximilian] ließ auch kainen brief nit ausgeen, es
> was die sach klain oder groß, er uberlaß zuvor denselben
> brief und underschrib alle brief mit seiner hand. Wie
> vleyssiglichen hat diser kunig regirt, dann man söliche
> regirung von kainem kunig geschriben findt! Er ist auch
> so ubertreffenlichen gewest mit angebung der brief und
> mit seiner gedachtnus, das er oftmalen newn, zehen,
> aintlif und zwelf secretarien zu ainer zeit, jedem
> secretarien ainen besonderen brief angeben hat, und die
> ganz regirung aller seiner kunigreich und land ist allain
> von ime beschehen, neben allen den grossen kriegen, die
> er in frembde nacion und land gefuert hat.[241]

This was certainly not the case. Not everything that left the Chancery with a royal visa was signed personally by Maximilian, and much Hofkanzlei business was concluded without using Court seals. The external evidence examined to this point, including the chancery ordinances, indicates that Maximilian was primarily interested in

retaining absolute control of the Court and Imperial Chanceries and
their activities. To do this he frequently intervened personally in
chancery matters.[242] There is nothing to indicate, however, that an
interest in any sort of language standardization, orthographic or
otherwise, was the basis for his interference in chancery affairs.
The chancery production was carefully controlled, but the controls,
as we have seen, were not of the sort historians of the German language have assumed.

It is remotely possible, however, that Ziegler and Maximilian
did develop and propagate an identifiable orthographic standard in
the Hofkanzlei. If so, their own holographs and the fair copies
penned by others that they endorsed should be evidence of this language. The preceding survey of validation practices shows that only
those documents bearing Maximilian's handwritten visas can be said to
have been approved by him personally. Similarly only fair copies
bearing Ziegler's manu propria signature, as well as his own holographs, can be said to have been endorsed by Niclas Ziegler. These
are the sorts of documents that would have to be examined to establish
the personal orthographic practices of the Emperor and his Senior
Secretary.

CHANCERY ACTIVITY UNDER MAXIMILIAN I

The organizational structure and internal procedures of the
Hofkanzlei and Reichskanzlei tell only part of the story of the Habsburg chancery system at the turn of the sixteenth century; they
introduce its activities without suggesting their import or indicating how closely chancery practice followed the routines prescribed.
Under Maximilian the Hofkanzlei became the center for most of the
Emperor's diplomatic and political activities, and chancery service
continued to offer remarkable opportunities for personal advancement.
Traditionally the chancery had been staffed with members of influential noble families who stood in close proximity to the Emperor, but
this practice began to change in the fourteenth and fifteenth centuries so that by Maximilian's time there were a number of bourgeois

members of the <u>Hofkanzlei</u> staff. Because of the immense power resting in the chancery in the late fifteenth century, it was the agency to which the politically and financially ambitious aspired.

A passage from the <u>Weißkunig</u> shows how important Maximilian himself considered the chancery to be; he felt that he had to control the chancery in order to be able to govern effectively. In the brief chapter entitled "Wie der jung weyß kunig lernet die handlung des secretari ambts," Maximilian describes how he ("der jung weyß kunig") had been taught by his father ("der alt weiß kunig") to control the chancery. The old king has learned through experience that a monarch who does not know how to deal with his chancery staff has difficulty ruling. For this reason he decides to teach his son what is seemly for a chancellor or secretary so that the boy will learn to know the basis for government and to recognize for what they are the self-seeking individuals who serve him. The chapter reaches its climax with a brief exchange between father and son. The father asks, "Son, do you understand the principle of government through the chancery (schriftliche regirung)?" The boy answers, "Whichever king places his trust in any person [. . .] not he but that person shall reign." The father is delighted that the young prince has understood the fundamentals of kingship.[243] Although the details of many of the accounts reported in the <u>Weißkunig</u> are greatly idealized and exaggerated, the attitudes expressed in the work are usually Maximilian's own. In this passage the significance he attaches to the chancery and the caution with which he views the ambitious individuals who staff it may be taken at face value.[244]

In the chancery ambitious men bridged the gap between social obscurity and political prominence in a single generation, while accumulating sizable fortunes. The structures and supervision of the chancery were rather flexible in this period, so that dominant personalities could and did shape the course of events. Bribery and political intrigues were common, and elevated positions at Court precarious. There are numerous success stories among the chancery biographies of this time. Some men who began as secretaries in the chancery managed, like Matthäus Lang, to ride the political wave and ended up as monied bishops and provosts. Many others, however, who came to make their fortunes at Court were broken by their service there. Hans Waldner, for example, onetime head of Frederick III's Hofkanzlei and later Austrian Chancellor under Maximilian, was dismissed from his post for misconduct and officially charged; he committed suicide.[245]   And Jakob Villinger, Maximilian's "Grand Tresorier" and "Generalschatzmeister," who spent much of his career borrowing money for the Emperor against his own assets,[246] died ten years after his sovereign in considerably reduced circumstances.[247]

The meteoric career of Frederick III's great Chancellor, Kaspar Schlick, is a particularly dramatic example of this phenomenon. It merits a brief aside because it shows what was possible in the chanceries of the period, and what it was that the ambitious literati sought. Probably beginning as a scribe in Emperor Sigismund's service in 1415, Schlick was the son of a burgher family from the Egerland. During the next twenty years he ascended through the ranks as Notary, Protonotary, and Vice Chancellor,[248] and eventually became Chancellor. He married a woman from a ducal family and, albeit on the basis of a forged document, himself ascended to the estate of Reichsgraf. He was the first member of the laity to hold the office of Reichskanzler, a position he occupied under several monarchs (including Sigismund, Albrecht II, and Frederick III). Needless to say, Schlick made enemies in this rise to power, not the least of whom were members of the College of Imperial Electors. After the election of Albrecht II, this body presumed to send the Emperor elect an emissary, requesting that Schlick not be named Chancellor; the petition was ignored.[249]   Schlick's case is a colorful example of a pattern that continued to be typical in the chanceries through the time of Maximilian.

During Maximilian's reign there was no Imperial diplomatic corps as such,[250] and for this reason any person prominent in public life might be called upon to undertake a state mission of greater or lesser importance. Since this diplomatic activity required central

coordination, it too became a function of the royal Chancery. In fact
this was one of the chief activities of the coterie immediately surrounding the Emperor. The rivalries that developed among the Chancery
diplomats were intense and ubiquitous.[251] As the many references in
the chancery ordinances imply, this infighting was not just a matter
of power and prestige, but also of cold cash. The following statement, contained in a letter dated 15 January 1501 from Eysenreich to
Duke Albrecht IV of Bavaria, attests to such malice in the chancery
and is undoubtedly quite accurate. "Wan sy sind auch nit all ainig,
di an der kgl. Mt. hof sind und wo ainer den andern hindern mag, ob
gleich das Ew. G. oder yemant anderß berurt, so geschicht solichs."[252]

In some cases Maximilian furnished his diplomats and others in
his service with clerical and secular titles that established them
socially.[253] As Jančar notes the titles "Sekretär" and "Rath" ("con-
silarius") were frequently dispensed in this way; the fact that more
secretaries are listed in the chancery registers than can actually be
accounted for in the chanceries indicates that some of these diplomats
never served regularly in the Hofkanzlei at all.[254] Other secretaries like Niclas Ziegler, however, held responsible positions in the
Chancery and were often used for diplomatic missions as well (see
"Marx Treytzsaurwein" and "Niclas Ziegler," chapter 3). In intercourse with foreign powers Maximilian often used what Heinz Gollwitzer
has called "neighborhood diplomats" ("Nachbarschaftsdiplomaten"), that
is, he enfeoffed his retainers with territories bordering on the areas
where he wished them to act on his behalf.[255] The financing of Maximilian's diplomatic missions, like that of so many of his other
undertakings, was precarious. Since his emissaries could never be
altogether certain that they would be reimbursed for expenses incurred
on his behalf, their leaving Court to undertake long and expensive
missions carried with it a double risk: first, the diplomat might be
ruined financially; second, he might become the victim of a political
intrigue while abroad.[256] Apart from these considerations, the
opportunities for income were usually greater in the Chancery itself.

As the chancery ordinances of 1498 imply, the actual channels through which Maximilian's affairs of state had flowed to that point were not necessarily those prescribed by the regulations. Nor did this change greatly after 1498. Generally speaking, matters of greatest significance were handled by Maximilian himself, the circle of close advisors who accompanied him on his travels, and by his Chancery at Innsbruck. The Hofordnung of 1498 gave formal status to the ad hoc group of counsellors who advised Maximilian, and the makeup of this council remained relatively constant. After the death of his father in 1493, Maximilian combined the Tirolean and Court Chanceries, and the Chancellor in Innsbruck became known as the "Tirolischer und Hofkanzler."[257] A branch of the standing chancery at Innsbruck accompanied Maximilian on his travels. Exactly who comprised this group at any given time is difficult to say. To some extent this can be determined by seeing which secretaries approved or drafted documents on the dates and in the places corresponding to those on Maximilian's own itinerary.[258] The endorsements on individual Urkunden establish which of the senior members of the Chancery accompanied Maximilian at any given time. Only in exceptional cases is it possible to determine by other means what additional personnel may have been in attendance. The production of the itinerant chancery is of particular interest in considering the handbook claims about the Habsburg chancery language because of all the staffs of all the Habsburg chanceries, this is the one with which Maximilian was most closely associated.

It appears that Maximilian's peripatetic administrative staff included members of the Hofrat as well as the Chancery. The advisors who were not traveling with the Emperor or on assignment, however, were based at Innsbruck. On 27 March 1503, for example, Maximilian wrote to his "Hofräte sammt und sonderlich" in Innsbruck,[259] so one may assume that at least part of the Hofrat was functioning in Innsbruck along with the rest of the Chancery at the time. Sigmund Adler asserts, however, that although instructions for the Council were sent almost without exception to Innsbruck, one should not think of a constant, permanently based Council membership. He says that "it is impossible to speak of a regular seat of the <u>Hofrat</u>, although one must assume on the other hand that the members were appointed permanently and not just for specific cases."[260] The description of the <u>Hofrat</u> might as easily be applied to the itinerant branch of the <u>Hofkanzlei</u> to which it contributed.

THE TRAINING OF CHANCERY PERSONNEL

In discussing the relatively standardized language of the Habsburg chancery and the supposed orthographic reform of Niclas Ziegler, historians of the German language overlook the education of chancery scribes. To some extent this is justified, because the majority of those who actually penned Habsburg chancery documents remain anonymous and are known to us only by their scribal hands. The scribes whose lives and training can be accounted for were diplomats and leaders in the chancery and thus belong to the upper-middle or highest tier of the chancery hierarchy. Their education is typical of their own chancery stratum but probably not of the staff as a whole. Although it is impossible to speak of the training received by individual lesser members of Maximilian's scribal staff, it is important to consider briefly the educational avenues that may have led them to the chancery and the circumstances of their learning to write administrative German. The handbook accounts suggest that the Habsburg documents from Maximilian's reign reflect the deliberate attempt of his staff to regularize the written language. What little we know about the lives of the scribes, however, indicates that many of those who set the tone in the chancery acquired their training elsewhere and joined Maximilian's service already knowing how to write <u>cancelleysch</u>. This is probably true of the lesser scribes as well, since there is very little evidence to suggest that the training of copyists was a major activity within Maximilian's chancery system. Thus the ways scribes learned to write may have contributed more to the complexion of the Habsburg dialect than did the atmosphere and regulations of the chancery itself.

The most sophisticated traditional education available in
Europe at the beginning of the sixteenth century was provided by the
universities. Members of the emerging class of administrators, who
served both the nobility and the cities, studied at one or more of
these institutions;[261] this was true of Maximilian's staff as well.
Matthäus Lang, Conrad Stürtzel, and Cyprian Serntein were among those
members of the Chancery who had attended universities. University
training was the exception, not the rule, for the Chancery staff as
a whole, however, and it probably had little impact on the orthographic features of the Habsburg chancery language under investigation. Those who could already write attended universities for the
advanced tuition they could not receive from local schoolmasters.
The basic writing habits of students, however, were firmly established
before they ever reached the universities. Thus tutors and lower
schools probably played a greater role in shaping the language that
all three levels of Maximilian's scribal staff wrote in chancery
documents than has generally been acknowledged.

Late medieval German schools were of two kinds: the first was
scholarly in its orientation and prepared students for the university,
the clergy, or both; the second was more pragmatic and prepared students for business. Church schools and city Latin schools comprised
the first group.[262] Synodal decrees from the eighth century onward
required the establishment of schools in conjunction with cathedrals
and churches,[263] and until the thirteenth century the teaching of
reading and writing was exclusively the domain of the Church. Scribes
trained in the Church schools staffed both clerical and noble chanceries.[264] By the end of the thirteenth century, the need for literacy in commerce had increased to the point where the Church schools
could no longer meet the need for instruction.[265] As a result two
kinds of secular schools developed in the cities: the Latin or
Trivialschulen and the more commercially oriented "kleine Schulen"
or "parvae scholae." Latin schools taught grammar, logic, and
rhetoric—the basics of the liberal education—and, depending on
the quality and reputation of the instructor, sometimes attracted

itinerant students. The "kleine Schulen," which included the Deutsch-
schulen ("dudesche Schriffscholen") and the schools of Rechenmeister
and Stuhlschreiber ("scribae cathedrales"), emphasized the fundamentals
of reading and writing as well as basic mathematics.[266] The children
of craftsmen and merchants attended these "little schools," whereas
the children of prominent bourgeois families were often tutored
privately.[267]

In cities private instruction was the alternative to the
schools; elsewhere private writing masters were the only teachers
available. The scribal profession in Germany in the late Middle Ages
was loosely organized but nevertheless showed definite stratification.
Larger cities, including Vienna, had guilds of penmen who supervised
the training of scribes.[268] Recently Herrad Spilling has divided the
scribes of the day into two categories: writing masters and other
members of the scribal fraternity.[269] Members of both groups served
as private tutors.

The term "writing master" ("Schreibmeister") as it occurs in
modern scholarship may refer to either or both of two groups of professional penmen. In broad terms the Schreibmeister were independent
penmen who made their living by writing, employed neither by towns nor
noblemen as notaries or scribes. In the more restricted sense
"Schreibmeister" refers to the great calligraphic artists ("Schreibkünstler"), like Johann Neudörffer, Leonhard Wagner, and Wolfgang
Fugger, who were active in the first decades after the invention of
printing.[270] In addition to teaching calligraphy, written style, and
other subjects such as mathematics, these latter penmen designed completely new alphabets for copyists and typographers. Schreibmeister
of both kinds were also known as "Modisten" because they instructed
students in various modes of writing, that is, they taught students
different scripts and styles of writing, and taught them which ones
should be used for which specific purposes. In the fifteenth century
the German term "Modist" was also sometimes used to mean a teacher for
children or of elementary subjects;[271] in this usage "Modist" is
synonymous with the unrestricted meaning of "Schreibmeister." The

Schreibmeister and Schreibkünstler were the best trained and most
capable of the independent penmen. Some are known to have had an
academic education including Latin and other foreign languages.[272]
The range of their professional competence was greater than that of
the second group of private writing teachers.

The other category of professional penmen includes independent
schoolmasters, public scribes or notaries, and copyists of liturgical
texts.[273] The schoolmasters (or schoolmistresses)[274] taught male and
female adults and children the basics of reading, writing, and arith-
metic. Students were usually taught to write only after they had
learned to read.[275] Schoolmasters (Schulmeister) taught their students how to compose and pen letters and Urkunden.[276] The instructional activity of schoolmasters and writing masters was similar;
they both provided elementary education. In the period before the
towns began hiring teachers regularly, many members of both groups
were itinerant. The public scribes, whose own skills were often
limited, made their living writing letters and Urkunden for the illiterate and those with meager writing skills. Unlike the writing
masters who wrote in many styles, public scribes like Benedictus
Schwerczer of Passau (who called himself a modist) could often only
write the dominant chancery script of the day.[277] Very little information has survived about the liturgical copyists. The advertisement
of a single liturgical penman has been traced to fourteenth-century
England. From this one may posit that such specialists must also have
existed in late fifteenth-century Germany and would have been yet
another possible source of instruction in writing; but since the
existing evidence itself has little to do with Germany in the period
under consideration and proclaims copying rather than teaching skills,
we will overlook these members of the scribal profession.

A few surviving advertisements and manuals written by the
Schreibmeister themselves provide most of what is known about how
writing was taught in Europe in the late Middle Ages.[278] What they
suggest about teaching in Germany is summarized above, but a few
specific features of these documents that pertain to our investigation

of the Habsburg chancery language require further consideration.
Typically the German writing masters offered samples of both book and
chancery scripts on their advertising placards. The chancery scripts
were written as mock legal documents ranging from private letters to
royal decrees and Urkunden relating to international matters.[279] The
Passau penman Benedictus Schwerczer, who worked primarily as a copyist
of official documents, actually used a fictive letter to Frederick III
on his advertising poster.[280] Other contemporary German teachers also
drew particular attention to their ability to teach chancery skills.
Their claims go beyond instruction in the scripts. In 1447 Hermann
Strepel, a Westphalian teacher, associates writing with learning in
general and mentions that learning has bearing on the literary diction
of the Bible and of canon and civil law; he offers to teach those who
wish to learn to write well the secrets of learning's sweetness "that
they may become good scribes in a short time."[281] Johannes Brune, who
worked as a teacher in Erfurt between 1493 and 1510, offers to teach
students chancery script ("cancelleysch") as well as the rules of
orthography and other skills.[282]

It has been suggested that the writing masters kept their
methods of instruction secret,[283] but this is not altogether true.
The surviving advertising placards and handbooks themselves offer some
information about their techniques. The advertisements show various
scripts used in the kinds of texts for which they were deemed appropriate: chancery scripts for Urkunden, bastarda and textualis scripts
for psalm verses or other liturgical texts.[284] Similarly Neudörffer's
celebrated calligraphic handbook, Ein gute Ordnung vnd Kurtze vnterricht [. . .] (1538),[285] presents a splendid collection of alphabets
used in the sorts of texts for which Neudörffer considers them suit-
able. He names the different styles, shows the stroking order for
the individual characters, and writes passages in these distinctive
scripts, demonstrating how they should be used. Many of his sample
texts are mock official letters similar to the handwritten examples
used by earlier penmen on their advertisements. Significantly one of
Neudörffer's samples, an official letter from a subject to his lord,

is labeled "Ein schriftlein zum Copirn" (fol. 65). This indicates
that students learned to write not only by carefully reproducing
series of individual characters and combinations of characters, but
also by copying entire sample texts. Erich Straßner confirms that
this was the pattern used by the schoolmasters of Nuremberg in the
fourteenth and fifteenth centuries: students first learned to form
individual characters; then they learned chancery conventions through
copy exercises.[286] The advertising placards also suggest something
about how students were taught to read. A Swabian schoolmaster from
the fifteenth century explains his method on his poster as an induce-
ment to prospective students. He promises to spare students the old-
fashioned techniques by which they were taught to read—first
pronouncing the names of individual letters and then drilling words
syllable by syllable. Instead he proposes to teach them acrophoni-
cally, using pictorial images to suggest the familiar sounds students
associated with them.[287]

Chancery scripts and simulated chancery texts figure promi-
nently in the advertisements and instructional materials of fifteenth-
and sixteenth-century German teachers of writing.[288] Thus almost any
novice penman during the period would have learned to write at least
one chancery script. Since students practiced by copying whole texts
in the chancery style, they would have become familiar with the format
and tone of various kinds of chancery communication, much as beginning
secretarial students today learn the basic form and diction of business letters from the exercises in their typing textbooks, whether or
not they ever receive specific instruction in letter writing. The
advertisements of the writing masters indicate that at least some of
these teachers taught composition actively. This means that even
moderately dexterous scribal students of the period should have been
able to compose documents in correct chancery script and according
to contemporary conventions of diction. Thus a scribe could easily
have joined Maximilian's staff with a command of one or more chancery
scripts and a working knowledge of the standard forms of contemporary
administrative communication. He could have acquired these skills in

any of the schools discussed and would have gained them from any of
the private teachers except perhaps the liturgical copyists.

Some of Maximilian's chancery scribes seem to have received
their training in his service. The references to this on-the-job
tuition are scanty and somewhat oblique, however. In the Reichskanzleiordnung of 1494, younger scribes are instructed to consult their
elders in matters of chancery style, and the senior scribes are
enjoined to teach them well. Maximilian himself, in the chapter of
his Weißkunig cited in "Chancery Activity under Maximilian I" above,
claims to have employed quite a number of secretaries whom he had
raised from their youth according to his wishes.[289] Marx Treytzsaurwein (see chapter 3) was one of these scribes who grew up in the
Emperor's service. In a letter introducing him to Charles V, Maximilian tells his grandson that Treytzsaurwein has served him "since
he was a youth" ("von Jugend auf").[290] An examination of his chancery
production compared with that of scribes in Maximilian's service
known to have been trained elsewhere allows one to see whether the
Habsburg chancery preparation is easily distinguishable.

The scribal training provided in Maximilian's chanceries would
have differed somewhat from the instruction afforded by city schools
and private tutors. Apprentice scribes in the chancery system would
have been exposed to accomplished penmen representing a variety of
scribal and academic backgrounds from several geographic regions.
Young scribes in the chancery engrossed drafts written by their
superiors, worked with Empfängerkonzepte written by outside petitioners, and helped maintain the registers. Thus they regularly copied a
greater variety of texts than the students of a local schoolmaster
would probably have encountered. In addition to their highly skilled
and widely diversified senior colleagues in the chancery, young
scribes also had the registers and the bound codices of chancery
drafts[291] to consult as they learned their craft.

The preceding survey of educational institutions in late medieval Germany indicates there were a number of ways Maximilian's
scribes could have become proficient in writing chancery German before

they entered his service. This is true for scribes of all ranks in
the chancery, for even the least sophisticated contemporary German
schools and tutors taught students the forms and scripts of the chancery as survival skills in literacy. Thus one may assume that all
Maximilian's scribes had been taught cancelleysch, most of them before
they entered his service, even though most of their biographies remain
unknown. The circumstances of this tuition probably caused the chancery German written in various geographic areas gradually to lose some
of its most pronounced dialectal features. The teachers doubtless
taught the same chancery German wherever they went, and students would
have learned to write as they were taught whether or not the orthography they learned reflected the phonology of their own local dialects.

The scribes who learned to write in Maximilian's own chancery
would also have been exposed to a number of linguistically homogenizing influences. They were instructed by professional scribes who had
received their training in different places and in different kinds of
schools; they had to copy texts prepared by these various members of
the chancery; they also engrossed Empfängerkonzepte submitted more or
less in chancery style from all over the Empire. Historians of the
German language draw attention to the relatively uniform variety of
chancery German written by Maximilian's scribes and assume that it is
the result of a particular, self-conscious linguistic effort in the
Imperial chanceries. The scribes' initial writing instruction, however, could in itself entirely account for this phenomenon. At least
some of the contemporary writing masters (Johannes Brune, for
example), like the grammarians of the first half of the sixteenth
century, were specifically concerned with the rules of orthography.
This means that the students of such instructors probably did to some
extent regularize the spelling of the diverse texts they engrossed.
The effect of this training would have been the gradual development
of somewhat supradialectal forms of chancery German. One of these is
described by Luther in the well-known Tischrede discussed in
chapter 1.

SUMMARY

The preceding survey of the Habsburg chancery system during
Maximilian's reign indicates that despite the Emperor's interest in
administrative reform, his main chancery, the Hofkanzlei, continued
to function in the traditional medieval manner. It was a single centralized clerical staff answerable directly to him. At some times
during this period it was combined with the Imperial Chancery, at
others it simply usurped a large measure of the latter's authority.
Because of the contention between the Archbishop of Mainz and the
Emperor over the administration of the Imperial Chancery during the
late Middle Ages, the use of the term "kaiserliche Kanzlei" to mean
the chancery with which Maximilian was most closely connected is somewhat misleading. Maximilian's own chancery, throughout his reign,
was the Court Chancery, particularly that portion of it which accompanied him on his travels. If he supervised or influenced the German
written in his chancery system, it would have been the German written
by this group.

The handbooks suggest that Maximilian was personally involved
with the production of his chanceries and that he instituted reforms
within them. The complaints of his chancery personnel,[292] the Weißkunig text, and the woodcuts Maximilian commissioned for the Weißkunig
that portray him dictating to his scribes and artists[293] leave little
doubt that the Emperor was personally engaged in the activities of his
chanceries. His interest in these matters seems to have been sporadic,
however. It is yet another example of his inability to delegate
authority consistently and of his pronounced desire always to be at
the helm of his own projects. There is no evidence to suggest that
Maximilian's intervention in chancery affairs had anything to do with
language standardization. Maximilian's reforms in the chancery system
affected the external configuration of these administrative offices.
Except for the introduction of his signature stamps (which were rarely
used), however, the internal procedures for executing documents

remained much as they had been under Frederick III and were rather typical of the late medieval German chancery tradition.

The administrative ordinances of 1494 and 1498 show that documents were carefully controlled within the Habsburg chanceries. Surviving evidence suggests that the controls were checks for diction and accuracy of content. The authentication procedures used in the chancery system make it impossible in many cases to determine which member of the staff approved a given document. Only those manuscripts bearing Maximilian's handwritten signature can be said to have been approved by him personally, and these represent but a small fraction of the total chancery production. Similarly, only those documents showing manu propria endorsements of individual chancery secretaries can be considered to have been approved by them personally. Seals, stamps, and other forms of validation existed in far greater numbers and were used more flexibly than the handbook accounts imply. For the most part they cannot be considered personal endorsements of a text because one does not know whose approval they represent. Where manu propria signatures do occur, one cannot be altogether certain which aspects of the documents the visas approve.

All the late medieval German educators who instructed students in the vernacular appear to have taught chancery German as a basic skill. The advertisements of the schoolmasters and writing masters emphasize the chancery scripts but also show that these teachers were interested in orthography and diction as well. In the absence of evidence that either Maximilian or his staff deliberately attempted to standardize the orthography of chancery documents, one should perhaps attribute such regularity as may be observed in the Habsburg manuscripts to scribal training outside the chanceries instead. Neither the chancery ordinances nor additional historical sources suggest that Maximilian's Hofkanzlei was a major center of scribal instruction, and it does not seem to have been characterized by a conscious interest in language regulation. The Chancery was Maximilian's own administrative staff and was concerned primarily with affairs of state. Document control within the Chancery appears to

have been motivated primarily by the desire to produce accurate legal
records and charters while minimizing the possibilities of forgery and
unauthorized diplomacy conducted by individual members of the Chancery.

3

THE CHANCERY LANGUAGE OF MAXIMILIAN I

Sixteenth-century references to Maximilian's chancery language have played a large role in the retention of this theme in the historiography of the German language. Misinterpretation of these early statements and the absence of a viable working definition of the chancery language have resulted in a certain amount of confusion about its nature and significance. Since many of the modern accounts of the Habsburg chancery language are based on a misreading of Luther's statement about it, a new characterization of the chancery language is needed to determine its role in the history of German and to assess current views of its importance. This characterization presents not only those features of the written language that are of interest for modern linguists, but also those considered significant by its contemporary advocates.

In the 1530s when Luther, Eck, and Frangk identified the chancery language of Maximilian I as an exemplary variety of written . German, they were all concerned with the non-chancery applications of the UG administrative language, and they were not referring to matters of style and diction.[294] Although each of these men was thoroughly familiar with the chancery usage of the day (all of them as a result of their educational backgrounds, Luther and Eck through their wide correspondence, and Frangk as a teacher of chancery style and conventions), their remarks about the chancery language (see chapter 1) refer to its use as a legitimate medium for literature and general

written communication. Luther speaks of the language of his own
writings, Eck of the German of his Ingolstadt Bible, and Frangk of
the German into which "many a noble and useful book" can be translated
and so made accessible to those who do not learn the "main languages"
(i.e., the classical languages).[295] In sixteenth-century terms each
of these men of letters is recommending Maximilian's chancery language
"orthographically."

    At this time Orthographia was a popular topic in Germany among
those involved either with teaching students to read and write the
vernacular or with disseminating ideas in the vernacular to a readership that ranged from the barely literate to the erudite. (Each of
the three proponents of Maximilian's chancery language mentioned
above was engaged in one or both of these activities.) Orthographia
was not just a concern of the few early linguists whose grammars and
reading manuals have survived, but, as the advertising placard of
Johannes Brune indicates,[296] it was also a subject offered by even
the lesser German writing teachers around 1500. In the following
statement from his Teutsche Grammatica (1534), Valentin Ickelsamer
indicated which aspects of the written language were "orthographic"
matters, although he declined to go into detail about errors of
"orthography" because others had already treated the question sufficiently:

> Souil hab ich wöllen anzaygen von dem überfluß/ mangel
> vnnd verwandlung der buchstaben des teütschen lesens/
> damit zühelffen vnnd zůdienen/ denen die nach der rechten
> weis vnnd art lesen wöllen lernen/ dann solche vnuolkom-
> menhait vnsers lesens/ werden sy wol mercken vnnd em-
> pfinden. Von den andern vngeschickligkaitten der Ortho-
> graphien/ ja mehr Cacographien da man die wörter mit zů
> wenig oder zůuil/ oder auch vnrechten buchstaben schreibt/
> als das wörtlin/ vnd mit zwaien/ n/ vnd on vnterschaide/
> den vnd denn/ in vnd inn/ Item das man den buchstaben/ e/
> überal anhenckt/ als sieben viesch/ vnd des wüsts
> vnentlich vil/ will ich nichts von schreiben/ Es habens
> andere gnůgsam thon/ vnd werden sich auch die teütschen
> hierinn nit Reformiern lassen. Ich waiß kain bessern
> rath darinn zůgeben/ dann meine obgesetzte zwů Regel/
> das man in allen wörtern/ der oren rath hab/ wie es
> aigentlich kling/ Vnd zum andern/ auff des worts rechte

signification oder bedeütung dencke vnd merck/ so wirdt
man nitt vil vnnützer oder vnrechter bůchstaben setzen/
was dann der gewonhait vnd dem gemainen brauch/ welchem
auch die Orthographia zeytten dienet vnd weichet/ wie
der Fabius sagt/ nachzůlassen vnd zů geben wer/ würdt
sich auch wol schicken.[297]

This is not an isolated statement; much of what Ickelsamer
expresses here is typical of the German linguistic thinking of his
time.[298]   It suggests that Orthographia as he and his contemporaries
used the term was not simply a matter of spelling words with the correct letters according to a rigid standard usage. It implied rather
the broader range of problems that are associated with representing
the sounds of German in written or printed symbols. It is in this
wider orthographic sense that we must look for those features of
Maximilian's chancery language that contemporary literati considered
to be distinctive, and for the purposes of the present investigation
we must attempt to characterize the written chancery dialect in such
terms.

Much of what we assume about the linguistic climate of early
sixteenth-century Germany is derived from the handful of grammars,
orthographies, and primers that survive from the period.[299]   Because
most of these, regardless of their varying titles, are designed to
teach the illiterate to read and write, the material they offer about
various linguistic phenomena is presented as part of a practical
course of instruction; it is therefore more applied than theoretical
in nature.[300] The specific instructions concerning spelling and
pronunciation and the explanations of particularly troublesome features of the contemporary German writing systems differ from grammar
to grammar, and they are frequently contradictory even within the
same work. For these reasons it would be impractical to attempt to
analyze the production of Maximilian's chancery in strict accordance
with the linguistic theory that can be extrapolated from these texts.
Nevertheless, if one looks beyond the superficial contradictions of
the individual treatises to the more basic concerns of their authors,
certain common attitudes and problems emerge in the texts. Considered together they show an incomplete understanding of the

relationship of the written symbol to its reference in the spoken language; they identify but do not account for umlauting; they confuse
umlauting and diphthongization. These texts probably reflect the same
sort of linguistic attitudes that caused Luther, Eck, and Frangk to
admire the Orthographia of Maximilian's chancery language. They are
therefore essential to a working definition of the chancery dialect
that attempts not only to describe its features but also to account
for its sixteenth-century reputation.

HANS MOSER'S SYNGRAPHIC ANALYSES

The area of modern linguistics that addresses itself particularly to the aspects of language implicit in the sixteenth-century
term "Orthographia" is graphemics. The graphemic method Hans Moser
selected for his 1977 examination of Maximilian's chancery language
is an approach indicated by the material itself. Moser's objectives
were to provide preliminary information about the general characteristics and the range of influence of the chancery language, supply
data for related diachronic studies in historical linguistics, and
develop a concept of the linguistic norm of the fifteenth and sixteenth centuries that avoided the superimposition of anachronistic
linguistic values, which has to this point resulted in the conclusion
that ENHG scribal practices were arbitrary.[301]

To date Moser's study has not received the attention it
deserves as a contribution to the history of the German language, and
it has attracted some rather pointed criticism from historical linguists.[302] There are problematic aspects of Moser's study, some to
be considered below; but these do not detract from its usefulness.
In the present investigation we have questioned from the outset
whether or not there was a single set of features that could account
for both the sixteenth-century and the modern reputation of Maximilian's chancery dialect. The extralinguistic evidence presented thus
far suggests that the assumptions of modern philologists about the
written language have little to do with the orthographic concerns of
Luther and his contemporaries. Moser's graphemic analysis provides

a plausible characterization of Maximilian's chancery language that
can be related fairly successfully to both the sixteenth-century and
the modern assertions about the dialect, thus eliminating much of the
confusion that has been perpetuated by the handbook accounts and per-
mitting us to view the written language in its historical context.
For this reason we will consider Moser's study in some detail.

Methodology

Moser's investigation of Maximilian's chancery language is
both graphemic and synchronic because he felt that a more traditional
diachronic study, attempting to relate the chancery data to MHG or
OHG systems of linguistic relationships, would be inefficient and
poorly suited to the material itself.[303]   His attempt is to approach
his topic by means of a method attuned to the linguistic attitudes of
the period under consideration. Through a synchronic analysis of the
writing system of Maximilian's chancery production, he seeks to derive
the contemporary scribal standard ("Normverständnis") toward which
Maximilian's scribes oriented themselves and in terms of which the
manuscript production of the chancery was written. He calls this part
of his study the "syngraphic" analysis because all the data considered here is from a single source, the manuscript production of Maximilian's chancery; in a second part of his investigation, the "heterographic" analysis, he compares the graphemic features of the Habsburg
chancery language developed in the syngraphic analysis to similar
features of other approximately contemporary written languages from
Upper and Middle Germany.

The syngraphic analysis is the core of Moser's investigation
and it is based on two principles he adopts from Wolfgang Fleischer:
(1) the German writing system is a system of signs intended to represent phonological content;[304] and (2) the grapheme, the basic unit of
the graphemic system, is a significans which has as its significatum
the phoneme.[305]   In writing, graphemes are realized as graphs
(letters) or combinations of graphs. A single grapheme may have
several allographic variants; these may occur in free variation or

they may be determined by their occurrence in specific words or positions.[306]   As Paul Roberge explained, "Etic units," in Moser's study,
"designate not different visual manifestations of a particular grapheme (e.g., cursive, majuscule, capitals [. . .]) but (normally) different representations of a common phoneme, regardless of whether the
graphs in question bear any physical resemblance to one another."[307]
Moser refers to variant visual representations of a single graph as
"different types of a typeme," i.e., as allotypes, and for the most
part finds them to be irrelevant to his investigation.[308]

Moser claims that in his investigative procedure "the first
indication of the graphemic significance of characters is their distinctive function in the writing system itself." He continues, however, by saying that this distinctive function is sometimes determined
through "phonological prescience" ("phonologisches Vorwissen") and
acknowledges that earlier and later graphic and phonological forms
("Prä- und Postgraphien bzw. -phonien") are an important aid in determining the phonological frame of reference of the graphemic system.[309]
Thus he acknowledges at the outset that his synchronic analysis is
utterly dependent on diachronic data and invokes what Herbert Penzl
has called "the diachronically definable principle of reality."[310]
Without actually entering the graphemic debate,[311] which is beyond
the concerns of our present inquiry, we will consider at a later
point to what extent these working assumptions may limit the validity
of Moser's data for the question at hand.

Through the establishment of oppositions that may be either
complete, suspendable in one direction, or suspendable in two directions, Moser develops the graphemic inventory of Maximilian's chancery language. The unidirectional oppositions that are suspended in
the direction of the archigrapheme[312] are the basis of most of his
discoveries about the developmental trends and the dynamics of the
variations that occur in Maximilian's chancery language during the
period covered by his manuscript samples (1486-1518). Moser explains
his concept of the "einseitig aufhebbarer Oppositionen" in terms of
its most dramatic example in Maximilian's chancery language. Using

the principle of diachronic verifiability, Moser presents three
developmental stages of the MHG graphemes <i̲> and <e̲i̲> in Bavaria
as shown in figure l.

	MHG	Maximilian's Chancery Language ENHG	Modern Bavarian NHG
1	î	ei, ey	ae
2	ei	ei, ey, | ai, ay	oa, a, etc.

FIGURE 1. The Unidirectional Neutralization[313]

The set of allographs shared by the two graphemes (those boxed by the
broken line in the figure) is the basis of the unidirectional neutralization.   In Maximilian's chancery language e̲i̲ and e̲y̲ may be written
as graphic reflexes of MHG <e̲i̲>, but a̲i̲ and a̲y̲ may not in accordance
with the chancery norm (see "The Basic Syngraphic Description" below)
be written for MHG <i̲>.[314]

Moser's characterization of Maximilian's chancery language is
based on an examination of about 340 manuscripts that were produced
by different units of the chancery system at various times during
Maximilian's reign. The total group of documents is subdivided into
five main text samples, each designed to evaluate the chancery writing system in terms of specific variables. In developing his basic
graphemic definition of the chancery language, Moser views the chancery as a "common sender" ("gemeinsamer Sender"), or single agent.
Since his study is concerned not only with identifying the writing
practices used by Maximilian's scribes, but also with determining to
what extent this orthographic system was influenced by and exerted
influence on other approximately contemporaneous forms of written
German, Moser bases his characterization of the language exclusively
on the outward-bound production of the chancery.[315]

On the basis of his investigation of the institutional structure and relationships of the Habsburg chancery system during

Maximilian's reign, Moser concludes correctly that the chancery to
investigate is the Hofkanzlei, and he bases his primary characterization of the chancery language on its production. The first of his
syngraphic analyses, and the working description of the chancery
writing system to which all other partial investigations are compared,
is an evaluation of thirty-four Hofkanzlei documents written between
1490 and 1493 that were intended for Austrian recipients (Corpus I,1).
The results of this investigation are then adjusted by comparing them
with those arrived at by examining fifteen additional documents from
the same chancery during the same period addressed to northern recipients (Corpus I,2). Moser chooses the period 1490-93 as the logical
beginning point for his manuscript analyses, because he feels that
these are the years when the separation of the local and central chanceries was accomplished and before the Imperial Chancery came into
existence.[316] Moser's second sample is a group of thirty-five Hofkanzlei documents from between 1515 and 1518 intended for both
southern and northern recipients; it represents the final developmental stage of the writing system used during Maximilian's reign. A
comparison of Corpora I and II permits Moser to identify evolutionary
trends in the scribal tradition over a period of almost thirty years.

  Having established a viable description of the chancery usage
for the span of Maximilian's reign on the basis of the first two
samples, Moser designs two additional samples to resolve some specific
issues about the chancery language of the sort discussed in chapter 1
of this study. Moser's Corpus III is a group of thirty-five holographs by fifteen known chancery personalities (III,1), and eleven
"doubles" (i.e., drafts and register entries, showing the same text
at two stages of its execution).[317] Moser's Corpus V is a group of
twenty-six documents dating from between 1494 and 1502 from the
Reichskanzlei of Berthold von Mainz. The largest sample is Corpus IV,
a group of 180 chancery manuscripts varying widely in date, variety,
and recipient. This voluminous and deliberately heterogeneous group
of manuscripts was designed as a test sample to ensure that the selection bases of the other samples had been broad enough to produce a

valid characterization of the written language. Of particular inter-
est in this sample is a group of texts from the years 1486-90 (the
"Vorphase") documenting the earliest stages of the scribal usage under
Maximilian.[318]

   After developing his initial characterization of Maximilian's
chancery language on the basis of sample group I,1, Moser adjusts
these findings to accommodate additional data from the manuscripts of
sample groups I,2; II; and IV. The supplementary information developed from samples III and V suggests how certain of the features
derived from the earlier samples should be interpreted; the corroborating data from sample IV establishes the validity of the earlier
findings. Together the results of the partial studies contribute to
the general graphemic characterization of Maximilian's chancery language, which Moser compares to other contemporary writing systems in
the heterographic analysis. It is this general description based on
the chancery usage between 1490 and 1493 that interests us most. We
will use Moser's own summary[319] of these results to answer some of
the questions that have been developed in chapters 1 and 2; beyond
this we will consider in detail only those aspects of his analysis
that may have colored the data he presents.

The Basic Syngraphic Description

   Before beginning his examination of individual graphemes, Moser
presents a complete inventory of the graphs and types occurring in
the first sample. In terms of his definitions, however, these lists
are essentially inventories of graphs alone, because many allotypic
variants are presented only in generalized forms. "Diacritical symbols used to mark vocalic graphs or combinations of graphs are
omitted from the outset if their graphemic irrelevance has been
established" (e.g., over y, ay, ey, and ye; over u/w in eu and ew).[320]
Moser considers these all to be one allotype of a typeme and treats
them as a single variant, that is, as the marked form of the graph.
Having established on the basis of an undescribed preliminary investigation that the several diacritical symbols used to mark u are variants

of a form and have no distinctive value, Moser generalizes the markers
and substitutes for all of them the acute symbol (´) above the marked
vowels in his analyses and sample texts. Capitalization is not taken
into account because it is considered a stylistic variant.[321]

The Graphemes

Moser presents the graphemic system from the beginning of Maximilian's reign (based on Corpus I with adjustments from Corpus IV) as
shown in figure 2.

Vowels

<ie>   <ue>
                                                                   ↓
<i><ee> → <e> ← <é> → <a>   <ó> → <o> ← → <u>
        <ei>   ←   <ai>
        <ew>   <au>

Consonants

a)   <b>   <d> ← → <t>   <g>
                                                      ↑
                                                      ↓
     <ph>   <z>   <k>
  <w>   <f> ← → <ff><ss> ← → <s> ← — <sch><j><h> — → <ch>
     <m>   <n> ← → <nn>
                          <l> ← → <ll>
                          <r> ← → <rr>
b)<x>

FIGURE 2. The Basic Graphemic System[322]

Graphemic Neutralization

Some of the graphemic oppositions shown above may be suspended
under certain circumstances. The unidirectional neutralizations
affecting vowels may occur in any environment. Other oppositions,
however, particularly those involving consonants, may only be suspended in specific positions. Moser describes the unidirectional
opposition <ei> ← <ai>, for example, as freely suspendable by contrast with the opposition <s> - <sch>, which only occurs initially
before particular consonants. The main conditions under which the
positionally determined neutralizations may occur he summarizes as
follows:[323]

(1) <u> - <o>   before -n as in sunst ∿ sonst; the pattern is
                    expanded to include a group of other specific words
                    in which the opposition is also suspended, e.g.,
                    kumen ∿ komen, mugen ∿ mogen.

(2) <d> - <t>   finally after -n as in land ∿ lant; the neutrali-
                    zation does not spread to other environments; it
                    results in a "neutralization variant"[324] (see
                    below), dt, that occurs in the same position (e.g.,
                    landt).

(3) <g> - <k>   in -ig + -lich and -ig/-ich + -heit/-keit, as in
                    kuniglich, pillichait; -g is occasionally written
                    as the neutralization variant gk word-finally;
                    <g> ∿ <k> after short vowels as in zu rugk.

(4) <h> - <ch>   finally as in hoch.

(5) <s> - <sch>   in absolute initial and morpheme-initial position
                    before -l, -m, -n, -w, -p, and -t, as in slosser
                    and besliessen.

The remaining neutralizations occur less regularly:

(6) <r> - <rr>   intervocalically and finally after vowel.

(7) <l> - <ll>   intervocalically and to some extent finally after
                    vowel.

(8) <s> - <ss>   intervocalically and to some extent finally after
                    vowel.

(9) <n> - <nn>   intervocalically.

(10) <f> - <ff>   intervocalically (weakly represented in Moser's
                    samples).

Moser notes that the most significant aspect of this pattern
of neutralizations is its predictability. In three cases, he says,
the neutralization process has resulted in specific neutralization
variants: <d> ∿ <t>, dt; <g> ∿ <k>, gk/gc; and <s> ∿ <ss>, sz.
Beyond the preceding list of regular neutralizations (i.e., those
that are in accordance with the scribal conventions of the Hofkanzlei
writing system), Moser notes that in Maximilian's chancery language

at this stage there is still a small group of words in -iren (-ieren)
showing the neutralization <i> ~ <ie>. Neutralizations not included
in the preceding list may also be regular in terms of the chancery
usage in specific words (as frembd ~ frombd), and irregular or uncon-
ventional neutralizations, as suggested above, are also possible, but
infrequent (see "Chancery Case Studies" below).[325]

Vocalic Marking

Moser observes that the tendency to mark umlaut environments
is not very pronounced in Maximilian's chancery language at this
stage and that the umlaut graphemes (<é>, <ó>) are subject to unidirectional neutralization. In the case of <é>, which represents the secondary umlaut of /a/ in this system, Moser shows two regular unidirectional neutralizations of the grapheme: <é> → <e> and <é> → <a>. He
justifies the graphemic status of <é> by explaining that the alternation of e ~ é ~ á ~ a is only conceivable in terms of the secondary
umlaut since the opposition <a> - <e> is otherwise clear and without
variants. Moser is not able to isolate distinctive graphemes for the
umlauted forms of /u/ and /ue/ and he warns the reader that in the
spellings ú and úe the diacritical hook is not necessarily an umlaut
symbol. ú is sometimes written to indicate umlauting, sometimes to
show diphthongization; ue and úe are also written to indicate diphthongs, although some reflexes of the MHG diphthongs are spelled u in
the sample.[326]

The Variants

Moser arranges the allographic variants as in figure 3 to correspond to the catalog of graphemes shown above. The underlined
forms are the variants he has used as graphemic designations; in most
cases these are the variants occurring with the highest frequency in
the sample.[327]

This visual presentation emphasizes Moser's phonemic understanding of the term grapheme and shows with particular clarity his
concept of the unidirectional neutralization. Thus e is shown as a
variant of <é>, but é is not shown as a variant of <e> because <e>,

in terms of the unidirectional neutralizations indicated, is without variants (see "The Merits of the Syngraphic Analysis" below). Moser notes the wide range in the number of variants associated with the individual graphemes: <e>, <o>, and <a> are practically without variants in this system, whereas the variants of the guttural affricate (those shown for both <g> and <k>) are so numerous as to approach unintelligibility ("Variation bis zur Unübersichtlichkeit").[328]

Vowels

ie, ye
                                                                              ue, úe, u, ú, v, v́
i, y, j   ee, e   e   é, e, á, a   a, (aa)   ó, o   o   u, v, ú, v́
                   ei, ey   ai, ay, ei, ey
                   ew, eu   au, aw
Consonants
   b,p,(pp)   d,dt   t,tt,(th)   g,gk,gc,(gg)
   ph,(pf)   z,cz/tz,c,t,tʃ,ts   k,c,q,ck,ckh,(ch),(dh)
w,u   f,v,u,ff   ff   s,ss,ʃ,ʃʃ,ʃs,(z)   ss,ʃʃ,ʃs,ʃz   sch,ʃch,ʃ,s   j(=I)h,ch   ch
   m,m̄   n,nn   nn   ng,nng
                               l,ll   ll
                               r   rr

FIGURE 3. The Variants

Many of the allographic variants, particularly those belonging to the consonantal graphemes, occur only in specific positions. Moser shows that the absolute initial position is the most restricted with respect to the variants. The following variants do not occur word-initially: all doublings except ee (as in eer); <i>: j; <d>: dt; <s>: z; <z>: tz/cz, c, t; <u>: ú, u; <g>: gk, gc; <h>: ch; <k>: ck, ckh. The following variants do not occur medially: <u>: v, v́; <s>: s, ss, (z); <h>: ch; <f>: v; <sch>: s; <k>: (ch, dh), q. A few isolated words and syllables form a group of regular exceptions within the chancery usage to these rules describing the distribution of allographic variants. These exceptions include: <t>: th (in thun, -thumb); <k>: ch (in churfúrst, marschalch); <k>: dh (in dhain).[329]

One of the most useful results of Moser's investigation of the
allographic variants is the definition he develops for the much-
maligned ENHG practice of Konsonantenhäufung or, as Ickelsamer put it,
"Cacographia." He says that since there is no rigid graphemic opposition between the single and double forms of many consonants, the
individual scribe may double the character at will in these optional
situations. He observes that although none of Maximilian's scribes
exercises the option consistently, they all seem to observe this convention: in a sequence of two consonantal graphemes the double
variant of only one may be written.[330] The application of this rule
shows that the form Hellffershellffer (see "Ziegler and the Chancery
Language of Maximilian I," chapter 1), which has been so popular
among historians of the German language as an example of the sort of
consonantal excess that Maximilian's chancery language is supposed to
have overcome, is indeed atypical of the chancery usage. This rule
also supports Moser's interpretation of the graphic combinations he
calls "neutralization variants" (above). The neutralization variants
often occur in combination with another doubled consonant (e.g.,
lanndt) in texts that feature no sequences of single doubled consonants (e.g., Hellffer). This suggests that the scribes did not consider the neutralization variants to be doubled consonants.

Moser's meticulous examination of the allographic variants
leads him to two other general observations about the writing system
that was employed in Maximilian's chancery. First, the tendency to
indicate vocalic length is quite weak. The sole vocalic grapheme
that may only represent a lengthened grade is <ee>; it occurs in but
a few short words and may also be expressed by its variant e. Beyond
this, vowel length may be indicated by the opposition of single and
double postvocalic consonants. No single graph (such as h or e) is
used as a sign of lengthening throughout the writing system. Second,
the same graphemic principles described to this point apply in both
stressed and unstressed syllables.[331]

The Common Practice as the Standard

The point-by-point analysis of Corpus I,1 not only leads Moser
to his basic description of the graphemic system of Maximilian's chancery language, but it also allows him to draw significant conclusions
about the sort of standard and the degree of consciousness of that
standard which the sample as a whole reflects. He concludes that:
(1) there is "a relatively simple system of graphemes that guarantees
unambiguous communication" ("ein [. . .] relativ einfaches System von
Graphemen, das eine zweifelsfreie Kommunikation garantiert");
(2) within that system the individual scribe has considerable latitude
in his choice of variants, in his choice between certain graphemes,
and in some cases in his decision whether or not to observe regular
oppositions; and (3) a certain number of deviations from the chancery
norm are tolerated.[332] In his comparison of Corpora I,1 and I,2
Moser establishes conclusively that the same variety of chancery
German was written to all external correspondents and that the chancery usage was not adjusted for northern and southern recipients.[333]
Moser characterizes the "chancery norm" in a way which is harmonious
with the linguistic thinking that produced it, and he demonstrates
dramatically (figure 4) the flexibility inherent in this definition:

> Diese Art von Norm ist von der heute üblichen, die
> keinerlei Variation erlaubt, grundsätzlich verschieden,
> aber weder 'willkürlich' noch 'verwildert'. Um Mißver-
> ständnisse zu vermeiden, wird für sie (wenn der Begriff
> 'Norm' nicht ausdrücklich näher charakterisiert wird)
> der Terminus 'Usus' vorgezogen. Usus bedeutet also
> 'elastische Norm' im beschriebenen Sinn, Norm, die
> innerhalb eines festen Rahmens verschiedene Möglich-
> keiten variierender Realisierung erlaubt.[334]

The sentence in figure 4, which can be read sixteen different ways,
shows clearly the amount and variety of leeway existing in the
"elastic norm" of the chancery writing system as it is characterized
by Moser.

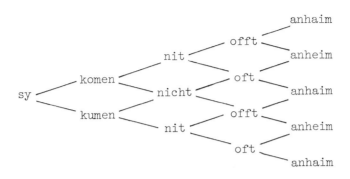

FIGURE 4. The "Elastic" Chancery Norm[335]

The Merits of the Syngraphic Analysis

Before proceeding to his other analyses, let us examine briefly
some of the reservations that have been expressed about Moser's investigative method and consider whether or not his technique invalidates
his description of the chancery writing system for the purposes of
the present study. Moser's approach derives essentially from the
graphemic method developed by Wolfgang Fleischer in his 1966 work on
the written language of Michael Weiße,[336] and from the investigative
technique of Herbert Penzl, from whom he adopts several of his termini
technici.[337]

In his Lautsystem und Lautwandel (1971), Penzl outlines the
philological method of historical phonological textual analysis that
is reflected to a considerable extent in Moser's examination of the
Habsburg chancery language. Penzl's basic premise is that synchronic
phenomena in historical languages must be explained and verified
diachronically. Assumptions about an individual stage in the evolution of a language, however, must be developed from the historical
texts themselves or from their writing systems. In Penzl's synchronic,
positivistic method of analyzing an historical ("nichtzeitgenössisch")
written text, the investigator must first determine the phonemic
system and then attempt to identify the allophones and describe the
spoken values ("Sprachlaute") indicated by the written symbols. The

phonemic and phonetic values for a given text are derived by subject-
ing the written evidence to an ordered set of analyses of its features.
Penzl proceeds on the hypothesis that German scribes sought to render
phonemic distinctions with the Latin alphabet and that one must therefore approximate the phonetic value of individual letters on the basis
of their assumed value in Latin. He then develops an inventory of
characters and symbols for each text; it reflects such features as
capitalization, punctuation, marking, and abbreviations. The analysis
of these graphs begins with the establishment of their distribution
patterns in all positions within words. Regular oppositions are determined through minimal pairs.[338]

      At this point the comparative analysis begins. The graphic
patterns of the individual text are compared with those of other contemporary texts and with those from earlier and later periods in the
development of the language in order to determine variation and alternation between graphemes. Graphic oppositions are considered to
reflect phonemic oppositions, and the assumed phonetic values ("Laut-
werte") of the Latin alphabet are used as a point of departure in
determining the phonetic values of the German graphs. Diagraphic
comparisons are used to establish whether a collapse or overlap
between graphs indicates a collapse of phonemes. Diachronic material
is used to clarify these issues.[339]

      In more general terms, Penzl asserts that "constant reference
to the facts of the historical past of a language [. . .] characterizes synchronic description in historical linguistics," and that "a
philologically exact interpretation of the text [. . .] is the pre-
requisite for synchronic analysis."[340] In applying these principles
to the matter of developing valid phonological data from historical
texts, Penzl considers three ways in which phonological textual
analysis has been undertaken to date: some scholars have considered
the written texts to be phonetic transcriptions (E. Sievers); others
have used historical texts as synchronic material for comparison with
a phonemic system developed on the basis of comparative diachronic
reconstruction (R. A. Hall, J. C. McLaughlin); and a third group of

scholars has derived phonemic systems directly from the written evidence itself (P. Valentin, W. Fleischer). Penzl considers only the third procedure appropriate.[341]

Depending on one's assessment of his technique, Moser's study falls into one of the latter two categories. The distinction between these two orientations, however, is simply one of degree. Both are phonemically oriented, and behind each hovers a generalized system of German phonemes that the investigator either derives from the texts deductively or "discovers" in the texts inductively. Both approaches are quite inductive, however, because even the discovery techniques employed by Penzl and Fleischer, for example, require that the investigator command considerable phonological prescience in order to isolate the multigraphic variants in the inventory of the writing system, identify the oppositions, and interpret the minimal pairs that establish the basic phonemic system. This should be considered in evaluating the critique of Moser's study.

Both Roberge and Straßner have objected to the phonemic orientation of Moser's analysis. Roberge has declared that Moser's definition "reduces the notion 'grapheme' to near vacuity" and that "the graphemic approach, as conceived by Moser, does not represent a viable interpretative paradigm" for the evaluation of Germanic texts.[342] Straßner has also questioned Moser's method for determining graphemes:

> Obwohl der Schrift eine 'relative Autonomie' zuerkannt wird, obwohl 'die lautlich/phonologischen Inhalte der graphischen Zeichen nur teilweise bekannt sind' und bei der Stützkonstruktion der Prä- und Postgraphien bzw. -phonien 'diachronische Tatsachen schon in die synchrone Analyse' hineinspielen (S. 56 f.), werden Graphe (Buchstaben) und Graphenverbindungen nicht als das Ausgangsmaterial angesehen, das es primär auf distinktive Funktionen hin zu analysieren gilt, ohne spekulative oder vom 'Vorwissen' her geprägte Interpretation. Die phonemorientierte Graphembestimmung wie der weitere Zusammenbau zu Graphemsystemen erfolgen nicht aus dem Material heraus, sondern werden von außen her an das Material herangetragen. Typisches äußeres Merkmal solchen Vorgehens ist die Terminologie der Phonemik, mit der unreflektiert operiert wird.[343]

As indicated, however, the degree to which an investigation of this sort, regardless of one's definition of grapheme, can be free of prescience and still have pertinence for comparative historical phonological studies is limited. The derivation of graphemes may appear to be more or less deductive, but the entire process of establishing the graphemic system is predicated on the researcher's diachronic knowledge of the language under investigation and on his expectations within this framework as he approaches his subject.[344]   Thus Straßner's objections to Moser's use of diachronic material is germane to the question of developing a more empirical graphemic method, but not to whether Moser proceeded correctly in terms of his chosen investigative orientation. Moser does not claim a paradigmatic value for his method; neither does he claim to have made any particular headway with basic graphemic issues. He simply adopts a method that will allow him to present the essential characteristics of Maximilian's chancery language in a way that can account for its sixteenth-century acclaim. The criticism of the phonemic orientation of the study overlooks the author's purpose to provide data that can be coordinated with related historical linguistic investigations. The inductive aspect of Moser's study is not a defect that calls his investigative method into question from a theoretical and a practical standpoint.

Nevertheless there are some troublesome aspects of Moser's study. His decision to generalize all diacritical markers to a single symbol and to eliminate altogether those markers he considers to be graphemically irrelevant gives the impression of a more ordered, less ambiguous, simpler orthographic system than Maximilian's chancery seems to have used. Reference to contemporary grammatical treatises shows that diacritical markers were used not only to identify certain characters visually (primarily u̲) but also to mark both umlaut and diphthong environments.[345]   Moser does not explain on what basis he establishes the graphemic relevance of the markers he retains; neither does he note that diphthongs were marked regularly according to the scribal practice of the period. This leads one to question the accuracy of his manuscript sample in this respect. In transcriptions

of texts from the period, markers should be retained above digraphic
diphthongs because they indicate an altered vocalic environment from
the standpoint of sixteenth-century German linguistic theory, whether
or not umlauting is also implied. In such cases the diacritical symbol
indicates the scribe's marking of a phonological and not just a visual
phenomenon. Further, it is often impossible to distinguish the u̲'s,
y̲'s, and w̲'s that were marked to identify the letters visually from
those marked to indicate umlauting or diphthongization.

For the most part Moser is consistent in defining his graphemes
according to the underlying phonemic systems he assumes. This is
convenient for purposes of comparison with related historical linguistic studies, but in some instances it seems to introduce an order
difficult to derive from the graphic data. In the case of the grapheme <é̲>, for example, Moser uses the marked vowel to indicate umlauting although this is not the way the umlaut is usually indicated in
the sample texts. Proceeding phonemically, Moser identifies two basic
e̲-graphemes in Corpus I,1. He uses the marked character é̲ to designate the secondary umlaut of /a̲/ and the unmarked character e̲ to
represent all other e̲-sounds in the system. (Later <e̲e̲> is added as
an adjustment of the system to indicate the lengthened grade of the
vowel.) The separation of the graphemes <é̲> and <e̲>, however, is
based more on phonological prescience than on unambiguous textual
data. Moser creates an independent grapheme <é̲> to represent the
secondary umlaut on the basis of minimal pairs like ré̲ten - re̲den and
of the coincidence of the marked e̲-forms in the sample with forms
containing the umlaut both in the historical language and in modern
Bavarian. He does so despite the fact that in the majority of
instances the secondary umlaut is spelled e̲, not é̲, in the sample.
He explains in accordance with his system of unidirectional neutralizations that e̲ should be considered the most frequent variant of <é̲>,
but that é̲ may not be considered a variant of <e̲>, even though é̲ is
written occasionally for an e̲-sound that does not result from umlauting.[346]

This treatment of the e-graphemes typifies the phonemic technique that Straßner has questioned, but it is useful to the historical
phonologist who needs a basis for categorizing the myriad marked and
unmarked e-spellings that occur in the Habsburg chancery texts and
other UG writing systems from the period. It blurs the fact, however,
that in the Habsburg writing system several phonemes are represented
by the same graph e, and that scribes did not find it necessary to
distinguish graphically between the several similar e-sounds that
characterize the Bavarian dialects. In separating the graphemes <é>
and <e> as he does, Moser distinguishes between phonemes that are only
partially distinct in the minds of the sixteenth-century scribes who
wrote them.[347]

Moser's similar phonemic treatment of the Bavarian labial stop,
which he represents with the grapheme <b>, is consistent with his
method, but it has apparently confused reviewer Roberge because it too
suggests an ordering principle that is not superficially evident from
the textual data. Roberge objects to Moser's interpretation of p and
pp as allographic variants of <b>, and suggests that the presence of
initial p in loanwords precludes the assignment of the graph to <b>.[348]
Roberge's argument would suggest that a new contrast has been introduced into the Bavarian phonemic system through these foreign forms.
The fact that loanwords containing an initial /p/ are frequently
spelled with b (e.g., babst, bábstlich, brobst)[349] by Maximilian's
chancery scribes argues against such a development, however, and confirms Moser's interpretation of the graphs.

In other respects Moser may have gone too far in his attempt to
explain the features of Maximilian's chancery language in terms of
systematic neutralizations. Roberge argues correctly that the assimi-
lation of n before labials (ent- in embieten) should not be described
as neutralization between <m> and <n>, and that the lexemic alternation niht/nit and the occurrence of epenthetic consonants in fursten-
tumb and frembd should not be called neutralizations. He is also
correct in saying that <x> in Maximilian is not a portmanteau
grapheme.[350]

None of these objections seriously limits the usefulness of Moser's characterization of the chancery language for our investigation. The phonemic definition of graphemes is practical in this case, although it is not without its theoretical drawbacks; once this phonemic orientation has been accepted, other objections to the inductive, diachronic aspects of Moser's study become pointless because they are inherent to his method. Moser's generalization and omission of diacritical markers in his sample texts and analyses is problematic because it alters a very characteristic feature of the chancery writing system before analysis begins. Moser does not explain on what basis which markers have been excluded, and his sample texts as well as his general remarks on the subject suggest that he does not view the characteristic marking of diphthongs in the chancery hands to be anything more than a marking of letters for the purposes of visual recognition. Even though this aspect of the chancery writing system is somewhat altered in Moser's investigation, however, the overall description provided by his syngraphic analysis is sufficiently valid for our purposes. It provides a set of features by which texts written in accordance with the usage of Maximilian's chancery can be identified and distinguished from those written in some other varieties of ENHG. In most respects the definition has been developed in a way that takes into account sixteenth-century German linguistic thinking. Hence we can use Moser's basic characterization along with the results of his other partial investigations to answer some of the remaining questions about the nature and significance of Maximilian's chancery language.

The Additional Syngraphic Analyses

Moser's comparison of the features of the text sample from the end of Maximilian's reign (Corpus II) with those presented in the basic syngraphic analysis shows the intensification of certain trends that were present in the earlier manuscripts. Over the two and a half decades that elapse between the samples, the unidirectional neutralization <u>ei</u> ← <u>ai</u> becomes a full opposition. The distinction between

the graphemes <u> and <ue> also becomes clearer. In the later texts
the digraphic spellings are used for the reflexes of the MHG diphthongs /uo/ and /üe/ in the great majority of instances, and this
tendency occurs even in a handful of words that normally resist the
digraphic spellings. The marked variant of each of the graphemes
occurs most frequently (ú, úe). Moser notes, however, that the marker
has no distinctive function in these cases. The most frequent variant
of the umlaut grapheme <é>, continues to be e, but in the later sample
á becomes the second most frequent variant spelling of the umlaut.
The alternation niht/nit disappears and nit becomes the regular chancery negation. The opposition <o> ← <ó> is intensified. The number
of possible graphemic neutralizations and variants in the guttural
range increases. The digraphs kh and ch occur as initial variants of
<k>, and ckh occurs more frequently as a medial variant of this
grapheme.[351]

    Moser interprets these changes, with the exception of the
increase in guttural forms and the ascendancy of the southern negation
particle, to be natural developments of the system itself: the opposition between <ei> and <ai> prevents the collapse of the two phonemes;
the increase of the á-variant of <é> strengthens the existing pattern
of marked vowels used to represent umlauted sounds (<ó>, e.g) at the
same time that it reduces the pressure on the overused letter e. He
concludes that taken together they represent a closing and consolida-
tion of the writing system.[352]

    The characteristics of the chancery language from the period
before 1490 differ in several respects from those developed in the
syngraphic analysis. In the Vorphase the unidirectional neutralizations <i> ← <ei>, <u> ← <au>, <u> ← <ew> still occur. Until 1489 the
unidirectional neutralization <u> ← <ú> represents a distinction
between the unumlauted monophthong (u) and the umlaut or diphthong
(ú), although there are unmarked spellings of the umlaut-diphthong
environments and marked spellings of the unumlauted /u/ from the
outset in this earliest period (cf. <e> and <é> in the syngraphic
analysis). In the Vorphase ai-spellings are rare. The following

neutralizations, which still occur in the earliest sample, are severely reduced or disappear in the basic syngraphic analysis: <u>i</u> ← <u>ie</u>, <u>d</u> ∿ <u>t</u>, <u>a</u> ∿ <u>o</u>. Moser feels that the features of this earlier stage of the chancery language confirm his conclusion that the developments in the scribal usage between 1490 and 1518 are the natural outgrowth of the system itself.[353]

In his examination of Corpus III, Moser considers the manuscript production of individual chancery personalities in various sorts of documents intended for both internal and external circulation. He assesses the written language of each of fifteen leading chancery personalities by comparing the features of their individual holographic production with the general description developed in the syngraphic analysis. In this way he determines how each used the flexibility inherent in the writing system. Not surprisingly he finds that no scribe makes use of the full range of orthographic options available to him in the system and that the written language of any particular scribe thus appears to be more regular than the chancery norm itself. The chancery German used in internal correspondence does not differ perceptibly from that used in the external correspondence on which the syngraphic description is based. Moser notes that the geographic origin of the writer generally has no effect on the variety of German he writes. There is a noticeable difference, however, in the scribal features of different kinds of chancery texts. Moser finds that orthographic patterns evident in highly stylized formal engrossed texts and in chancery drafts resemble each other and adhere fairly closely to the chancery norm. Letters, on the other hand, show fewer consonant doublings and more modern spellings.[354]

One of the secretaries whose scribal production Moser examines in this partial investigation does not write according to the chancery norm. Johann Storch is one of the group of scribes whom Moser associates with Mainz and the Imperial Chancery at the earliest stages of Maximilian's reign. He was a member of the <u>Reichskanzlei</u> in 1486 and around 1494 seems to have joined the <u>Hofkanzlei</u>. In 1505 his written German looked quite different from the chancery norm and

showed several of the neutralizations associated with the Vorphase.
By 1513, however, Storch's orthography had begun to look much more
like the norm. Moser describes Storch as a secretary who had not
mastered the chancery usage and suggests that over time he was unable
to resist the dominant conventions of the chancery. In comparing the
first two samples to the Vorphase documents, Moser also suggests that
the relative consistency of the chancery scribal practice for the
main period of Maximilian's reign indicates an established usage
("ein fester Kanzleibrauch") toward which individual scribes oriented
themselves.[355]

The case of Storch is puzzling. It is unlikely that a professional penman who was active in the Habsburg chanceries for nearly
thirty years would only have learned to adjust his orthography to the
chancery norm in the last decade of his service if there had been any
compulsion for him to do so. As we have seen in chapter 2, young
penmen in this period learned to write various styles and scripts and
were taught to be sensitive to questions of orthography. If Storch
wrote as he had always written for his first twenty years in the
chancery, there was probably no need for him to change his writing
pattern. The changes in his orthography after 1505 should probably
be seen as the gradual adoption of forms Storch saw produced regularly
in the chancery around him, and not as a late attempt by the secretary
to master the orthography of his younger colleagues. By comparison
with the chancery norm, the orthography of Storch reflects a somewhat
older scribal tradition. The differences between his usage and the
norm may be explained as a difference of scribal generations in the
chancery.

In a final syngraphic investigation Moser examines the graphemic features of Berthold's Reichskanzlei production between 1494 and
1502. He discovers, as one might expect on the basis of the inter-
dependency and overlapping personnel of the Imperial and Court Chanceries, that the scribal usage is a variant of the Hofkanzlei norm.
In the Reichskanzlei production, ai- and ue-spellings occur infrequently and cannot be considered independent graphemes in this sample.

This may be explained in part by the fact that the period covered by the Reichskanzlei sample is only about a third as long as that represented by Corpora I and II. In his investigation of Corpus V, Moser compares expedited texts to the corresponding entries in the Reichskanzlei register. He notes that the registrar, like the copyists who engrossed chancery drafts, permitted himself considerable orthographic leeway.[356]

Summary

The syngraphic analyses indicate that the basic graphemic system shown in figures 2 and 3 above dominated the production of Maximilian's chancery after 1490. The same orthography was used for internal chancery communication and for external correspondence intended for northern and southern recipients. The scribal usage of individual scribes is found to be more regular than the chancery norm because the description Moser developed is a composite of many personal writing patterns. An individual's written German is considered to be in accordance with the chancery usage if his orthography features oppositions, neutralizations, and variants within the range covered by the general description. Moser has observed that normally the geographic origin of an individual scribe does not affect his writing conventions.

It may be, however, that on a larger scale the regional training if not the geographic derivation of chancery personnel may have influenced the tone of the graphemic system. In speaking of exceptions to the chancery usage, Moser relates the writing patterns of Johann Storch and of the Reichskanzlei scribes represented in Corpus V to their "mainzische Herkunft."[357] The reference here is not to their actual geographic origins, however, but rather to the first chancery tradition with which they can be associated, that of the Reichskanzlei. Their exceptional scribal practices are probably evidence of scribal training from an earlier period and perhaps also from a different geographic region. They are not indications of a different scribal standard maintained in the Imperial Chancery. The fact that

the new members of the Hofkanzlei staff, who were added from the late
eighties onward, were predominantly UG and were at least in part
trained in Upper Germany (see "Chancery Case Studies" below) may have
affected the way the graphemic system of the chancery language continued to develop during Maximilian's reign.   The older scribes or
scribes from the MG border areas who had learned to write an orthography that did not feature the Bavarian ai- and ue-spellings probably
continued to function without retooling orthographically.   When new
blood was introduced into the chancery system by Maximilian, however,
it was brought in primarily from his own UG region and employed in
his own Hofkanzlei.   This concentration of more recently trained Upper
Germans in the central chancery may account in part for the perceptible change in the orthographic features of the written language
between 1486 and 1493.

CHANCERY CASE STUDIES

The fact that contemporaries considered Maximilian's chancery
language to be superior on the basis of its orthography answers many
of the questions about the written dialect that have persisted in the
histories of the language.   And Moser's definition of the flexible
chancery norm makes it possible to some extent to identify documents
written in accordance with the Habsburg usage.   The questions remaining to be answered about the writing system have to do with linguistic
self-consciousness in the chancery itself and with the reputation and
influence of the chancery language outside the Habsburg administrative
network and beyond the EUG region.   Although we cannot be certain
about the attitude of Maximilian's scribes toward the German they
wrote, Moser has suggested that they adhered consciously to the
loosely defined chancery usage and adjusted their writing habits to
conform to it.   The following case studies may help clarify this
issue by providing information about the chancery as a scribal school,
the activities and orthography of Niclas Ziegler, the chancery language as a "literary instrument," and the significance of chancery
endorsements.

The surviving holographs and other endorsed chancery documents
of Marx Treytzsaurwein, Hans Ried, and Niclas Ziegler bring into
sharper focus some of the trends Moser identified in his examination
of the manuscripts of individual chancery personalities (Corpus III)
and clarify chancery attitudes toward the written language. Each of
these chancery writers can be associated closely with Maximilian himself, and each served for some time either in the Court Chancery or
in the Tirolean Chancery as a diplomatic secretary or copyist during
Maximilian's reign. Together they represent at least two and possibly
three different scribal schools, and two of the three scribes were
deeply involved with Maximilian's literary projects as well as with
affairs of state. A brief look at the background and scribal practices of each figure reveals the nature and extent of his compliance
with the chancery norm as Moser defines it.

The manuscript production of each is evaluated in terms of
Moser's characterization of the Habsburg chancery language outlined
above. In order to speculate about the scribal tradition and educational background these men represent, I include a cursory summary of
the biographical information available about each. The characterization of the individual scribal usages is based on the complete range
of their holographic materials that were available to me. Portions
of these documents are included in the manuscript sample (appendix 2);
they are referred to by number in the text.

Marx Treytzsaurwein

Maximilian's private secretary, Marx Treytzsaurwein, is best
remembered for his editorial efforts on some of the Emperor's literary
projects. The most important of these were the semiautobiographical
works Theuerdank and Weißkunig. Treytzsaurwein served for more than
a decade as both a scribe and an administrator, however, before he
became involved with Maximilian's literary undertakings, and his
diplomatic production from this earlier period shows him to have been
a member of the itinerant chancery that accompanied Maximilian on his
journeys. Treytzsaurwein is of particular interest because he is the

only one of the scribes whom Maximilian claims to have raised from
their youth in the chancery (see "The Training of Chancery Personnel,"
chapter 2) whose name is known to us. This makes his personal scribal
usage and its relationship to the chancery norm as described by Moser
particularly significant. If Maximilian's chancery was in any active
sense a scribal school, then Treytzsaurwein's written German is an
unadulterated example of the orthographic standard it prescribed. If
it was no more than a scriptorium in which a somewhat distinctive EUG
Gemeindeutsch evolved as the by-product of routine chancery concerns
and activities, Treytzsaurwein's personal scribal usage is an exceptional example of that Habsburg language.

Marx Treytzsaurwein belonged to the renowned Treytz family of
smiths and armorers and was born in Mühlau near Innsbruck sometime
after 1450. Little is known about his youth, but there is no reason
to assume that Maximilian's statements about his early service in
the chancery are incorrect. The first surviving documentary reference to Treytzsaurwein is from an instruction of Maximilian's dated
5 September 1501, in which the Emperor praises the faithful and useful services of his chancery scribe and awards him a portion of the
landholdings that have become vacant through the death of Balthasar
Kessler's widow. This suggests that in 1501 the scribe, who might
already have been in the chancery for as many as twenty-five or thirty
years, was well known to Maximilian and that his chancery services
were valued highly. Between 1501 and 1510 Treytzsaurwein received
substantial gifts from the Emperor, including partial interest in a
vineyard and a mine, operating expenses for the foundry he owned, and
not least of all Schloß Schneeberg.[358]

The chanceries with which Treytzsaurwein was associated during
these years were Maximilian's Hofkanzlei and the Tirolean Chancery at
Innsbruck. Documentary evidence shows that Treytzsaurwein was often
on assignment between 1504 and 1510 conducting the Emperor's private
business from Brabant to Bavaria,[359] and that Maximilian had come to
depend on his presence at Court. In one instance in 1505, for
example, when Treytzsaurwein had been unable to travel with the Court,

Maximilian wrote an urgent letter saying that he was unable to manage
without him, and that he was to hire someone at the expense of the
Raitkammer to oversee his affairs so he could come to Strassburg and
remain at Court for some time. This is not an isolated incident.[360]

Between 1510 and 1511 Treytzsaurwein was severely ill, and both
his health and fortune were undermined. In July 1511 he appealed
pitiably to Maximilian for assistance. The Emperor advanced him two
hundred gulden and within a year the private secretary had recovered
and was in Vienna hard at work on Maximilian's literary projects. The
illness and the move to Vienna marked the beginning of a new phase of
Treytzsaurwein's career. From this point there is no further documentary evidence to connect him with Innsbruck,[361] and in the years that
followed Treytzsaurwein appears to have worked on at least eleven of
Maximilian's literary manuscripts.[362] The first of these, the
Triumphwagen, was completed in 1513; and the unfinished Weißkunig
manuscript, on which he resumed work in 1526, must have been among
the last of his literary efforts. After his move to Vienna Treytzsaurwein also assumed a more prominent position in the administrative
hierarchy of the Habsburg chancery system; he became Chancellor of
the regional chancery for Lower Austria and held this post until his
death in 1527.[363]

The following aspects of Treytzsaurwein's biography make him
significant for our investigation. A Tirolean, he was a native of
the SB dialectal region who apparently received his first and only
scribal training in Maximilian's chancery. The absence of documentary
evidence of his service before 1501 suggests that he actually worked
his way up through the ranks of the chancery and is probably one of the
few identifiable personalities from Maximilian's staff who would have
begun his service at the lowest rather than the middle level of the
administrative ladder (see "The Imperial Chancery Ordinance [Reichs-
kanzleiordnung] of 1494," chapter 2). Only after some years of
service does he seem to have achieved the status of secretary, which
required him to endorse chancery documents.[364] He was an approximate
contemporary of Maximilian's and seems always to have been attached

to the Emperor's own entourage until he moved to Vienna in 1512. Thus
in Treytzsaurwein's case we need not assume that he had first learned
another older or different scribal usage or had first served in
another chancery. Treytzsaurwein was the chief scribe of Maximilian's
original literary works, some of which he adapted from drafts prepared
by others and some of which he took down as dictation and reworked.
If the literary language that is supposed to have been forged in Maximilian's chancery was anything more than an orthographic system,
Treytzsaurwein's literary manuscripts should reflect this. The language of his diplomatic holographs may be considered a pristine example
of the chancery usage, and the language of his literary production
the best example of that usage as it was adapted in the chancery for
literary purposes.

To date I have discovered five diplomatic holographs by Treytzsaurwein.[365] Of these only [7] and perhaps [11] have been attributed
to him previously. One of the manuscripts is an expedited chancery
draft ([8]); two are engrossed fair copies, one a mandate ([6]), and
one a letter ([9]), each of which bears the Proprialvermerk and can
be assumed to have been commissioned by the Emperor if not actually
dictated by him;[366] and two are personal letters from Treytzsaurwein,
one to Maximilian ([7]), and one to Serntein ([11]).

In many respects the scribal usage reflected in Treytzsaurwein's diplomatic holographs conforms to Moser's first (1493) characterization of Maximilian's chancery language,[367] and it shows some of
the trends that become evident in the chancery documents from the end
of the Emperor's reign (Corpus II). Treytzsaurwein regularly writes
the dominant variant e for the secondary umlaut of /a/ (<é>) and only
once uses the variant á, which gained ground in chancery writings
toward the end of Maximilian's reign. In the few occurrences of the
MHG diphthong environments /uo/ and /üe/ in these texts, Treytzsaurwein always writes the digraphic variant. In these documents the
opposition <ei> - <ai> is complete. Even these short texts, however,
feature several additional graphemic neutralizations and variants that
Moser did not find to be typical of the chancery norm. These include:

(1) <a> ∿ <o>   in O̲m̲b̲r̲a̲s̲ ("Ambras") ([6])

(2) <e> ∿ <ó> ∿ <o>   in M̊o̲s̲s̲i̲n̲g̲, M̲ö̲s̲s̲i̲n̲g̲, M̲o̲s̲s̲i̲n̲g̲h̲a̲n̲d̲l̲s̲ ([6])

(3) <o> ∿ <á>   in B̲r̲ä̲b̲s̲t̲ ("Probst") ([6])

(4) <ew> ∿ <au>   in h̲a̲u̲p̲t̲l̲a̲ü̲t̲e̲n̲ ("Hauptleuten") ([8])

(5) <h̲>: x̲ in h̲ + s̲   in S̲e̲x̲t̲e̲ ("sechste") ([9]),
                        w̲a̲x̲t̲ ("wächst") ([11])

(6) <ph>: p̲f̲f̲, p̲p̲f̲   in k̲u̲p̲f̲f̲e̲r̲ ([6]), k̲u̲p̲p̲f̲e̲r̲ ([7])

(7) <w̲> ∿ <b̲>   in a̲l̲b̲e̲g̲ ([11])

The orthography Treytzsaurwein uses in his own correspondence to Maximilian and to Serntein matches that which he writes in the texts commissioned in the Chancery. In the most characteristic features (the treatment of MHG /ī/, /ei/, /uo/, and /üe/, this orthography conforms to the chancery norm. Treytzsaurwein's personal usage, however, does show many spellings that Moser does not list as regular variants in the chancery writing system.

Manuscripts written by others and endorsed by Treytzsaurwein show scribal features similar to his own but, as one would expect, not matching his own orthography in every respect.[368] The few diplomatic documents of this sort that I have been able to locate actually conform more closely to Moser's characterization of the chancery norm than Treytzsaurwein's own holographs do. This fact, along with Moser's discovery that the orthography of chancery drafts and that of their corresponding register entries do not match, supports the assumption that chancery endorsements were only controls for content.

Treytzsaurwein's literary manuscripts provide a different sort of information about Maximilian's chancery language. The manuscript sample includes matching excerpts from two successive T̲h̲e̲u̲e̲r̲d̲a̲n̲k̲ drafts that Treytzsaurwein wrote between 1513 and 1514. The first of these ([12]) is taken from that portion of a T̲h̲e̲u̲e̲r̲d̲a̲n̲k̲ fair copy which Treytzsaurwein penned himself; the second ([13]) is from a rough somewhat expanded draft that is entirely in Treytzsaurwein's hand and is based on the earlier manuscript. Treytzsaurwein's role in the

Theuerdank project was that of editor rather than author. He corrected, recast, and amplified material written or dictated by someone
else. The Theuerdank manuscripts [12] and [13] are a second reworking
of material written by Maximilian's Silberkämerer, Siegmund von
Dietrichstein, in or before 1512. Dietrichstein's poem, Unfallo,
appears to have been expanded by the author or by a second person
before Treytzsaurwein began his work on it. Treytzsaurwein's primary
task in this project was to organize the existing material in accordance with the overall plan Maximilian was developing for his complete
autobiography.[369] His revisions are distinguished by a pronounced
lack of poetic flair, and the poem as we read it today is essentially
the 1517 edition of the humanist Melchior Pfintzing and not this
revision by the chancery secretary.

Only the efforts of the chancery-trained diplomatic secretary,
however, are of interest to us here. If a supradialectal literary
language was forged in Maximilian's chancery as Waterman and others
have suggested, Treytzsaurwein's Theuerdank manuscripts should display
it in pristine form. The literary material they present was new at
the time when Treytzsaurwein wrote. The model from which he worked
cannot have been more than a year or so old, and its author, Dietrichstein, and patron, Maximilian, were also natives of the EUG region.
For these reasons we may assume that Treytzsaurwein's model was for
the most part free of the linguistic archaisms of an older scribal
tradition and of non-Bavarian dialectal influences (cf. "Hans Ried"
below). The language of the Theuerdank manuscripts, then, is EUG from
the early sixteenth century, and it reflects Maximilian's own narra-
tive concerns as well as the orthographic and literary habits of two
of his subjects, Dietrichstein and Treytzsaurwein. The fact that
Pfintzing apparently had to go back to the original Unfallo text to
complete his work on the Theuerdank suggests that the drafts under
consideration are primarily the work of Marx Treytzsaurwein and did
not resemble Dietrichstein's original too closely. In examining them
we will be concerned not only with the graphemic characteristics of
the texts and the way these compare to Treytzsaurwein's scribal usage

in the diplomatic texts, but also to a lesser extent with questions
of diction that might be seen as evidence of a literary consciousness
in the chancery.

In the Theuerdank manuscripts Treytzsaurwein's basic conformity
to the chancery usage, as defined by Moser, is confirmed. Here as in
the diplomatic texts his orthography reflects many of the developmental trends that continued between 1493 and 1518. In [12] and [13] e
is again the dominant variant of <é>. Marked variants in a representing the secondary umlaut do occur somewhat more frequently in these
texts than in the diplomatic manuscripts, but they still account for
only about a quarter of the attestations of the umlaut environments.
As in the diplomatic manuscripts, Treytzsaurwein regularly uses the
digraphic spelling ue to represent the MHG diphthongs /uo/ and /üe/,
although a few monographic spellings occur as minority forms. Treytzsaurwein consistently writes the variant s initially before m, p, t,
and w and the variant sch initially before l and n to represent the
grapheme <sch>. In [12] the opposition <ei> - <ai> is complete; in
[13] the opposition is almost complete.

The Theuerdank texts examined show only a few graphemic variants that are irregular according to Moser's definition of the chancery norm:

(1) <ei> ∿ <iy>   in driyen ([12])
(2) <f>: bf   in glaubhabftig ([13])
(3) <ng>: nckh, ngkh, nngk, nngkh   in lanckh ([12]); langkh ([13]);
                                     aufgangkh ([12] and [13]);
                                     lanngk ([13]); lanngkh ([12])

Treytzsaurwein's literary manuscripts, both the fair copy and
the rough second draft, feature a scribal usage that is very close to
the chancery norm. The only difference occurring with any frequency
is the number of variants Treytzsaurwein writes postvocalically for
the velar nasal grapheme <ng>. Moser does not show any of the combinations in c, k, h, given in (3) above to be regular variants of <ng>
in this position, although he draws attention elsewhere to the great
proliferation of guttural variants in the chancery language toward

the end of Maximilian's reign.[370] In terms of Moser's graphemic
system and his argument for ng as an independent grapheme, however,
the spellings -nckh, -ngkh, and -nngkh in the preceding examples must
be seen as variants of the nasal and not of the guttural.

From an orthographic point of view it is interesting that the
Theuerdank, a brand-new SB romance, was cast from the outset by its
EUG creators in the identifiably southeastern but not markedly dialectal written language of the Habsburg chancery. This is probably the
result of the orthographic training of the three Upper Germans associated with these drafts. From a stylistic point of view the drafts
are unremarkable at best and seem to have escaped being written in
cancelleysch only by the fact that they are composed in verse.
Clemens Biener characterized the text in this way: "Die zusätze die
P ([13] in appendix 2) aufweist, zeigen die charakteristischen
eigentümlichkeiten des alten kanzleibeamten und geheimsekretärs, der
einmal einen abstecher ins gebiet der poesie macht und dabei doch
kanzleischreiber bleibt."[371]

Treytzsaurwein's revisions consisted mainly of minor adjustments in grammar and phraseology. They rarely represent a stylistic
improvement. In fact they usually destroy the regular four-beat
rhythm of the rhymed couplets. The following examples are typical
and reflect Treytzsaurwein's editorial concerns. The lines from [13]
in each case show his additions to the text.

[12]		[13]	
2^r	An Reichtümb vnnd parem gelt	1^r	An Reichtumb schain vnd parem gelt
3^r	versehen würden nach pilli-chait	3^r	versehen vnd versorgt wurden nach pillichait
4^r	Der Künig samelt Ainen Rat	3^v	Der Künig samelt gar pald ainen Rat
4^v	Ee Sÿ ainen Ratschlag mach-ten		Ee sy ainen entlichen Ratslag machten
	der Ieder were an Adel groß	4^r	der Ieder were An Adl vnd tugent groß

Most of Treytzsaurwein's additions to the text are padding of this
sort. He either lengthens the line by making a compound element, or
he adds modifiers to existing sentence elements. Only occasionally
does he recast a line or make a significant grammatical change:

7^r Er was des alten weysen Kůnigs 5^v Sein Vater was kunig Andach-
     Sůn bekant   tige genannt
     Vnd aůch mechtig von steten   Vnnd großmechtig von steten
     vnd großen landt   vnnd landt

18^r oder Er seinen leib verlor 12^r Oder derselb seinen leib
                                              mueset verlieren
     darůmb solich huet von Inen   Vnd darumb ain soliche huet
     ward aufgelegt   von Inen aufgelegt

    Treytzsaurwein's product does not show any particular belle-
tristic sensitivity or reflect a chancery preoccupation with literary
style. He is not even able to preserve the simple <u>Vierheber</u> of the
MHG romances to which the meter of the <u>Theuerdank</u> is intended to
allude. This and the other features of his clumsy style suggest that
if the term "literary language" is a legitimate designation for Maximilian's chancery dialect, it may not be applied to the stylistic
aspects of the literary works produced by the chancery members.

Hans Ried

    Hans Ried, Maximilian's customs collector on the Adige, is
known to Germanists primarily as the copyist of the remarkable
<u>Ambraser Heldenbuch</u>. Over the last century philologists have debated
about his fidelity to his sources, his industry as a penman, and his
social station, agreeing only on the excellence of his calligraphy.
Our present interest in Ried, however, stems from the fact that he,
like Treytzsaurwein, served for decades as a scribe in the chanceries
of Tirol before being selected by Maximilian to copy the poems that
are preserved in the <u>Rysenpuech</u>. As in the case of Treytzsaurwein, a
few of Ried's nonliterary manuscripts survive. A comparison of the
scribal usage of Ried's literary and nonliterary texts offers additional information about one scribe's perception of the Habsburg
chancery orthographic norm. It may help to determine in what sense
Maximilian's written dialect was developed into a literary tool by his

administrators and suggest answers to long-standing questions about
how Ried treated the materials he copied.

Although Ried is not attested in documentary evidence before
1496, recent studies by Martin Wierschin and Helmut Weinacht provide
a relatively certain outline of the copyist's life that enables us to
interpret various aspects of his written language.[372]   Ried was from
a South Tirolean noble family that had its ancestral seat at Burg
Ried on the Talbera.   The Rieds had served as liegemen to the lords
of Wangen since the first half of the thirteenth century.[373]   Hans
Ried was probably born around 1465,[374] and we may assume on the basis
of a letter written by his widow in 1516 after his death, in which she
reminds Maximilian how her husband had served him for more than
thirty years,[375] that Ried must have begun his chancery work some
time before 1485.   Wierschin infers from the statement that Hans Ried
first served in the chancery of Maximilian's uncle, Sigmund of Tirol,
where the young scribe and the young prince may both have been taught
to write by Wernher Ried.[376]   In any event, Hans Ried does not appear
to have begun to write for Maximilian until after the abdication of
the Archduke in 1490.

The earliest surviving documentary references to Ried are from
1496 and 1498 and have to do with a payment to the scribe of two
measures ("Schäffl") of salt.[377]   What services Ried had performed to
earn this sum we do not know.   In 1500 Ried was appointed tariff
collector on the Adige near Bolzano, and his holograph to Maximilian
underwriting this commission ([3]) is the first of two surviving diplomatic letters that can be attributed to him with certainty.[378]   This
document, like the later letter, bears the Ried seal, a fact confirm-
ing the assumption that Hans belonged to this family of minis-
teriale.[379]   At the end of 1501 Florian Waldauf von Waldenstein[380]
was given permission to have Ried come from Bolzano to write two
copies of the long deed of foundation for "die heÿlig Capellen vnser
lieben frauen" that Waldauf and his wife were endowing at Hall near
Innsbruck.   Weinacht notes that Waldauf's letter is the first surviving reference to Ried's calligraphic talent.[381]   Waldauf, who was

made a protonotary by Maximilian in 1488, had begun his own career in
the chancery of Sigmund of Tirol.[382] His familiarity with Ried's pen-
manship supports the idea that the copyist probably first served as a
scribe in Sigmund's chancery; it is likely that Waldauf knew him from
that period, since Ried was not working in Maximilian's Innsbruck chancery at the time of Waldauf's request. Ried went to Innsbruck to copy
the Stiftbrief but apparently returned to Bolzano afterward.[383]

At the time Maximilian first mentioned the Heldenbuch project
in 1502, Ried was not the copyist of his choice. Only two years
later did Ried become involved with the project; and, as Weinacht
notes, he could not have given the work his undivided attention before
1507-08, when he ceased to supervise the customs collection on the
Adige.[384] Exactly how and where Ried spent the years between 1508 and
1511 has not yet been established. In February 1511 Paul von Liechtenstain wrote to the Council of the Raitkammer in Innsbruck about Ried,
who was then instructing Liechtenstain's son in "Schreiberey" in that
city. Liechtenstain wanted to know if the Council was about to give
Ried another assignment and was informed that the Kammer intended to
have him pen various "old Imperial patents and other letters, particularly those pertaining to Austria" ("alte kayserliche freyheitn
vnnd annd brieve. Sonnderlich was gen Österreich gehört") that Maximilian wanted recopied. Nevertheless, Ried apparently returned to
Bolzano sometime after February 1511 and spent the rest of the year
there working on the Heldenbuch. He was instructed by the Raitkammer
to be in Innsbruck by New Year's Day 1512, however, to begin copying
the Urkunden.[385]

Although no trace of these copies or of other chancery documents either in Ried's hand or bearing his endorsement has been discovered for the period after 1511, Ried probably served in the Innsbruck chancery from 1512 to 1514. In March of 1514 he was given
back his post as tariff collector on the Adige in recognition of the
services he had rendered Maximilian in his chanceries ("so er vnns
in vnnser Canntzleyen gethan"), and because his eyesight was failing.
He seems to have continued to discharge these duties and copy the

<u>Heldenbuch</u> texts in Bolzano until his death sometime before June of 1516.[386]

Hans Ried and his scribal production are significant in several respects for the present investigation. An approximate contemporary of Maximilian's and a native of the SB dialectal region, Ried, unlike Treytzsaurwein, seems to have received his initial scribal training or experience in the chancery of Sigmund of Tirol rather than that of Frederick III or Maximilian. This different initial exposure may or may not have colored his own scribal usage. As a chancery scribe, Ried never seems to have risen beyond the lowest levels of the middle tier of the three-part chancery hierarchy despite his calligraphic prowess. Although Waldauf, Liechtenstain, and Maximilian himself sought Ried out for particular writing jobs, he apparently never served in the chancery as anything more than a copyist, for to date no documents originating in the chancery have been discovered with any sort of visa by Hans Ried.[387]   This means that while he served in the chancery he did not share the final proofreading responsibilities of the secretaries.

Ried's holographs are of interest because they show how a scribe trained in the regional chancery tradition used <u>cancelleysch</u> in writing his own letters ([3]), in copying another contemporary legal document composed by a fellow Tirolean ([4]), and in copying literary texts that may have represented various dialectal regions and different stages of the development of the German language ([14]-[16]). These last texts from the <u>Ambraser Heldenbuch</u> are particularly impor- tant. To date it has only been possible to speculate intelligently about the sources of the codex. Examining Ried's copies in terms of his own regular graphemic practices may suggest something about the orthographic patterns of his models.

Only four Ried holographs are currently known: the underwrit- ing letters of 1500 and 1514 in which Ried accepts the position of tariff collector on the Adige; the <u>Waldauf'scher Stiftbrief</u>; and the monumental <u>Ambraser Heldenbuch</u>. All of these are fair copies. The following characterization of Ried's own orthography is based on his

first brief underwriting letter ([3]). Observations about the orthography he uses in the Stiftbrief are based on several extracts from
that lengthy text ([4]).[388] Observations about the orthography of
the Heldenbuch are based on selections from three of the works contained in the codex; [14] is from a poem composed during the MHG
Blütezeit; [15] and [16] are from poems composed later in the thirteenth century.[389]

The orthographic pattern of Hans Ried's first letter to Maximilian ([3]) conforms in almost every respect to Moser's characterization of the Habsburg chancery norm. In the majority of instances
Ried writes e for the secondary umlaut of /a/ although he also uses
the variant á in this environment (e.g., Iärlich). He uses both
digraphic and monographic spellings for the MHG diphthongs /uo/ and
/üe/, but the monographic spellings in this brief text occur only in
forms of tůn (MHG tuon) and zu (MHG zuo).[390] Ried writes only the
variant s of the grapheme <sch> initially before l, p, t, and w; the
grapheme does not occur initially before m or n in this text. The
opposition <ei> - <ai> in the text is complete except for a single
occurrence of the form main (<MHG mîn); the word is spelled mein-
elsewhere in the letter. The only irregular neutralization indicated
is <b> ∿ <w> in albeg; Treytzsaurwein also writes this form occasionally, and Moser has also noted that this neutralization sometimes
occurs in Habsburg chancery texts.[391]

In the much longer Waldauf'scher Stiftbrief ([4]), which is
presumably Ried's fair copy of a draft provided to him by Florian
Waldauf, the orthographic pattern looks somewhat different, and the
differences are probably not only to be attributed to the greater
length of the deed of foundation. As in his own letter Ried usually
writes the variant e for the secondary umlaut of /a/. In the Stiftbrief, however, he writes the variant é almost as frequently, and he
uses the variants á and a in one or two isolated instances. In the
Stiftbrief Ried writes both monographic and digraphic spellings for
the MHG diphthongs /uo/ and /üe/; the digraphic spellings occur only
slightly more frequently than the monographic ones. The opposition

<ei> - <ai> is complete except in the words geist- and heil-, in
which the spellings ei and ai vary freely. The ei-spellings of these
words occur more frequently than the forms in ai. Ried regularly
writes the variant s of the grapheme <sch> initially before l, m, n,
p, t, and w; abschneyde (but aufgesnitne) is the only exception to
this pattern that occurs in the portion of the text examined.

    Although the broad features of Ried's orthography in the Stift-
brief are certainly within the chancery norm, he does write several
variants and neutralizations that Moser does not consider to be typical of the chancery graphemic system. These include:

(1) <e>: é   in stet ("steht," 3rd sg. pres. ind. of stên)

(2) <i> ∿ <ie>   in hawßwiert, Hiert, Liechter; verdinstlich,
                           dinst, dinstberkait

(3) <ó> ∿ <e>   in anherig, Gewenndlich

(4) <o> ∿ <é> ∿ <e> in Kirchbrêbst, kirchprêbst, kirchprebst

(5) <ei> ∿ <i>   in Driualtigkait

(6) <k>: kh   in sterkh, merkhlich, dannkhperkait, volkh [392]

The differences between the Stiftbrief orthography and that of Ried's
underwriting letter suggest that he has picked up some of the spellings from his SB model in [4] but has not found them to be sufficiently irregular to change them. Aside from the atypical variants
and neutralizations listed, the Stiftbrief shows particularly strongly
the Bavarian confusion of /b/ and /p/; many loan words in /p/ are
spelled with b in this text.

    Ried's literary texts from the Ambraser Heldenbuch raise
several interesting questions. Because the sources of this remarkable
codex have never been satisfactorily identified, it is tempting to try
to work backward through the manuscript texts themselves to arrive at
assumptions about the number, age, and dialects of their sources. The
documentary evidence relating to the Heldenbuch project has not suggested how many models Ried used, how old they were, or where they
originated.[393] We do not know whether he worked from MHG manuscripts,
for example, or from earliest NHG texts already featuring an orthography very similar to his own.

Thornton's 1962 investigation of Ried's scribal usage showed
clearly that the entire Heldenbuch was written in the "Tiroler
Schriftdialekt der Lutherzeit," but it failed to offer any information
about the relationship of the scribe and his orthography to his
sources. In his 1969 edition of the Kudrun, Franz Bäuml drew attention to the fact that Ried used two distinct forms of minuscule r in
copying this Heldenbuch text. Bäuml described the first as a letter
written basically in the Textura form but with a split vertical shaft
and interpreted it as a preform of the later Kurrentschrift r. He
called the second round or cursive form the "Arabic-2 type" of r
("Typ arabisch-2"), presumably because of its visual similarity to
the numerical symbol.[394] At more than a dozen places in the poem,
Bäuml showed that Ried had mistakenly written s or z for r or r for
s or z. In each case he posited that Ried had confused an "Arabic-2"
r with one of the other minuscule forms.[395] There are enough of
these examples to support Bäuml's assumption that the manuscript
source from which Ried copied did feature the Arabic-2 minuscule r.
This single paleographic feature, however, does not bring us any
closer even to the immediate source of the Kudrun. The so-called
Arabic-2 minuscule r is a feature common to various scripts written
in Germany from the High Middle Ages forward. It occurs in the
Gothic book hands of Latin manuscripts from the twelfth and thirteenth
centuries, in the Cistercian script used in Latin manuscripts during
the thirteenth century, and in the Textura scripts of both Latin and
German vernacular manuscripts in the fourteenth century.[396]

Thus we have no concrete sense of the age of Ried's sources.
We do not know, for example, whether it was Ried who in adapting MHG
to an EUG Gemeindeutsch produced such false ENHG-MHG rhymes as
reichen: gewaltigklichen ([14]), or whether he simply copied the
work of an earlier adaptor. An exhaustive orthographic comparison of
the Heldenbuch texts to each other and to Ried's diplomatic holographs
may eventually help to answer these questions.

In [14], an excerpt from the Heldenbuch text of Hartmann's
"Büchlein," Ried's orthography essentially matches both the chancery

norm and the graphemic pattern of his own underwriting letter ([3]).
The only slight difference in usage is that he writes sch more frequently than s initially before l, m, n, p, t, and w in this text.
There are no irregular neutralizations or variants in the selection
examined. In [15], an excerpt from the Heldenbuch text of Herrant
von Wildon's "Diu getrew Kone," Ried's orthography is in all respects
within the chancery norm and very similar to the graphemic pattern of
his own letter. In this text Ried writes both e and á with almost
equal frequency to indicate the secondary umlaut of /a/, and he also
uses é to indicate this environment; once he writes the é for an [e]
that is not the result of umlauting. He uses the monographic u more
frequently than ue to indicate the MHG diphthongs in this text, but
both forms occur quite often. Since he writes the variant s before
initial w but sch before initial m, there is no clear pattern of
<sch>-spellings in the text. The opposition <ei> - <ai> is complete
here as it is in [14]. In the passage from Helmbrecht ([16]), Ried's
orthography is only slightly different from that of the preceding
Heldenbuch texts. Here Ried uses á in the great majority of instances
to mark the secondary umlaut of /a/; é is the second most frequent
variant, and e is written only once to indicate this environment. The
opposition <ei> - <ai> is complete. Monographic and digraphic spellings are written with equal frequency for the MHG diphthongs /uo/ and
/üe/. Ried writes s initially before p, t, and w and sch before l.
The only irregular neutralization that occurs in the text is <au> ∿ <u>
in schut ("schaute," 3rd sg. pret. ind.).

    In general terms the orthography of Ried's own letter ([3])
and that of his texts from the Ambraser Heldenbuch ([14]-[16]) match
so closely that they can be called the same, and the orthography of
the Waldauf'scher Stiftbrief ([4]) is very similar. The graphemic
pattern of each text falls generally within the chancery norm defined
by Moser. The few irregularities occurring in the Stiftbrief text
suggest that Ried was influenced here by his written model.

    If Ried's usage was affected even slightly by the Stiftbrief
draft, it is curious that the literary sources of the Heldenbuch did

not color the orthography he wrote in the poems. There are two possible explanations for this. The first is the unlikely eventuality that all the poems Ried copied were already written in a fairly uniform Gemeindeutsch similar to his own. The second is that Ried took his various models, which presumably included some MHG texts, and wrote them with the same ENHG orthography he used in his own letter.

The relative orthographic uniformity of the Heldenbuch[397] suggests that Ried himself must have been the orthographic adaptor of at least some of the poems it contains. The fact that the scribal usage in the Heldenbuch is closer to Ried's own than is the pattern of the Stiftbrief indicates that the orthography of the literary models was probably farther from Ried's written German than was the language of Waldauf's draft. The literary source texts probably varied so widely that Ried felt obliged to recast them in a uniform sort of written German. Ried not only copied the Heldenbuch texts, but he also seems to have homogenized them orthographically. In penning the fair copies of the Stiftbrief, on the other hand, Ried limited his work to copying the text; the language of the contemporary draft that Waldauf, his Tirolean countryman and fellow Kanzlist, supplied him was probably so similar to his own cancelleysch that Ried felt no need to change it.

The minor variations in orthography from text to text within the Heldenbuch that are revealed by comparing [14]-[16] are insignificant. In order for these to be explained as reflections of the orthographic patterns of the sources, one would have to assume that Ried was in each case writing from a model already so like his own written German that he copied it essentially without orthographic alteration, as he did the Stiftbrief. This is most unlikely. The orthographic variation among individual poems in the Heldenbuch should be seen as gradual developments in Ried's own scribal usage over the several years in which he copied the texts for the codex.

Niclas Ziegler

Niclas Ziegler's orthography is of particular interest because
of the acclaim it received from Johann Eck and has continued to enjoy
in the histories of the German language. It is also significant for
our study because it represents the scribal usage of a senior member
of the chancery staff whose duties were for the most part administrative and political. The surviving evidence indicates that although
Ziegler did actually pen texts in exceptional circumstances (when the
issue treated was particularly sensitive or when the chancery or he
himself was on the road, for example), his regular duties in the chancery were supervisory. Unlike Treytzsaurwein and Ried, he seems to
have become a secretary, and thus a proofreader and controller of the
documents penned by lesser scribes, almost as soon as he entered
Maximilian's service.

Christa Kohlweg's recent investigation of the Ziegler brothers
in the service of Maximilian now provides considerable biographical
information about the chancery secretary. Niclas Ziegler, the son of
a Swabian draper who came to Nördlingen in 1471, was probably born
between 1472 and 1475. By 1493 he was already in Maximilian's chancery. Unfortunately, nothing is known about Ziegler's youth, and to
date it has been impossible to establish whether or not he attended
a university.[398]   For this reason one can only speculate about where
he may have received his scribal training. A comparison of Ziegler's
career in the chancery to those of Treytzsaurwein and Ried, however,
suggests that Ziegler was probably not one of the scribes who acquired
their training in Maximilian's entourage. He probably came to the
chancery already knowing how to write exceptionally well, because by
1493, when he was perhaps not quite twenty, he was already being used
by Maximilian as a diplomat and was receiving significant considerations from the Emperor for services rendered. This is certainly a
different pattern from that of Treytzsaurwein, who served Maximilian
all his life but did not begin to receive Imperial gifts or to gain
the rights of a chancery secretary until he was middle-aged. Thus,

we can deduce that Ziegler probably learned his <u>cancelleysch</u> outside
of Maximilian's chancery but that the variety of German he wrote was
considered to be perfectly acceptable in the <u>Hofkanzlei</u>.

The earliest documentary evidence of Ziegler's activities in
the Habsburg chancery is from 1493. In a letter to the Mayor and
Town Council of Nördlingen, Maximilian asks that a public office be
bestowed on Ziegler's brother-in-law in recognition of the services
his chancery secretary, Niclas Ziegler, is performing in the <u>Hof</u>-
<u>kanzlei</u>. At the end of that year Ziegler was sent to Groningen to
negotiate a settlement for the Emperor between that city and the
Ostergo. Over the next four years Ziegler's status in the Chancery
continued to increase; he received various fiefs and other tokens of
the Emperor's appreciation, and in the <u>Hofordnung</u> of 1498 he was named
Secretary to the <u>Hofrat</u> (see chapter 2). Between 1498 and 1500,
Ziegler's position at Court became stronger and he spent much time in
the immediate proximity of the Emperor, traveling with him and report-
ing back to the main chancery at Innsbruck. In the summer of 1500
Ziegler assumed the functions of the Senior Secretary (<u>Oberster</u>
<u>Sekretär</u>) and became second only to Serntein in the chancery hier-
archy. Contrary to the statements by Kluge and subsequent historians
of the German language, Niclas Ziegler never rose above this office
during Maximilian's lifetime. Nevertheless, the influence Ziegler
wielded from his post as Secretary for the next two decades is a
matter of record.[399]

As a result of his efforts to help Maximilian's grandson
Charles secure the Imperial throne, a campaign that began at the 1518
Diet of Augsburg and continued into the next year, Ziegler became Vice
Chancellor of the Empire.[400] Although he was active in this office
for only about a year, that year coincided with the memorable 1521
Diet of Worms and was undoubtedly the high point of Ziegler's career.
It is also the only point at which it is possible to make any connec-
tion between Ziegler and Eck that might account for the reference in
the Ingolstadt Bible. Although Ziegler did not resign his office

until the year before his death in 1526, he left Court and gave up his active chancery service in 1522.[401]

As I have stated in detail elsewhere, Eck and Ziegler appear never to have met or to have corresponded with each other, and it is probable that Eck, who was about ten years younger than Ziegler, never saw a holographic document by Maximilian's secretary. The most likely basis for Eck's assessment of Ziegler's orthography is the text of the 1521 Edict of Worms and the Publikationsmandat with which it was circulated throughout German-speaking Europe. Due to a series of coincidences, Niclas Ziegler himself translated the Edict from Latin into German in a single night in the spring of 1521. Printed versions of this text were distributed throughout the Empire along with the brief mandate of publication, which bore Ziegler's handwritten signature. Eck, who did not attend the Diet but was active as a papal nuncio and inquisitor in the cause against Luther in Germany, was in correspondence with Girolamo Aleander, the papal representative to the Diet, and would have been aware of Ziegler's role both in the drafting of the earlier Dezembermandat and in the translation of the Edict itself.[402]

It is unclear what Eck found to be so distinctive about Ziegler's orthography that he cited it publicly ten years after the Vice Chancellor's death. It is also curious that he praises Ziegler's orthography, which he could only have known from printed documents, in the same Vorrede in which he disparages the printers who have not preserved his own orthography. Eck's praise of Ziegler is probably to be explained politically. The Ingolstadt Bible is dedicated to Matthäus Lang, who had been an eminent member of Maximilian's chancery and who had in 1517 been commissioned along with Eck and Konrad Peutinger by the Emperor to confer about a plan for a popular discussion of theological doctrine;[403] by 1536 Lang had become the Archbishop of Salzburg. Eck probably sought to curry favor with this powerful prince of the Church, and his remarks about Ziegler's orthography should be seen in this light.[404]

Whether or not Ziegler's orthography deserves the particular attention it has received, it is of interest for the present investigation for several reasons: it represents the scribal usage of a chancery member from the highest tier of the staff hierarchy, it features the orthography of a secretary originally from the Swabian rather than the SB dialectal region, and it is probably a second example of the cancelleysch written by a scribe who was not trained in the Habsburg chancery itself. Ziegler's case also brings us back to a question raised in chapter 1 by Fabian Frangk's Orthographia: how and in what form did Maximilian's chancery language acquire its contemporary reputation? It seems that Eck's assessment of Ziegler's German is based on printed samples of his writing. If this is correct, then Ziegler's German should be characterized according to the printed texts of the Publikationsmandat and the official edition of the 1521 Edit of Worms.[405] Before considering this possibility further, however, let us examine the scribal usage of Ziegler's holographic production and see how it compares with that of Treytzsaurwein and Ried.

To date, with the assistance of the Wiesflecker regesta and Hans Moser's study, I have discovered a total of ten Ziegler holographs.[406] The four of these that are included in the manuscript sample are the basis of the present characterization of Ziegler's scribal usage; of these, [1], [2], and [5] are drafts, and [10] is a fair copy. Because these are all rather brief diplomatic texts and feature what is essentially the same orthographic pattern, they are considered together.

Ziegler's orthography, different from Ried's and Treytzsaurwein's, shows the unidirectional opposition <ei> ← <ai> rather than the full opposition of these graphemes. Ziegler regularly writes e for the secondary umlaut of /a/, once writes a marked e in this environment, and never uses the a-variants of this grapheme. He writes the monographic u for the MHG diphthongs /uo/ and /üe/ with only one exception in these texts, and s for <sch> initially before w and n. Ziegler's orthography shows only two minor neutralizations

that are irregular according to Moser's characterization of the Habsburg chancery norm:

(1) <u>a</u> ∿ <u>o</u>   in <u>Morggraf</u> ([2])
(2) <u>ei</u> ∿ <u>i</u>   in <u>bẙ</u>, <u>fryburg</u>, <u>fritag</u> ([2]);
                 <u>Braůnswig</u> ([10])

 Ziegler's orthography, like that of Ried and Treytzsaurwein,
falls easily within the limits of Moser's general definition of the
chancery norm. It is a little different, however, from the patterns
of the two SB scribes. In continuing to write <u>ei</u> occasionally for
the MHG diphthong /<u>ei</u>/, <u>i</u> for MHG /<u>ī</u>/ (though for the most part only
in proper nouns), <u>e</u> for the secondary umlaut of /<u>a</u>/, and <u>u</u> for the
MHG diphthongs /<u>uo</u>/ and /<u>üe</u>/, Ziegler produces what seems a conservative version of the Habsburg chancery orthography, although he was at
least ten years younger than Ried and perhaps as much as twenty-five
years younger than Treytzsaurwein. His holographs do not show any of
the developmental trends that Moser observed in his comparison of
documents from the end of Maximilian's reign with those from around
1490. The pattern of Ziegler's orthography matches that of the documents in Moser's first syngraphic analysis, and it does not appear to
undergo any significant change during his years of service in the
chancery.

 Like Treytzsaurwein, Ziegler endorsed a number of chancery
documents that he did not copy himself. An examination of six of
these shows that they all conform unusually closely to the chancery
norm but do not match Ziegler's own scribal usage in every respect.[407]
The variants <u>e</u> for the secondary umlaut of /<u>a</u>/ and <u>u</u> for the MHG
<u>u</u>-diphthongs are predominant in all these texts, but about half of
them show the complete opposition <ei> - <ai>. This reaffirms the
assumption that chancery controls were primarily for content and not
for rigid orthographic conformity.

 In comparing the scribal usage of Ziegler's holographs to the
orthography of the first edition of the Edict of Worms and its
<u>Publikationsmandat</u>, one aspect of the typography of the printed texts

must be taken into account. In both imprints three distinct vocalic
markers are used with considerable regularity: a diaeresis symbol is
used to mark the umlauted forms of MHG /u/ and /uo/ (e.g., Künigen,
fürstenthūb, Bücher) and also to mark the diphthong eü (e.g.,
Deütschen, Durchleütigē); e is printed as a superscript to indicate
the umlauting of MHG /a/, /o/, and /uo/ (e.g., Bȧbst, Gȯtlich, Bu̇cher);
and in accordance with contemporary sixteenth-century German typographic conventions o is used to mark u where u represents the ENHG
reflex of MHG /uo/ (e.g., ersůcht, Auffrůr, gůtten).[408] This pattern
of vocalic marking in the printed texts presents the umlauting of MHG
/u/ and /uo/ fairly clearly, and it also distinguishes between the
unumlauted ENHG reflexes of these two phonemes.[409] The distinctive
typographic marking of the monographic u gives it a relatively
unambiguous meaning in the printed texts that it does not have in the
handwritten chancery texts featuring the u-hook. This orthographic
clarity may have appealed to Eck, although there is nothing particularly distinctive about it.

　　　Aside from the different implication of the vocalic markers in
the printed and handwritten texts, the orthographic pattern of the
Publikationsmandat looks very much like that of Ziegler's holographs.
It features the unidirectional opposition <ei> ← <ai> and the exclusive use of the variants e and u for <é> and <ue> respectively, and
it shows no irregular variants or neutralizations. Although the
orthography of the longer Edict also conforms to the scribal norm of
Maximilian's chancery in most respects, it is much less regular than
that of the Mandate or of Ziegler's holographs. Like that of
Ziegler's holographs, the orthography of the Edict features e and u
as the dominant variants of <é> and <ue>; but it also shows forms in
which the secondary umlaut of /a/ is spelled a, å, or ȧ, and forms in
which the MHG diphthong is spelled ue or ůe. The variants s and sch
of <sch> occur with almost equal frequency initially before l, m, n,
and w. The opposition of <ei> and <ai> is incomplete in the Edict,
and the printed text shows a more arbitrary distribution of ai- and

<u>ei</u>-spellings of MHG /<u>ei</u>/ than do Ziegler's holographs. Ziegler tends
to write <u>ai</u> for MHG /<u>ei</u>/ and <u>ei</u> for MHG /<u>ī</u>/.[410]

The text of the Edict also shows the following irregular
neutralizations and variants (these are isolated occurrences and are
limited to related forms of the specific words in which they occur):

(1) <ei> ∿ <i>   in <u>abzuschnyden</u>

(2) <ue>: <u>ie</u>   in <u>betriegen</u>

(3) <b>: <u>bp</u>   in <u>Babpst</u>

(4) <ch>: <u>g</u>   in <u>negst</u> ("nächst")

(5) <d> ∿ <t>   in <u>außdilgung</u>, <u>verdiglt</u>, etc.; <u>vndertruckung</u>,
                      <u>Buchtrucker</u>, <u>vnderdruckung</u>, <u>Druck</u>; <u>notturft</u>

(6) <f>: <u>ff</u>   morpheme-initially in <u>geffallen</u>

(7) <f>: <u>vh</u>   in <u>vheyndtschrifften</u>, <u>vheinde</u>

Both the holographic and printed versions of Ziegler's orthography conform in most respects to Moser's definition of the Habsburg
chancery norm. Ziegler's own scribal usage more closely resembles
the graphemic pattern of chancery documents from the early years of
Maximilian's reign than it does that of documents from the closing
years. Ziegler's own orthography may be interpreted as either
slightly more archaic or as slightly less Bavarian (or both) than the
orthographies of Treytzsaurwein and Ried. The orthography of the
Edict does not match Ziegler's, but neither does it fall outside the
loosely defined chancery norm. It resembles Ziegler's usage in
several respects, including the incomplete opposition of <ei> and
<ai>, but the occurrence of the variants <u>ue</u> and <u>á</u> (<u>a</u>) for <ue> and
<é> respectively make the orthography appear somewhat more modern and
more Bavarian than Ziegler's own.

Summary

The scribal habits of Treytzsaurwein, Ried, and Ziegler offer
answers to some of the questions raised by the histories of the German
language about the way Maximilian's staff viewed the administrative
German it wrote; they raise new questions about the basis of the
sixteenth-century reputation of the chancery language; and they show

clearly the extent to which Moser's characterization of the written
language generalizes its orthographic features. The manuscript production of these scribes not only indicates that the Habsburg chancery
staff acknowledged an orthographic norm, but it also suggests how much
leeway was permitted within this convention.

The fact that Treytzsaurwein and Ziegler both endorsed chancery
documents with orthographies that do not match their own indicates that
the scribes themselves found a limited amount of variation in the
written language acceptable and that they did not insist on a rigid
standardized orthography in the sense of modern German Rechtschreibung.
This practice of chancery endorsement reflects the same attitude
toward document control that Moser observed in the case of register
entries. The entries may differ orthographically from the drafts and
fair copies on which they are based, but, once again, the supervisory
scribe approves the content of the document without objecting to the
orthography, even though it may not be altogether like his own.

The manuscript production of Hans Ried shows further that Maximilian's scribes sometimes recast their models in their own orthographies and sometimes worked in the manner of modern diplomatic copyists, reproducing the text of the original more or less letter by
letter. Ried's manuscripts suggest that he did both and that the
choice of copying technique depended on the language of the model.
In the case of the Waldauf'scher Stiftbrief, Ried, working from a
written text, wrote an orthography slightly different from his own
and from that of the Habsburg chancery as characterized by Moser.
This suggests that he copied the text as he found it and saw no need
to adjust the orthography. On the other hand, the orthography of the
Ambraser Heldenbuch is essentially Ried's own. Here he apparently
found the orthographic patterns of his literary models to be so far
from the acceptable standard that he changed them all to the version
of the norm that he wrote. The slightly different orthographies of
Ried's various holographs indicate that there were limits to the
orthographic flexibility that Maximilian's scribes accepted:
Waldauf's draft fell within them; the literary texts did not. In the

absence of the _Heldenbuch_ source texts, however, we can only assume
that these models featured orthographies Ried perceived to be either
too archaic (MHG) or too different dialectally.

We may assume, on the basis of Ried's holographs and of the
nearly four hundred chancery documents Moser examined to produce his
characterization of the written language, that there was an acknowledged orthographic norm in Maximilian's chancery. But it is difficult
to say how chancery personnel perceived and observed this standard, or
how orthographic variations within the chancery or within the manuscript production of a single scribe should be interpreted in terms
of this norm. As we have seen above, even the orthographies of
Treytzsaurwein, Ried, and Ziegler do not match the chancery norm in
every respect unless one invokes Moser's rule that allows individual
scribes to write irregular forms within the chancery norm, a provision
that to a certain extent vitiates his general definition.[411]

Treytzsaurwein's orthography should be considered the quint-
essential example of the Habsburg chancery usage because he was trained
in the chancery and was from the outset responsible to Maximilian himself. That the younger Ziegler came into the chancery writing a
slightly different orthography and did not alter it during his period
of service indicates that the variety of _cancelleysch_ Treytzsaurwein
learned in the chancery was not the only acceptable one (as Ried's
copy of the _Stiftbrief_ also confirms) and that scribes trained elsewhere were not required to retrain in order to serve in the chancery.
This means that if Maximilian's chancery was in any sense a scribal
school, its orthographic prescriptions were quite loose and its orthography similar to that produced in other contemporary EUG chanceries.
Treytzsaurwein's and Ried's orthographies are, after all, essentially
the same.

Moser has suggested that the geographic origin of individual
scribes is irrelevant in accounting for their scribal usage.[412] This
assumption may not be altogether correct. The chancery production as a
whole has a rather predictable orthography that should be called
regional rather than specifically dialectal. Slight differences

between the personal orthographies of individual scribes within the
norm, however, may perhaps be explained in terms of the scribes' geographic origins. If one compares the orthographies of Treytzsaurwein
and Ziegler, for example, one might describe Treytzsaurwein's orthography as more modern because it more closely resembles the chancery
usage from the end of Maximilian's reign, and Ziegler's as more conservative because it approximates the chancery usage from the beginning
of the reign. On the other hand, Treytzsaurwein may distinguish more
completely between <u>ei</u> and <u>ai</u> than Ziegler and prefer the digraphic
spellings of MHG /<u>uo</u>/ and /<u>üe</u>/ to the <u>u</u> that Ziegler writes because
the phonological distinctions these spellings imply are more pronounced
in his native SB than they are in the Swabian of Ziegler's native
region (see "Hans Moser's Heterographic Analyses" below).

These case studies also clarify the extent to which the southeastern <u>Gemeindeutsch</u> was developed into a literary language in the
Habsburg chancery. Maximilian's scribes were involved both with his
literary copying projects and with the composition of the various
parts of his autobiography. There is no indication, however, that
they were concerned with the development of a belletristic medium in
the sense that the <u>Sprachgesellschaften</u> were a little more than a
century later. Although it is fairly certain that Hans Ried transcribed the models for the <u>Ambraser Heldenbuch</u> in his own chancery
orthography, the uneven literary tone of the texts preserved in the
codex suggests that he did little or no editorial revision of the
poems. Treytzsaurwein's work on the <u>Theuerdank</u> and <u>Weißkunig</u> projects
was qualitatively different. He was involved with the composition of
new works of literature and worked from contemporary written drafts
and outlines dictated by Maximilian himself. The excerpts of the
<u>Theuerdank</u> drafts included above, however, show that Treytzsaurwein's
creative skills were limited and that his editorial concerns had to
do primarily with the content of his texts. They do not attest to any
general stylistic interests, nor do they indicate an attempt to
develop the language of the chancery into a medium for belles lettres.

In order to posit that German was transformed into a "literary instrument" in Maximilian's chancery, one must define that term as "written language" or "writing system," as the Soviet and French scholars who work on such subjects often do.[413] To the extent that Maximilian's chancery language featured an efficient and somewhat distinctive orthographic system, it might be considered an important developmental stage in the evolution of the modern German written language. Maximilian's chancery did not, however, contribute significantly to the development of German as a belletristic medium. This explanation makes further investigation of the chancery language as a national language, an "Einheitssprache," or a standard language unnecessary.

The case of Niclas Ziegler and Johann Eck raises new questions about how Maximilian's chancery language came to enjoy its sixteenth-century reputation and about the form in which its proponents knew it. There is no doubt that the written dialect was considered to be worthy of emulation in its own time. For various reasons (see "The Chancery Languages of Maximilian I and Frederick the Wise" below) it was probably more popular even than the few surviving references to it suggest. To date scholars concerned with the Habsburg chancery language have emphasized the manuscript production of the chancery system, assuming correctly that any agency as prolific and politically significant as Maximilian's chancery, which produced close to a hundred thousand documents during his reign,[414] must have had an impact on other contemporary administrative writing. Eck's reference to Ziegler and Frangk's references to the imprints of Johann Schönsperger as well as to the writings of Maximilian's chancery indicate, however, that the chancery language was also admired in its printed form. Maximilian used the printing press not only to produce his autobiographical Theuerdank and other literary projects, but also to publish various political proclamations as well as the proceedings of the Imperial Diets.[415] These publications must also have contributed to the contemporary reputation of the chancery language.

As Eck's disparaging remarks in the <u>Vorrede</u> to his Bible indicate, sixteenth-century German printers often changed the orthography
of the original when they set a text in type. Although we no longer
have the manuscript drafts of the 1521 Edict of Worms and its
<u>Publikationsmandat</u>, we may assume with fair certainty that both were
written in German originally by Ziegler.[416]   Thus the orthography
should match that of Ziegler's holographs if it has not been altered
by the printers. The Mandate features an orthography that is essentially Ziegler's; the orthography of the Edict is similar to Ziegler's
but not the same. This means that the typesetters made changes, and
that some of the contemporary statements about the chancery language
are based at least in part (Eck's statement, for example) on altered
printed versions of the writing system—versions featuring orthographic variants and neutralizations beyond those identified by Moser,
and characterized by a system of vocalic marking less ambiguous than
those used in contemporary chancery scripts.

HANS MOSER'S HETEROGRAPHIC ANALYSES

To understand what Luther meant when he claimed that the chanceries of Frederick the Wise and Maximilian I wrote the same kind of
German, we must consider in general terms how closely the orthographies of the Wettin and Habsburg chanceries resembled each other at
the beginning of the sixteenth century and how typical each was of the
contemporary German written in its own region. The extralinguistic
material examined in chapter 1 indicates that Maximilian's chancery
language enjoyed a certain prestige among literati from various parts
of Germany in the early sixteenth century. Comparison of the Habsburg
chancery norm with various contemporary German orthographic systems
may suggest whether the supraregional reputation of Maximilian's chancery language reflects an actual influence that it may have exerted
on the German written outside the EUG area.

In his heterographic analyses, Hans Moser undertook such a
survey by adapting data from existing investigations of related German
written languages to his graphemic method and comparing them with his

characterization of the Habsburg chancery norm. Although the degree
to which Moser was able to adapt this material was in some cases
limited by the investigative orientations of the other studies, his
results are sufficiently detailed to provide an excellent basis for
evaluating some of the assertions put forward by the histories of the
German language about the significance of the Habsburg chancery dialect. Moser compared his findings with the orthographic patterns of
two MG chancery languages, that of the Dresden chancery as represented
by the city scribe, Michael Weiße, who wrote during the mid-sixteenth
century,[417] and that of the Saxon Electoral chancery between 1486 and
1546.[418] He also compared the Habsburg chancery norm with the orthographies of two versions of the same non-chancery text, the Regula
bullata;[419] the first of these is a Bavarian translation from around
1486, the product of a single scribe; the second is an EMG translation
dated 1496.[420]

The Upper German Written Languages

Moser's graphemic comparison of the vocalic and consonantal
systems of Maximilian's chancery language with those of the Bavarian
Regula shows them to be the same in almost every respect. The only
significant difference between the vocalic patterns is the absence of
the umlaut graphemes (<é>, <á>, <ó>) in the Bavarian text. Moser
explains this as a scribal idiosyncrasy and reminds the reader that
the option not to mark umlaut environments also existed within the
Habsburg chancery norm.[421] The absence of umlaut graphemes from the
Regula text means that the secondary umlaut of /a/ normally appears as
e here; e is also the most frequent variant of <é> in the Habsburg
chancery texts from the beginning of Maximilian's reign. The e-
spelling of the umlaut was also typical of Frederick III's chancery
language, and of the MG and Nuremberg scribal traditions as well.[422]
Moser indicates that ee did not have graphemic status in the Regula
text, but this is an insignificant difference as the form is only
weakly attested in Habsburg chancery texts, and its graphemic status
there is debatable. The consonantal systems of the two EUG written

languages are almost identical. Moser proposes that the only significant difference between the two is the intervocalic opposition
<u>h</u> - <u>ch</u> that is beginning to emerge in the Habsburg language but
is not evident in the <u>Regula</u> text.[423]

In some respects Moser's comparison of these two graphemic
systems is problematic because he does not consider the neutralizations and variants in the case of the Bavarian <u>Regula</u> to the extent
that he does in his syngraphic analysis of Maximilian's chancery
language and in his comparison of the Habsburg language with the EMG
usage (see "The Middle German Written Languages" below). This
limited treatment gives the impression that the German of the <u>Regula</u>
is farther removed from certain Bavarian dialects than is actually the
case. Like Treytzsaurwein's written German, the text does feature the
neutralizations <u>a</u> ∿ <u>o</u> and <u>b</u> ∿ <u>w</u> that Moser considers to be
dialectal and atypical of the chancery usage. The neutralizations
are minority forms in the texts in which they occur, but they should
be taken into account as one reads that both the languages of Maximilian's chancery and of the <u>Regula</u> are "mundartfern."[424]

In an additional brief comparison of the Habsburg chancery norm
with a Swabian version of the <u>Regula bullata,</u> Moser notes that the
vocalism of this text matches that of the Bavarian translation, except
that the former shows the unidirectional rather than the complete
opposition of <u>ei</u> and <u>ai</u>.[425] The Swabian vocalism, then, matches
that of the chancery language from the beginning of Maximilian's
reign, and it approximates that of Niclas Ziegler.

The Middle German Written Languages

Whereas the orthographies of the Bavarian and Swabian <u>Regula
bullata</u> manuscripts are close to the Habsburg chancery norm, the EMG
version of this non-chancery text manifests an orthographic system
substantially different from the systems of the EMG chancery languages
(both that of Michael Weiße and of the Saxon Electoral chancery). The
difference is most striking in the vocalism of the EMG orthographies.
The chancery writing systems show the NHG diphthongs <u>ei</u>, <u>ew</u>, and

<aw> as the dominant reflexes of MHG /ī/, /iu/, /öu/, /ū/, and /ou/.[426] The EMG Regula bullata, which was written within the period covered by Gerhard Kettmann's sample texts from the Saxon Electoral chancery, shows the older MHG forms <i>, <u>, <ū̂>, and <ou>. Both of the EMG chancery languages show the unidirectional opposition <ei> ← <ai>, whereas the non-chancery text shows no ai-variants of MHG /ei/ whatsoever.[427] This particular distinction, however, should be understood in terms of the chronological development of the vocalic systems of these EMG languages. The vocalism of the Regula is the most archaic of the three; since it does not yet show the NHG diphthong /ei/ < MHG /ī/, there is no confusion between the MHG and NHG ei-diphthongs. Both of the other orthographies show all three NHG diphthongs. As the new ei-forms increase in frequency in the written language, so do the ai-spellings of the MHG diphthong. This can be seen most clearly in the Electoral orthography. The steady increase of the new ei-spellings of MHG /ī/ in EMG chancery texts after 1500 is followed by a marked upswing in the number of ai-spellings of MHG /ei/ after 1520.[428]

Another distinctive feature of these EMG chancery languages is their tendency to distinguish vocalic length. In the Electoral language and in Weiße's orthography h is used and e may be used as a sign of lengthening after vowels: the graphic sequences ie and ee indicate long vowels in both systems; and in the Electoral language e written after a and o may signal lengthening as well.[429] Umlauting, on the other hand, is only weakly indicated in these three EMG orthographies. In each the secondary umlaut of /a/ is spelled e. The umlauting of /o/ is weakly indicated in the Regula text by the marked letter ö̂ but is not indicated in either of the chancery orthographies.[430] In Weiße's orthography the unidirectional neutralization <u> ← <ue> represents an opposition between the reflexes of MHG monophthongal and diphthongal forms that may or may not also feature umlauting[431] (this is the same sort of opposition that Moser found in the Habsburg chancery norm);[432] but in the EMG Regula bullata and in the Electoral chancery language the patterns of u-marking (u vs. ü, ů̂, etc.) and

u-spellings (u vs. ue) are more ambiguous and cannot be considered to
show the regular tendency to indicate umlauting.[433]

The consonantal systems of the three EMG orthographies that
Moser compared are quite similar to each other. In most respects they
also resemble the UG orthographies just examined. All three of the
EMG writing systems feature a complete opposition between <b> and <p>,
although the sample texts for each show a number of forms in which p
is written initially for <b>. In the Dresden chancery language and
the EMG Regula these p-spellings can for the most part be explained
as loan words.[434] The opposition <b> - <p> in these orthographies is
the single consonantal feature that distinguishes them most clearly
from contemporary UG writing systems. Michael Weiße's chancery German
features three geminate graphemes that do not have graphemic status
in either of the other EMG or in the UG orthographies examined: <bb>,
spelled pp in the texts; <dd>; and <mm>.[435] Weiße writes these double
forms regularly to indicate a preceding short vowel. This practice
is a logical extension of the tendency to indicate vocalic length that
is evident in the EMG vowel systems examined. Only Maximilian's chancery language and the Wettin orthography feature the grapheme <ff> as
a reflex of Gmc. /p/; in the Habsburg language it also appears to
signal a preceding short vowel, but in the Electoral chancery language,
curiously enough, it does not.[436]

Beyond these differences in the total number of graphemes that
the individual EMG and UG consonantal systems contain, there are minor
but distinctive differences in the ways that the writing systems regularly represent particular graphemes. In the Dresden and Electoral
chancery languages, as in the orthography of the Bavarian Regula, the
labial affricate is <pf>; in the Habsburg chancery language and the
EMG Regula, it is <ph>. The dental affricate is <z> in the Habsburg
and Electoral chancery languages, <zc> in Michael Weiße's orthography,
and <cz> in the Bavarian and EMG Regula texts.[437]

Neutralizations and Variants

A comparison of certain neutralizations and variants that are restricted to specific words or positions provides additional bases for comparing the individual EMG and UG written languages.

Maximilian's chancery language features a number of regular neutralizations between <u> and <o>, the most significant one occurring before nasals (see "Graphemic Neutralization" above). Moser notes that the indigenous UG spellings show u in this environment; whereas o-spellings occur relatively early in Swabia, the only scriptorium to write these forms in the Bavarian region during the second half of the fifteenth century was the Imperial chancery. Noordijk also observed that these MG forms in o occurred with greater frequency in Frederick III's chancery than in the Bohemian chancery of Emperor Sigmund. Maximilian's chancery continues this MG practice. The Habsburg orthography in this feature matches that of the Wettin chancery, which regularly writes o before nasals.[438]

In the early years of Frederick III's reign, the Habsburg chancery scribes often neutralized the opposition <d> - <t> after l, a practice seen also in the contemporary written languages of Vienna and of the Austrian ducal chanceries. Maximilian's chancery language did not preserve this feature of the inherited writing system, but instead wrote the typically UG -lt-. The EMG writing systems considered above, however, all feature the neutralization, but to different degrees: in the orthography of the EMG Regula the typically MG variant -ld- dominates; in Michael Weiße's writing system the UG -lt- dominates; and in the manuscripts from the Wettin chancery -lt- occurs most frequently. The UG -lt-spelling became regular in the Electoral chancery earlier than it did in other MG writing systems that adopted it.[439]

Neutralization of the opposition <d> - <t> after n medially in the EMG and UG written languages shows a somewhat different pattern. Aside from a few exceptional forms such as unter and hinter, Maximilian's chancery scribes regularly maintain the opposition in this

environment and write the NHG -nd- (or the neutralization variant
-ndt-), which was atypical of the Bavarian region at this time. Of
the EMG writing systems examined, only the orthography of the Regula
shows this opposition to be essentially intact; here the typical MG
spellings in -nd- occur almost without exception. Both of the EMG
chancery languages show the neutralization of this opposition in
medial and in absolute final position. Moser interprets these t-
spellings in the MG chancery languages as a southern influence and
as evidence of the elevated stylistic level of the written
languages.[440]

The treatment of certain graphemic variants is also distinctive
in the EMG and UG written languages. Toward the end of Maximilian's
reign the variants gkh, gkch, kh, ckh, and kch of the grapheme <k>
occur more frequently in Habsburg chancery texts, although they
remain minority forms. These h-variants are typically Bavarian and
do not occur regularly in the written languages of other regions.
Moser suggests that where these forms occur, particularly in initial
position, outside the Bavarian region, they might be interpreted as
evidence of the influence of the Imperial Chancery. Except in the
word Churfurst, these h-variants do not come into the Electoral chancery language until after 1520. Moser maintains that the pattern of
variants written in the Habsburg chancery for the grapheme <ph> is
also distinctive. He indicates that whereas pf had become the dominant spelling in the Wettin chancery after 1440 and had been gaining
ground in Swabia and Bavaria since the early fifteenth century, ph-
spellings were regular in the Habsburg chancery language throughout
Maximilian's reign, and pf-variants were in the minority; the variants
ppf and pff typical of pf-regions are not supposed to have occurred in
Maximilian's chancery at all.[441] This is not altogether accurate.
Treytzsaurwein himself, the most Habsburg of the Habsburg scribes,
wrote these variants. Nevertheless, Moser's observation is generally
correct. The ph-spellings that dominate in Maximilian's chancery
language are an anachronism and distinguish the Habsburg writing
system from other contemporary UG and EMG orthographies.

Taken together, the EMG writing systems considered here differ from the UG ones primarily in their regular indication of vocalic length, their failure to indicate umlauting, and their maintenance of the opposition <u>b</u> - <u>p</u>. Of these EMG orthographies, the chancery languages show all three NHG diphthongs, whereas the non-chancery <u>Regula</u> text maintains the MHG vocalism. In this most significant respect, the EMG chancery languages are more modern and more similar to the UG writing systems than the orthography of the EMG <u>Regula</u> is. This feature in itself is a legitimate basis for the conclusion that the language of the Saxon Electoral chancery at the beginning of the sixteenth century was easier to distinguish from other EMG orthographies than Maximilian's chancery language was from other varieties of EUG <u>Gemeindeutsch</u>.

The Chancery Languages of Maximilian I and Frederick the Wise

Having seen how the Habsburg and Wettin chancery languages relate to the scribal traditions of their respective regions, let us consider briefly how the two orthographic systems that Luther cited compare with each other. As Moser has shown, several of the distinctive features shared by these writing systems emerged first in the chancery of Maximilian and then developed ten or fifteen years later in the Electoral chancery,[442] so that the Wettin chancery orthography of 1520 is closer to the Habsburg usage of 1495 than to the general usage of Maximilian's chancery in 1519. This staggered development, however, need not particularly concern us here, where we are interested in comparing the general similarities of the two systems not only from a modern descriptive point of view, but also as Luther and his contemporaries would have seen them.

The sequential development that Moser identified is, of course, defined graphemically. In certain respects, however, the surface patterns of the neutralizations and variants shown by documents written in the two chancery orthographies remain more similar to each other than do the actual graphemic systems of the two languages. In graphemic terms, for example, the Habsburg chancery language lacks a

distinctive grapheme <p>, whereas the Wettin chancery maintains the
opposition <b> – <p> throughout the entire period covered by Moser's
and Kettmann's studies. Both languages, however, show many instances
of p for <b> initially in both loanwords and non-loanwords. A literate sixteenth-century observer would probably have noted this superficial similarity, but he would not have perceived a basic (graphemic)
difference in the patterns of p- and b-spellings in the two chancery
languages. Contemporary assessments of the chancery usages will have
been based on the actual pattern of variants occurring in the texts,
not on the graphemic systems they implied; and the surface appearance
of these orthographies was quite similar between 1495 and 1530. For
these reasons we will generalize the staggered graphemic development
of the two writing systems and compare their surface features at the
points within this time span at which they are most similar.

Vocalism

     In many respects the vocalism of the Wettin and of the Habsburg
chancery orthographies is quite alike. Both systems feature all three
MHG diphthongs. In the Habsburg language all are present at the
beginning of the period under investigation; in the Wettin language
MHG <i> > <ei> shortly before 1500, and as the new diphthong increases
in frequency in the documents, so does the occurrence of <ai> < MHG
<ei>. In Maximilian's chancery language the relationship of <ei> to
<ai> begins as a unidirectional opposition and gradually develops into
a full opposition. In the Saxon language the opposition of the two
graphemes remains unidirectional. From a contemporary point of view,
the pattern of ei- and ai-spellings in the two orthographies would
probably have been seen as a matching feature and the ai-spellings
considered southern, although their clarifying function in the MG
written language makes their occurrence as logical there as it is in
UG orthographies.

     Although we have noted that the Wettin orthography tends not to
mark umlaut environments and the Habsburg usage does, this distinction too is sharper in a graphemic analysis than in a comparison of

the surface features of the writing systems. Although the Habsburg
orthography does develop distinctive graphemes toward the end of
Maximilian's reign to indicate the secondary umlauting of /a/, the
unmarked e is the variant Habsburg scribes write most frequently in
this environment throughout Maximilian's reign; this is also the form
written regularly by the Wettin scribes. The distinctive Habsburg
umlaut graphs that do not occur in the Saxon orthography are the
marked vowels á, é, and ó; these are minority forms. The umlauting
of /ŏ/ is not indicated orthographically in the Wettin writing system;[443] in the Habsburg chancery language it occurs as the unidirectional opposition <o> ← <ó>, the marked vowel representing the
umlauted form.

The MG tendency to indicate vocalic length orthographically
produces some spellings that distinguish the Saxon writing system
clearly from Maximilian's. The digraphs ae and oe do not occur in
the Habsburg chancery language, nor do the combinations of vowel + h
where h functions as a sign of lengthening. These spellings are typical of the Electoral chancery language.[444] Moser notes that in the
Saxon writing system <i> represents the short and <ie> the long monophthongal vowel; in the Austrian chancery language <i> - <ie> continues
the opposition between the MHG monophthong /i/ and the MHG diphthong
/ie/.[445] This is another valid modern linguistic distinction between
the two systems that may not have been so apparent to the contemporary
writers of the orthographies.[446] The problem of vocalic length was
only beginning to be addressed by contemporary grammarians, and even
those who came from regions where the writing systems tended to distinguish between long and short vowels had difficulty explaining the
inconsistent notational conventions that were used to reflect lengthening.[447] Thus the distribution of i and ie in the two orthographies
would probably have seemed much the same to many sixteenth-century
readers, and only the spellings ae, oe, and vowel + h would have
seemed to be distinctive vocalic indicators of the Electoral chancery
language.

In the Habsburg and Electoral writing systems, as in most of
the ENHG orthographies, <u> and <ue> and their diversely marked variants represent a special case. In Maximilian's chancery language the
opposition <u> ← <ue> is essentially a monophthongal-diphthongal distinction, as Moser presents it.[448] He is unable to isolate independent umlaut graphemes for the two phonemes /ü/ and /üe/ because of
the highly contradictory conventions governing u-marking in the
contemporary orthographies.[449] In the Saxon Electoral orthography,
u is the dominant variant for both MHG /uo/ and /ue/ throughout the
period under consideration. After 1530, when the üe-spellings do
begin to appear with some frequency, they are, according to Kettmann,
to be construed as evidence of southern influence and not as an
extension of the MG tendency to indicate vocalic length by the addition of a Dehnungszeichen to a monographic vowel.[450] The tendency
toward monographic u-spellings is typical of the Wettin chancery
language, then, and different from the Habsburg chancery norm. The
ue-variants that do develop in the MG chancery language after 1530
would have been perceived by MG writers as imported forms.

In Maximilian's chancery language the opposition <u> - <o> is
frequently neutralized before nasals in a particular group of words
(e.g., sunst ∿ sonst, kunig ∿ könig, etc.),[451] so that the Austrian
chancery regularly writes the MG forms in o in these cases. This
pattern is a continuation of a practice that developed in the chancery of Frederick III when the chancery staff included a number of MG
scribes; it does not represent the adoption of MG forms into the
Habsburg language during Maximilian's reign. These MG forms are
another feature that the two chancery languages share. The Wettin
chancery regularly writes the MG o before nasals in this group of
words; Maximilian's chancery often does.

Consonantism

As mentioned previously, the most distinctive difference
between the consonantal systems of the Wettin and Habsburg chancery
languages is the absence of the graphemic opposition <b> - <p> in the

southern orthography; this distinction is of far greater interest to
modern linguists than it would have been to contemporary observers.
Superficially the two languages would have appeared to match with
regard to this orthographic feature. Maximilian's chancery language
shows many instances of p for <b> in loanwords and non-loanwords alike,
but the frequency of the p-spellings is lower in the Habsburg language
than in some other contemporary Bavarian writing systems. And despite
the regular opposition <b> - <p> in the Saxon Electoral chancery
language, numerous forms occur in Kettmann's sample corpus where p is
written for <b> and even a few instances where b is written for <p>
(e.g., Briester), as in the Habsburg chancery orthography.[452]

Both chancery languages feature the opposition <f> - <ff>, but
the geminates bb, dd, and mm do not have graphemic status in either
system. In the Wettin orthography bb does not occur, and dd occurs
rarely; mm, which occurs occasionally in the Habsburg orthography,
increases in the Saxon chancery language only after 1530.[453] In these
respects the two chancery orthographies are quite similar, and the
Electoral orthography is atypical of contemporary MG writing systems.

The Habsburg and Wettin chancery languages show several other
minor consonantal differences that are rather insignificant in terms
of a modern graphemic comparison, but they make the orthographies
appear superficially different and permit one to distinguish the two
with relative ease. In the Habsburg language, the labiodental affricate is usually spelled ph, in the Wettin language pf. Although each
of the languages shows isolated occurrences of the other spelling, the
ph-forms are distinctively southern and archaic. In both orthographies, k has graphemic status, and in this feature they match at a
graphemic level. The variants of the k-grapheme, however, look rather
different in the two orthographies. The Austrian orthography shows a
number of variants in h (ckh, kh, ch, etc.) that are identifiably
southern and occur only rarely in the Saxon orthography beginning
around 1520. Similarly, the Wettin orthography shows a distinctive
variant of the z-grapheme. Though both orthographies feature <z>,
the digraph zc is a Wettin variant that does not occur at all in Maximilian's chancery language.[454]

In the Habsburg chancery language the opposition <u>d</u> - <u>t</u> is preserved after <u>l</u>, and the southern spellings in -<u>lt</u>- are normal. In the Saxon orthography the opposition is neutralized, and the UG spelling -<u>lt</u>- dominates. Similarly, Maximilian's chancery language generally preserves the opposition <u>d</u> - <u>t</u> after <u>n</u>. In this environment the Habsburg scribes typically write the MG variant -<u>nd</u> or the neutralization variant -<u>ndt</u>. In the Electoral chancery orthography this opposition is neutralized; both forms occur, and the neutralization variant is also well attested.[455] In these features also, then, the two writing systems look quite similar; in one case the UG chancery prefers an MG variant, and in the other the MG chancery writes typically UG forms.

Summary

The preceding comparison and the earlier summary of Moser's heterographic analysis[456] show that from a graphemic standpoint Luther's suggestion that the chanceries of Maximilian I and Frederick the Wise wrote essentially the same language is accurate. Although Maximilian and the Saxon Elector do not appear to have played any personal role in bringing this about, the chancery orthographies are remarkably similar in documents from the first decades of the sixteenth century. Looking beyond the graphemes to the distribution of variants in the EUG and EMG manuscript samples, the superficial likeness of the writing systems in many ways appears greater still. A cursory examination of early sixteenth-century German linguistic treatises suggests that contemporary literati are more likely to have been struck by the similarity of the systems' graphemic variants than to have been aware of the differences in the graphemic patterns, which Moser has delineated so carefully.

Accounting for the similarities in the orthographic systems of the Wettin and Habsburg chancery languages during this period is another matter. Each system includes some forms that are not typical of the region to which it is indigenous; these forms set the chancery orthographies apart from the other, more purely dialectal, forms of

German written in the same regions. On the whole, the Wettin chancery language shows more atypical forms than the Habsburg chancery language does. Kettmann lists a number of additional minor southernisms (for the most part additional variations and neutralizations) that expand our catalog of the atypical orthographic features of the Saxon chancery language. He notes that UG forms began to be adopted in the Wettin chancery around the mid-fifteenth century and that the practice continued well into the sixteenth century. There was a particular upsurge in the number of southern features in the Wettin language around 1520, right after the death of Maximilian, when Frederick the Wise began his term as Imperial Regent (Reichsverweser) and, because of Luther, became deeply involved in Imperial Diets taking place in southern Germany.[457]

Several explanations offered by linguistic historians for the presence of nonindigenous forms in the regional chancery orthographies have become standard. The chancery languages are by definition written professional languages; they are produced only by educated speakers and are thus both a formal and an artificial variety of the language. They are essentially conservative and resistant to innovation.[458] To some extent the scribal usage of a chancery reflects the geographic and educational backgrounds of its personnel; thus a regionally diversified staff may contribute to a chancery orthography that is a mixture of dialectal forms. In addition the physical location of chanceries in dialectal transition zones, where a more widespread process of language adjustment and leveling occurs, may result in dialectally heterogeneous chancery orthographies; writing systems of this kind may appear to be the product of deliberate standardization or of the avoidance of pronounced dialectal features, even though such acute characteristics are actually not typical of the language of the interface areas.[459] Taken together, these factors account almost completely for the development of the Habsburg chancery language during the reign of Maximilian I as it has been described in this chapter.

During the reign of Maximilian's father Frederick III, the Habsburg chancery staff included a number of MG scribes, some of whom

had served in the Luxemburg chancery. The MG forms that occur in the
Habsburg writing system during Maximilian's reign entered the orthography during his father's time and were retained by the next generation of scribes. The retention of these forms (the continued writing
of s̲ for <sch̲> initially before l̲, m̲, n̲, and w̲; and ph̲ for <ph>
throughout the sample, e.g.) is evidence of the conservative nature
of the scribal usage. The relatively low frequency with which certain
acutely Bavarian dialectal features occur in the language (<a̲> ∿ <o̲>;
<b̲> ∿ <w̲>; <d̲> ∿ <t̲>; p̲ for <b̲>; kch̲, gkch̲ for <k̲>, e.g.) indicates
not only that the chancery orthography, as Moser suggests, reflects
the level of language that is farthest removed from the lowest linguistic stratum,[460] but probably also that the basic stock of this written
language was from one of the dialectal transition areas (Middle
Bavaria or Swabia) and not from a part of the EUG region (Tirol or
South Bavaria, e.g.) that featured the most pronounced dialectal
forms. The fact that the orthographies of Niclas Ziegler and the
Swabian Regula match the Habsburg chancery usage more perfectly than
does the orthography of the South Bavarian Treytzsaurwein supports
this argument. As the percentage of southern scribes in the Habsburg
chancery grew, the orthography of Maximilian's chancery language
became more similar to that of other forms of German written in the
EUG region and less like that of the MG written languages. No new MG
forms were added to the chancery orthography during Maximilian's reign.
There was, however, an overall increase in the number and frequency
of southern forms. The most significant changes in this respect—the
increase in ai̲-spellings, the development of the complete opposition
<ei> - <ai>, and the continuing development of the umlaut grapheme
<é> (<á>)—may be viewed as structural changes that improve the
clarity and efficiency of the orthographic system itself. Other
changes, such as the proliferation of the guttural variants in h̲, in
no way streamline the chancery orthography; these forms instead
reflect the influence of the local Bavarian dialects or of more typically dialectal Bavarian orthographies on Maximilian's chancery
language.

It is more difficult to account for the UG features of the Wettin chancery language in these terms. Although the Saxon chancery, like the Habsburg chancery, functioned in a dialectal interface area, had a dialectally heterogeneous staff, and corresponded with all parts of German-speaking Europe, its orthography does not appear to have followed the almost predictably conservative developmental pattern evident in the Austrian chancery language. The early adoption of the NHG diphthongs in the orthography of the Saxon Electoral chancery can be explained by the chancery's location in a dialectal transition zone and by its regular correspondence with regions that wrote the diphthongs. But the increase in other southern features in the Wettin orthography, features having no parallel developments in the local MG dialects, suggests that some other sociolinguistic dynamic is at work here. Whereas the MG features of Maximilian's chancery language reflect a time when the Hofkanzlei was heavily staffed with MG scribes, the UG features in the orthography of Frederick the Wise appear to have been deliberately affected.

Although it is possible to explain many of the southern features in the Wettin chancery language in terms of the leveling and adjustment that occur naturally in dialectal transition zones, there is evidence to support a different explanation. The continued increase of UG forms in that language during the first half of the sixteenth century, when the Habsburg language was becoming more dialectal, suggests that the UG scribal tradition, although not necessarily the Habsburg chancery norm itself, was viewed as a prestige language in MG at this time. The MG scribes seem to have oriented themselves toward a southern writing standard, whereas the UG scribes wrote essentially in the manner of their own region.[461]

SUMMARY

The sixteenth-century German literati who recommended Maximilian's chancery language were advocating the orthographic system used by the Habsburg scribes. Their statements are based on this writing system as they knew it from printed documents and from actual chancery

manuscripts; and they recommended the language in both its handwritten and printed forms.

Hans Moser's graphemic analysis of the manuscript production of
Maximilian's chancery between 1490 and 1518 provides a detailed definition of the Habsburg scribal usage that can be integrated well into
the broader range of ENHG phonological studies. His characterization
of the Habsburg orthography also provides a basis for comparison with
other ENHG writing systems. In some respects, however, his presentation of the orthography, while extremely useful for modern linguistic
purposes, blurs the image of the chancery language that its contemporaries—those who described it as a superior variety of written
German and who are responsible for its inclusion in modern histories
of the German language—would have had. Nevertheless, Moser's
meticulous graphemic characterization of the Habsburg chancery language and his comparison of the Imperial Chancery usage to other ENHG
writing systems allows one to make tentative assumptions about how
Maximilian's chancery language was viewed by those who wrote it as
well as those who read it. His syngraphic analyses show clearly that
from a modern point of view the orthographic norm of Maximilian's
chancery was quite flexible but still generally identifiable.

The case studies of Treytzsaurwein, Ried, and Ziegler amplify
the image of the chancery norm that Moser developed. These scribes
appear to be the products of three different scribal schools, although
each writes an orthography that in most respects falls within the
chancery norm as defined by Moser. The two older scribes, Treytzsaurwein and Ried, who are Tiroleans, write orthographies that essentially
match the Habsburg chancery norm from the end of Maximilian's reign.
The younger Swabian, Ziegler, writes a typically Swabian orthography
that matches the Habsburg orthography from around 1490. Thus even
though none of the three scribes writes an acutely dialectal orthography, their regional origins may actually be evident in their individual writing patterns. The fact that none of the scribes appears to
have adjusted his personal usage during his period of service in the
chancery indicates that each penman considered his written German

already to be in compliance with the chancery standard as he understood it.

An examination of the manuscripts endorsed by Treytzsaurwein
and Ziegler in their capacity as chancery secretaries shows they
approved diplomatic documents that fall within the range of Moser's
norm but that did not match their personal scribal usages. This
finding supports the contentions that the acknowledged norm was quite
flexible and that chancery visas testified only to the accuracy of a
document's content but did not approve orthography or style. Ried's
manuscript production, however, suggests that there were limits to
the degree of orthographic variation that Maximilian's scribes tolerated. In the Waldauf'scher Stiftbrief, Ried copies a legal document
in a variety of contemporary Bavarian similar to but not exactly like
his own usage or the chancery norm. He apparently finds the orthography completely acceptable, however, because he does not adjust it.
This is not the situation with the Ambraser Heldenbuch texts that
Ried writes in his own orthography. Since one may assume that the
source texts from which Ried copied would not all have been written
in Maximilian's chancery language, the fact that Ried's copies are
all in his own orthography means that he adjusted or translated at
least some of his models, presumably those he felt were too far from
the current scribal usage. Since none of these models has to our
knowledge survived, we cannot speculate about what the contemporary
scribe would have felt to be beyond the flexible limit of the chancery
writing system. We can only assert that there was such a limit and
that the recognition of it resulted in Ried's writing the entire
Ambraser Heldenbuch in his own orthography, a decision that has probably obscured the actual sources of the codex forever.

Ried adapted the Heldenbuch sources into his own orthography
because they did not conform to the Habsburg chancery norm. The
individual orthographies of Treytzsaurwein, Ried, and Ziegler, on the
other hand, each show forms that are according to Moser's characterization atypical of Maximilian's chancery language, although these
orthographies conform to the norm in most respects. This raises some

questions about the definition of the norm. Moser's characterization
of the Habsburg chancery language is a descriptive one based essentially on the anonymous manuscript production of scribes from the
beginning of Maximilian's reign. Features are considered to be characteristic on the basis of their frequent occurrence in the manuscript
sample. Infrequent neutralizations and variants are considered to be
atypical of the usage.

In evaluating the accounts put forward by the historians of the
German language, however, we are concerned not only with the description but also with the prescription of the chancery norm. It has been
suggested that the chancery prescribed the usage evident in its manuscript production. If this was the case, none of the variants and
neutralizations written by favored scribes like Ried, Treytzsaurwein,
and Ziegler can be considered irregular. If a norm was prescribed in
the Habsburg chancery, certainly Treytzsaurwein must have written it,
since he received all of his scribal training there. Yet his orthography, like Ried's, includes the Bavarian dialectal forms that occur
infrequently in Moser's sample. There is no extralinguistic evidence
that Maximilian's chancery was in any active sense a scribal school,
just as there is no indication that it fostered the development of
German as a belletristic medium. The variation in the individual
usages of these three scribes would seem to confirm that indeed
neither was the case. Not only do they each write forms that occur
infrequently in the total chancery production, but they also find
similarly infrequent orthographic features acceptable enough to adopt
without alteration (consider Ried's copy of the Waldauf'scher Stiftbrief). This indicates that the flexible norm that Hans Moser
described was even more elastic than his characterization indicates.
His description shows what was typical of the usage but not all that
was acceptable within it. As the catalog of possible Habsburg orthographic features increases, however, it becomes more difficult to
distinguish the chancery writing system from other contemporary varieties of written EUG. It also becomes more difficult to guess on
what basis contemporary admirers of Maximilian's chancery language
distinguished it from other similar UG written languages.

Moser's heterographic analysis brings this latter issue into sharper focus. It shows that although Maximilian's chancery language is identifiably EUG, it was not so pronouncedly Bavarian as it might have been, and it even retained some distinctively MG features that had come into the chancery orthography during the reign of Frederick III. In most respects the graphemic pattern of the Habsburg chancery language matched that of the contemporary Swabian and Bavarian writing systems, with which it has been compared. It also resembled the graphemic pattern of the Saxon Electoral orthography to a surprising degree. This resemblance was due primarily to the fact that the Saxon chancery language had adopted a number of UG forms during the first years of the sixteenth century. The number of UG forms in the Wettin chancery language distinguished it to a degree from other contemporary MG orthographies, giving it a somewhat supradialectal appearance in its own region. By contrast, the Habsburg orthography was by the end of Maximilian's reign becoming progressively more southern in character and more like the other indigenous writing systems of EUG. This development supports the interpretation that the MG features in the Habsburg chancery language around 1500 were the result of historical coincidence rather than deliberate affectation. The increase in southern forms in the Wettin chancery language during the first decades of the sixteenth century, however, suggests the deliberate adoption of certain features of a prestige writing system.

CONCLUSION

In describing "the most common German language," the language
that Maximilian and Frederick the Wise "pulled together into a single
particular language" and that "all the princes and kings in Germany"
emulated, the German he himself wrote, Luther was speaking orthographically. His remarks have to do with a writing system—a convention
for rendering German sounds in roman letters—and not with literary
style or language level. Luther was not claiming to write the lexicon,
syntax, or diction of the chanceries, but only to use their spelling
system, which was, he asserted, employed by noble and free city chanceries throughout the Holy Roman Empire.

From an orthographic point of view, Luther's implication that
the Habsburg and Wettin chanceries wrote the same variety of German
is surprisingly accurate. In the first decades of the sixteenth century, Habsburg scribes wrote the most pronounced features of the SB
dialects only as minority forms in their chancery orthography, and
they continued to use certain MG spellings that had already been
standard in the orthography during the reign of Frederick III. This
gave the writing system a mildly supradialectal appearance, although
its general characteristics were decidedly EUG. At the same time the
Wettin chancery language, although predominantly MG, included a number
of southern forms. Thus it too had a somewhat supraregional tone.

The reason for the occurrence of nonindigenous forms in the
orthographies was different in each case. In the Habsburg language

they were residual elements of the MG usage that had characterized
Imperial Chancery communications during the Luxemburg period. In the
Electoral chancery the explanation is somewhat more complicated. Some
forms occurring in the Wettin chancery language that do not occur in
other contemporary EMG writing systems may be interpreted either as
imported southern forms or as early evidence of a gradual modernizing
trend in the late medieval writing systems of the region. The NHG
diphthongs fall into this category. Other features, such as kh- for
<k> and p- for <b>, can only be seen as adopted southern orthographic
forms.

No new MG features were added to the Habsburg orthography
during Maximilian's reign. Between 1490 and 1519 the writing system
added more SG spellings that reflected dialectal pronunciations common
to the EUG region, and the orthography came to look more like the
other written languages of the southeast. This does not represent a
"relapse into linguistic particularism,"[462] as has been claimed. It
is rather the continuation of a development that began when Austrian
personnel joined the chancery staff under Frederick III and that continued throughout Maximilian's reign, when South Germans came to dominate the Hofkanzlei. The gradual attrition of MG features in the
orthography and the simultaneous increase in UG forms that improved
the structural efficiency of the writing system should be understood
in terms of the history of the Imperial Chancery before 1519 and in
light of the general development of the ENHG written languages in the
south. It should not be seen as the result of the later politicization of language, which has been associated with the Reformation. The
increase in the number of UG features in the Wettin chancery language
in this period cannot be explained to the same extent in terms of
chancery personnel and gradual evolutionary trends in the writing
system. In the early sixteenth century the Wettin scribes appear to
have affected certain UG orthographic characteristics that were not
indicative of parallel developments in the spoken dialects of Middle
Germany.

During the reigns of Maximilian and Frederick the Wise, the
orthographies of the Austrian and Saxon chancery languages, which were
evolving along somewhat different lines, converged so that they looked
very much alike at about the time Luther made his assessment.   Then,
following their own developmental trends, they diverged again.   The
superficial similarities between the writing systems around 1530 were
great enough to justify Luther's contention that they were a single
written language.   But Luther's explanation of how this language came
into being and how it was viewed in contemporary German scriptoria is
less accurate, and it has resulted in some confusion in the histories
of the German language.

Neither Maximilian, Frederick the Wise, nor their chancery personnel consciously attempted to shape the chancery languages nor to
make them similar to each other.   Maximilian and Frederick did not,
as Luther suggests, pull the two orthographies together into one language.   There is no extralinguistic evidence to suggest that the
Habsburg chancery was concerned with language standardization, with
the development of a supradialectal writing system, or with the creation of a "literary instrument," although Luther's remarks have led
historians of the German language to pursue these issues.   Luther also
seems to have mistaken the direction in which dialectal influence was
moving in the ENHG written languages during the first decades of the
sixteenth century.   He indicates that the Saxon chancery orthography,
his own model, was the model for all the princes, noble courts, and
free cities in the Empire.   This statement suggests that the Wettin
usage was more widespread than it actually was; it implies that it
was typical of contemporary MG writing systems; it does not distinguish between the usage of this most elevated of chanceries and that
of the scriptoria of the cities and the lesser nobility; and it presents the Saxon chancery as the trend setter of the day.   Luther's
statement does not mention the number of southern features in the
Wettin orthography, which was increasing even at the time he wrote.[463]
Luther did model his usage on the Wettin writing system, but the Saxon
orthography included significant features adopted from the writing

systems of the south.   Luther was apparently unaware of the southern cast of the Wettin language, which distinguished it from some other contemporary varieties of MG.

Maximilian's chancery was not a major scribal school, although some of its members, like Marx Treytzsaurwein, received all of their training there and others, like Hans Ried, instructed private pupils in writing.   The orthographic reform that is supposed to have been carried out under the auspices of Maximilian and Niclas Ziegler never took place, and none of the chancery members—with the possible exception of Hans Krachenberger, about whose linguistic activities little is known—demonstrated any particular interest in the development of the written German language.   The rigid chancery procedures, which were observed quite strictly, included a number of document controls; but all of these were intended to ensure the accuracy of the content of the registers and the individual Urkunden.   One of the chancery ordinances does refer to the "style of the chancery," but this was a matter of traditional administrative diction, not of orthography.

Despite this lack of prescriptive attention to orthographic matters in the chancery, however, the Habsburg scribes wrote what is from a modern point of view a remarkably consistent orthography.   This writing system, which may not be understood in the rigid terms of modern Rechtschreibung and which was even more flexible than Hans Moser's characterization indicates, shows that the individual scribes were quite conscious of orthographic matters as they wrote.   Although the orthographic system permitted a wide range of personal scribal variations, the scribes' choices were neither unlimited nor random, and the scribes for the most part stayed well within the range of options included in the chancery norm as Moser has delineated it.

Accounting for the orthographic conformity of Habsburg chancery documents from Maximilian's reign is complicated by the fact that we know only in very general terms how sixteenth-century penmen perceived the orthographies they read and wrote.   We know, for example, that contemporary men of letters considered Maximilian's chancery language to be a particular variety of written German that could be

distinguished not only from the German written in other dialectal
regions but also from the inferior orthography of the UG city scribes.
Statements to this effect were made not only by the Middle Germans,
Luther and Frangk, to whom the Habsburg chancery language may have
seemed somewhat foreign, but also by an educated native of the UG
region, Eck, who would have been familiar with the varieties of German
that were being written in the southeast at the time. And the evidence
from the Habsburg chancery manuscripts themselves indicates that Maximilian's scribes tolerated only a certain amount of deviation from the
implicit norm. Hans Ried's manuscript production indicates that he
found the UG usage of Florian Waldauf, for example, to be acceptable
without alteration, although it does not quite match the modern characterization of the norm; whereas the elusive sources of the Ambraser
Heldenbuch seem to have fallen outside the acceptable range of variation and therefore had to be recast in the chancery orthography.

The difficulty is that we do not know what sort of contrast
these contemporary references to Maximilian's chancery language imply
because the negative examples with which the Habsburg usage might be
compared either do not survive (as in the case of the Heldenbuch
sources) or are not specified (as in the case of Eck's city scribes).
Thus we do not know which features of the Habsburg orthography contemporaries considered to be superior and which features of other writing
systems were considered to be inferior. And what is more important,
we do not know how similar or dissimilar contemporaries would have
felt individual UG scribal usages (like those of Ziegler, Ried, and
the Bavarian Regula scribe) to be. Would they have seen these individual orthographies as similar variants of the same usage (as we are
inclined to), would they have perceived them as examples of a single
orthography, or would they have viewed them as distinct scribal
usages? We cannot know, and the contemporary linguistic treatises
afford little assistance in this matter.[464]

Even Moser's valuable characterization of the Habsburg chancery
usage can only be of limited assistance here. It describes from the
most appropriate modern linguistic point of view the characteristics

of a large corpus of manuscripts known to have been produced in Maximilian's chancery system.　In doing so, however, it generalizes certain
superficial features of the orthography that contemporaries may have
considered to be distinctive.　Further, Moser's definition of the flexible orthographic norm is so elastic that it becomes difficult to
differentiate between documents written in Maximilian's chancery language and those written in other contemporary varieties of Bavarian.
Moser generally selects as the designations of the individual graphemes those variants that occur most frequently in the sample.　It is
this inventory of graphemes that essentially characterizes the regular
chancery usage as he presents it.　But for most of the graphemes Moser
also lists variants that he finds to be typical of the usage and that
fall within the limits of the norm.　Beyond this he notes that
irregular forms are also permitted in the chancery usage.[465]　And
indeed, the individual orthography of so regular a Habsburg scribe as
Treytzsaurwein can only be fit into Moser's characterization of Maximilian's chancery language if one invokes the provision for irregular
forms.

　　According to Moser, the Habsburg usage is generally Austro-
Bavarian in character, represents the elevated level of language
farthest removed from the basic spoken language, and lacks a number
of more pronouncedly dialectal features common in other contemporary
EUG texts.[466]　The dialectal features he lists, however, do occur in
the manuscript production of Habsburg scribes who cannot be considered
atypical.　This means that the Habsburg usage is distinguished from
other EUG orthographies only by the relative frequency of the occurrence of these features that modern scholars consider to be most
characteristic of the SB dialects, and by a few MG forms.　Moser's
characterization of the Habsburg norm is useful in comparing the
Austrian chancery orthography with significantly different writing
systems from other dialectal regions.　It can hardly be used, however,
to distinguish between contemporary varieties of EUG.　Neither does
it permit one to identify unequivocally documents that are written in
the Habsburg chancery language; and thus it cannot be used to provide

conclusive answers about the influence and range of impact of the
chancery orthography.

The fact that Moser's characterization cannot provide any absolute criteria for identifying the Habsburg scribal usage should be
understood not as a deficiency in his analysis, but as an indication
of the evolutionary state of the EUG written languages at the beginning of the sixteenth century. Even without knowing precisely which
features of the prevalent writing systems contemporaries considered
to be inferior or "cacographic" (and we shall probably never know
this), we should perhaps assume that with the exception of its atavis-
tic MG forms Maximilian's chancery language was more like other EUG
orthographies of the day than either the accounts in the histories of
the German language or the remarks of Luther, Frangk, and Eck might
lead one to suspect. Perhaps the Habsburg usage was less distinctive
or easily recognizable even in the early sixteenth century than we
have supposed. If so, the significance of its reputation among contemporary literati should be reconsidered.

It is impossible to know how similar a sixteenth-century
observer would have considered the personal orthographies of the Habsburg scribes to be. The fact that the individual usages are for the
most part consistent within the manuscript corpus of a single penman
but show variations from scribe to scribe supports the extralinguistic evidence that the scribes learned their orthographies from different teachers. The great majority of the Habsburg scribes whose
individual manuscript production has been investigated wrote their own
orthographies without noticeable adjustment throughout the entire
period of their chancery service. This indicates that their skills
at the time they took up their duties were considered satisfactory
and that they were under no compulsion to adapt their orthographies
to any more rigid or specific chancery standard. It also means that
from the point of view of the chancery itself, the individual usages
were not only acceptable but in a general sense equivalent.

The question, then, is how the scribes who acquired their
skills outside the chancery came to write what is both in modern and

to some extent in sixteenth-century terms the same language. The
answer would seem to be the modists and writing masters. Cancelleysch
—that is, both chancery scripts and diction—was the basic writing
skill that vernacular writing teachers of all levels taught in Germany
toward the beginning of the sixteenth century. Although the more
accomplished penmen offered instruction in a variety of scripts and
styles, all writing masters taught at least one chancery language. At
the outset of Maximilian's reign many of the Hofkanzlei scribes were
from Upper Germany, and by the end of his reign the staff was almost
completely UG. These copyists probably acquired their earliest writing skills in the south or from writing masters who taught the EUG
Gemeindeutsch as the fundamental writing skill.

     Two other factors would also have contributed to the relative
homogeneity of the Habsburg chancery scribal usage. First, the southern orthographies, as is evident from the number of UG forms taken
over into the MG writing systems of the day, were considered to be
prestigious and were emulated even outside the UG region. The recommendation of the Habsburg chancery language by Luther and by Frangk
in the 1530s, as the politicization of regional languages was beginning to occur, attests to this fact as well; even the Protestant
reformers admired the cancelleysch of the south. In the years prior
to the Reformation, literacy and more particularly proficiency in
chancery skills were important tools of upward social mobility.
Unlike the grammarians of the second quarter of the sixteenth century,
who taught reading skills in order to provide individuals with access
to fundamental religious texts, the earlier writing teachers emphasize
in their advertisements the production of correctly written texts and
the advantages of being able to produce them. Since the southern
orthographic forms were particularly esteemed around 1500 and continued to be popular in the north well into the sixteenth century, it
is probable that the southern orthography is the one writing masters
preferred to teach and ambitious pupils sought to learn, especially
in Upper Germany where the writing system was indigenous.

This alone, however, would not account for the similarity of usage one finds in documents from Maximilian's chancery. As Eck implied, even among the contemporary UG orthographies some varieties were considered superior and others inferior; the Habsburg writing system was recognized as a good orthography. Although most novice penmen in the south would have learned some sort of UG orthography at this time, the quality would have varied widely. Maximilian's administrative system was doubtless the most illustrious group of chanceries in the SG region at the end of the fifteenth century, and the opportunities for advancement which it presented to young scribes were as great as those available to professional penmen anywhere in the Empire. Indeed, as we have seen, in Maximilian's chancery the sons of drapers and armorers were able to outstrip the sons of noble houses by relying first on their scribal skills and then on their political acumen. All the young scribes of the region would have aspired to positions in one of the scriptoria in the Habsburg chancery system, and it in turn would have been able to select its staff from the best talent available. Presumably it chose scribes who already wrote in the approved way, that is, who wrote more or less according to the orthography Moser has described. The great attraction of the Imperial Chancery would also have caused aspiring penmen throughout the region to write and teach this orthography. The prestige of the southern orthographies in general and the particular attraction of the Habsburg chancery for ambitious scribes would have resulted in one or more varieties of UG cancelleysch being taught as the basic written language in southern Germany. Together these factors may account for the orthographic homogeneity of the Habsburg writing system between 1490 and 1518.

Maximilian's chancery language was the most prestigious UG writing system at a time when southern orthographic features in general were admired throughout Germany. It seems to have differed from other prevalent EUG orthographies only by degree, and contemporaries would probably have had as much difficulty distinguishing it absolutely from similar Bavarian orthographies as modern scholars do. When Luther

and Frangk refer to Maximilian's chancery language, each recommends
it as a good or useful variety of German. Neither suggests that it is
particularly different from other kinds, however; they only say it is
exemplary. It is likely that they recommend Maximilian's orthography
not because it is radically different from others, but rather because
it is one to which almost any literate person in the Empire could have
had access. Written and printed diplomatic and literary documents
from Maximilian's chancery were disseminated throughout the Empire in
considerable numbers during his reign. They would have been more
widely available than examples of other, possibly equally good, scribal
usages. When Eck refers to Maximilian's orthography, comparing it
with the lesser varieties of UG written by the city scribes, he is
writing to Lang, a master of the chancery usage and one to whom the
differences in the orthographies mentioned would have been apparent.
Even here, however, there is no suggestion that Maximilian's orthography is markedly different from other sorts of UG.

It is difficult to assess the direct influence of Maximilian's
chancery language on other contemporary German writing systems around
1500 because it is almost impossible to distinguish the Habsburg
orthography incontrovertibly from other prevalent varieties of EUG
Gemeindeutsch. Not every orthography that matches Moser's characterization of the Habsburg norm can or should be associated with the
chancery writing system. Maximilian's chancery language was a particularly well-known form of the popular SG orthographies that were gaining ground in other dialectal regions at this time; and as such it
was singled out for mention by contemporaries. These few references
are not sufficient grounds for assuming that all documents written
in orthographies matching the Habsburg chancery norm can be connected
with the chancery or seen as evidence of the influence of the chancery
orthography. Because of its attraction for ambitious scribes, Maximilian's chancery probably did influence the kind of cancelleysch that
southern writing masters taught and that students of the region sought
to learn at the beginning of the sixteenth century. It cannot, however, be seen as the single source of all the similar EUG orthographies

of the period, and we will probably not know finally how to interpret its role among the EMG and EUG written languages of the late fifteenth and early sixteenth centuries until more is understood about the dynamics of prestige language phenomena.[467]

In the meantime Maximilian's chancery language continues to merit a place in the histories of the German language not only because of the praise accorded it by contemporaries, but also because it was in fact a rather streamlined and somewhat supradialectal writing system. It should be seen as the most renowned of several similar varieties of EUG _Gemeindeutsch_. It owed its contemporary reputation, however, more to its wide distribution and the trememdous political status of the Habsburg chancery than to the uniqueness of its orthographic features. As one of the SG writing systems that influenced EMG orthographies during the fifteenth and sixteenth centuries, Maximilian's chancery language may be said to have contributed to the development of the NHG orthographic system. Its influence, however, was neither so widespread nor so specific as Luther and the histories of the German language have claimed.

Appendix 1

Index to the Manuscript Sample

In the following index each numbered item corresponds to the text of the same number transcribed in appendix 2. In the case of the literary manuscripts and the <u>Waldauf'scher Stiftbrief</u>, the documentation indicates the folios or sections actually examined to produce the descriptions of the chancery usage of individual Habsburg scribes included in chapter 3. These selections have had to be shortened in appendix 2. The index entries offer, in the order listed below, as much of the following information as is known about each manuscript:

(1) The date the manuscript was written and the location of its origin.

(2) The classification of the manuscript (e.g., letter, mandate, deed, etc.) or, in the case of a literary text, its title.

(3) The stage of execution that the text represents (e.g., draft, fair copy, etc.).

(4) The name of the scribe who penned the text.

(5) The variety of signature (formal or informal) or other endorsement formula, if any, found on the manuscript.

(6) Any notation on the document indicating which chancery controls the text has passed (e.g., "Rta," "rata," "Exp," "Epp," etc.).

(7)   The present location of the manuscript. HHSA refers to the
Österreichisches Staatsarchiv; TLA to the Tiroler Landesregierungsarchiv. Other archives and libraries are cited with
their complete titles. Where I have worked from facsimile
plates ([14]-[16]), both the actual location and the printed
editions of the manuscripts are listed.

(8)   A summary of the content of the text (diplomatic manuscripts
only).

DIPLOMATIC MANUSCRIPTS

1.   1498 June 22 Freiburg. Diplomatic letter. Draft. Niclas
Ziegler. No signature. "Ept." Vienna, HHSA, Maximiliana 4d,
fol. 92.

   Maximilian informs the Hofkammer that he has promised to
split a fief between his Secretary Niclas Ziegler and Hofmarschall Heinrich Graf zu Fürstemberg, and then later to grant
them each an entire fief.

2.   1499 September 7 Reutlingen. Diplomatic letter. Rough final
draft. Niclas Ziegler. Signature: "Niclas Ziegler" (informal).
"Epp." Incomplete text. Innsbruck, TLA, Maximiliana I/41,
fol. 293.

   Ziegler writes privately to Serntein concerning Maximilian's financial difficulties. He also complains that he has not
been allowed to use the official Chancery seal. Ziegler marks
the letter "In sein Hennd," an indication of the sensitive
nature of its content.

3.   1500 February 7 Innsbruck. Diplomatic letter. Fair copy.
Hans Ried. No signature. Sealed with Ried's personal seal.
Innsbruck, TLA (LRA), Schatzarchiv No. 1225 (UR 604).

   Hans Ried acknowledges his appointment by Maximilian
to the office of Customs Collector ("Zollner") at Bolzano.

4.   1501 December 29 Hall i. Inntal. Deed of foundation establishing Vnser lieben Frauen Capelle at Hall. Fair copy, one of

four original copies. Hans Ried. Signatures and brief statements by Florian and Barbara Waldauf von Waldenstein in their
own hands. Innsbruck, Stadtarchiv, Urkunde 587, Items 1-4,
87-91, 204-08.

> The deed establishes the chapel at Hall and includes
detailed instructions for the maintenance of the church, the
support of the priest, the order of services, etc.

5. 1505 January 6 Gmunden. Diplomatic letter. Very rough draft.
Niclas Ziegler. Signature: "Niclas Ziegler" (informal).
Marginal notes, also by Ziegler. Vienna, HHSA, Maximiliana 9a/1,
fols. 7-8.

> Niclas Ziegler writes privately to Chancellor Serntein
concerning various items of chancery business. Ziegler mentions
Serntein's remarks about Hanns Renner, Maximilian's displeasure
at Paul von Liechtenstain's frequent journeys, and Maximilian's
financial difficulties (which he is treating with great
secrecy).

6. 1505 September 27 "Fewr" in Brabant. Diplomatic mandate. Fair
copy. Marx Treytzsaurwein. Signatures: "M Treytzsaurwein,"
"M ppria" (formal); "p Reg p s." "Comissio dñi Regis ppria."
Vienna, HHSA, Maximiliana 9b/1, fol. 202.

> Maximilian writes to the Haußcamerer at Innsbruck, to
Sigmund Spreng, Probst at Ambras, to Vlrich Moringer, Camermaister at Innsbruck, and to Gilg Fronnhaimer, Zollner at
Rattenberg, concerning the "Catzennloer's" handling of the
brass trade at "Müllein" (i.e., Mühlau). An accounting is to
be made of the foundry's financial transactions and a report
sent to Treytzsaurwein at Court.

7. 1506 January 5 Linz. Diplomatic letter. Fair copy. Marx
Treytzsaurwein. Signature: "M TreytzSaurwein," "M ppria"
(formal). Vienna, HHSA, Allgemeine Urkundenreihe.

> Treytzsaurwein agrees to deal with Hanns von Stetten on
behalf of Maximilian in a matter originally assigned to Paul

von Liechtenstain. Treytzsaurwein will apparently be required
to spend two hundred gulden. Maximilian has procured fifty
tons of copper for Treytzsaurwein at a price of two hundred
gulden.

8. 1506 July 7 Vienna. Diplomatic mandate. Draft. Marx Treytzsaur-
    wein. Signature: "Marx tr" (informal). "Exp." Vienna, HHSA,
    Maximiliana 10a/2, fol. 98.

    Maximilian announces to his commanders a forthcoming
eight-day cease-fire with the Hungarians. Because he does not
know whether the Hungarians will honor the agreement, he gives
orders to be implemented in the event they do not. Treytzsaurwein notes that Maximilian wants either Serntein or Maister
Vincentz (Rogkner) to have twelve copies of the letter prepared
by noon.

9. 1506 December 13 Traunstein. Diplomatic letter. Fair copy.
    Marx Treytzsaurwein. Signatures: "M Treytzsaurwein," "p M
    ppria" (formal); "p reg p s." "Comissio dñi Regis ppria."
    Vienna, HHSA, Maximiliana 10b/2, fol. 30.

    Maximilian commands his Camermaister at Innsbruck, Vlrich
Moringer, and his goldsmith, Benediet, to join him at once at
Rattenberg.

10. 1507 November 10 Cologne. Diplomatic letter. Fair copy.
     Niclas Ziegler. Signature: "Niclas Ziegler." "p. m. p."
     (informal). Closing seal. Innsbruck, TLA, Maximiliana VI/I,
     fol. 104.

    Maximilian wishes to engage the services of Duke Heinrich
von Braunschweig to command the Imperial forces. Ziegler,
after conferring with Braunschweig's Chancellor and Marschall,
feels that the Duke's services may be had for less than the
asking price. Ziegler outlines in detail to Maximilian what
he believes will be an acceptable counterproposal.

11. 1511 July 30 Mühlau b. Innsbruck. Diplomatic letter. Fair copy.
Marx Treytzsaurwein. Signature: "Marx treitzsaurwein"
(informal). Vienna, HHSA, Maximiliana 19a/1, fol. 129.

      Treytzsaurwein informs Chancellor Serntein that he is
unfortunately unable to comply with Maximilian's summons to
appear "von haus aus" because he is currently without the funds
to maintain his household. Having eaten his seed corn in the
previous year during his illness and having already pledged all
of his possessions, he is now utterly destitute. The illness
has ruined him physically and financially. Treytzsaurwein asks
Maximilian to pay him two hundred gulden for his services during
the coming year. In return he will come to Vienna and do the
Emperor's bidding. If he has not recovered by the end of the
year, he will make no further requests of Maximilian.

LITERARY MANUSCRIPTS

12. 1513 Vienna. Theuerdank MS. O. Fair copy. Marx Treytzsaurwein.
Vienna, Nationalbibliothek, VNB Codex 2867, fols. 1-19.

      This copy of the Theuerdank draft was prepared entirely
by Treytzsaurwein and was intended for Emperor Maximilian.

13. 1513-14 Vienna. Theuerdank MS. P. Rough draft for printer?
Marx Treytzsaurwein. Vienna, Nationalbibliothek, VNB Codex
2806, fols. 1-12.

      This copy of the Theuerdank draft was prepared by Treytz-
saurwein from MS. O.

14. 1504-16 Bolzano. Ambraser Heldenbuch. Fair copy. Hans Ried.
Hartmann von Aue: "I. Büchlein." Vienna, Nationalbibliothek,
VNB Codex 2663, fols. XXII$^{r/c}$ - XXVI$^{v/a}$. Facsimile: Codices
Selecti, 43 (1973).

15. 1504-16 Bolzano. Ambraser Heldenbuch. Fair copy. Hans Ried.
Herrant von Wildon: "Diu getrew Kone." Vienna, National-
bibliothek, VNB Codex 2663, fol. CCXVII$^{r/a - r/b}$. Facsimile:
Codices Selecti, 43 (1973).

16. 1504-16 Bolzano. <u>Ambraser Heldenbuch</u>. Fair copy. Hans Ried.
Wernher der Gartenaere: <u>Helmbrecht</u>. Vienna, Nationalbibliothek,
VNB Codex 2663, fols. CCXXV$^{r/b}$ - CCXXIX$^{r/a}$. Facsimile: <u>Codices
Selecti</u>, 43 (1973).

Appendix 2

The Manuscript Sample

In transcribing the following texts, I have attempted to reproduce a group of diplomatic and literary manuscripts by members of the chancery of Maximilian I to be used by researchers concerned with either the Renaissance treatises on the German language, the ongoing graphemic discussion, or both. Because it was the orthography of the Habsburg chancery language that resulted in its contemporary acclaim, I have deliberately avoided standardizing the texts in most respects. Certain orthographic features characteristic of the German written in the Habsburg chancery are obscured in editions that have been normalized excessively for the convenience of modern readers. Although the transcriptions in the sample are not in the strict sense diplomatic since they do not reflect all the allotypic variants of individual letters that occur in the manuscripts, they do preserve the orthographic variants that are discussed in the contemporary grammars and appear to have had significance either to the penmen or the language theorists of the day. Thus punctuation, capitalization, and vocalic marking are retained in the transcriptions regardless of their import for modern linguistic analysis.[468] The sample is intended to complement the text volume of Hans Moser's 1977 study in that it includes literary texts produced by chancery scribes, and it retains various orthographic features Moser considered irrelevant in terms of his graphemic method.

In the transcriptions individual letters are capitalized
according to the manuscripts. Punctuation is treated in much the
same way; wherever a virgula or a point occurs in the text, it is
transcribed. Superscripts are reproduced as they appear except for
the u-hook, which is indicated by the symbol (°) throughout the
sample.

In both the cursive hands of Maximilian's chancery scribes and
the Vorfraktur of the Waldauf'scher Stiftbrief and the Ambraser Heldenbuch, certain majuscule and minuscule letters appear in various forms,
often within the same manuscript written by a single scribe. For the
most part allotypic variants of this kind (i.e., more than one shape
used to represent the same letter), different from those produced by
vocalic marking, are of interest only from the standpoint of paleography or calligraphy.[469] They were not generally considered worthy of
mention by the early grammarians, and they have no significance for
modern graphemic analyses. The alternative forms of minuscule r in
the chancery scripts (the Kurrentschrift r and the Arabic-2 r), for
example, fall in this category.[470] The grammarians do not discuss the
different shapes of r, and the variant forms do not appear to reflect
any phonological opposition; to the extent that the distribution of
these forms can be predicted, it is explained on paleographic grounds.

Only in the case of the minuscule s is allotypic variation of
this kind discussed by the sixteenth-century language theorists, and
here, as elsewhere in these early linguistic treatises, the distinction between the symbols and the sounds they were intended to represent is rather fuzzy.[471] In the manuscripts written by Maximilian's
chancery scribes the minuscule s is represented by a total of three
single characters and, in combination with z, a ligature. In the cursive hands of the diplomatic manuscripts and the Theuerdank drafts
([1]-[3], [5]-[13]) a long s (ſ) is used initially, medially, morpheme-
finally, in medial doublings, and in combination with z medially and
finally;[472] a round s (σ) is used in absolute final position and is
very occasionally doubled at the end of a word.[473] In the book hand
of the Waldauf'scher Stiftbrief and the Ambraser Heldenbuch as well as

in the cursive hands of certain diplomatic texts from the chancery not
included in the present sample,[474] the long and round s occur as
described above; and a third minuscule s, a short s (s),[475] alternates
in absolute final position with the round s. In his discussion of the
various s-graphs,[476] Moser proceeds on the assumption "that there is a
phonological opposition between the broad and narrow s-sounds that is
only partially realized graphemically" in the writing system of Maximilian's chancery.[477] His analysis of the s-spellings that occur in
his text selection supports this premise and justifies his generalization of all types of minuscule s found in the manuscripts to the single
letter s in his transcriptions. In the following transcriptions and
in the excerpts from them cited in the text, I adopt this practice so
that s represents ſ, σ, and s; and ss represents ſſ, σσ, ſσ, ſs, and
ss. The character ß is used for the ligature s + z.

Abbreviations in the chancery manuscripts are usually indicated
in one of three ways. In words that occur frequently in the diplomatic texts, certain letters are normally omitted. Thus dz, for
example, is often written for "daz," Ao for "Anno," and so forth.
Where the resolution of such shortened forms is immediately obvious,
I present the abbreviations just as they appear in the manuscript,
without adding the missing letters. Where the resolution is less
apparent, I supply the missing letters and underline them. The second
form of abbreviation occurring in the chancery texts is the common
Nasalstrich, an unattached tilde or bar that is usually written above
that letter before or after which an omission has been made. This
normally indicates the gemination of the nasal or the addition of e
before the nasal above which the tilde appears. These abbreviations
are resolved throughout the sample, and in all cases the added letters
are underlined.

The third and perhaps most characteristic form of abbreviation
used in the chancery manuscripts is a long final stroke or hook.
Three common varieties of this final hook occur in the manuscripts
from Maximilian's chancery. (1) A hook beginning at the line and
rising to the left usually represents -er or -r. It is sometimes

written after the letter it would actually precede if the word were
spelled out completely. Thus H̲rn + the abbreviation represents
"H̲errn" and would appear this way in the sample. Occasionally this
r̲-hook is written beginning at the line and rising to the right.
(2) A long stroke beginning at the line, dropping below it to a sharp
point, then rising again to cross the line and hook above it usually
stands for -e̲n or -n̲. It is distinct from the r̲-hook in both form
and function. (3) A long curved stroke dropping below the line and
trailing off to the right indicates that the last syllable of the
word has been omitted. This abbreviation replaces a syllable composed of e̲ or some other unstressed vowel plus a nasal; it is sometimes used to represent the -u̲m in the Latin "datum," for example.
I resolve these abbreviation hooks throughout the sample and indicate
that I have done so by underlining the letters added. The spellings
used in the resolutions of abbreviations are based on unabbreviated
forms of the same words found elsewhere in the same manuscript when-
ever possible (although the same word may be spelled differently
within a single text) or elsewhere within the manuscript sample.

Where I have been unable to decipher a word within a text, I
have indicated the omission thus [...] with each dot representing an
omitted letter, or I have enclosed my attempted transcription in
[square brackets]. Ellipses in the transcriptions are indicated thus
[---]. Marginalia are set off within <angle brackets> and inserted
into the text at the points indicated in the manuscript.

DIPLOMATIC MANUSCRIPTS

[1] Maximilian etc/
     Erwirdig̲er fůrst. andĕchtig̲er. Edl̲er vnd lieb̲er
     get[reẘer] Wir haben. vnse̲rm hofmarschalch hein-
     rich̲en Grafe̲n Zu fůrstemberg. vnd vnnse̲rm secretarj
     Niclase̲n Ziegler/ Erstlich halben teil/ eines
     v̊llig̲en lehe̲n. vnd nachmals. Dafůr ein gantz
     lehe̲n. so vns auch heimgefall̲en ist/ laut dis̲er
     [huiten] bylass̲en Zedl/ Zulass̲en Zůgesagt/ In d̲er

gestalt. dz vns dz Erst lehen gantz Zusteen solle/
damit vnser new furgenomen ordnunng gehalten werde/
Nů haben Sẙ vns ẙtz. angeZaigt/ dz die lehen. so
weilend Iob Kirhstetter vns weilend Kunig lasslaen
als hertzogen Zu osterreich emphangen hat/ Vns
auch. heimgefallen seẙen/ vnd wir Inen dieselben
lehen <souil der seinen> auf Ir diemůtig bete/ fůr
baide obgemelte lehen die wir Inen vormals Zuleyhen
Zůgs[agt] hetten/ vnd nů vns allein Zusteen sollen
aus gnaden verlihen/ demnach Emp[helen] wir Euch
ernstlich. dz Ir denselben vnserm hofmarschalch.
vnd secretarj darůber einen. lehensbrief vnd vnser
hofcamer ordnůnng fertiget vnd gebet/ darin tůt Ir
vnser ernstlich meynung/ datum/ frẙburg. An freitag
vor Iohannis Baptista/ A o 98/
An die hofcamer

[2] [--1 line--] glauben ganntz dhein gelt bẙ K. Mt.
dann wir nit wol Zerung haben můgen. Wo Ich aber
etwas erfar/ sol darInn dhein vleiss gespart
werden/ darumb wellet mich entschuldigt haben/ Ich
kan. oder waiss. Euch des hofwesens nichts sonndrs
Zuschreiben/ denn das der hertzog von Maẙlannd mit
seinen kinden heraus gen Insprugg Zewcht/ vnd
villeicht gar gen Vlmen. dahin Ku. Mt. auf nechsten
fritag oder Mitich kummet/ franckreich vnd Mailand.
werden In gar vertreiben/ Ist warlich mitsampt
dem. das der Sweytzer Krieg. widerumb angeen sol.
Ku. Mt [...] got schicken Zum pessten./ Ku. Mt
wirdet trewlich geraten einen tag Im Reich Zehalten.
Vnd die anstossenden fleckhen Zubesetzen/ Vnd das
pesst sunst steet Ku. Mt. auf disem handl/ gewiss-
lich ein swerer abfall. Aber ich kan nit merckhen.
das es seiner Mt. angenem sein welle/ Sein. Mt.

hat ytz den nechsten Grafen Platen. vnd Steten.
auch Edlleuten. mit der anzal wie Zu Costentz
abgeredt ist/ dz sich auf viij^M Mann lauffet/ den
nechsten In dz Hegew Zu Ziehen aufgepoten. auf
Mathey. wirdet vom pundt ein tag Zu Vlmen gehalten/
Morggraf fridrich will den Krieg wider die Nurm-
berger anfahen/ der pundt hat Im hilff Zugesagt/
Ist ytz Zu villingen weg vnd als man sagt Heim/
sein volck ligt noch Im leger/ Ku. Mt. arbait
vast. In zubehalten vnd sein furnemen anZustellen/
Graf Wolfgang hat noch am hof dheinen tittl nach
verwesung/ Ich verstee Zolner. sol an Herrn Veyten
<solihen> stat sein/ Wo Ich dz sigl gehept. het Ich
etwas mugen fertigen. Also hab Ich es andern
leuten muessen Zu schickhen das ist mir spotlich.
auch lenger vnleidlich <[---] darzu [auch] Ewr
nachteil>. Ewre zwen schreiben haben mir Zu fryburg
nichts hellffen wellen/ Wo Ir ein vertrawen In mich
setzen. als mit dem sigl. der Kunig. vnd hertzog
fridrich getan haben/ wolt Ich mich dermassen
gegen Euch halten/ dz Ir darab ein gefallen hetten/
Ich mayne/ auch Ir solten das tun/ wie Ir mir
Zugesagt habt/ Datum Reutlingen. an Sambstag. vnser
frawen Abend Nativitatis. A o 99
Herr Ziprian von Serntein
Ku Mt Pt Secretarj etc In sein Hennd

[3] Ich Hanns Ried Bekenn offennlich mit disem brief.
Als der Allerdurleuchtigist grosmechtigist furst.
vnd herr herr Maximilian Romischer kunig etc mein
allergnedigister herr. mich bis auf seiner kuni-
gklichen Maiestat widerrueffen Zu derselben Zollner
Zu Botzen am Eysagk aufgenomen. Vnd mir darauf
vber den gewonlichen alten Sold. wie der vormals
anndern seiner Ku Mt. Zollnern an demselben Zoll

gegeben ist. vnd mir auch alle Jar. v̈ntz auf seiner
Kü Mt. wolgefallen dauon geben werden sol. bis auf
derselben seiner Kü gnaden widerrüeffen. Nemlich
Acht guldin Reinisch Zu ainer pessrůng. doch allain
ditz Iars Zugeben Zůgesagt hat. Daz Ich dargegen
seiner Kü Mt beÿ meinen trewen. vnd Eeren Zůgesagt.
vnd versprochen hab. wissenntlich mit dem briefe Also
daz Ich denselben seiner Kü Mt. Zoll am Eÿsagk. nů
hinfür von seiner künigklichen gnaden wegen
treůlichen. vnd vleissiklichen. Jnnhaben. verwesen.
vnd alles gelt. so seinen Ku gnaden ÿe ZuZeiten
daran geuallen wirdet. aigentlich. vnd ordenlichen
aufschreiben. Vnd das albeg von stůndan in gegen-
wůrtikait seiner Ku Mt Gegen Zollners daselbs. in
die verslossen Truhen. so mir seiner Ku Mt Ambtman
daselbs Zu Botzen. Hanns Abmstorffer/ oder wer der
kunfftiklich ist. antwurt. legen sol. der seiner Ku
Mt. alsdann dasselb gelt. Iärlich auf seiner
gnaden Raitcammer Zu Ynsprugk verraiten/ Vnd Zu
derselben hannden ausrichten wirdet. dartzů dann
der bemelt Irer gnaden Ambtman. auch Ich. als
Zollner. vnd derselben seiner Mt. Gegenschreiber
in derselben Ambthauss ÿeder ein Slüssl. Zu Derselben
Truhen haben söllen. Ich sol vnd wil auch an
demselben Jrer Kü Mt. Zoll nichts entziehen. noch
ÿemands entziehen lassen. sonnder Jrer gnaden
herrlikait. gerechtikait. vnnd gewaltsam Dabeÿ
vestiklichen hanndthaben allenthalben seiner Mt
nůtz. vnd frůmmen fůrdern schaden wennden. Vnd sünst
alles das tůn. daz die notdurfft desselben seiner
Ku Mt. Zolls erfordert Vnd ein getreẅer Zollner Vnd
diener. seinem herrn Zutůn schuldig. vnd phlichtig
ist/ in massen Ich seiner Ku Mt. darůmb gelobt. vnd
gesworn. Vnd mich des auch sonnderlich gen seinen Ku

gnaden hiemit verschriben vnd verpürgt hab. Des Zu
Vrkhůnd han ich disen brief mit meiner aigen hannd
geschriben. Vnd mein Jnsigl hiefůr gedrugkt
Beschehen an freitag vor sand Apolonien tag Anno
dominj. Fůnfftzehenhundert Iar.

[4] Herrn Florian Waldauf von Waldenstain. vnd Frảwen
Barbaran seiner Eelichen Hawsfrảwen Stiftbrief
antreffend die heÿlig Capellen vnser lieben frauen
zu Hall im Yntal aůch das Predigambt/ bede
Caplaneÿen/ das tẻglich gesungen Salůe regina/ vnd
Recordare virgo mater etc aůch andern gotsdienst.
so Sÿ in sand Niclasen kirchen daselbst zů Hall im
Yntal. gestift vnd aufgericht haben. Nach Cristi
gebůrde Tawsendt fůnfhundert vnd im Ersten Iar.

Thůmbrebst Thůmbdechandt. Vnd das Erwirdig Capitl zů
Brichsen. vnd Bůrgermaister vnd Rat der Stẻte Hall
im Yntal vnd Insprůgg. sind der obgemelten heyligen
Capellen. vnd aller Ordnungen Stifftůngen vnd Sachen
in disem Stiftbrief begriffen. vnd darczu aůch des
grossen heÿlthůmbs/ vnd der Bebstlichen Rȯmischen
vnd ander Indulgentzen gnaden vnd Ablass. damit die
heÿlig Capellen begabt ist. ewige conserůatores
Execůtores volfůerer behalter vnd hanndthaber etc

Der Prediger. Caplan. Kirchbrẻbst. vnd Mesner. der
heÿligen Capellen zů Hall im Yntal. sind diser
ȯrdnůngen Stifftůngen vnd Sachen ewige sollicitatores
maner vnd aufseher etc.

1 In dem namen der Heiligen vngetailten Driůaltikait
got des Vaters. got des Sůns. vnd got des heiligen
Geists. in ainem ainigen ewigen gȯtlichen wesen
ainen daůon vnd daraůs aller gewallt vnd mẻchtigkait
alle gůttat vnd volkomne gab. alle kůnst krafft.
Sterkh. vnd v̇bůng Zů gůet gotliche gnad vnd

Parmhertzigkait flewsset. der driůalltig in
personen. einiger ewiger got in der Natůr vnd wesen.
důrch sein Våterlichs ewigs wort den Sůn gottes
gleich Im. beschaffen hat. Himel vnd Erdtrich. vnd
alle Creatůr Zů offenbarůng vnd erclerůng seiner
Maiestat glori vnd Eere gőtlichs wesen. aůch Zů
verordenter hilff/ nůtz. trost. lůst. vnd stětter
vnderteniger dinstberkait Zů dienen dem Menschen.
damit Er willigklicher mit ganntzem Hertzen vnd
gmůt genaigt wůrde. gehorsam vnd dienst Zůbeweisen.
seinem Schőpfer der In vber alle Creatůr gewirdiget
vnd geadelt. vnd in seiner Schőpfůng nach seiner
gotlichen pildung vnd gleichnůss geformirt hat Also
daz Im nit allain Irdisch Creatůr. Sonnder aůch
himelische geist. die heiligen Enngl Zůbehůetung vnd
beschůtzůng. von anfang seiner gepůrd bis in sein
letzt Ende Zůgegeben sind/ vnd vber das alles. hat
got der vater aůs besonnder lieb vnd vnaůssprech-
licher milltikait seinen Sůn das ewig Våterlich
wort/ am letzten Zů End der wellt geschikht/ dem
Menschen Zůdienen. vnd nemlichen den weg der
seligkait důrch sein hailsame gőtliche Lere Zů
Lernen.
[--85 items--]

87   Es sol aůch dartzů derselb Wochner/ aůch ein ẙeder
vorgerůrter Briester/ alle Freẙtag das ganntz Iar/
oder an ainem andern tag in ẙeder Wochen in seiner
Mess vns obgemelt Stiffter vnd Stiffterin/ vnd aller
vnser voruordern Seelen. aůch all getreẘ fůrdrer
steẘrer vnd hanndthaber vnser lieben fraẘen Capellen
vnd diser vnser Stifftůng lebentig vnd tod/ vnd
dartzů all gelaẘbig Seelen in seiner gedechtnůss
haben/ vnd ẙeder fůr vns vnd dieselben in ẙeder
Wochen ain mal ein gewőndliche Collecten/ nemlichen

Omnipotens sempiterne deůs/ qui viůorům dominaxis
simůl et mortůorům etc einlegen/ vnd dartzů die
obgemelt vnser lieben frawen Capellen vnd vnsern
gestifften gotsdienst ordnůngen vnd stifftůngen/
aůch die obberůrten Bebstlichen vnd annder
Indůlgentzen gnaden vnd ablas/ vnd das merkhlich
gross Heÿlthůmb/ vnd dartzů in sonderhait der
Capellen hanndtraichůngen Zůstend vnd gefelle/ in
allen Iren Predigen peichthören vnd annderswo mit
allem getrewen vleiss fůrdern vnd Befolhen haben/

88   Vnd fůr das alles. sol ein ÿeder kirchherr/
denselben Siben gesellen/ aůch allen Caplånen vnd
Briesterschaft im Wÿdem/ vnd dartzů dem Schůel-
maister/ alle freÿtag das gantz Iar daran nit
panfast geůallen wůrden. aůf Zwen Tisch im Widem.
nemlichen aůf ÿeden Tisch ain gůete grosse aůf-
gesnitne Sůppen/ ein gůet gemůess/ vnd prots genůeg/
vnd dartzů aůch yedem Briester. vnd dem Schůelmaister ain Trincken gůets weins haller mass/ fůr
ein Collacion geben.

89   Aber an Freÿtėgen in der Vasten. den Qůattember
Freÿtėgen. vnd alsofft im Iar an freÿtėgen Panfast
geůallen wůrden. sol der kirchherr an ÿedem
denselben freÿtėgen/ ÿedem obbestimbten Briester.
vnd aůch dem Schůelmaister fůr ain Collacion geben/
ain Trincken gůts weins. vnd dartzů aůf ÿeden
obberůrten Tisch/ fůr Zwen krewtzer prot/ vnd ѵber
das alles. sol der kirchherr in sonnderhait dem
obbestimbten Wochner alle abent in seiner Wochen.
Zů dem nachtmal oder Collacion. geben ain Trincken
gůets weins. bringt Im am freÿtag Zů der Collacion
Zwaÿ Trincken wein. alles Haller mass. Welicher aber.
oder weliche aůs den obberůrten Briestern vnd

personen in obbestimbter Procession nit gewesen
wėren. vnd das obgemelt Respons vnd Antiffen in der
Capellen nit hetten singen verhellffen. dem. vnd
denselben. sol der kirchherr die obbestimbt Collacion. aůf denselben Freẙtag Zůgeben nit schůldig
seinn. Sẙ wėren dann aůf dieselb Stůnd mit dem
Hochwirdigen Sacrament/ oder dem heiligen Ȯl
aůsganngen/ oder mit der Taẘff oder anndern
Phȧrrlichen rechten vnd gescheften der kirchen
beladen gewesen/

90   Darůmb vnd fůr sȯliche obbestimbte speisůng vnd
Collacion/ sol der Ersam Rat dem obgenanten kirch-
herrn alle Iar aůf den heiligen Weichnachtabent
aůsrichten vnd geben/ benantlichen Sechtzehen Marck
perner.
[--119 items--]

[5]   Besonnder lieber Herr/ Eẘre schreiben hab Ich
vernomen/ vnd die vom landsrechten Zů ȯsterreich
werden durch dz Regiment Zů lẙnntz allen beschaid
haben/

So wirdet dem von Harrdegg/ auf sein [......]
herniden beschaid/

.K. Mt. hat dz gescheft. Andreen von der Důrr seins
pawshalben Zugelassen/ wie Er begert vnd Blasy
wirdet Euch dz furderlich Zů senden/

So will Ich den brief an den Cardinal sancte Crucis
furderlichen fertigen/ Vnd Euch Zu schicken dieweil
Ir den alwegen/ Durch den Sniter hinein bestellen
mȯgt

Graf Adolfs diener ist noch vnabgefertigt am hof/

Renners halben hab Ich Eẘr schreiben nit verstanden/
In beswerůngsweise/ Vnd mȯgt Euch entlich Zů mir

versetzen dz Ich Euch alles dz tun will so Euch vnd
der Kantzley Zů Eer vnd nůtz dienet/ Bit Euch mich
etlich beủelhen zehaben/

Ku. Mt. hat etwas verdrieß/ dz herr Pauls so oft
vrlaủb begert/ seẙt daran. als aủs Euch selbs/ dz
Er kain vnlust auf sich lad/ Ku. Mt. ist wol Zůfriden/
Das Er Ytz gen freẙsingen reẙt.

der von Wirtzburg ist abgefertigt/ Wie Ir ab
hiebeẙligenden copeẙen vernemen werdet/ Nủ hab Ich
sunst kaine vnd bedarff der teglichs/ tut so wol.
schickht mir die von stund wider auf der posst damit
Ich die gewiss In v. tagen hab. <Ich will Euch die
copeyen bey der nechsten post schickhen>

Wirtzburg hat sich mit der K. Mt. vertragen vnd
iiij^M gldn par geben vnd iij^M guldin schuld
nachgelassn/ ist nủ Zumal der Bairischen Hilf freẙ/
<es ist In grossem geheim gehandelt>

Ich gedenck K. Mt. werde morgen hinweg/ vnd also hie
vmb Iagen. vnd beleiben/ bis von dem von Wirtzburg
antwort kummet/ Aber Ich verstee nit annders. dann
Ku. Mt. werde gen augspurg/ Vnd da die sachen
Richten/ Aber Zuuor gen Insprugg/

Herr Reinprecht von Reyhemburg hat Zů Ried bey vij^C
pferden. vnd iij^M Zů fuss gủter dienstleủt/ vnd Herr
Adam dorringer mit prandt grossen schaden tan/
nemen wz Sy finden/ Vnd werden ain Eerlichen kerab
machen. Ich versich mich nit/ dz .K. Mt. dabeẙ sein
werde/

Ich hoff wir wellen noch mer fur dz Interesse
Zůwegen bringen/ Das den landen hervnder auch
gelegen seẙ/ Datum Gmunden an der Heiligen drey
Kunig tag/ A. 5.

[6] Maximilian von gots gnaden Romisch Kunig Zuallenn-
tzeitten merer des Reichs etc

Getrewen lieben/ Nachdem der Catzennloer den Mössing
hanndl bißherr von vnns gehabt/ Auch Er die Mössing
hutten Zů Müllein gepawen/ Vnnd mit Ime deßhalben von
vnnsern wegen kain Raittung beschehen ist/ Deßhalben
wir vntzher kain grüntlich vnnderrichtung gehabt
haben/ Sein wir dardurch gevrsacht worden/ solichs
mössungs hanndls halben mit gedachtem Catzenloer
enntliche Raittüng thůn Zulassen/ vnd den mössing
hanndl an ein Enndt Zůstellen vnnd aůfZürichten/ Danns
vnns aůs etlichen vrsachen/ Die vnns furgefallen/
mercklich daran gelogen wil sein/ Vnnd Eůch Zů
solicher Raittüng verordennt/ Demnach Emphelhen wir
Eůch mit Ernnst vnnd wellen/ Das Ir gedachten Catzenloer auf einen Kurtz bestimbten tag. Nemlich nach
vber anntwurttung ditz briefs in Zehen tagen fůr Euch
erfordert Auch vnnsern Zeůgmaister Barthlmen
freyßleben dartzu nemet/ der dann bißher in derselben
sach gehanndlt/ Vnnd darümb ain wissen hat/ Vnd mit
gedachtem Catzennloer des Mossinghanndls halben/ was
Er von vnns Kupffer vnd Mössing emphanngen/ Auch
welher massen/ Vnnd in was cossten Er die mössing
hutten Zů Müllein gepaůt hab/ grüntlich raittüng
thüet/ Vnnd auch von Ime aigentlich vernemet/ Wie Er
sich hinfuro mit dem mössing hanndl hallten welle/
Vnnd vnns solichs alles in schrifft auf der posst
furderlichen Zůschickhet/ Auch bestellet/ das
dieselben Ewre brief vnnserm Secretarien Marxen
Treitzsaurwein in sein hanndt gewißlich geanntwurt
werden/ Vnnd damit in dhainen weg nit vertziechet/
Damit wir weÿtter der notturfft nach dardůrch der
mössing hanndl nit nidergelegt werde/ hännoln mugen/
Das ist vnnser Ernnstliche maynüng/ Wir haben auch
vnnserm gemeltem Zeugmaister vnd dem Catzenloer

soliche raittung verkunndt vnnd Zůgeschriben/
Wollten wir Eůch nit verhallten/ Geben Zu der Fewr
in Brabanndt am Sibenund Zwaintzigisten tag
Septembris Anno domini etc xv^C vnnd im funfften
vnnsers Reichs im Zwaintzigisten Iarn

Vnnsern getrewen lieben Ruědolfen harber vnnserm Rat
vnnd haußcamerer Zů Innsprůgg Sigmunden Sprengen
vnnserm phleger vnd Bräbst Zů Ombras. Vlrichen
Moringer vnnserm Camermaister Zů Innsprůgg Vnnd
Gilgen fronnhaimer vnnserm Zollner Zu Rattemberg.

[7] Ich Marx Treitzsaurwein/ Romischer Kunigclicher
Maiestat Secretarj/ Bekenn mit Diser meiner hanndt-
schrifft Das Ich/ Ku/ Mt Zugesagt hab/ das geschefft
so sein Mt/ auf herrn paulsen von liechtenstain
ausgeen hat lassen mit Hannsen von Stetten Zuhandln
mit Zwaẙ hundert gulden Zugeben/ wider von herrn
paulsen heraus Zubringen vnnd seiner Maiestat Zů
Anntwurten/ Dann mir sein Mt vmb solich Zway
hunndert gůlden funftzig Zenntner Kuppfer
verschaffen hat/ Zu vrkundt hab Ich mich auch mit
meinem hanndtzaichen vnder schriben/ Datum Zu
Lynntz am funfften tag Ianuary Anno etc im Sechsten
Iar/

[8] Wir Maximilian etc Embietten allen vnnd jegklichen
vnnsern haüptlaüten vnnd phlegern so diser vnnser
brief furkumbt vnnser gnad vnnd alles guet/

Nachdem Zwischen/ vnns/ vnnd den Hunngern/ ain
Anstanndt Nemlich Achttag furgenomen der sich dann
am nechstkunnfftigen phintztag anfahen solle/ Vnnd
dieweil aber nit aigenntlich wissend ist ob die
Hungern den selben Anstanndt hallten werden oder
nit/ Demnach Emphelhen wir Euch allen vnnd ainen
Ieden in sonnderhait Ernnstlich/ ob die hunngern in

der Zeit/ oder nach Ausganng des Anstanndts in vnnser
lannd Zů Ziechen vnnder steen/ oder darein Ziechen
wurden/ Das Ewr Ieder auf dem Sloss oder in der Stat
Darynnen Er ist alsdann kreẙtschůss Nemlich dreẙ
schůss Zů stundan aůf ain ander thue damit sich
vnnser volckh versamel/ vnnd sich vor mercklichen
schaden ver[....]ten můgen / Auch dem Vienden Irm
furnemen ain abpruch gethan/ vnnd wider Zůruckh
getriben/ vnnd habt in solichen <Ewr> sonnder gut
vleissig auf sehen. Das vnnser volckh mit den
Kreẙtschůssen Zu rechter Zeit gewarnet werden/ Das
ist vnnser Ernnstlich maynung/ Geben Zu Wien am vij
tag Iueli Ano xv^C vnd Im vj vnsers reichs Im xxi Iarn.

Kn Mt beuelh ist das der von Serntein oder maister
Vincentz diser brief xii sollen schreiben lassen/
Also das die heut vmb xii vr ferttig. sein vnd
darnach Zu Stundan gen hof tragen/ so welle seine Mt
die Zaichnen

[9]   Maximilian von gots gnaden Romischer Kunig etc

Getrewer/ Wir Emphelhen Dir mit Ernnst/ das dů
mitsampt vnnserm Goldschmidt dem Benedieten von
stundan Zů vnns gen Rattemberg am Ẏn/ kumest/ vnd
nit verZiechest Daran tuest dů vnnser Ernnstliche
maẏnung/ Geben Zů Trawnstain am xiij tag Decembris
Anno etc Sexte/ vnnsers Reichs im xxj Iarn.

[10] Allergnedigister Kůnig. Es hat Hertzog Heinrich von
Braůnswig der Elter. sein Cantzler vnd Marschalch
ytz hie. beẙ mir gehebt/ vnd anzaigen lassen/ Er seẙ
willig. des Reichs veldhaůbtmanschaft anzenemen.
Soferr Im .3. oder .4.^C pferd gehalten. vnd Er vmb
den sold vergwist werde/ aber an der Kriegscamer
will Er sich nit settigen lassen/ wart deshalben
antwort/ Nů acht Ich. Er were Zůbewegen. Das Er mit

i.j^C pferden als haubtman angenomen. Vnd vmb den sold.
auf der Bischof vnd Stet lubegg Goszlar. Northawsen
Mülhawsen. Hildeszheim. Münster osnabrugg. vnd was
vmb sein landtschaft ist/ hilf. vnd ansleg. Ytz Zů
Costentz. aufgelegt/ verweist wurde/ dar Inn mag ewr.
Ku. Mt. nach Irem gefallen handlen. vnd beüelch tůn/
Warlich wo es sůnst. in seinem vermůgen were da. an
seiner person. Kain mangl. dann Er. als seine Ret
sagen. lust vnd begird het/ bey Ewr. Ku. Mt. Zů
sein/ Er wart anheim. auf mein ferrer schreiben/
Beuilch mich damit ewr. Ku. Mt. als meinem
allergnedigisten herrn/ datum. Cölnn. am .x. tag
Noůembris. Anno etc vij.

[ll] Genediger Herr. mein willig geflissener dienst sein
Euch Zuuor/ Alls Ir mir für gehallten habt/ Wie. Kay.
Mt maynůng seÿ/ Dieweil Ich also mit Krannckhait
beladen seÿ mich von haůs aůs Zubestellen/ Auf solich
furhallten hab Ich mich seÿder bedacht/ vnnd kan nit
in mir finden das Ich kain bestellung Zů diser Zeit
von haus aůs annemen muge/ Nemlichen aůs den vrsachen
Ich hab kain haußhaben/ so mag Ich kain haußhaben
hallten dann Ich hab das Korn so mir Ietzo waxt vor
ainem Iar in meiner Krannckhait geessen/ vnnd hab da
haimet gar kain vnderhalltůng dann Ich meine gueter
scher alle versetzt vnd gar nichts mer hab/ Dann die
Krannckhait hat mich an leib vnd guet verderbt/
vnnser Herr welle mich wider Reich machen/ Vnd
solichem nach hab Ich mir den weg fur genomen/ mich
bedunckht es were für Kay. Mt. vnd fur mich Nemlichen
Ich wolt Ietzo gen Wienn Ziechen vnd daselbst ain
Iar beleiben vnd das mir die. Kay. Mt. auf ain Iar
Lang i.j^C gulden beÿ dem Vitzthumb Zů wienn verordent
het/ Nemlich das Er mir hundert gulden alspald Ich
hinab kome gäb vnd die andern hundert gulden in dem

halb_en Iar so möcht Ich mich dester mit mynder
costenn auß hallt_en/ Wurde Ich dann in Demselb_en
Iar von meiner Krannckhait gar erledigt so mocht
mich Kay. Mt. prauch_en nach. seiner Mt gefall_en Wurde
Ich dann nit gesundt/ so wolt Ich seh_en vnd/ mich
in die sach schickhen/ Das Kay. Mt. auch kain_en
weit_ern vncoss_ten auf/ mich ausgäb/ Das sein. Mt.
mich Ietzo mit den ij^C guld_en nit laß Ich v_ermain
sein Mt. solt damit nit beswert sein/ so verhof Ich
Zu got ganntz Vngezweiflt Ich welle in demselb_en
Iar gesundt werden/ Ich hab mir biß her den schad_en
gethan/ Das Ich albeg in xiiij tag_en gesundt hab
well_en werden/ Damit hab Ich mir nit Recht ausgewart
als mir not/ gewest were/ Vnnd an Sannd Barthlmes
Abend oder den annd_ern tag Darnach het Ich auf dem
wasser ain guete fuer bis gen Passaw/ Damit beuelh
Ich mich Euch als mein_em gn_edigen Herr_n/ Datum Zů
Mullein am xxx tag Iuly A_nno etc xi Iar.

Item so mag mich Kay. Mt. in der Stat Wienn in
seiner .Mt. sach_en wol prauch_en/ Damit were Ich auf
das Kunfftig Iar geferttigt dem Ackher hab Ich alle
mein abferttigung beuolh_en Euch anzu zaigen/

Herr_n Ziprian von Serntein Cantzler etc mein_em
gn_edigen Herr_n

LITERARY MANUSCRIPTS

[12] Das ist der fürwittich
1^r   den Marx Treÿtzsaür-
     wein mit schrifft
     vnd gemäl in ordnung
     gestelt hat

     Item an das Enndt ain gemäl/
1^v Ain Kunig der da sitzt in seiner

[12] .Mt. vnnd ain Iůnnckfraw
kunigclich beklaidt/ die vor Ime
steet/

Das gemäl ist nit
gemacht

Hie hebt sich an das p̈uech ge-
2ʳ nannt Tewrdannck. vnd im
anfang ist beschriben der
künig Rüemreich. darnach
sein Tochter Erenreich/ Vnd
darnach der Thewrdannckh
was Er mit seiner hanndt
volpracht/ Vnd was wider-
wärttigkait Er von driÿen
valschen haüptleůten. Mit-
namen der Erst fürwittich.
der ander Vnfallo der drit
Neÿdelhardt. gehabt hat/
Wie hernach volgt/

Ietz hebt sich an von
künig Rüemreich

Vernemet das ain mächtiger Künig was
der so gar in kunigclichen Eeren sasz
Seins geleichen lebt hart in der Welt.

An Reichtůmb vnnd parem gelt.
großlannd vnd leůt het Er fürwar

In großem Reichtumb saß Er manige Iar.
2ᵛ sein lannd vnnd leůt Er wol Regiret
Alsdann einem Künig pillich gepiret
der kunig von Rüemreich hieß Er
Er het ainen gemahl als Ich ler
Beÿ der Er kainen Erben nit gewan

[12]   dann ain tochter aůf dise Welt schon

dem kunig starb der gemahl sein

darůmb sein hertz lide swere pein

Erlichen bestätet Er Sÿ Zů der Erdt

Nůn het der Edl kunig werdt

die Ainig tochter vorgemelt

Irs gleichen lebt hart in der welt

damit Sÿ got sonderlich begabet het

Die tochter weÿßlichen paren tet.

3^r Sy was ganntz schon Zůchtig vnd klůeg

vernůnfft vnnd weÿßhait het Sÿ genůg

In allen tügenten gar wol gethan

der Eren ain hochwirdige Cron.

Sÿ was geschickt in manicher sach

Nůn wardt der Künig alt vnnd swach

der Kunig von Růemreich vorgenannt

Merckt wie sein herrschaft/ in seinem landt

Mit bit. den Kunig strennget an.

das Er seiner tochter lobesan.

verheiraten solt als gotlichen was

dardůrch seine landt vnd leůt destpas

versehen wůrden nach pillichait

Vil werber wůrden da dem kunig berait

Item an das Enndt ain gemäl

3^v das ain kunig mit seinen Räten

ainen großen Rat halt/

Das gemäl ist nit gemacht

Wie der kunig Ruemreich

4^r sein tochter Erenreich

Zuüerheiraten ainen Rat samelt

Der Kůnig samelt Ainen Rat

vnd sagt Inen Zů der selben fart

Wie oft Er wůrde gestrennget an

[12] seiner tochter Zů geben ainen Man
damit versehen würde das gantz Reich
darůmb Ratet mir alle geleich
vnd bedenckt Eůch mit gůetem hertzen
Es ist hier Innen ganntz nit Zů schertzen
Als Ir mir verphlicht vnd verpůnden seÿt
Vnd wellet nit praůchen gůet oder Neid
Sy sagten alle mit ainer styme
das würde praůchen weÿße Sÿnne/

Sy wolten thůn nach Irn verstanndt

4ᵛ was Nutz were dem ganntzen lanndt
Mit trewen wolten Sẙ das Erwegen
Vnnd Irn trewen Rat darzů geben
Sÿ teten mit allen vleis betrachten
Ee Sÿ ainen Ratschlag machten
Sÿ waren weÿß vnd darzů klueg.
der Werber vmb die tochter waren genüg
Sy gaben dem kunig Irn Ratschlag Zů erkennen
Vnnd teten Ime Zwelf personnen nennen
der Ieder were an Adel groß
Aůch Ieder seiner tochter genosz
daraůs solle der kunig Er kießen
Zů Welhem sein hertz tet fliessen/

Das solt Er Inen alsdann verkündten

5ʳ so möcht man darnach weiter Rat findten
Der kunig bedacht sich gar wol.
Wie dann ain weÿßer man thůn sol.
Er was in der wal ganntz Irrig
vnnd sein hertz haimlichen vnrůeig
Er het geren den pessten erwelet
das der selb nach Ime würde gezelet
Ain adenlicher vnnd Thewrman
das sein tochter damit möcht bestan

[12]   der kunig alda nichts beschlosz

Die sach was Ime Insonnderhait groß

Er Redt Ich wils Ietz got lassen walten

vnd solichs in meiner gedachtnůs behalten

Vnnd so got mir schickt mein letste stundt

5^v   alsdann solle aus sprechen mein Mündt

Welhen Ich meiner tochter erkieset han

derselbe solle sein Ir Eelicher Man

Item an das Enndt/ ain gemäl

das ain kunig in ainem garten

bey ainem graben vor ainer

Stat ligt in seinen harnasch

vnd stirbt/ Vnd vil volk beẙ

Ime ist/ Zů Roß vnd fueß

Das gemäl ist nit gemacht

[---]

[13]   Hie hebt sich an das puech genannt

1^r   Thewrdannckh/ vnd im anfanng

ist begriffen/ Der Kung Ruemreich

Darnach sein tochter Ern reich/ vnd

Dar nach der Thewr dannckh/ was

Er mit seiner hanndt volpracht/ vnd

was wider warttigkait Er von

Diesen valschen hauptleuten

Mitnamen/ Der Erst furwittich

Der annder vnfallo Der Drit Neidl

hardt gehabt hat/ wie hernach

aus dem gemal vnd geschrifft

vernomen wirdt

Rot   Ietzo hebt sich an Kung Ruemreich

Vernemet Das ain mechtiger Kung

was/ der so gar in Kungcliher Ern saß

[13] seines gleichs lebet hart in der Welt
An Reichtumb schain vnd parem gelt
groß lannd vnd leut hat Er furwar
In grosem Reichtumb saß Er mang. Iar
sein land vnd leůt Er gantz wol regiret
als ain<u>em</u> weisen Kung pillichen gepuret
Der Edl Kung von Ruemreich hieß Er
Er het ain<u>en</u> lieb<u>en</u> gemahl als Ich ler
bey der Er kain<u>en</u> Mans Erben nit gewan
Dann ain tochter auf dise welt schon
Dem Kung starb der lieb gemahl sein
Darůmb sein hertz lide sond<u>er</u> swere pein

Eerlichen bestatet Er Sy Zu der Erdt
3^r Nun het der obgedacht Edl Kunig werdt
Die Ainig sonderlich schon tochter vorgemelt
Ires geleichen lebet hart in der welt
Damit Sy got Insonders begabet het
Die tochter got weißlichen p̈ären tet
Sy was gantz schon Zůchtig vnd Klůeg
vernůnfft vnnd weißhait het Sÿ genůeg
In allen tugendten gar wol gethan

Der Eren ain sondere hoch wirdige Cron
Sÿ was geschickht in manicher sach
Nun wardt der Kunig Allt vnd swach
Der Kunig von Růemreich vorgenant
Merckht wie sein her<u>r</u>schaft in seinem lanndt
Mit großem bete. den Künig strennget an
Das Er sein Zarte tochter gar lobesan
verheiraten solt. als gotlichen was
Dardůrch seine lannd vnd leůt destpas
versehen vnd versorgt wurden nach pillichait
vil werber wůrden da dem Kunig berait

Ietzo ain halb plat lär

[13]   Wie der Kunig Růemreich sein tochter
Rot   Erenreich Zuuerheiraten ainen Rat samelt

3^v   Der Kůnig samelt gar pald ainen Rat
        vnnd sagt Inen Zu derselben fart
        Wie oft Er wůrde von Inen gestrenget an
        seiner lieben tochter Zůgeben ainen Man/
        Damit versehen wurde das ganntz Reich
        Darumb Rattet mir in trewen alle geleich
        vnnd bedennckht Euch mit gůetem hertzen
        Es ist hier Innen ganntz nit Zů schertzen
        als Ir mir verphlicht vnd verpunden seẏt
        vnnd wellet nit prauchen guet oder Neidt

        Sẙ sagten alle mit ainer Stẙme
        das wurde praůchen weẙße Sÿnne
        Sẙ wolten thůn nach Irm verstanndt
        was Nutz were dem ganntzen lanndt
        Mit trewen wolten Sẙ das Er wegen
        vnnd Iren trewen Rat darZů geben
        Sẙ teten mit allen vleiss betrachten
        Ee Sy ainen entlichen Ratschlag machten
        Sy waren weẙß und darZů klůeg
        Der werber vmb die tochter waren genůg
        Sy gaben dem Kunig Irn Ratschlag Zuerkennen
        vnnd teten Ime Zwelf personnen nennen

        der Ieder were An Adl vnd tugent groß
4^r   Auch Ieder seiner lieben tochter genoß
        Daraus solle der Kunig selbs Er kießen
        Zu welhem sein hertz saget vnd tet fließen
        Das solt Er Inen alsdann ver kündten
        So mocht man darnach weiter Rat finden
        Der Kunig bedacht sich selbs gar wol

[13]   Wie dann ain weißer Man thůn soll/

Er was in der Wal ganntz Irrig

vnnd sein hertz haimlichen gar vnrůeig

Er het geren daraus den pessten erwelet

das derselb nach Ime auch wurd geZelet

Ain Adennlicher vnnd Thewrer man

das sein tochter damit möcht bestan

der Kunig alda ganntz nichts beschloß

die sach was Ime In sonnderhait groß

Er Redt Ich wils Ietz got lassen walten

vnd solichs in meiner gedachtnůs behalten

vnnd so got mir schickht mein letste stůndt

Alsdann solle aussprechen mein Mundt

Welhen Ich meiner tochter erkießet han

derselb solle sein Ir Eelicher Mann

Jetzo ain halb plat lär

[---]

[14]   Ein schồne Disputatz. Von der

Liebe. so einer gegen einer schồnen

frawồen gehabt vnd getan hat

XXII^{v/a}   Mẏnne waltet grosser krafft:

Wann sy wirt sighafft:

an thumben vnd weẏsen:

an alten vnd greẏsen:

an Armen vnd an reichen:

gar gewaltigklichen:

bezwang Sy einen Iüngeling:

daz Er alle seine ding:

muesset mit gewalt ergeben:

Vnd nach Irem gepote leben:

So daz Er Zemasse ein weẏb:

durch schone synne:

vnd durch Irn leẏb:

[14] mÿnnen begunde:

da sy im des nicht begunne:

daz Er Ir were vnndertan:

Sy sprache er solte Sÿ erlan:

[--14 lines--]

Owe hertze vnd dein sÿ̊n

werest du icht annders denn ich bin:

du hettest wol verschuldet vmb mich:

daz ich klaget v̊ber dich:

allen den ich des getraw:

daz sÿ̊ mein schad geraw:

daz sy mich rechen an dir:

vnd wie es dartzů stat mir:

Zwar ich tě̊t dir den todt.

vnd gulte dir alle solhe not:

die du mir offt bringest:

Wann du mich laÿder Zwingest:

mit deiner kreffte wes du wil:

Wann des gewaltes ist souil:

des dir an mir verlassen ist:

daz mir kaines mannes list:

fride daruor mag gegeben:

Ich muesse in deinem gewalte leben:

daz ich dem nicht enntwencken mag:

des gewÿnne ich manigen schwä̊ren tag:

wann dich wil nicht genů̊egen:

wes du mir magst zů̊gefů̊egen:

nach geender rew:

das ist ein vntrew:

seÿdt du in mir gehauset hast:

vnd dein ding an mir begast:

die vnder Ir vnd freüden missezimpt:

Wann Sÿ mir die freů̊de gar benÿmbt:

[--314 lines--]

[14]
XXIII^{r/c}   Mochte ich nu wissen das:

wauon ich deinen hass:

von ersten gearnet hette:

Vil gernne ich dich påte:

daz du es durch got verkůrest:

vnd vnns baide nicht verlůrest:

Wann es dir schaden begÿnnet:

wann mir dein Zerÿnnet:

wer sol den streit nu schaiden:

vnnder vnns baiden:

Wann dü thů es durch gotes Eere:

vnd richt dich nicht sere:

hab ich dir icht getan:

des lass mich dir Ze puesse stan:

vnd richte selbs v̊ber mich:

so Eerest du dich:

Du magst mich gerne emphahen:

la dir nicht verschmahen:

meine dienst vnd mein freůntschafft:

vnd důnck mich sölher krafft:

vnd mit solhen dingen:

die ich můg volbringen:

so diene ich dir als ich sol:

vnd kumet vnns baiden auch wol:

[---]

[15]   Ditz půechel haysset die getrew Kone.

CCXVII^{r/a}   Wir sůllen von lieben dingen sagen.

Vnd laider måre gar gedagen.

Wann sy tůnd wee dem hertzen gar.

ich han alle meine Iar.

mit laiden måren heer verzert.

dauon Ich freůden bin beheert.

[15] Wann gůte måre machent fro.

die leiden han getan mir so.

daz ich Ir willikliche empier.

wo die wal stat an mir.

da wel ich daz mir rechte kůmbt.

Vnd mich an meinen freůden frůmbdt.

Nu ist das mein maists laÿd.

daz mir die wal ist gar versait.

seyt mir niemand nicht wil sagen.

daz mir von recht můge behagen.

so bin aber Ich so wolgemůt.

daz ich vil lieber sage gůt

daz daz mir nicht gezåm

vnd yemand sein freůde nåm.

dauon wil ich ein mare sagen.

daz euch von rechte můss behagen.

Hie hebt sich an das půechel

Ein Reůtter het ein schön weÿb.

die was im lieb als sein leib.

das was billich Ir schöne was.

durchleůchtig als ein spiegl glas.

dartzů was sy den vollen gůt.

wo ein weib ist so gemůt.

daz sÿ beÿ schöne gůete hat.

der leib billich Ze loben stat.

die raine was so erber.

daz Ir man kain hertzen swår.

von den dingen nie gewan.

dauon möcht er Sÿ gern han.

Sy was an Züchten so volkomen.

daz nie nicht ward von Ir vernomen.

daz man fůr vnzucht möchte han.

darumb was aůch lieb Ir man.

[15] Sy pot es seinen freunden wol.
     den gesten als ein frům̊b weib sol.
     Ir wirt was an dem leibe ein man.
     daz er was nicht so wol getan.
     als er es gern het gesehen.
     von Im wil ich der warhait iehen.
     Er was gerumphen vnd klain.
     der reů̊tter vor den leů̊ten schain.
     als es wer hundert Iaralt.
     daz es doch nicht gegen Ir entgalt.
     Er daucht sÿ̈ schǒner als Absolon.
     vnd stercher dann Sampson.
     in Irem hertzen ward nie man.
     den Sy fů̊ᵃr In wolte han.
     das machet Ir grosse frům̊ᵃbkait.
     das annder Er was gar berait.
     Zů̊ alle die das ẙmmer man.
     an allen eren mag began.
     das tet er alles vǒᵃlliklich.
     als ob Er wᵉᵃr ein Kaÿ̈ser rich.
     gewesen vnd ein der schǒᵃneste man.
     den alle die welt ye gewan.
     willig seines mů̊tes.
     seines leibes seines gů̊tes.
     Was er gar den vnndertan.
     an den Eere solte began.
     dauon ward sein vnflě̊tikait.
     in allen lannden hingelait.
     Nu kam es nach gewonhait.
     Das dem Reů̊ᵃtter ward gesait.
     Von ainem Vrlauge gros.
     [---]

[16]   Das puech ist von dem Måyr Helmprechte

CCXXV^{r/b}   Ainer sagt was Er gesicht.

der annder sagt was Im geschicht.

der drit von mÿnne.

der Vierd von gewẙnne.

der fůnfft von grossem gůte.

der Sechst von hohem můte.

Hie wil ich sagen was mir geschach.

daz ich mit meinen augen sach.

Ich sach das ist sicherlichen war.

eines gepaurn Sůn der trůg ein har.

das was raide vnde fal.

ob der achsel hin Ze tal.

mit lennge es volliklichen gie.

in ein hauben er es vie.

die was von pilden wåhe.

Ich wån yemand gesehe.

so manigen Vogl auf hauben.

Sytteche vnde tauben.

die waren alle darauf genået.

Welt Ir nu ho̊ren was da stået.

Ein Mayr der hiess Helemprecht.

des Sůn was derselbe knecht.

Von dem das måre ist erhaben.

sam den Vater nennet man den knaben.

Sy bede hiessen Helmprecht.

mit einer kurtzen rede schlecht.

Kůnde ich euch das måre.

was auf der hauben wåre.

Wunders erzeůget.

das måre euch nicht betreůget.

Ich sag es nicht nach wane.

hinden von dem spane.

nach der schaitel gegen dem schopfe.

[16]

CCXXV^{r/c}   Recht enmitten auf dem Kophe.

der Lůn mit Voglen was bezogen.

recht als sy wåren geflogen.

aus dem Specht harte.

auf gepauren swarte.

kam nie pesser haube tach.

dann man auf Helmprechte sach.

demselben geůtoren

was gegen dem Zeswen oren.

auf die hauben benået.

Welt Ir nu horen was da stet.

[--800 lines--]

CCXXVII^{r/b}   Ir solt fůllen vnns den maser.

ein åffe vnd ein narre waser.

der ye geseut seinen leib.

fůr gůten wein vmb ein weib.

Wer liegen kan der ist gemait.

triegen das ist hofischait.

[---]

Notes

INTRODUCTION

1. Martin Luther, D. Martin Luthers Werke. Kritische Gesamtausgabe: Tischreden, I (Weimar: Hermann Böhlaus Nachfolger, 1912), 524-25; all references to this edition of Luther's works are hereafter cited as WA (Weimarer Ausgabe).

2. Jakob Grimm, Vorreden zur Deutschen Grammatik von 1819 und 1822, ed. Hugo Steger (Darmstadt: Wissenschaftliche Buchgesellschaft, 1968), pp. 36-37.

3. See Glenn Elwood Waas, The Legendary Character of Kaiser Maximilian (New York: Columbia University Press, 1941), chs. 4, 5, 7.

4. Cf. Hans Eggers, Das Frühneuhochdeutsche, Vol. III of Deutsche Sprachgeschichte (Hamburg: Rowohlt Taschenbuch Verlag, 1969), p. 29:

> So jedenfalls ist in Frankreich und in England die
> Entwicklung verlaufen. Die von den altfranzösischen
> und den mittelenglischen Dichtern in Wechselwirkung
> mit den Kanzleien und Schreibstuben geprägte Kultur-
> sprache wurde zur sicheren Grundlage aller weiteren
> sprachlichen Entwicklung. Auch in den Niederlanden
> legte der gelehrte Dichter JACOBUS VAN MAERLANT
> (ca. 1225-1291), der gleichzeitig Stadtschreiber, d.h.
> Vorsteher der städtischen Kanzlei in Damme war, den
> Grund, auf dem die niederländische Kultursprache
> erblühte.

5. See Christel Schulte, "Gibt es eine oberdeutsche Form des Frühneuhochdeutschen?" in <u>Zur Entstehung des Neuhochdeutschen</u>, ed. Ilpo Tapani Piirainen (Bern and Frankfurt a. M.: Herbert Lang and Peter Lang, 1972), pp. 31-56.

6. Leo Santifaller's article, "Bericht über die Regesta Imperii," <u>AAWien</u>, 106 (1969), 299-331, gives a brief history of the efforts that have been made to prepare complete <u>regesta</u> of the diplomatic documents of the Holy Roman Empire from its beginning forward. Various scholars have or have had the responsibility for preparing the <u>regesta</u> for individual periods. Hermann Wiesflecker and his colleagues at the University of Graz are currently involved with the preparation of the Maximilian <u>regesta</u>.

7. Hans Moser, <u>Die Kanzlei Kaiser Maximilians I.: Graphematik eines Schreibusus</u>, Innsbrucker Beiträge zur Kulturwissenschaft, Germanistische Reihe, Vol. 5, Innsbruck, 1977, Pts. I-II.

8. Elaine C. Tennant, "The Habsburg Chancery Language (1440-1519)," Diss. Harvard 1977.

9. The 1517 Schönsperger edition of Maximilian's <u>Theuerdank</u> and the 1537 edition of Johann Eck's so-called Ingolstadt Bible (see note 41) are examples of such works.

10. Joseph Chmel, ed., <u>Urkunden, Briefe und Actenstücke zur Geschichte Maximilians I. und seiner Zeit</u> (Stuttgart: K. Fr. Hering & Comp., 1845). This was about the only published source of materials from Maximilian's chancery available during the nineteenth century. Also see note 108.

11. Friedrich Maurer, "Zur vor- und frühdeutschen Sprachgeschichte," <u>DU</u>, 3 (1951), 5-20.

12. R. E. Keller's <u>The German Language</u> (New Jersey: Humanities Press Inc., 1978) is a particularly fortunate example of this development.

CHAPTER 1

13. Virgil Moser, Historisch-grammatische Einführung in die frühneuhochdeutschen Schriftdialekte (Halle a. d. Saale: Verlag der Buchhandlung des Waisenhauses, 1909), p. 14:

> Aber schon unter [. . .] Friedrich III. (1439-93) voll-
> zog sich ein völliger umschwung. Tief im Bayrischen
> sprachgebiet, zu Gratz, lag die hauptkanzlei; kein
> wunder, dass wir hier fast alle jene züge, die uns schon
> bei Ludwig d. Bayern entgegengetreten sind, wiederfinden,
> wobei sich die herzoglichen und kaiserlichen urkunden in
> nichts voneinander unterscheiden.

In a statement discussed in the section "Frederick III and the Habs-burg Chancery Language" in this chapter, Eggers (note 4) presents quite a different view of Frederick's chancery language (pp. 139-41). He argues that Frederick's Imperial chancery in Vienna and his House chancery at Graz functioned independently of each other and produced different varieties of written German. Neither Moser's nor Eggers' statement indicates a very thorough knowledge of the operations of the Habsburg chanceries. In this period the court and the chancery were closely associated with each other and with the person of the Emperor. At various times during his long reign, Frederick III was in residence at Wiener Neustadt, Vienna, and Linz, but he preferred Graz and often spent years at a time there. Because of Frederick's presence in Graz, both House and Imperial affairs were conducted by the Graz chancery. For this reason the Graz chancery should properly be considered Frederick's "hauptkanzlei." See chapter 2 for a detailed examination of chancery structure and operations. For further information on the functioning of Frederick's court and chancery at the various cities of his residences see Fritz Popelka, Geschichte der Stadt Graz, I (Graz: Verlag Styria, 1959), 63; Josef Mayer, Geschichte von Wiener Neustadt, 2 pts. in 3 vols. (Wiener Neustadt: Selbstverlag des Magistrats Wiener Neustadt, 1924-27), II, 100-14; and Karl Gutkas, Geschichte des Landes Niederösterreich (St. Pölten: Niederösterreichisches Pressehaus Druck- und Verlags-gesmbH, 1974), p. 131.

14. These are the works to which I refer. The dates given in parentheses are, unless otherwise noted, those of the first editions in order to enable one to trace questions of possible influence. As working editions, however, I have used the latest available to me. These dates are given in square brackets. Complete documentation appears in the bibliography.

Jakob Grimm, Deutsche Grammatik (1819); Karl Müllenhoff, Denkmäler [. . .] (1864, 2nd ed.); Wilhelm Scherer, Zur Geschichte der deutschen Sprache (1868); Heinrich Rückert, Geschichte der neuhochdeutschen Schriftsprache (1875); Konrad Burdach, Die Einigung der neuhochdeutschen Schriftsprache (1884); Otto Behaghel, Die deutsche Sprache (1886) [1968]; Friedrich Kluge, Von Luther bis Lessing (1888) [1888, 1918]; Adolf Socin, Schriftsprache und Dialekte im Deutschen (1888); Karl von Bahder, Grundlagen [. . .] (1890); Otto Behaghel, "Geschichte der deutschen Sprache" (1891); Sigmund Feist, Die deutsche Sprache (1906) [1933]; Virgil Moser, Historisch-grammatische Einführung [. . .] (1909); Emil Gutjahr, Die Anfänge der neuhochdeutschen Schriftsprache [. . .] (1910); Hermann Hirt, Geschichte der deutschen Sprache (1919); Friedrich Kluge, Deutsche Sprachgeschichte (1920); Hans Naumann, Geschichte der deutschen Literatursprachen (1926); Adolf Bach, Geschichte der deutschen Sprache (1938) [1970]; Wolfgang Jungandreas, Geschichte der deutschen Sprache (1947); Hugo Moser, Deutsche Sprachgeschichte (1950) [1969]; John Waterman, A History of the German Language (1966); Hans Eggers, Das Frühneuhochdeutsche (1969); Wilhelm Schmidt et al., Geschichte der deutschen Sprache (1969) [1970]; Fritz Tschirch, Geschichte der deutschen Sprache (1969); Johannes Erben, "Frühneuhochdeutsch" (1970); Peter von Polenz and Hans Sperber, Geschichte der deutschen Sprache (1970, 7th ed.); Hans Rupprich, Das ausgehende Mittelalter [. . .] (1970); R. E. Keller, The German Language (1978).

15. See Hans Rupprich, Das ausgehende Mittelalter, Vol. IV, Pt. 1 of Geschichte der deutschen Literatur, ed. Helmut de Boor and Richard Newald (Munich: C. H. Beck'sche Verlagsbuchhandlung, 1970), p. 412.

16. Ernst Martin, rev. of <u>Das Leben des Heiligen Hieronymus</u> <u>in der Übersetzung des Bischofs Johannes VIII. von Olmütz</u>, ed. Anton Benedict, <u>ADA</u>, 6 (1880), 313-17; Hermann Paul, "Gemeindeutsch," <u>BGDSL</u>, 12 (1887), 558-60; Arno Schirokauer, "Zur Bedeutung von 'Gemein-deutsch,'" <u>PMLA</u>, 63 (1948), 717-19; and Stanley Werbow, "Die gemeine Teutsch," <u>ZDP</u>, 82 (1963), 44-63.

17. Werbow (note 16), p. 48.

18. Werbow (note 16), p. 50. Also see Friedrich Ranke, "Ulrich von Pottenstein," <u>VL</u>, 3 (1943), cols. 921-22. The context in which this statement appears supports Werbow's reading of it.

19. Cod. Vind. 12460, Suppl. 109, fols. 1-91^r, 1464.

20. Erika Bauer, ed., <u>Heinrich Haller Übersetzungen im "gemeinen Deutsch" (1464)</u>, Litterae, Göppinger Beiträge zur Text-geschichte, Vol. 22, Göppingen, 1972, pp. 7-9.

21. Martin (note 16), p. 316.

22. Paul Pietsch, <u>Martin Luther und die hochdeutsche Schrift-sprache</u> (Breslau: Verlag von Wilhelm Koebner, 1883), pp. 16-19.

23. Pietsch (note 22), p. 18.

24. Bauer's (note 20) identification of Heinrich Haller as the 1464 translator may now make it possible to determine what he intended with the phrase "zuo ainer schlechten gemainen theutsch [pringen]." The Heinrich Haller manuscripts afford a rare opportunity to investigate an individual's written language. Haller's holographic draft of his translation, his holographic fair copy, and a contempo-rary copy of the translation in another hand have all survived. See Bauer for description and discussion of these manuscripts.

25. See Bauer (note 20), pp. 7-8.

26. Schirokauer (note 16), pp. 717-19.

27. Schirokauer (note 16), pp. 717-18.

28. Conrad Gesner, <u>Mithridates</u> (Zurich: [Christophorus] Froschoverus, 1555), fol. 37^v. According to Konrad Burdach's <u>Die Einigung der neuhochdeutschen Schriftsprache</u> (Leipzig: J. B. Hirsch-feld, 1884), p. 21, n. 27, the Gesner phrase appeared unchanged on fol. 42^r of the 1610 edition.

29.   Josua Maaler, <u>Die Teütsch spraach</u> (Zurich: Christophorus Froschouerus, 1561), "Praefatio," fol. 4^V.   I quote here directly from Maaler.   Schirokauer in regularizing the Maaler text has been somewhat inaccurate.   The original reads:

> Porrò cùm diuersae sint dialecti linguae Germanicae,
> aliae plus, aliae minùs inter se differunt: quaedā
> adeò, ut se inuicem colloquentes non intelligant: cū
> in pronunciatione ferè solùm & paucis literis mutatis
> discrimen existat.   Ex his illam qua superiores Germani
> utūtur, aliqui optimā & precipuā, minimeq́; corruptā
> esse iudicant.   Sunt qui tractui circa Lipsiam elegan-
> tioris sermonis (quo Lutherus etiā libros suos condi-
> derit) primas deferant: alij potiùs Augustanis, alij
> Basiliensilium linguam magna ex parte probant.   A
> nostra quidem, id est, superioris Germanicae, & ueluti
> cōmuni Germanica lingua, quantùm & in quibus diuersae
> dialecti differant, pluribus in Mithridate nostro
> ostendi [. . .].

30.   Schirokauer (note 16), p. 718.

31.   Burdach (note 28), pp. 20-21.

32.   Christel Schulte (note 5) reviews the regional languages as described by Virgil Moser, Mirra Guchmann, Werner Besch, and Emil Skála in the section of her article entitled "Abgrenzung und Einteilung des oberdeutschen Sprachraumes" (pp. 37-47).

33.   Although V. Moser, Guchmann, and Besch each view the written languages of the dialectal transition zones somewhat differ-ently, they are unanimous in identifying the written language of the southeastern (Austro-Bavarian) region as one of the distinctive varieties of German written during the period under consideration. Their analyses of the regional written languages are reviewed by Schulte (note 5), pp. 37-47.

34.   Karl Müllenhoff and Wilhelm Scherer, "Vorrede zur zweiten Ausgabe," <u>Denkmäler deutscher Poesie und Prosa</u>, 3rd ed. (Berlin: Weidmannsche Buchhandlung, 1892), pp. XXIX-XXX.   The pagination is from the second (1864) edition.

35.   Heinrich Rückert, <u>Geschichte der neuhochdeutschen Schriftsprache</u> (Leipzig: T. O. Weigel, 1875), II, 182.

36.   Burdach (note 28).

37. Burdach (note 28), pp. 1-2.

38. See notes 28-29.

39. Hans Volz reminds the reader that Eck's Bible was neither printed in Ingolstadt nor in Bavarian (<u>Vom Spätmittelhochdeutschen zum Frühneuhochdeutschen</u> [Tübingen: Max Niemeyer Verlag, 1963], pp. XXII-XXIII, nn. 59, 61):

> Gegenüber der von Keferstein (und auch noch von <u>F</u>. <u>Kluge</u> <u>Von Luther bis Lessing</u> [. . .] und von <u>Vogel</u> [. . .]) vertretenen irrigen Auffassung, daß Ecks Bibel bayrisch gefärbt sei, wiesen <u>E</u>. <u>Schröder</u> [. . .] und <u>M</u>. <u>H</u>. <u>Jellinek</u> nachdrücklich darauf hin, daß diese Bibel in Schwaben (Augsburg, nicht Ingolstadt) gedruckt und der Grundcharakter der Sprache Ecks schwäbisch sei. (n. 59)

This is pertinent to research on Eck's written language but has no direct bearing on the present investigation. For the sake of simplicity I continue to refer to the first (1537) edition of Eck's translation by its popular title, "The Ingolstadt Bible." See note 41.

40. Friedrich Kluge, <u>Von Luther bis Lessing</u> (Strassburg: Verlag von Karl J. Trübner, 1888), p. 28.

41. Johann Eck, <u>BJbel: Alt vnd new Testament</u> (Ingolstadt: Görg Krapf, 1537), Dedication ("Vorrede"), n. pag. For further information concerning this edition see Theodor Wiedemann, <u>Dr. Johann Eck, Professor der Theologie an der Universität Ingolstadt</u> (Regensburg: Verlag von Friedrich Pustet, 1865), pp. 615-25. When Kluge quotes this passage (note 40, p. 29), he alters the orthography considerably and makes minor omissions.

42. Friedrich Kluge, <u>Von Luther bis Lessing</u>, 5th ed. (Leipzig: Verlag von Quelle & Meyer, 1918), pp. 34-35.

43. "Unter Maximilian begann aber nicht nur die Regelung, sondern auch die Ausbreitung einer modernen Sprache" (note 42, p. 35).

44. Adolf Socin, <u>Schriftsprache und Dialekte im Deutschen nach Zeugnissen alter und neuer Zeit</u> (Heilbronn: Verlag von Gebr. Henninger, 1888), pp. 169-70.

45. Moser (note 13), p. 26

46. Emil A. Gutjahr, <u>Die Anfänge der neuhochdeutschen Schriftsprache vor Luther</u> (Halle a. d. Saale: Verlag der Buchhandlung des Waisenhauses, 1910), p. 176.

> Das soziale 'mittelste dûtsch', das im XIII. und XIV.
> Jahrhundert als Geschäfts- und Kanzleisprache, aber
> auch als Literatursprache sich 'in me lande zcu Sach-
> sen' überall Geltung verschafft, ist zunächst die
> obersächsische Sprache des ostmitteldeutschen Stadtadels
> z. B. zu Halle und zu Prag, in der Zukunft aber auch
> die hochdeutsche (md.-obd.) Sprache der allgemein
> 'sechsischen Cantzelei', d. i. die gemeindeutsche Sprache
> sowohl der Kanzleien der Kaiser aus luxemburgischem (bes.
> Karls IV.), aus bayrischem (bes. Ludwigs des Bayern) und
> aus österreichischem (bes. Maximilians I.) Hause, aber,
> nach Luthers Angabe, auch aller übrigen Fürsten und
> Städte in Deutschland.

47. Hans Naumann, <u>Geschichte der deutschen Literatursprachen</u> (Leipzig: Verlag von Quelle & Meyer, 1926), p. 22. "Zum Unterschied von der ahd. und mhd. Kultursprache ist der Charakter der neuen zunächst ein gemeinsprachlicher, amtlicher, praktischer, erst in zweiter Linie ein literatursprachlicher."

48. Adolf Bach, <u>Geschichte der deutschen Sprache</u>, 9th ed. (Heidelberg: Quelle & Meyer, 1970).

49. Eggers (note 4).

50. Keller (note 12).

51. Some of Maximilian's literary projects are discussed in conjunction with the manuscript production of Treytzsaurwein and Ried in chapter 3.

52. Fritz Tschirch, <u>Geschichte der deutschen Sprache</u>, II (Berlin: Erich Schmidt Verlag, 1969), 92-93.

53. Cf. Grimm (note 2) quoted in my introduction, and Eggers (note 4), p. 187.

54. See, for example, Ludwig Erich Schmitt, "Zur Entstehung und Erforschung der neuhochdeutschen Schriftsprache," <u>ZMF</u>, 12 (1936), 208. Also see the introduction to his <u>Die deutsche Urkundensprache in der Kanzlei Kaiser Karls IV. (1346-1378)</u> (Halle a. d. Saale: Max Niemeyer Verlag, 1936).

55. John T. Waterman, A History of the German Language (Seattle: University of Washington Press, 1966), p. 117.

56. Eggers (note 4), p. 152.

57. Wilhelm Schmidt et al., Geschichte der deutschen Sprache, 2nd ed. (Berlin: Volk und Wissen Volkseigener Verlag, 1970), pp. 95-97.

58. Keller (note 12).

59. Ernst Wülcker, "Lauteigentümlichkeiten des Frankfurter Stadtdialects im Mittelalter," BGDSL, 4 (1877), 9.

60. Otto Behaghel, Geschichte der deutschen Sprache, 5th ed. (Berlin: Walter de Gruyter & Co., 1928), p. 190.

61. Sigmund Feist, Die deutsche Sprache, 2nd ed. (Munich: Max Hueber Verlag, 1933), p. 175.

62. Walter Henzen, Schriftsprache und Mundarten, 2nd ed. (Bern: Francke Verlag, 1954), p. 50.

63. Ferdinand Jančar, "Das Kanzleiwesen unter Maximilian I.," Prüfungsarbeit, MS, Institut für österreichische Geschichtsforschung, University of Vienna, 1897, p. 7.

64. Peter von Polenz and Hans Sperber, Geschichte der deutschen Sprache, 7th ed. (Berlin: Walter de Gruyter & Co., 1970), p. 76.

65. Ernst Wülcker, "Die Entstehung der kursächsischen Kanzleisprache," ZVThürG, n.s., 1 (1879), 349-76.

66. Chmel (note 10).

67. Kluge (note 42), pp. 30-31.

68. ____ Gass, "Theodor Bibliander (Buchmann)," ADB, 2 (1875), 612.

69. Theodor Bibliander, De ratione communi omnium linguarum & literarū (Zurich: Christoph[orus] Frosch[overus], 1548), p. 27.

70. Fabian Frangk, Orthographia, in Quellenschriften und Geschichte des deutschsprachlichen Unterrichtes bis zur Mitte des 16. Jahrhunderts, ed. Johannes Müller (Gotha: Verlag von E. F. Thienemann's Hofbuchhandlung, 1882), p. 93. Further references to Frangk's Orthographia are to Müller's edition of the 1531 text.

Concerning the desirability of a complete German grammar, Frangk writes:

> DAs wir Deutschen/ neben andern Nation jnn vnser sprache/
> nicht so gantz vngeschickt befunden würden/ hab ich den
> jungen deutscher zung/ vngeübten/ vnd den recht regulirts
> deutschs liebhabern/ diesen kurtzen vnderricht/ zur
> anweisung/ sich darinnen zuüben/ fürschreiben wollen/ Wie
> wols on schaden/ ja meins bedunckens/ hoch von nöten/ weer/
> Das ein gantze Grammatica hierinn beschrieben würd/ wie
> jnn Krichischer/ Latinischer vnd andern sprachen gescheen/
> Denn so wir ansehen den emssigen vleis/ so die Latiner
> allein/ jnn jrer zungen fürgewandt/ vnd vnsern vnuleis/
> bey der vnsern/ da gegen stellen/ solten wir billich
> schamrot werden/ das wir so gantz ablessig vnd sewmig
> sein/ Vnser edle sprach so vnwert vnd verachtlich halten/
> Weil sie dennach jhe so lustig nützlich vnd tapffer jnn
> jrer red mass/ als jndert ein andere befunden wird/

71. Frangk (note 70), p. 94.

72. Socin (note 44), p. 165.

73. "Maximilian I. (1493-1519) baut nur wenig an dieser sprache weiter. [. . .] So können wir das hohe lob, welches ihm und seinem kanzler Ziegler gerade wegen seiner orthographischen reform-bestrebungen, schon seit Luthers zeit bis tief ins 17. jh. hinein, zu teil wird, kaum verstehn" (note 13, p. 15).

74. Henzen (note 62), p. 91.

75. Dirk Gerardus Noordijk, <u>Untersuchungen auf dem Gebiete der kaiserlichen Kanzleisprache im XV. Jahrhundert</u>, Diss. Amsterdam 1925 (Gouda: T. van Tilburg, 1925), pp. 154-67.

76. Hugo Moser, <u>Deutsche Sprachgeschichte</u>, 6th ed. (Tübingen: Max Niemeyer Verlag, 1969), and "Die Entstehung der neuhochdeutschen Einheitssprache," <u>DU</u>, 3 (1951), 58-74.

77. Eggers (note 4), p. 143.

> Die Wiener Entwicklung sei noch etwas weiter verfolgt.
> Unter Kaiser MAXIMILIAN I. (1486-1519) bleibt die alte
> Tradition im wesentlichen bewahrt; allerdings wird der
> bairisch-österreichische Einschlag in der Schreibsprache
> etwas stärker. Der Kaiser, selbst mit dem 'Theuerdank'
> und dem 'Weiskuning' als Dichter hervorgetreten und ein
> Sammler und Förderer der deutschen Literatur, war auch
> um die Gestaltung der Sprache bemüht, darin lebhaft
> unterstützt von seinem Kanzler NIKLAS ZIEGLER. Die

Sprache, die sie pflegten, wurde als das 'Donauische' oder die 'Donausprache' bekannt und galt weithin als Vorbild. Dabei dürften die Bewunderer die mundart- lichen Züge, die dieser Sprache eigneten, nicht so sehr beachtet haben wie die Orthographiereform, die ZIEGLER durchsetzte. Bis zu seiner Zeit war die Unsitte der Doppelschreibung von Konsonanten, über die bereits WYLE sich beklagt, mächtig ins Kraut geschossen. ZIEGLER setzte sich für Vereinfachung ein (z. B. <u>Helfershelfer</u>, <u>Zeiten</u> statt <u>Hellffershellffer</u>, <u>Czeyten</u> [. . .]) und lenkte damit die weitere Entwicklung in vernünftigere Bahnen. Dies vor allem scheint den Ruhm von MAXIMILIANS Kanzleisprache begründet zu haben. Jedenfalls waren sich die Zeitgenossen bewußt, daß von der kaiserlichen Kanzlei starke Impulse ausgingen.

78. Polenz (note 64), p. 76.

79. Kluge (note 40), pp. 26-27; Socin (note 44), p. 165; Henzen (note 62), p. 91; Bach (note 48), p. 250; and Rupprich (note 15), p. 136.

80. Müller (note 70), pp. 310-11.

81. Rudolf von Raumer, <u>Geschichte der germanischen Philologie vorzugsweise in Deutschland</u> (Munich: R. Oldenbourg, 1870), p. 62.

82. Joseph von Aschbach, <u>Geschichte der Wiener Universität</u>, II (Vienna: Wilhelm Braumüller, 1877).

83. Engelbert Klüpfel, <u>De Vita et Scriptis Conradi Celtis</u> (Freiburg i. Br.: Libraria Wagneriana, 1827), p. 179.

84. Anton Maria Kobolt and Benefiziat Gandershofer, <u>Ergän- zungen und Berichtungen zum Baierischen Gelehrten-Lexikon</u>, II (Landshut: Verlag bei Franz Seraph Storno, 1824), 176-77.

85. Michael Denis, <u>Wiens Buchdruckergeschichte bis M.D.L.X.</u> (Vienna: Christian Friedrich Wappler, 1782).

86. Joannes Cuspinianus, <u>Austria</u> (Basel: Joannes Oporinus, 1553), p. 593.

87. See Denis (note 85), p. 299. An undated work of Cuspinianus', which according to Denis must have appeared before 1500, is dedicated to Krachenberger.

88. See Lewis W. Spitz, <u>Conrad Celtis: The German Arch- Humanist</u> (Cambridge: Harvard University Press, 1957), pp. 57-58, and Aschbach (note 82), pp. 288-89, among others.

89. Elias Caspar Reichard, Versuch einer Historie der deutschen Sprachkunst (Hamburg: Johann Adolf Martini, 1747), pp. 15-16. This work is something of a period piece and is dedicated to the "hochlöblichen deutschen Gesellschaften in Leipzig, Jena, Göttingen, Greifswald und Helmstädt." As Müller warns, it is less than reliable (note 70, p. 311, n. 49).

90. Hermann Maschek, "Ladislaus Suntheim," VL, 4 (1953), col. 347.

91. Bibliotheca Institvta et Collecta, Primvm a Conrado Gesnero: Deinde in Epitomen redacte, & nouorum Librorum accessione locupletata, tertiò recognita, & in duplum post priores editiones aucta, per Iosiam Simlerum: Iam verò postremò aliquot mille, cùm priorum tùm nouorum authorum opusculis, ex instructissima Viennensi Austriae Imperatoria Bibliotheca amplificata, per Iohannem Iacobum Frisium Tigurinum, [3rd ed.] (Zurich: Christophorvs Froschovervs, 1583), p. 531, col. 1.

92. Conrad Gesner died in 1565; Josia Simler in 1576.

93. The second edition was apparently published under the direction of Simler in 1574. It was entitled Bibliotheca Institvta et Collecta primvm a Conrado Gesnero, Deinde in Epitomen redacta & nouorum Librorū accessione locupletata, iam, vero postremo recognita, & in duplum post priores editiones aucta, per Iosiam Simlerum Tigurinum, [2nd ed.] (Zurich: Christophorus Froschovervm, 1574). The Sunthaym reference occurs on p. 442, col. 2.

The first complete edition of the catalog appeared between 1545 and 1555. Each volume appeared under a separate title and all four were published by Christoph Froschauer in Zurich. The volumes are: Bibliotheca Vniversalis, sive Catalogus omnium scriptorum locupletissimus, in tribus linguis, Latina, Graeca, & Hebraica [. . .], 1545; Pandectarum sive Partitionem universalium Conradi Gesneri Tigurini, medici & philosophiae professoris, libri X̄X̄Ī, 1548; Partitiones Theologicae, Pandectarum Vniversalium Conradi Gesneri Liber ultimas, 1549; Appendix Bibliothecae Conradi Gesneri, 1555.

94. Conrad Gesner, <u>Pandectarvm</u> [. . .] (Zurich, 1548), fol. 35^V, col. 2.

95. The entries differ only in typeface. The word "Germaniam" is abbreviated in the second edition and not in the third. I have removed the italics in quoting the entry because they vary in the two editions and have no bearing on the statement.

96. Dr. Eheim has done extensive research on Ladislaus Sunthaym. His work on Maximilian's <u>Hofkaplan</u> includes: "Ladislaus Sunthaym: Leben und Werk," Diss. Vienna 1949; "Die älteste Topographie von Österreich," <u>Jahrbuch für Landeskunde von Nieder-Österreich</u>, 33 (1957), 7-25; and "Ladislaus Sunthaym: Ein Historiker aus dem Gelehrtenkreis um Maximilian I.," <u>MIÖG</u>, 67 (1959), 53-91.

97. "Wir glauben uns durch solche Thatsachen die Berechtigung erworben zu haben, auf des Kaisers Anregung auch die Anfänge theoretischer Normirung der Sprache zurückzuführen" (note 40, p. 26).

98. Kluge's use of the title "kaiserliche[r] Kanzler" ("Imperial chancellor") to describe Niclas Ziegler is somewhat mis-leading. The term "Kanzler" is sometimes used loosely in German as a synonym for "Kanzlist," meaning "chancery scribe" or "member of the chancery staff." In this sense it is accurate to describe Ziegler as "der kaiserliche Kanzler," since he did serve for a time on the staff of the Imperial Chancery (<u>Reichskanzlei</u>). He never attained the office of <u>Reichskanzler</u> or <u>Erzkanzler</u> (Imperial Chancellor or Arch-chancellor), however, a position traditionally held by the Archbishop of Mainz. Historians of the German language who present Ziegler simply as "Maximilian's chancellor" or "Maximilians Kanzler" (Bach [note 48], p. 250; Eggers [note 4], p. 143; Waterman [note 55], p. 114, e.g.) fail to make this distinction and imply that Ziegler occupied a more influential position in the chancery than he did. See "The Imperial Archchancellor under Maximilian I" and "The <u>Hofordnung</u> of 1498," chapter 2.

99. Portions of the material on Ziegler presented here and in subsequent chapters are taken from my essay, "An Overdue Revision in the History of Early New High German," <u>DVLG</u>, 55 (1981), 248-77.

100.   Kluge (note 40), p. 27.

101.   Moser (note 13), p. 15.

102.   Bach (note 48), p. 250.

103.   Henzen (note 62), pp. 91, 99; Waterman (note 55), p. 114; Schmidt (note 57), p. 97; Rupprich (note 15), p. 136; Eggers (note 4), p. 143; and Polenz (note 64), p. 76.

104.   Thomas P. Thornton. "Die Schreibgewohnheiten Hans Rieds im Ambraser Heldenbuch," ZDP, 81 (1962), 52-82.

105.   The footnote in the fifth edition (note 42, p. 31, n. 2) that is supposed to give additional information about Niclas Ziegler in fact refers to a passage in Joseph von Aschbach's Geschichte der Wiener Universität (note 82, p. 421, n. 2) concerning Hans Krachenberger.

106.   Heinrich Ulmann, Kaiser Maximilian I., 2 vols. (Stuttgart: Verlag der J. G. Cotta'schen Buchhandlung, 1884-91).

107.   The notes appear on pp. 69 and 817. Kluge must have read this work with great attention as the index did not appear until 1891, when it was published along with the second volume of the biography.

108.   Victor von Kraus, Maximilians I. vertraulicher Briefwechsel mit Sigmund Prüschenk Freiherrn zu Stettenberg (Innsbruck: Verlag der Wagner'schen Universitaets-Buchhandlung, 1875).

109.   Tennant (note 99), pp. 268-69, n. 38.

110.   Tennant (note 99), p. 268, n. 37.

111.   Ulmann (note 106), I, 817.

112.   See Ernst Wülcker, "Luthers Stellung zur kursächsischen Kanzleisprache," Germania, 28 (1883), 195; Socin (note 44), p. 163; Behaghel (note 60), p. 190; Bach (note 48), p. 250; and Waterman (note 55), p. 114.

113.   Otto Behaghel, Die deutsche Sprache, 14th ed. (Halle a. d. Saale: Max Niemeyer Verlag, 1968), p. 40.

114.   Wülcker (note 65), p. 366.

115.   Wülcker (note 112), p. 195.

116.   Socin (note 44), p. 163; Bach (note 48), p. 250; and Waterman (note 55), p. 114.

117. Eggers (note 4), p. 181:

Dem Leseeifer der Reformationszeit kann man freilich
ebenfalls keine unmittelbare Wirkung auf die Sprachent-
wicklung zuschreiben, wohl aber eine mittelbare.
Wenigstens dem aufmerksamen Leser müssen sich gewisse
Sprachmuster einprägen, ein Gefühl für Anlage und
Gliederung deutscher Texte, für wiederkehrende
Wendungen und Ausdrucksweisen, für Satzbau und Wort-
wahl. Auch Unterschiede im Schreibgebrauch können der
Aufmerksamkeit nicht entgehen, und einer Zeit, die das
'gemeine Deutsch' als Ziel erfaßt hat, muß daran gelegen
sein, nicht nur eine gemeinverständliche, sondern auch
eine nach allgemeinen Grundsätzen geregelte Sprache anzu-
streben. Für solches Streben gibt es eine bemerkenswerte
Fülle von Beweisen.

118. Luther (note 1).

119. Paul (note 16), p. 558.

120. Werbow (note 16), p. 53.

121. Johannes Erben, "Luther und die neuhochdeutsche Schriftsprache," in Deutsche Wortgeschichte, ed. Friedrich Maurer and Friedrich Stroh, 2nd ed., I (Berlin: Walter de Gruyter & Co., 1959), 448.

122. Martin Luther, D. Martin Luthers Werke. Kritische
Gesamtausgabe: Tischreden, V (Weimar: Hermann Böhlaus Nachfolger,
1919), 512.

123. Erben (note 121), pp. 446-47.

124. See Eggers (note 4), pp. 153-54, for example.

125. Werbow (note 16), p. 53. In this passage Werbow cites
Carl Franke, Satzlehre, Vol. III of Grundzüge der Schriftsprache
Luthers, 2nd ed. (Halle a. d. Saale: Verlag der Buchhandlung des
Waisenhauses, 1922), p. 380.

126. Günter Feudel, "Luthers Ausspruch über seine Sprache (WA
Tischreden I, 524)—Ideal oder Wirklichkeit?" BGDSL (Halle), 92
(1970), 72.

127. See Fabian Frangk, Ein Cantzley vnd Titel buchlin
(Wittenberg: Nickel Schirlentz, 1531), sig. A 2-3; and Orthographia
(note 70), p. 93.

128. Titel buchlin (note 127), sig. A 2-3; and Orthographia
(note 70), p. 95.

129. Hans Schönsperger the Elder (1481-1523) was an Augsburger who worked for a time as a printer in Nuremberg. He is particularly noted for his edition of the Theuerdank, printed in Nuremberg in 1517. This first edition of the work is supposed to have been prepared under the supervision of Maximilian's chancellor, Melchior Pfintzing, who was also one of the authors of the text. See Constantin Karl Falkenstein, Geschichte der Buchdruckerkunst in ihrer Entstehung und Ausbildung, 2nd ed. (Leipzig: Verlag von B. G. Teubner, 1856), pp. 159-61.

130. See Elaine C. Tennant, "'Vom mangel vnd fähl vnsers A be cees/ im Teutschen lesen,'" Codices manuscripti, 7, No. 3 (1981).

131. See Kluge (note 40), p. 31, for example.

132. Eggers (note 4), p. 184:

Aber wenn auch in der Praxis das Ziel noch keineswegs
erreicht wird, so ist doch hier erstmalig eine Forderung
ausgesprochen, die auf einheitliche Regelung abzielt.
Wenn außerdem die Schrift wiederholt aufgelegt und
andern Orts nachgedruckt wird, so äußert sich darin das
Bedürfnis der Zeit nach Vereinheitlichung des Sprach-
gebrauchs. FRANCK ist kein Sonderling, kein einsamer
Rufer, sondern er findet Gehör und weist Wege, die auch
andere einschlagen.

133. See Tennant (note 130) concerning Johann Kolroß, for example.

CHAPTER 2

134. Jančar (note 63), p. 4.

135. See "The Training of Chancery Personnel" in this chapter.

136. See Moser (note 7), pp. 26-29.

137. Jančar (note 63), p. 41:

Von den übrigen zahlreichen Secretarien, welche in den
Registerbüchern angeführt werden, lässt sich nicht
bestimmen, wo sie zugetheilt waren. Schon damals [um
1515] ist dieser Titel, sowie der eines Rathes
(consiliarius) in manchen Fällen eine blosse Rangs-
bezeichnung geworden für Personen im königlichen
Dienste, deren Thätigkeit in der Kanzlei sich aber
nicht nachweisen lässt und manchmal auch gerade zu
ausgeschlossen ist, z. B. wenn diplomatische Agenten
diesen Titel führen.

138. Harry Bresslau, <u>Handbuch der Urkundenlehre für Deutsch-</u>
<u>land und Italien</u>, 3rd ed., 2 vols. (Berlin: Verlag Walter de Gruyter
& Co., 1958), I, 1-2. "U r k u n d e n nennen wir [. . .] auf-
gezeichnete Erklärungen, die bestimmt sind, als Zeugnisse über
Vorgänge rechtlicher Natur zu dienen" (p. 1).

139. Cf. Heinrich Otto Meisner, <u>Urkunden- und Aktenlehre der</u>
<u>Neuzeit</u>, 2nd ed. (Leipzig: Koehler & Amelang, 1952), pp. 60-85.

140. See Jančar (note 63), pp. 46-47; and Meisner (note 139),
pp. 60-61.

141. Bresslau (note 138), II, 149.

142. Wilhelm Bauer, "Das Register- und Konzeptswesen in der
Reichskanzlei Maximilians I. bis 1502," <u>MIÖG</u>, 26 (1905), 277.

143. Meisner (note 139), p. 64.

144. Moser (note 7), p. 21.

145. In this regard consider Rudolf IV and the so-called
<u>privilegium maius</u>, for example. See Gutkas (note 13), pp. 95-97.

146. Moser (note 7), pp. 21-22.

147. Bresslau (note 138), I, 103.

148. Bauer (note 142), p. 254.

149. Gerhard Seeliger, "Die älteste Ordnung der deutschen
Reichskanzlei. 1494. Oktober 3. Mecheln," <u>ArchZ</u>, 13 (1888), 1-7. The
original <u>Reichskanzleiordnung</u> has been lost, but the text is preserved
in two manuscripts from the second half of the sixteenth century.
Seeliger's edition was done from these. Notation in the text refers
to the section numbers of the Ordinance according to this edition.

150. The titles "Imperial Chancery" and "Court Chancery" are
capitalized in the text when they refer directly to the <u>Reichskanzlei</u>
and <u>Hofkanzlei</u>, respectively. The terms "Imperial chancery" or
"Imperial chanceries" refer to the "kaiserliche Kanzlei" or to the
Imperial chancery system in general.

151. Jančar (note 63), p. 21.

152. Bauer (note 142) cites a case heard before the <u>Reichs-</u>
<u>kammergericht</u> in 1524. It concerned an Imperial fief that was being
held by France. In order for the opposing claims to be evaluated the

court needed to examine chancery documents that Maximilian's senior chancellors had taken with them when they left the chancery. Thus the Räte of the Esslinger Reichsregiment wrote to Archduke Ferdinand and asked that a search be made for the missing documents among the papers of Maximilian and Frederick in Vienna and Innsbruck. The Räte also asked that the investigation include the papers of the former secretaries Stürtzel, Serntein, Ziegler, Renner, etc. or of their estates. Jančar (note 63, p. 15) notes that Maximilian was the founder of an archive in Innsbruck, albeit an incomplete one.

153. It should be remembered that missives in this period were sometimes sent in wrappers, but more often they were simply folded with the message to the inside, sealed with wax, and addressed on the back. See frontispiece.

154. See "Seals" in this chapter and Wilhelm Erben, Die Kaiser- und Königsurkunden des Mittelalters in Deutschland, Frankreich und Italien (1907; rpt. Munich: R. Oldenbourg Verlag, 1967), p. 275.

155. Bauer (note 142), p. 277.

156. It is unfortunate that none of the registers in which these fees were recorded has survived. See Jančar (note 63), pp. 48-49, 62.

157. See Ulmann (note 106), I, 293, 313, 804 ff.

158. Georg Voigt, Enea Silvio de' Piccolomini, als Papst Pius der Zweite, und sein Zeitalter, I (Berlin: Verlag von Georg Reimer, 1856), 278-79.

159. Voigt (note 158), p. 279.

160. Gerhard Seeliger, Erzkanzler und Reichskanzleien: Ein Beitrag zur Geschichte des deutschen Reiches (Innsbruck: Verlag der Wagner'schen Universitäts-Buchhandlung, 1889), pp. 21-25.

161. Seeliger (note 160), pp. 45-46.

162. Seeliger (note 160), p. 49.

163. Seeliger (note 160), p. 56.

164. Seeliger (note 160), p. 57.

165. Seeliger (note 160), p. 52.

166. See Bresslau (note 138), I, 536-37; and Seeliger (note 160), p. 58.

167. Seeliger (note 160), pp. 59-61.

168. Seeliger (note 160), pp. 62-65.

169. Seeliger (note 160), pp. 66-67.

170. Jančar (note 63), p. 7.

171. Jančar (note 63), p. 7:

Bis auf Friedrich III. war die Reichskanzlei die einzige, welche alle Beurkundungsgeschäfte der Herrscher, auch für ihre Erb- und Hauslande besorgte. Seit Frühjahr 1442 wurde eine österreichische Kanzlei für die Erblande Friedrichs abgesondert. Sie hatte besondere Beamte und eigene Beurkundungsformen. Doch halfen sich die Beamten gegenseitig, nur die Expedition war immer getrennt. Schon damals wurde in der österreichischen Kanzlei die Unterfertigungsformel: commissio domini regis (imperatoris) consequent festgehalten, während die Reichskanzlei die Formel: ad mandatum d. r. anwendete. Daneben sind aber auch schon unter Friedrich III. Ansätze zu einer Hofkanzlei vorhanden, indem Urkunden über wichtige Staatsangelegenheiten, als Verträge, Vollmachten udgl. zum grössten Theile, auch wenn sie das Reich betraffen, nicht in der Reichskanzlei, sondern von eigenen Secretären des Kaisers, welche sein Vertrauen besassen, ausgefertigt wurden.

172. See Seeliger (note 160), p. 69; and Bresslau (note 138), I, 531.

173. Seeliger (note 160), p. 70.

174. Seeliger (note 160), pp. 70-72

175. Jančar (note 63), p. 16.

176. Jančar (note 63), p. 13.

177. Jančar (note 63), p. 10:

Die Kanzleigeschäfte aller dieser Behörden [des Regimentes zu Linz, des Hof- oder Kammergerichtes zu Wiener Neustadt, des Hofkammers zu Wien, des Rechenkammers zu Wien, des Hauskammers zu Wien, des Hofrathes zu Wien] leitet der österreichische Kanzler, der dem Hofrathe und dem Regimente angehört. Er besetzt die Kanzlei des Regimentes und des Hofgerichtes. Man sieht, der Name 'österreichische Kanzlei' ist eigentlich ein Sammelname und bezeichnet die unter gemeinsamer Leitung stehenden Hilfsämter der niederösterreichischen Behörden.

178. Jančar (note 63), pp. 8-10.

179. Jančar (note 63), pp. 11-12.

180. See Jančar (note 63), p. 18; and Moser (note 7), p. 14.

181. Jančar (note 63), p. 38.

182. Hermann Wiesflecker, Reichsreform und Kaiserpolitik, Vol. II of Kaiser Maximilian I. (Vienna: Verlag für Geschichte und Politik, 1975), p. 305.

183. Jančar (note 63), p. 20.

> Berthold wollte eben nicht blos Leiter der Kanzlei sein, er fasste seine Stellung bedeutsamer auf. Als ein activer Politiker und Oberhaupt der fürderhin Opposition wollte er die Reichsgeschäfte möglichst unabhängig von den wechselnden und immer unberechenbaren Entschliessungen des Königs machen; daher sein Streben, die Kanzlei als einen wichtigen Theil der Executive dem königlichen Einflusse zu entziehen.

184. Wiesflecker (note 182), pp. 305-07.

185. Seeliger (note 160), pp. 75-76.

186. Kraus (note 108), pp. 107-08.

187. See Wiesflecker (note 182), pp. 306-07.

188. See Bauer (note 142), p. 272; and Jančar (note 63), pp. 20-22.

189. Thomas Fellner, Die österreichische Zentralverwaltung, 2 vols. (Vienna: Adolf Holzhausen, 1907), I, 26.

190. Seeliger (note 160), pp. 83-84.

191. Jančar (note 63), pp. 23-24.

192. Seeliger (note 160), pp. 85, 212-13.

193. All references to the 1498 ordinances are to the texts as they appear in the second volume of Fellner's Zentralverwaltung (note 189), including the variant readings, which are of particular interest with regard to the Hofordnung (II, 6-16).

194. See Fellner (note 189).

195. The dating of this fragment has been the subject of considerable discussion. Neither Seeliger (note 160, pp. 80, 193) nor Jančar (note 63, pp. 33-34) agrees that the Instruktion was issued along with the Hofordnung in February 1498. Jančar, emphasizing that the internal procedures prescribed in the fragment differ from

those in the February ordinance and that the fragment still stresses separation of Reich and Erblande affairs, dates the text between 1495 and 1496. Fellner, however, argues convincingly that the Instruktion was conceived in conjunction with the Reichskanzleiordnung in September 1498 (note 189, II, 50-51).

196. Fellner (note 189), II, 6-16.

197. Fellner (note 189), II, 7-8.

198. Despite his professed desire to be consulted only in matters of the greatest importance, Maximilian is known to have concerned himself regularly with the routine business of his artists and scribes. This was sometimes a source of irritation to his staff. In a letter from Cyprian Serntein to Paul von Liechtenstain dated 3 April 1509, the Chancellor complains that the Emperor insists on "assigning, reviewing, and correcting everything himself" ("alle ding selbst angeben durchsehen und corrigiren"; Kraus [note 108], p. 121) in the Chancery. The artists and ghostwriters for his literary projects had similar difficulties. See Tennant (note 99), p. 257, n. 17.

199. Fellner (note 189), II, 9-10.

200. Wiesflecker (note 182), pp. 307-08.

201. Ulmann (note 106), I, 826-27:

Eine Reihe von Anordnungen aus der nächsten Zeit beweist das Inslebentreten der reformirten Regimentsordnung. Während des Reichstags in Freiburg fungirt der Hofrath neben den vom König mit 'etlichen besonderen Räthen' gepflogenen Berathschlagungen. Als aber im Spätherbst Friedrich von Sachsen halb und halb im Zorn den Hof des Königs verließ, muß auch die Hofrathsordnung allmählich in Abgang gekommen sein.

202. Fellner (note 189), II, 10-11.

203. Fellner (note 189), II, 11:

[21.] Item das eilft sol haben ein slössel, wol vermacht. Darein sol man legen das sigel und secret verspert, und denselben slüssel sol haben der canzler oder obrist secretari. Und der gros kasten, darinne die cleinen kestlin steen, sol haben vier gutte slösser, das eins nicht sei als das ander; zu denselben slossen sol haben der genannt herzog Friderich zu Sachsen einen slüssel an unserer statt, der hofmeister den andern und der hofmarschalh den dritten und der canzler oder

obrister secretari den vierten slüssel zum sigeltruhelin;
und sol solh truhen nit geoffent werden dann in gegen-
würtickeit der merer teil der rete.

204. See "Seals" in this chapter.

205. Jančar (note 63), p. 22.

206. Jančar (note 63), p. 50.

207. Fellner (note 189), II, 48-49.

208. Fellner (note 189), II, 49.

[1.] Von erst sollen dheinerlei brieve von unsern als
rhömischen königs wegen in das hailig reich geschrieben
werden dann in unser romischen canzlei, so itz der
erwirdig Berchtold erzbishove zu Meintz des hailgen
römischen reichs in Germanien erzcanzler unser lieber
neve und churfürst in verwesung hat [. . .].

209. Fellner (note 189), II, 49, [2.]-[6.].

210. See note 195.

211. Fellner (note 189), II, 51.

212. Fellner (note 189), II, 52.

213. Fellner (note 189), II, 53-54.

214. These procedures applied only to official documents
originating in the Chancery. The private correspondence of the
secretaries was not, of course, subject to these controls; neither
were many of the internal communications between members of the
Chancery.

215. See note 171.

216. Jančar (note 63), pp. 55-56.

217. Jančar (note 63), p. 33.

218. Fellner (note 189), II, 51.

219. Consider, for example, the document dated 20 September
1498, Innsbruck, which Rudolf Horber ("Hawscamerer zu innsprugk")
sealed with his own seal on behalf of Niclas Ziegler. Vienna, HHSA,
Allgemeine Urkundenreihe.

220. For example, the fair copy of a diplomatic mandate dated
17 March 1503, Antwerp, shows Niclas Ziegler's formal signature in
this position. Vienna, HHSA, Maximiliana 7b/1, fol. 63.

221. An engrossed mandate dated 7 January 1503, Wesel, shows both Niclas Ziegler's formal signature at the lower right of the plica and the King's visa "p reg p s" at the upper left. Vienna, HHSA, Maximiliana 7b/1, fol. 1.

222. Many scholars resolve this notation "per regem per se." In the abbreviation, however, the two p's are written differently. The first is crossed in the manner commonly used to represent "per" (see A. Cappelli, Dizionario di Abbreviature, 1973, pp. 256-57); the stroke used to cross the letter is a second line and not a continuation of the character itself. The second p shows a line that extends from the character itself, dropping downward to the left of the stem of the p and forming a loop. This second form may also be resolved "per" but more frequently represents "pro" (Capelli, loc. cit.). Because the two p's are written differently in the notation, I take them to indicate different words; thus I resolve the second abbreviation as "pro" throughout my text except in quoted material. Jančar explains that this form of Maximilian's handwritten endorsement developed from the formula "per regem fridericus etc.," which was used by his father; the notation "p reg p s" was used throughout Maximilian's reign (note 63, p. 57).

223. Burkhard Seuffert, Drei Register aus den Jahren 1478-1519 (Innsbruck: Universitäts-Verlag Wagner, 1934), pp. 344-45.

224. A treaty between Maximilian and Ulrich of Württemberg dated 6 May 1510 shows the Emperor's "great signature" along with those of Ulrich and Chancellor Serntein; Vienna, HHSA, Allgemeine Urkundenreihe. On an official letter to the Abbess of Goss dated 25 November 1496, Pontremoli, Maximilian's abbreviated manu propria signature, "M. R. Kunig etc., p m p," appears as the only chancery endorsement; Vienna, HHSA, Allgemeine Urkundenreihe.

225. See note 224.

226. This work is frequently cited, "Friedrich Wilhelm Cosmann, Von dem großen Namenshandzeichen Maximilians I., [Diss.] Mainz 1786, n.p.," according to the name of its Defensor (Cosmann), which appears on the title page of the work. The study is Franck's,

however, and it is preserved as MS. 14484 in the Österreichische Nationalbibliothek in Vienna (Seuffert [note 223], p. 346, n. 34).

227.   See note 224.

228.   See Seuffert (note 223), p. 345. For further information concerning the Imperial monograms and their use see Berthold Sutter's "Die deutschen Herrschermonogramme nach dem Interregnum: Ein Beitrag zur Diplomatik des Spätmittelalters," in Festschrift Julius Franz Schütz, ed. Berthold Sutter (Graz: Hermann Böhlaus Nachfolger, 1954), pp. 246-314. This article includes illustrations of the monograms of Frederick III and Maximilian I.

229.   For additional information on Maximilian's Stempel-schneider and their activities, see Helmut Jungwirth "Münzen und Medaillen Maximilians I.," in Ausstellung Maximilian I. Innsbruck, ed. Erich Egg (Innsbruck: Verlagsanstalt Tyrolia, 1969), p. 66.

230.   Seuffert (note 223), pp. 346-48. Jančar (note 63, pp. 57-58) disputes the idea that a stamp was used and suggests a stencil or template ("Schablone") instead. At least some of the documents mentioned by Seuffert, however, show definite embossing, indicating that stamps were used. This is particularly apparent in the case of the per Cesarem stamp on a document dated 1 May 1518, in which Maximilian grants the Abbess and Convent Zum Heiligen Geist an annual allowance; Vienna, HHSA, Allgemeine Urkundenreihe.

231.   These are Seuffert's resolutions of the abbreviations on the stamps; see note 222. Seuffert's Tafel 48 is a photograph of the stamp "$\overset{e}{u}$ per Cesarem" as it appears on a manuscript dated 24 July 1516; Vienna, HHSA.

232.   Seuffert (note 223), pp. 345-48.

233.   Hans Moser (note 7, pp. 205-07) makes similar observations, not about endorsements, but about the various scripts in which individual scribes penned different kinds of texts.

234.   Niclas Ziegler, for example, used his noncalligraphic signature to endorse the Publikationsmandat circulated throughout Germany with the 1521 Edict of Worms. See Tennant (note 99), p. 273, n. 41.

235. Franz-Heinz Hye, "Die Siegel Maximilians I. von 1486 bis
1519, ihre historisch-politische und ihre kanzleigeschichtliche
Bedeutung," NumZ, 82 (1967), 86-107. This article provides the most
complete list and description now available of the official Habsburg
seals used during Maximilian's reign. It also discusses briefly the
history of each seal and the sorts of documents on which it has been
found. The illustrative table of newly discovered seals accompanying
Hye's text completes the series of Habsburg seals pictured in vols. 3
and 4 of Otto Posse's Die Siegel der deutschen Kaiser und Könige
(Dresden: Verlag von Wilhelm Baensch, 1909-13).

236. The Secretsiegel used in 1491-92 was a ring seal or
signet; Maximilian's secreth described in the Hofordnung of 1498 was
not. See Jančar (note 63), pp. 55-56.

237. Hye (note 235), pp. 96-97, 102.

238. The following manuscripts, like the Urkunde mentioned in
note 219, document this flexible usage of seals in Maximilian's chancery system: 7 September 1499 Reutlingen, Innsbruck, TLA,
Maximiliana 1/41, fol. 293; 15 August 1500 Augsburg, Vienna, HHSA,
Allgemeine Urkundenreihe; and 7 March 1501 Linz, Vienna, Hofkammer-
archiv, Gedenkbuch I, p. 231, fol. 113^{V}.

239. See note 238, 7 September 1499 Reutlingen.

240. See note 219, and Jančar (note 63), pp. 49, 56.

241. Der Weißkunig, ed. Alwin Schultz, JbKhS, Vol. 6, Vienna,
1888, p. 70.

242. Cf. note 198.

243. Der Weißkunig (note 241), p. 70:

Auf ein zeit betrachtet der alt weiß kunig der welt
lauf und befand durch sein regirung, wo ein mechtiger
kunig in dem canzler ampt und in dem secretari ampt
nit erfaren und kundig were, das demselben kunig je
zu zeiten nachtail daraus erwuechsen Nemlichen aus
den ursachen, das ein kunig nit albegen sein gemuet
offenwaren und auch sein regirung und sein vertrawen
in ain ampt oder person setzen solle; es ist genueg
davon gemeldt. Aus sölicher bewegung nam der alt
weiß kunig seinen sun ain zeit zu ime und prauchet
ine mit der schreiberey, was dann ainem canzler und

secretari zugehöret, das dann aines jeden kunigs maist
regirung ist, dardurch er sich möcht erkunden den grund
der regirung und erkennen lernen die aigennutzign. Der
alt weiß kunig prauchet ine in sonderhait vast darynnen,
und der sun was ganz vleyssig, und in kurzer zeit begriff
er die haupt artikl: darab het der vater ein sonderliche
grosse frewd. Und auf ain zeit sprach der vater zu ime:
'sun versteestu aber den grund der schriftlichen regirung?'
Der sun gab dem vater die antwurt: 'welher kunig in ain
person sein vertrawen setzt, und hat in seiner handlung
mit seiner schönen red bei ime gelauben, derselb und nit
der kunig regirt. Welher kunig die unwarhaftigen und
aigennutzig nit erkennt, demselben kunig wird sein gelt
und reich in vil tail getailt. Welher kunig die
warhaftigen und die in der rechten eer lebn nit lieb hat,
derselb kunig ist ein verzerer seins volks und ein
austilger der gerechtigkait.' Der Vater was diser red
gar fro, das sein sun den grund der regirung verstund
[. . .].

244. Regrettably Maximilian was unable to put into practice
the principle of "government through the chancery" that he understood
so well in theory. In many instances it was indeed the <u>Kanzlisten</u>
and not the Emperor who ruled. The bitter complaints of several contemporary observers who were unable to get through the "hedge"
("Hecke") of secretaries to Maximilian himself still survive. See,
for example, Ulmann (note 106), I, 293, 804 ff.

245. Jančar (note 63), p. 38.

246. See Peter Krendl, "Über Hosenbandorden, 'Feder' und
andere burgundische Kleinodien Karls des Kühnen," <u>ZHVSteierm</u>, 72
(1981), 13 ff.

247. See Moser (note 7), pp. 36-37.

248. This office should not be confused with that of the same
title later held by Niclas Ziegler.

249. Bresslau (note 138), I, 527-34.

250. Walter Höflechner, "Beiträge zur Geschichte der Diplomatie und des Gesandtschaftswesen unter Maximilian I. 1490-1500,"
Diss. Graz 1967. Höflechner shows that diplomatic activity was
highly organized and stratified during Maximilian's reign, but that
it could not yet be thought of as a distinct branch of government.

251. Consider Ziegler's letter to Serntein concerning the chancery seal (quoted under "Seals" above), for example. Also see Christa Kohlweg, "Die Brüder Ziegler im Dienste Kaiser Maximilians," Diss. Graz 1978, pp. 40 ff. ("Das Rankespiel am Hofe König Maximilians").

252. Heinz Gollwitzer, "Zur Geschichte der Diplomatie im Zeitalter Maximilians I.," HJb, 74 (1955), 189-99; Eysenreich is quoted on p. 194, n. 10.

253. Consider Ladislaus Sunthaym, for example.

254. See note 137; and Gollwitzer (note 252), p. 189.

255. One member of Maximilian's entourage who functioned as a "neighborhood diplomat" was Hofkanzler Conrad Stürtzel, whose fief was near the lands of the Swiss Confederation (Gollwitzer [note 252], p. 190).

256. Gollwitzer (note 252), pp. 189-90, 195.

257. See Wiesflecker (note 182), p. 306. The use of this double title persisted until the end of Maximilian's Imperial reign. Correspondence to Chancellor Serntein was addressed using both titles. Consider, for example, a letter dated 9 June 1516 (TLA, Maximiliana XIV/1516/2, fol. 58) addressed to "Zipprian von Serntein, vnnserm hof vnnd Tirolischen Canntzler."

258. Victor von Kraus, "Itinerarium Maximiliani I. 1508-1518: Mit einleitenden Bemerkungen über das Kanzleiwesen Maximilians I.," AÖG, 87 (1899), 229-318. Maximilian's own itinerary sometimes differed from that of his traveling chancery members. Kraus shows that in some of these instances the distances between their locations were less than a day's ride and that both parties could have ended up at the same point on a given day despite the locations indicated on their separate documents (p. 267). The locations given in the colophons of the manuscripts are the places where the texts were actually penned. Thus it is possible, even in the case of documents that were prepared at the spoken command of Maximilian, that the copyist and the Emperor were in different places when the texts were engrossed.

259.   Sigmund Adler, Die Organisation der Centralverwaltung unter Kaiser Maximilian I. (Leipzig: Verlag von Duncker & Humblot, 1886), p. 62.

260.   Adler (note 259), pp. 65-69. See esp. p. 69:

Diese Nachrichten beweisen deutlich, daß von einem festen Sitze des Hofrathes keine Rede war, während andererseits anzunehmen ist, daß die Mitglieder nicht bloß fallweise sondern ständig ernannt waren.

261.   See Robert Peter Ebert, "Social and Stylistic Variation in Early New High German Word Order: The Sentence Frame ('Satzrahmen')," BGDSL, 102 (1980), 361, 387; and Keller (note 12), p. 342.

262.   Carl Wehmer, "Die Schreibmeisterblätter des späten Mittelalters," in Miscellanea Giovanni Mercati, Vol. VI, Studi e Testi 126, Vatican City, 1946, pp. 152-53.

263.   Klaus Leder, "Nürnbergs Schulwesen an der Wende vom Mittelalter zur Neuzeit," in Albrecht Dürers Umwelt (Nuremberg: Selbstverlag des Vereins für Geschichte der Stadt Nürnberg, 1971), p. 30.

264.   See Wehmer (note 262), p. 152; and James Westfall Thompson, The Literacy of the Laity in the Middle Ages, University of California Publications in Education, Vol. 9, Berkeley, 1939, p. 71.

265.   S. H. Steinberg, "Medieval Writing-Masters," The Library, 4th ser., 22 (1941), 3-4.

266.   Wehmer (note 262), p. 153.

267.   Leder (note 263), p. 33.

268.   Steinberg (note 265), pp. 3-4.

269.   Herrad Spilling, "Schreibkünste des späten Mittelalters," Codices manuscripti, 4 (1978), 97-119.

270.   See Spilling (note 269), p. 98; and Carl Wehmer, "Schreibmeister von einst," Archiv für Buchgewerbe und Gebrauchsgraphik, 76 (1939), 37-58.

271.   Steinberg (note 265), p. 11

272.   Erich Straßner, Graphemsystem und Wortkonstituenz, Hermaea, Germanistische Forschungen, n.s., Vol. 39, Tübingen, 1977, p. 18.

273. Spilling (note 269), p. 103.

274. See Spilling (note 269), p. 103; Ebert (note 261), p. 362; and Straßner (note 272), p. 19, concerning the education of girls and women.

275. Spilling (note 269), pp. 103-06.

276. Wehmer (note 262), p. 153.

277. Spilling (note 269), pp. 103-05.

278. Steinberg (note 265), p. 2.

279. Spilling (note 269), p. 99.

280. Spilling (note 269), p. 105.

281. Strepel's advertisement is translated in this way by Steinberg (note 265), p. 10:

> To all scholars who wish to learn to write well in a
> short time! Come ye to Hermann Strepel who wish to be
> quickly instructed in it. For there is the source of
> learning that does not dry up in winter nor in summer.
> How useful and how necessary is the glorious knowledge
> of learning. It is the crowned science the help of which
> is wanted by the upper, middle, and lower classes. It
> bears upon the literary diction of the New and Old Testa-
> ments, the Canon and Civil Laws, and all literature. It
> is seated on the chair of honour in the courts and
> palaces of kings, potentates, and princes, and there
> procures most honourable places to its lovers and pupils.
> Let them come to me who want to be embraced by it: for
> I shall open to them the secrets of its sweetness as
> best as I can, in such a way that they may become good
> scribes in a short time, with the help of God's grace.
> For the dullness of any work is softened by diligence.

282. Brune's advertising placard is quoted by Steinberg (note 265), p. 19:

> Wer yemandes der noch rechter außgemeßener kunst und art
> lernen wolde [schreyben], geleichen nach den rechten
> regulen der orthographien text ader nottel subtil[er art]
> cancelleysch ader sußt von mancherley namhafftigen notteln
> igliche mit irer und[irscheyd und] allerley ercze auß der
> federn schreyben unde uff gutte subtile art illuminiren
> unde [. . ., kom]me zu Johanni Brune wonhafftig zcu dem
> bunten lawen bey sante Maria Magd[alenen, und wird] eyn
> iglicher gutlich undirweyseth.

283. See Leder (note 263), p. 34; Straßner (note 272), p. 19; and Ebert (note 261), p. 361.

284. Spilling (note 269), p. 99.

285. My remarks about Neudörffer's handbook are based on an examination of a microfilm of his Anweysung einer gemeinen handschrift (that is, Ein gute Ordnung vnd Kurtze vnterricht der furnemsten grunde aus denen die Jungen Zierlichs schreybens begirlich mit besonderer Kunst und behendigkeyt vnterricht vnd geůbt mogē werden). The work, which comprises 118 folios, is usually dated 1538, although it contains plates dated as late as 1543 (e.g., fol. 101). For a visual analysis of the most salient features of Neudörffer's Anweysung and the educational tradition from which it emerged, see Michael Baxandall, The Limewood Sculptors of Renaissance Germany (New Haven: Yale University Press, 1980), pp. 145-49.

286. Straßner (note 272), p. 19:

> Der Schreibunterricht beginnt mit praktischen Anweisungen
> über die Wahl der Feder, ihre Zubereitung und die richtige
> Körperhaltung. Dann wird mittels der 'Zerstreuungen' die
> Entwicklung der Buchstaben gezeigt und gelehrt. Es folgen
> Kopierübungen, vor allem nach Briefmustern an Fürsten und
> Städte, Urkunden, Privilegien und Verträge. Auf diese
> Weise werden die Schüler mit der Praxis der Kanzlei, mit
> den ständig wiederkehrenden formelhaften Wendungen, aber
> auch mit der deutschen Grammatik und dem deutschen Stil
> vertraut. Daneben wird Buchhaltung und Rechnen vor allem
> mit dem Rechenbrett gelehrt.

287. The dating of this text is approximate. See Spilling (note 269), p. 104.

288. Consider Fabian Frangk's Titel buchlin (note 127), for example. This "do-it-yourself" manual is intended to teach the beginning penmen of Frangk's native region the correct formal aspects of chancery correspondence for that area.

289. Der Weißkunig (note 241), p. 70:

> Als derselb jung weiß kunig zu seinen jaren und in sein
> regirung kam, da het er gar vil secretari, den er dann
> allen genug zu schaffen gab, und zoch dieselben secre-
> tarien albegen von jugent nach seinem willen auf.

290. David Schönherr, "Über Marx Treytz-Saurwein, Geheimschreiber K. Maximilians I., dessen Heimath u. Familie," AÖG, 48 (1872), 361.

291. According to the <u>Hofordnung</u> of 1498, Chancery drafts were to be saved so that they might be bound and deposited every six months (Jančar [note 63], pp. 34-35).

292. See note 198.

293. See frontispiece, <u>Der Weißkunig</u> (note 241), p. 69 ("Die geschicklicheit des jungen w[eißen] k[unigs] in angebung durch seine eynige person in mangerley sprachen vil seinen secretarien auf einmal"); and p. 75 ("Den lust und die geschicklicheit, so er in angebung des gemelds gehabt, und bey seinen ingeni die pesserung desselben").

CHAPTER 3

294. Frangk (note 70), p. 95.

REcht deutsch schreiben aber/ wird hie nicht genohmen/
odder verstanden/ als Rein höflich deutsch/ mit geschmück-
ten verblümbten worten/ ordentlich vnd artigk nach dem
synn odder meinung eines jdlichen dings/ von sich
schreiben (Welches mehr der redmas vnd Rethoriken
zustendig/ vnd der halben jnn der Redkündiger schule
gehörig/ da wirs auch bleiben lassen) Sondern/ Wenn ein
jdlich wort/ mit gebürlichen buchstaben ausgedruckt (das
ist) recht vnd rein geschrieben wird/ also/ das kein
buchstab müssig/ odder zuuiel noch zu wenig/ Auch nicht an
stat des andern gesetzt nach versetzt Dar zu nichts
frembdes/ abgethanes/ so einen missestant oder ver-
finsterung geberen möcht eingefürt werd/ Welchs sonst die
Latiner vnd Krichen/ Orthographiam/ wir aber/ Recht buchstäbig Deutsch schreiben/ nennen wollen. [. . .] Weil nuh
ein jdlich wort mit gebürlichen buchstaben sol ausgedruckt
vnd geschrieben werden/ So mus man die buchstaben vorhin
wol wissen zeunderschieden.

295. Frangk (note 70), p. 93.

Denn so wir ansehen den emssigen vleis/ so die Latiner
allein/ jnn jrer zungen fürgewandt/ vnd vnsern vnuleis/
bey der vnsern/ da gegen stellen/ solten wir billich
schamrot werden/ das wir so gantz ablessig vnd sewmig
sein/ Vnser edle sprach so vnwert vnd verachtlich halten/
Weil sie dennach jhe so lustig nützlich vnd tapffer jnn
jrer red mass/ als jndert ein andere befunden wird/ Vns
vngelerten Layen auch (vnd die wir der heuptsprachen
nicht geübt nach kündig) so viel an jr/ als jndert einer
andern gelegen ist/ Weil wir dieselben heubt sprachen
allzugleich nicht erlangen noch erlernen mögen/ Vnd so

viel Edler nützbarlicher bücher vnd künste jnns deutsche
zebringen vnd zuuerdolmetschen sein/ die vns/ vber den
lust vnd nutz zum teil auch/ zewissen hoch von nöten
weeren.

296. See note 282.

297. Valentin Ickelsamer, Teutsche Grammatica, in Müller's
Quellenschriften (note 70), p. 142.

298. See Müller (note 70), p. 142, nn. 139-40.

299. Many of the most significant of these works, including
Ickelsamer's Die rechte weis auffs kürtzist lesen zu lernen (1527,
1534) and his Teutsche Grammatica (1534), Johann Kolroß' Enchiridion
(1530), Fabian Frangk's Orthographia (1531), Peter Jordan's Leyen-
schul (1533), Johann Elias Meichßner's Handbüchlin (1538), and
Ortholph Fuchßperger's Leeßkonst (1542), are reprinted with extensive
commentary in Müller's Quellenschriften (note 70).

300. Consider, for example, Ortholph Fuchßperger's Leeßkonst
(1542), in which the author tells his student that each letter has a
shape, a sound, and a designation, but does not explain to him what
the significance of these features is or how they relate to each
other. See Müller (note 70), pp. 171-72.

301. Moser (note 7), pp. 4, 54, 58.

302. In their reviews of Die Kanzlei Kaiser Maximilians I.,
Paul Roberge (MGS, 6 [1980], 153-59) and Erich Straßner (BGDSL, 102
[1980], 76-79) allow their criticism of what they find to be methodological difficulties in Moser's study to overshadow its significant
factual contribution to ENHG research. Thus far only Emil Skála in
his brief review (Germanistik, 19 [1978], 294) and Gerhard Kettmann
in his more detailed assessment (DLZ, 102 [1981], cols. 723-25) have
accorded Moser's investigation the praise it deserves.

303. Hans Moser, "Zur Kanzlei Kaiser Maximilians I.:
Graphematik eines Schreibusus," BGDSL (Halle), 99 (1978), 36:

> Die Orientierung an einem mittelhochdt. oder althochdt.
> Bezugssystem wäre unökonomisch, vor allem aber dem
> Gegenstand selbst nur grob angepaßt: dem Schreibteil-
> nehmer der Zeit waren diese Bezugssysteme fremd, er
> orientierte sich an einem zwar historisch bedingten.
> aber synchron verstandenen Regelsystem.

304. Moser (note 7), p. 55.

305. Wolfgang Fleischer, <u>Strukturelle Untersuchungen zur</u>
<u>Geschichte des Neuhochdeutschen</u>, Sitzungsberichte der Sächsischen
Akademie der Wissenschaften zu Leipzig, Philologisch-historische
Klasse, Vol. 112, No. 6, Berlin, 1966, p. 12.

306. Moser (note 7), p. 55.

307. Roberge (note 302), pp. 155-56.

308. Moser (note 7), pp. 85-86.

309. "Im U n t e r s u c h u n g s v e r f a h r e n ist
deshalb erstes Indiz der graphemischen Geltung von Zeichen die dis-
tinktive Funktion auf der Schreibebene selbst" (note 7, p. 57); also
see Moser (note 7), pp. 57-58; (note 303), p. 38.

310. Herbert Penzl, <u>Lautsystem und Lautwandel in den althoch-</u>
<u>deutschen Dialekten</u> (Munich: Max Hueber Verlag, 1971), p. 15:

> Wir finden in jeder genügend durch Texte belegten und
> bekannten Sprache Laute, Formelemente (Morpheme), ferner
> Verbindungen dieser Elemente zu größeren Einheiten, die
> wir als Wörter, Wortgruppen, Sätze, Satzverbindungen
> bezeichnen. Die historische Sprachwissenschaft beschreibt
> diese Sprachlaute, Morpheme, Wortschatzeinheiten, syntak-
> tischen Gebilde nichtzeitgenössischer Sprachstufen.
> Selbst wenn die Beschreibung synchronisch bleibt, ist aber
> stets ein diachronisch definierbares Realitätsprinzip
> wirksam. Wir sprechen nur dann von historischer Lautlehre,
> historischer Formenlehre (Morphologie), historischer
> Syntax, historischer Lexikologie (Wortschatzkunde), wenn
> der Wandel, die Entwicklung oder der Ursprung entweder
> die Kriterien für die synchronische Beschreibung abgeben
> oder wenn die Darstellung überhaupt diachronisch ist.

311. This debate has centered on the methods used to determine
graphemes. Of the Germanic linguists conducting graphemic research in
the last twenty years, Ilpo Tapani Piirainen in his <u>Graphematische</u>
<u>Untersuchungen zum Frühneuhochdeutschen</u> (Studia Linguistica Germanica,
Vol. I; Berlin, 1968) has made the most rigorous attempt to develop a
method in which graphemes are determined without reference to
phonetic or phonemic parallels. His intention is to separate the
purely graphemic phase of textual analysis from those that are not
directly related to graphemics ("nicht-graphemgebunden") and establish graphemic research on a more objective, exact (i.e., statistical),

and reliable scientific basis (p. 20). He opposes the method of Karl
Lachmann and his twentieth-century successors, who, he claims, ignore
the graphemic level as a system and proceed directly to present the
so-called phonetic values of the text (p. 21). In the statement that
follows, Piirainen explains the advantages for historical linguistics
of a non-phonemically-based graphemics. This orientation has provided the theoretical premise for critiques of more recent phonemi-
cally-based graphemic studies (consider the reviews by Roberge and
Straßner [note 302], for example), but it has not resulted in a
significant methodological shift among researchers who analyze written texts that are, after all, reflections of phonetic and phonemic
systems.

> So sehr die historische Sprachwissenschaft auch die
> Diachronie betont, kann die Graphematik darüber hinaus
> ermöglichen, Vergleiche zwischen zwei Texten durch-
> zuführen, die weder zeitlich, räumlich noch in irgend
> einer anderen Weise miteinander zusammenhängen. Ist
> das graphematische System der beiden Texte gleich
> dargestellt, so ist es irrelevant, wann, wo und wie die
> Texte entstanden sind. Wichtig ist allein, was in dem
> einen Text den Erscheinungen in dem anderen entspricht
> bzw. nicht entspricht. Würde dieses nicht auf der Basis
> der Graphematik, sondern mit abgeleiteten phonematischen
> Werten geschehen, so wäre eine solche Forschung nicht
> mehr objektiv und als wissenschaftliche Arbeit unbrauchbar.
> (p. 24)

312. See Moser (note 303), p. 40.

313. Moser (note 7), p. 58; (note 303), p. 38. This diagram,
which appears to present the development of graphemes, is somewhat
confusing. The variants shown for the MHG and ENHG periods are characteristic of their respective contemporary writing systems, whether
or not they are accurate phonetic spellings of the acoustic values
they were intended to represent (one suspects, for example, that the
ei written in Bavaria was pronounced [ɛi] and not [ei] in that region
even during the MHG period); the variants shown for the modern
period, however, are essentially phonetic spellings, which are found
regularly only in the orthographies of such dialect poets as Hans
Kloepfer; they are not characteristic of the hochdeutsche Rechtschreibung that is the dominant writing system in Bavaria today,

where the fit between the standard orthography and the Bavarian
sounds it represents is now even worse than it was in the MHG period.

314. In considering Moser's findings I use his notational conventions: /slashes/ to indicate phonemes; <angle brackets> to indicate graphemes; a hyphen (-) to indicate oppositions; a tilde (∿) to
indicate neutralizations; and an arrow (→) to indicate the direction
in which an opposition is suspended. Opposing arrows (← →) indicate
that an opposition may be suspended in either direction. A broken
arrow (- →) indicates that the regular suspension of an opposition
only occurs in specific positions. In the text underlining is used
to cite forms as they appear in the manuscripts. In the manuscript
sample (appendix 2) underlining is used to distinguish my resolutions
of scribal abbreviations from the alphabetic spellings otherwise written by the scribes. When citing forms from my own transcriptions in
the text, I preserve the vocalic markers as they appear in the manuscripts (° is used for the frequent u̲-hook) but categorize the forms
according to Moser's graphemic designations. For further explanation
of my transcriptional practices, see appendix 2.

315. Moser (note 7), pp. 59-60.

316. Moser (note 7), pp. 62-63, 66-68. Moser refers here to
the independent Reichskanzlei under Berthold von Mainz; the Reichskanzlei as it had existed under Frederick III (see chapter 2) continued largely unchanged until 1494.

317. These "doubles" are not reproduced in Moser's volume of
texts.

318. Moser (note 7), pp. 63-65, 70-83, 198.

319. Moser (note 303).

320. Moser (note 7), p. 85:

Solche diakritische Zeichen wurden allerdings von
vornherein weggelassen, wenn ihre graphemische Irrele-
vanz feststand: z.B. über y̲, ay̲, ey̲, y̲e, über dem u̲/w̲
von au̲, aw̲, eu̲, ew̲. Sie sind in diesem Fall als ver-
schiedene Typen eines Typems zu rechnen, das nur als
e i n e Variant angeführt werden muß.

321. Moser (note 7), pp. 85-86, 106.

322. Moser (note 7), p. 136; (note 303), p. 40. This diagram and figure 3 present the general features of the Habsburg chancery orthography between 1490 and 1493. The relationships between the graphemes and their variants indicate dominant tendencies of the   . chancery writing system. As Moser is careful to show in his detailed development of this characterization, however, there are exceptions— in some cases isolated, in others frequent—to most of the patterns of usage indicated here. For Moser's discussion of individual graph- emes see note 7, pp. 87-135.

323. Moser (note 303), pp. 40-41.

324. Moser (note 303), p. 41.

325. Moser (note 303), p. 41.

326. Moser (note 303), p. 42.

327. Moser (note 7), p. 139; (note 303), p. 42.

328. Moser (note 303), p. 43.

329. Moser (note 303), p. 43.

330. Moser (note 303), p. 44.

331. Moser (note 303), pp. 44-45.

332. Moser (note 303), p. 45.

333. Moser (note 7), pp. 160-63.

334. Moser (note 303), p. 45.

335. Moser (note 303), p. 46.

336. See Fleischer (note 305).

337. See note 310.

338. Penzl (note 310), pp. 14-19, 31. Also see Penzl's "Althochdeutsch /f/ und die Methoden der Lautbestimmung," ZMF, 31 (1964), 289.

339. Penzl (note 310), pp. 31-40.

340. Penzl (note 310), p. 14:

Die stetige Rücksichtnahme auf die Tatsachen der historischen Vergangenheit der Sprache, soweit sie erkennbar sind, charakterisiert die synchronische Beschreibung in der historischen Sprachwissenschaft. Eine philologisch genaue Interpretation der Texte,

die das einschlägige sprachliche, wirklich 'reale'
Material darstellen, ist dabei nicht nur eine
wertvolle Hilfe, sondern geradezu die Vorbedingung
für die synchronische Analyse.

341. Penzl (note 310), p. 35.

342. Roberge (note 302), pp. 156-57.

343. Straßner (note 302), p. 77.

344. Even Piirainen, who argues explicitly for the determination of graphemes without reference to phonetic and phonemic parallels, begins his study with an undescribed "preanalytic phase" ("präanalytische Phase") in which he considers each graph to decide whether it is "functionally relevant" ("funktionell relevant") by itself or in combination with other graphs as a grapheme or variant (note 311, p. 20). He does not indicate on what non-phonetic, non-phonemic basis he makes these decisions·so fundamental to the remainder of his investigation. And later in his introduction, after stating that his non-phonemically-based graphemic method will permit the comparison of any two texts, regardless of their historical relationship to each other, Piirainen nevertheless explains that he will compare the graphemic system he develops for the writings of Hans Krafft to "'Normal Middle High German'" ("das 'Normal-Mhd.'") as if the latter actually represented the MHG graphemes and even though it is based on phonemic values (note 311, pp. 24-25). Thus despite his theoretical protestations to the contrary, phonemic considerations seem to have intruded themselves into Piirainen's graphemic study at these two critical junctures.

345. See Tennant (note 130), pp. 74-91.

346. Moser (note 7), pp. 87-88.

347. See Tennant (note 130), pp. 89-91.

348. Roberge (note 302), p. 156.

349. See Moser (note 7), p. 191; and Hans Ried's copy of the Waldauf'scher Stiftbrief (appendix 2:[4]).

350. Roberge (note 302), pp. 156-57.

351. Moser (note 303), p. 46.

352. Moser (note 303), p. 47.

353. Moser (note 303), pp. 47-48.

354. Moser (note 304), p. 49. Although the individual scribes wrote their personal orthographies without much alteration, except in the level of formality, for all chancery purposes, Moser notes that Chancellor Serntein used the u-hook consistently as an umlaut marker in letters but not in drafts.

355. Moser (note 7), pp. 9, 40; (note 303), pp. 47, 49.

356. Moser (note 7), pp. 231-34; (note 303), p. 49.

357. Moser (note 303), p. 50.

358. Schönherr (note 290), pp. 358-64.

359. See appendix 2:[6], [7]; Innsbruck, TLA, Maximiliana XIV/1505, fol. 169; and Vienna, HHSA, Maximiliana 9b/2, fol. 160, for example.

360. Schönherr (note 290), p. 362.

361. Schönherr note 290), p. 368.

362. Treytzsaurwein is credited with having worked on the following texts, which are preserved in the manuscript collection of the Österreichische Nationalbibliothek in Vienna: Maximilian's Liber memorialis and Gedenkpüechel (MSS. 2900 and 7425.1); three Theuerdank texts (MSS. 2806, 2867, 2889); three Weißkunig texts (MSS. 2892, 3032, 8145.3); two sets of notes relating to the Weißkunig (MSS. 7326, 7425.2); and the Triumphwagen (MS. 8119).

363. Schönherr (note 290), pp. 368-69.

364. The index to the WMR includes references to individuals mentioned in Habsburg chancery documents and to those who served as endorsing agents for these materials. Treytzsaurwein does not appear in the index until 1501; this reference is to the instruction award-ing him landholdings that have reverted to Maximilian through the death of Kessler's widow (Innsbruck, TLA, Geschäft von Hof, 1501/II, fol. 40^V). The index first shows Treytzsaurwein as the endorsing agent of a chancery document in 1504 (Innsbruck, TLA, Maximiliana XIV/1504, fol. 15).

365. Appendix 2:[6], [7], [8], [9], [11].

366. Since both of these documents were written while the Chancery was on the road, it is likely that Maximilian dictated them himself.

367. The texts are too brief to confirm all aspects of Moser's description.

368. See, for example: Innsbruck, TLA, Maximiliana XIV/1504, fol. 15; Innsbruck, TLA, Maximiliana XIV/1505, fol. 169; and Vienna, HHSA, Maximiliana 9b/2, fol. 160.

369. Clemens Biener, "Die Fassungen des Teuerdank," ZDA, 67 (1930), 177-78, 190.

370. Moser (note 7), pp. 134, 139; (note 303), p. 46.

371. Biener (note 369), p. 190. Treytzsaurwein's drafts of the Weißkunig, a prose work that Maximilian actually dictated in the chancery chambers, show even more clearly the scribe's penchant for chancery diction. See Clemens Biener, "Entstehungsgeschichte des Weißkunigs," MIÖG, 44 (1930), 84 ff.

372. Martin Wierschin, "Das Ambraser Heldenbuch Maximi-lians I.," Der Schlern, 50 (1976), 429-44, 493-507, 557-70; and Helmut Weinacht, "Archivalien und Kommentare zu Hans Ried, dem Schreiber des Ambraser Heldenbuches," in Deutsche Heldenepik in Tirol, ed. Egon Kühebacher (Bolzano: Verlagsanstalt Athesia, 1979), pp. 466-89.

373. Wierschin (note 372), p. 499.

374. Weinacht (note 372), p. 483.

375. David Schönherr, "Der Schreiber des Heldenbuchs in der k. k. Ambraser Sammlung," Archiv für Geschichte und Alterthumskunde Tirols, 1 (1864), 105-06.

376. Wierschin (note 372), p. 500; and Hermann Wiesflecker, Jugend, burgundisches Erbe und Römisches Königtum bis zur Alleinherr-schaft, Vol. I of Kaiser Maximilian I. (Vienna: Verlag für Geschichte und Politik, 1971), pp. 73-74.

377. See Weinacht (note 372), pp. 472, 474, 482. This pay-ment seems to have had a contemporary value of about sixteen florins. At this time the lowest salary paid an Imperial advisor was fifty florins and the leaders of the Innsbruck government (e.g., Paul von

Liechtenstain) were earning a thousand florins annually (Kohlweg
[note 251], p. 34). In 1594 a cord of wood sold for nineteen florins
in Vienna. See Dorothy Gies McGuigan, The Habsburgs (Garden City:
Doubleday & Co., 1966), p. 414.

378. The other is the underwriting letter that he penned in
1514 when he resumed his duties as tariff collector on the Adige.
See Weinacht (note 372), pp. 474, 480-81.

379. Wierschin (note 372), p. 500.

380. See Wieland Schmidt, "Florian Waldauf von Waldenstein,"
VL, 4 (1953), col. 769; and Ernst Verdroß-Droßberg, Florian Waldauf
von Waldenstein, Schlern-Schriften, Vol. 184, Innsbruck, 1958.

381. Weinacht (note 372), pp. 473-77.

382. Franz Unterkircher, "Kommentar," Ambraser Heldenbuch,
Codices selecti, Vol. 43, Graz, 1973, p. 6.

383. Weinacht (note 372), p. 477.

384. Unterkircher (note 382), "zu Regest Nr. 6"; and Weinacht
(note 371), p. 478.

385. Weinacht (note 372), pp. 480-81.

386. Weinacht (note 372), pp. 481-82.

387. The index to the WMR includes a number of references to
documents in which Ried is mentioned; these are listed and abstracted
in Weinacht's essay (note 372). The only documents discovered to
date that show Hans Ried as the endorsing agent, however, are the
underwriting letters from 1500 and 1514.

388. The Stiftbrief consists of nineteen large folios.

389. An accurate graphemic analysis of the orthography of the
Heldenbuch would, of course, require an examination of the entire
codex. Because that is beyond the scope of the present investigation,
I have compared the orthographic patterns of these excerpts to
Thornton's (note 104) earlier findings.

390. See Moser (note 7), pp. 94-95; and Tennant (note 8),
pp. 251-52.

391. Moser (note 7), p. 185.

392. In the Stiftbrief Ried frequently writes kh as a final variant of <k>; in Moser's sample this variant only occurs in word- and morpheme-initial position (note 7, p. 181).

393. Unterkircher's (note 382) and Wierschin's (note 372) essays review the surviving documentary evidence relating to the Heldenbuch project and offer thoughtful speculations about the sources of the codex.

394. Franz H. Bäuml, ed., Kudrun: Die Handschrift (Berlin: Walter de Gruyter & Co., 1969), pp. 29-30.

395. See Bäuml (note 394), pp. 71, 130, 133, 148, 157, 179, 268, 293, 305, 336, 355, 395, 446, 482, 519-20. It is important to remember, however, that Ried was a professional penman, renowned for his calligraphic prowess, who regularly wrote both forms of the minuscule r himself. In the Stiftbrief as well as in the Heldenbuch, both occur in fairly free variation. It would be surprising, then, that Ried should have misread a character that was a regular feature of his own script unless one assumes that he copied the Kudrun text during the last two years of his life when his eyesight was failing.

396. See, for example, Ernst Crous and Joachim Kirchner, Die gotischen Schriftarten (Leipzig: Klinkhardt & Biermann, 1928), pp. 15, 41-42; and pls. 3, 7-8, 13-14.

397. Thornton (note 104), pp. 62-82.

398. Kohlweg (note 251), pp. 2-4, 17.

399. Kohlweg (note 251), pp. 27-34, 40, 47-106 passim; and Tennant (note 99), pp. 263-64.

400. Seeliger (note 160), p. 90; Kohlweg (note 251), p. 122; and Tennant (note 99), pp. 263-65.

401. Kohlweg (note 251), pp. 47-129 passim; and Tennant (note 99), pp. 264-67.

402. Tennant (note 99), pp. 266, 272 ff.

403. Heinz Otto Burger, 'Dasein heißt eine Rolle Spielen' (Munich: Carl Hanser Verlag, 1963), p. 24.

404. Tennant (note 99), pp. 272-79.

405. Tennant (note 99), pp. 273-74.

406. For the complete list see Tennant (note 99), pp. 268-69, n. 38.

407. These texts were compared graphemically to the Ziegler holographs: Innsbruck, TLA, Maximiliana XIV/1503, fols. 1-2; Vienna, HHSA, Maximiliana 7b/1, fols. 1, 62-63; Vienna, HHSA, Maximiliana 9a/1, fol. 5; and Vienna, HHSA, Maximiliana 16/2, fol. 147.

408. Tennant (note 130), pp. 75-80, 86-90.

409. For the probable phonetic values of these spellings in specific ENHG orthographies, see Tennant (note 130), pp. 76, 78.

410. Tennant (note 99), pp. 270, 274.

411. Moser (note 303), p. 41.

412. Moser (note 303), pp. 48-49.

413. Fleischer (note 305), p. 9.

414. Tennant (note 99), p. 276, n. 44.

415. See Peter Diederichs, Kaiser Maximilian I. als politischer Publizist, Diss. Heidelberg 1931 (Jena: Eugen Diederichs Verlag, 1932); and Tennant (note 99), p. 275.

416. Tennant (note 99), pp. 266-67. The fact that Ziegler translated directly from the Latin eliminates the possibility that the diction and orthography of the Edict derive from a German model.

417. On Weiße see Fleischer (note 305).

418. Gerhard Kettmann, Die kursächsische Kanzleisprache zwischen 1486 and 1546, Deutsche Akademie der Wissenschaften zu Berlin, Veröffentlichungen des Instituts für deutsche Sprache und Literatur, Series B, Vol. 34, Berlin, 1967.

419. Norbert Richard Wolf, Regionale und überregionale Norm im späten Mittelalter, Innsbrucker Beiträge zur Kulturwissenschaft, Germanistische Reihe, Vol. 3, Innsbruck, 1975, pp. 8, 16-18, 268 ff.

420. Wolf (note 419), pp. 8, 17-18.

421. Moser (note 7), pp. 242-44.

422. Noordijk (note 75), pp. 69-70; and Moser (note 7), p. 244.

423. Moser (note 7), pp. 257-59.

424. Moser (note 7), p. 246; and Wolf (note 419), pp. 56, 58, 165, 175.

425. Moser (note 7), p. 246; and Wolf (note 419), pp. 16, 193-94.

426. Kettmann (note 418), pp. 104-07, 113; and Moser (note 7), p. 247.

427. Moser (note 7), pp. 248-49; Kettmann (note 418), pp. 107-08; and Wolf (note 419), p. 220.

428. Kettmann (note 418), pp. 97-98, 107-08.

429. Moser (note 7), pp. 247, 250; (note 303), pp. 53-54; and Kettmann (note 418), pp. 96, 286.

430. Wolf (note 419), pp. 217-18; Fleischer (note 305), p. 24; and Kettmann (note 418), pp. 78, 101.

431. Fleischer (note 305), p. 27.

432. Moser (note 303), p. 42.

433. Wolf (note 419), pp. 218-19; and Kettmann (note 418), pp. 118-21.

434. Fleischer (note 305), pp. 36-37; and Wolf (note 419), pp. 225-26.

435. Fleischer (note 305), pp. 38, 43, 54. Cf. Wolf (note 419), pp. 225-26, 228-29, 238-39; and Kettmann (note 418), pp. 194, 209, 251.

436. Moser (note 7), pp. 114-16, 260-61; and Kettmann (note 418), p. 204.

437. Moser (note 7), pp. 257-58; and Kettmann (note 418), pp. 198-200, 242. Kettmann's study is not organized graphemically. To compare his data with Moser's I have used Moser's principle of selecting the most frequent variant as the graphemic designation. Thus the dental affricate in the Electoral orthography is <z>, although Kettmann also records the variants cz, t, tz, and zc.

438. Moser (note 7), p. 253; Noordijk (note 75), p. 69; and Kettmann (note 418), p. 85.

439. Noordijk (note 75), p. 75; Moser (note 7), pp. 266-67; Wolf (note 419), p. 228; Fleischer (note 305), p. 44; and Kettmann (note 418), pp. 219-20.

440.   Moser (note 7), pp. 267-68; Wolf (note 419), pp. 217-19, 222-26, 228; and Fleischer (note 305), pp. 44-45.

441.   Moser (note 7), pp. 264-66; and Kettmann (note 418), pp. 181-82.

442.   Moser (note 303), pp. 52-54.

443.   Kettmann (note 418), pp. 78, 101.

444.   Moser (note 7), p. 85; and Kettmann (note 418), p. 286.

445.   Moser (note 303), p. 53.

446.   Ickelsamer, for example, in his discussion of "Caco-graphia" quoted in the introduction to this chapter, objects to the arbitrary addition of certain extra letters to words not requiring them. One such letter is e, and as incorrect forms he cites sieben and viesch. In neither of these forms is the root vowel a reflex of the MHG diphthong /ie/, and the ie-spellings of these words would not have been typical in either the UG or the EMG orthographies of the day. The spellings are, as Ickelsamer indicates, mistakes. In citing them he is drawing attention to the misspelling of a short vowel, but his remarks are apparently isolated perceptions and not part of a consistent system for indicating vocalic length orthographically. In neither of his grammatical treatises does he address the subject of vocalic length as such, nor does he include ie in his catalog of diphthongs. See Tennant (note 130), pp. 74-77.

447.   In this regard consider Fabian Frangk; see Tennant (note 130), pp. 84-85.

448.   Moser (note 303), p. 53.

449.   See Tennant (note 130), pp. 69-70, 75, 78-80, 84-87.

450.   Kettmann (note 418), pp. 118-21.

451.   Moser (note 303), p. 52.

452.   Moser (note 7), p. 261; Kettmann (note 418), pp. 192-98.

453.   Moser (note 7), p. 185; Kettmann (note 418), pp. 133-34, 194, 209, 251.

454.   Moser (note 303), p. 42; Kettmann (note 418), pp. 242-43.

455.   Kettmann (note 418), pp. 219-20, 224-26.

456. Also see Kettmann's comparison of the Electoral chancery language with the southern orthographic tradition (note 418, pp. 289 ff.).

457. Kettmann (note 418), pp. 289-90.

458. Moser (note 7), pp. 262-63, 279

459. See among others Adolf Socin (note 44), pp. 169-71; Werner Besch, "Zur Entstehung der neuhochdeutschen Schriftsprache," ZDP, 87 (1968), 425-26; and Klaus J. Mattheier, "Wege und Umwege zur neuhochdeutschen Schriftsprache," ZGL, 9 (1981), 274-84.

460. Moser (note 303), p. 52.

461. See Mattheier (note 459), p. 280.

CONCLUSION

462. Eggers (note 4), p. 187. Eggers' complete statement is quoted in "'Gemeines Deutsch' in the Handbook Accounts," chapter 1.

463. See Mattheier (note 459), pp. 284 ff., esp. pp. 300-03.

464. Fabian Frangk, for example, recommends Maximilian's chancery language in his Orthographia, but elsewhere in the same treatise speaks against the vocalism that the writing system features. See Tennant (note 130), p. 83.

465. Moser (note 303), p. 45.

466. Moser (note 303), pp. 51-52.

467. See Mattheier (note 459), pp. 292-303.

APPENDIX 2

468. On the practice and theory of vocalic marking in ENHG texts see Tennant (note 130).

469. Bäuml's edition of the Kudrun text from the Ambraser Heldenbuch (note 394) provides a diplomatic transcription of one of the literary texts penned by Hans Ried and detailed description of its paleographic features.

470. See Bäuml (note 394), pp. 29-30, and the discussion in chapter 3 of Hans Ried's scribal usage.

471. Consider, for example, Johann Kolroß' discussion of the letter s in his 1530 Enchiridion. See Müller (note 70), pp. 74-75.

472. This pattern corresponds to the usage Moser identified in his chancery sample. See his detailed analysis of this feature (note 7, pp. 117-22).

473. Bäuml calls this s the final or "schluß" s of the German Kurrentschrift (note 394, p. 30).

474. Consider, for example, two fair copies, one dated 1498 September 20 Innsbruck, the other 1500 August 15 Augsburg, that are preserved in the Allgemeine Urkundenreihe, HHSA, Vienna.

475. Bäuml calls this s the round or "rundes" s (note 394, p. 30).

476. Moser identifies only two of the three minuscule s-graphs; his discussion does not include the short s.

477. "Wir gehen davon aus, daß zwischen breitem und schmalem s-Laut eine phonologische Opposition besteht, die graphemisch nur partiell realisiert wird" (note 7, p. 117).

Selected Bibliography

Adler, Sigmund. Die Organisation der Centralverwaltung unter Kaiser
　　Maximilian I.: Auf urkundlicher Grundlage dargestellt. Leip-
　　zig: Verlag von Duncker & Humblot, 1886.

Ambraser Heldenbuch. Ed. Franz Unterkircher. Codices selecti,
　　Vol. 43. Graz, 1973.

Aschbach, Joseph von. Geschichte der Wiener Universität. Vol. II.
　　Vienna: Wilhelm Braumüller, 1877.

Aventinus, Johannes. Baierische Chronik. Ed. Georg Leidinger.
　　Jena: Eugen Diederichs, 1926.

Bach, Adolf. Geschichte der deutschen Sprache. 9th ed. Heidelberg:
　　Quelle & Meyer, 1970.

Bach, H[einrich]. "Die Entstehung der deutschen Hochsprache im
　　Frühneuhochdeutschen." ZMF, 23 (1955), 193-201.

Bäuml, Franz Henry. Kudrun: Die Handschrift. Berlin: Walter de
　　Gruyter & Co., 1969.

———. "Die Kudrun Handschrift." Diss. University of California
　　at Berkeley, 1957.

Bahder, Karl von. Grundlagen des neuhochdeutschen Lautsystems:
　　Beiträge zur Geschichte der deutschen Schriftsprache im 15.
　　und 16. Jahrhundert. Strassburg: Verlag von Karl J. Trübner,
　　1890.

Bauer, Erika, ed. Heinrich Haller Übersetzungen im "gemeinen Deutsch"
　　(1464). Litterae, Göppinger Beiträge zur Textgeschichte,
　　Vol. 22. Göppingen, 1972.

Bauer, Josef von. "Ladislaus von Suntheim und die Anfänge
     genealogischer Forschung in Österreich." Jahrbuch der k. k.
     heraldischen Gesellschaft "Adler", 14 (1904), 60-83.

Bauer, Wilhelm. "Das Register- und Konzeptwesen in der Reichs-
     kanzlei Maximilians I. bis 1502." MIÖG, 26 (1905), 247-79.

Baxandall, Michael. The Limewood Sculptors of Renaissance Germany.
     New Haven: Yale University Press, 1980.

Bebermeyer, Gustav. "Vom Wesen der frühneuhochdeutschen Sprache
     (1350-1600)." Zeitschrift für Deutschkunde, 43 (1929), 697-
     707.

Behaghel, Otto. Die deutsche Sprache. 14th ed. Halle a. d. Saale:
     Max Niemeyer Verlag, 1968.

_____. "Geschichte der deutschen Sprache." In Grundriß der
     germanischen Philologie. Ed. Hermann Paul. 2nd ed. Vol. I.
     Strassburg: Karl J. Trübner, 1901, pp. 650-780.

_____. Geschichte der deutschen Sprache. 5th ed. Berlin: Walter
     de Gruyter & Co., 1928.

Benzing, Joseph. Buchdruckerlexikon des 16. Jahrhunderts (deutsches
     Sprachgebiet). Frankfurt a. M.: Vittorio Klostermann, 1952.

_____. Der Buchdruck des 16. Jahrhunderts im deutschen Sprach-
     gebiet: Eine Literaturübersicht. Leipzig: Otto Harrassowitz,
     1936.

Bernt, Alois. Die Entstehung unserer Schriftsprache. Vol. XI of
     Vom Mittelalter zur Reformation. Ed. Konrad Burdach. Berlin:
     Weidmannsche Buchhandlung, 1934.

Besch, Werner. "Schriftzeichen und Lautmöglichkeiten der Lautbestim-
     mung an deutschen Handschriften des späten Mittelalters."
     ZDP, 80 (1961), 287-302.

_____. "Zur Entstehung der neuhochdeutschen Schriftsprache."
     ZDP, 87 (1968), 405-26.

Bibliander, Theodor. De ratione communi omnium linguarum & literarū.
     Zurich: Christoph[orus] Frosch[overus], 1548.

Biener, Clemens. "Dialektstudien an den Diktaten zum Weißkunig."
     Teuthonista, 4 (1927-28), 32-43.

Biener, Clemens. "Die Fassungen des Teuerdank." ZDA, 67 (1930),
     177-96.

_____. "Die Schreibgewohnheiten der Kanzlisten Kaiser Maximi-
     lians I." Teuthonista, 5 (1929), 241-60.

_____. "Entstehungsgeschichte des Weißkunigs." MIÖG, 44 (1930),
     83-102.

Bresslau, Harry. Handbuch der Urkundenlehre für Deutschland und
     Italien. 3rd ed. 2 vols. Berlin: Verlag Walter de Gruyter
     & Co., 1958.

Brinkmann, Hennig. "Hochsprache und Mundart." WW, 6 (1955), 65-76.

Burdach, Konrad. Die Einigung der neuhochdeutschen Schriftsprache.
     Leipzig: J. B. Hirschfeld, 1884.

Burger, Heinz Otto. 'Dasein heißt eine Rolle spielen': Studien zur
     deutschen Literaturgeschichte. Munich: Carl Hanser Verlag,
     1963.

Cappelli, Adriano. Dizionario di Abbreviature latine ed italiane.
     6th ed. Milan: Editore Ulrico Hoepli, 1973.

Chambers, W. Walker, and John R. Wilkie. A Short History of the
     German Language. London: Methuen & Co Ltd, 1970.

Chmel, Joseph, ed. Urkunden, Briefe und Actenstücke zur Geschichte
     Maximilians I. und seiner Zeit. Stuttgart: K. Fr. Hering &
     Comp., 1845.

Crous, Ernst, and Joachim Kirchner. Die gotischen Schriftarten.
     Leipzig: Klinkhardt & Biermann, 1928.

Cuspinianus, Joannes. Austria. Basel: Joannes Oporinus, 1553.

Denis, Michael. Wiens Buchdruckergeschichte bis M.D.L.X. Vienna
     Christian Friedrich Wappler, 1782.

Diederichs, Peter. "Kaiser Maximilian I. (1459-1519)." In Deutsche
     Publizisten des 15. bis 20. Jahrhunderts. Ed. Heinz-Dietrich
     Fischer. Munich: Verlag Dokumentation, 1971, pp. 35-42.

_____. Kaiser Maximilian I. als politischer Publizist. Diss.
     Heidelberg 1931. Jena: Eugen Diederichs Verlag, 1932.

Ebert, Robert Peter. "Social and Stylistic Variation in Early New
     High German Word Order: The Sentence Frame ('Satzrahmen')."
     BGDSL, 102 (1980), 357-98.

Eck, Johann. Dedication ("Vorrede"). BJbel: Alt vnd new Testament.
     Ingolstadt: Görg Krapf, 1537.

Egg, Erich, ed. Ausstellung Maximilian I. Innsbruck. Innsbruck:
     Verlagsanstalt Tyrolia, 1969.

_____, and Wolfgang Pfaundler, eds. Kaiser Maximilian I. und Tirol.
     Innsbruck: Verlagsanstalt Tyrolia, 1969.

Eggers, Hans. Das Frühneuhochdeutsche. Vol. III of Deutsche Sprach-
     geschichte. Hamburg: Rowohlt Taschenbuch Verlag, 1969.

Eheim, Friedrich. "Die älteste Topographie von Österreich."
     Jahrbuch für Landeskunde von Niederösterreich, 33 (1957),
     7-25.

_____. "Ladislaus Sunthaym: Ein Historiker aus dem Gelehrtenkreis
     um Maximilian I." MIÖG, 67 (1959), 53-91.

_____. "Ladislaus Sunthaym: Leben und Werk." Diss. Vienna 1949.

Erben, Johannes. "Die sprachgeschichtliche Stellung Luthers." BGDSL
     (Halle), 76 (1955), 166-79.

_____. "Frühneuhochdeutsch." In Sprachgeschichte. Vol. I of
     Kurzer Grundriß der germanischen Philologie. Ed. Ludwig Erich
     Schmitt. Berlin: Walter de Gruyter & Co., 1970, pp. 386-440.

_____. "Luther und die neuhochdeutsche Schriftsprache." In
     Deutsche Wortgeschichte. Ed. Friedrich Maurer and Friedrich
     Stroh. 2nd ed. Vol. I. Berlin: Walter de Gruyter & Co.,
     1959, pp. 439-92.

_____. "Zur Normierung der neuhochdeutschen Schriftsprache." In
     Festschrift für Karl Bischoff. Ed. Günter Bellmann, Günter
     Eifler, and Wolfgang Kleber. Cologne: Böhlau Verlag, 1975,
     pp. 115-29.

Erben, Wilhelm. Die Kaiser- und Königsurkunden des Mittelalters in
     Deutschland, Frankreich und Italien. 1907; rpt. Munich:
     R. Oldenbourg Verlag, 1967.

Falkenstein, Constantin Karl. Geschichte der Buchdruckerkunst in
     ihrer Entstehung und Ausbildung: Ein Denkmal zur vierten
     Säcular-Feier der Erfindung der Typographie. 2nd ed.
     Leipzig: Verlag von B. G. Teubner, 1856.

Feist, Sigmund. _Die deutsche Sprache_. 2nd ed. Munich: Max Hueber
    Verlag, 1933.

Fellner, Thomas. _Die österreichische Zentralverwaltung_. 2 vols.
    Vienna: Adolf Holzhausen, 1907.

Feudel, Günter. "Luthers Ausspruch über seine Sprache (WA Tischreden
    1, 524—Ideal oder Wirklichkeit?" _BGDSL_ (Halle), 92 (1970),
    61-75.

Fichtenau, Heinrich. _Die Lehrbücher Maximilians I. und die Anfänge_
    der Frakturschrift. Hamburg: Maximilian Gesellschaft, 1961.

_____. "Die Schulbücher Maximilians I." _Philobiblon_, 3 (1959),
    2-8.

_____. "Maximilian I. und die Sprache." In _BNGÖst, Festschrift_
    für Adam Wandruszka. Ed. Heinrich Fichtenau and Erich Zöllner.
    Vienna: Hermann Böhlaus Nachf., 1974.

Fleischer, Wolfgang. _Strukturelle Untersuchungen zur Geschichte des_
    Neuhochdeutschen. Sitzungsberichte der Sächsischen Akademie
    der Wissenschaften zu Leipzig. Philologisch-historische
    Klasse, Vol. 112, No. 6. Berlin, 1966.

_____. "Zum Verhältnis von Phonem und Graphem bei der Heraus-
    bildung der neuhochdeutschen Schriftsprache." _WZUJ_, 14 (1965),
    461-65.

Franck, Peter Anton von. _Von dem großen Namenshandzeichen Maximi-_
    lians I. bey Unterzeichnung der Urkunden in teutschen Reichs-
    sachen. [Diss.] Mainz 1786? Mainz: Die Kurfürstl. priv.
    Hof- und Universitätsbuchdruckerey bey Johann Joseph Alef,
    1786.

Frangk, Fabian. _Ein Cañtzley vnd Titel buchlin_. Wittenberg: Nickel
    Schirlentz, 1531.

_____. _Orthographia_. See Johannes Müller.

Franke, Carl. _Satzlehre_. Vol. III of _Grundzüge der Schriftsprache_
    Luthers. 2nd ed. Halle a. d. Saale: Verlag der Buchhandlung
    des Waisenhauses, 1922.

Gass, _____. "Theodor Bibliander (Buchmann)." _ADB_, 2 (1875), 612.

Genzsch, Hans Albrecht. Untersuchungen zur Geschichte der Reichs-
    kanzlei und ihrer Schriftformen in der Zeit Albrechts II. und
    Friedrich III.. Diss. Marburg 1930. Hamburg: Hartung & Co.,
    1930.

Gesner, Conrad. Bibliotheca Vniversalis [. . .]. 4 vols. Zurich:
    Christophorvs Froschovervs, 1545-55.

_____, and Josia Simler. Bibliotheca Institvta et Collecta [. . .].
    2nd ed. of Gesner's Bibliotheca Vniversalis. Zurich: Chris-
    ophorus Froschovervs, 1574.

_____, _____, and Johann Jacob Frisius. Bibliotheca Institvta
    et Collecta [. . .]. 3rd ed. of Gesner's Bibliotheca Vniver-
    salis. Zurich: Christophorvs Froschovervs, 1583.

_____. Mithridates. De differentiis linguarum tum veterum
    quae hodie apud diversas nationes in toto orbo terrarū in usu
    sunt. Zurich: [Christophorus] Froschovervs, 1555.

Gollwitzer, Heinz. "Zur Geschichte der Diplomatie im Zeitalter
    Maximilians I." HJb, 74 (1955), 189-99.

Grimm, Jakob. Deutsche Grammatik. 4 vols. Göttingen: Dieterische
    Buchhandlung, 1819-37.

_____. Geschichte der deutschen Sprache. 4th ed. 1880; rpt.
    Hildesheim: Georg Olms Verlag, 1970.

_____. Vorreden zur Deutschen Grammatik von 1819 und 1822. Ed.
    Hugo Steger. Darmstadt: Wissenschaftliche Buchgesellschaft,
    1968.

Guchmann, M. M. Der Weg zur deutschen Nationalsprache. 2 pts.
    Trans. from the Russian by Günter Feudel. Deutsche Akademie
    der Wissenschaften zu Berlin, Veröffentlichungen des Instituts
    für deutsche Sprache und Literatur, Series B, Vol. 1. Berlin,
    1964-69.

Guden, Karl Friedrich A. Chronologische Tabellen zur Geschichte der
    deutschen Sprache und National-Literatur. Leipzig: Verlag
    von Gerhard Fleischer, 1831.

Gutjahr, Emil A. Die Anfänge der neuhochdeutschen Schriftsprache vor
    Luther. Halle a. d. Saale: Verlag der Buchhandlung des Waisen-
    hauses, 1910.

Gutkas, Karl. Geschichte des Landes Niederösterreich. St. Pölten:
    Niederösterreichisches Pressehaus Druck- und VerlagsgesmbH,
    1974.

Harnack, Otto. Das Kurfürstencollegium bis zur Mitte des vierzehnten
    Jahrhunderts: Nebst kritischem Abdrucke der ältesten Aus-
    fertigung der Goldenen Bulle. Giessen: J. Ricker'sche Buch-
    handlung, 1883.

Heffner, Carl. Die deutschen Kaiser- und Königs-Siegel nebst denen
    der Kaiserinnen, Königinnen und Reichsverweser. Würzburg:
    Verlag der Stahel'schen Buch- und Kunsthandlung, 1875.

Henzen, Walter. Schriftsprache und Mundarten. 2nd ed. Bern:
    Francke Verlag, 1954.

Hirt, Hermann Alfred. Geschichte der deutschen Sprache. Munich:
    C. H. Beck'sche Verlagsbuchhandlung, 1919.

Höflechner, Walter. "Beiträge zur Geschichte der Diplomatie und des
    Gesandtschaftswesen unter Maximilian I. 1490-1500." Diss. Graz
    1967.

Hye, Franz-Heinz. "Die Siegel Maximilians I. von 1486 bis 1519, ihre
    historisch-politische und ihre kanzleigeschichtliche Bedeutung."
    NumZ, 82 (1967), 86-107 and pl. 12.

Ickelsamer, Valentin. Teutsche Grammatica. See Johannes Müller.

Jancar, Ferdinand. "Das Kanzleiwesen unter Maximilian I." Prüfungs-
    arbeit, MS. Institut für österreichische Geschichtsforschung.
    University of Vienna, 1897.

Jellinek, Max Hermann Geschichte der neuhochdeutschen Grammatik von
    den Anfängen bis auf Adelung. 2 vols. Heidelberg: Carl
    Winter's Universitätsbuchhandlung, 1913-14.

Jungandreas, Wolfgang. Geschichte der deutschen Sprache. Vol. II of
    Geschichte der deutschen und der englishen Sprache. Göttingen:
    Vandenhoeck & Ruprecht, 1947.

Jungwirth, Helmut. "Münzen und Medaillen Maximilians I." In
    Ausstellung Maximilian I. Innsbruck. Ed. Erich Egg. Innsbruck:
    Verlagsanstalt Tyrolia, 1969, pp. 65-72.

Keller, R[udolf] E[rnst]. _The German Language_. New Jersey: Humani-
    ties Press Inc., 1978.

Kettmann, Gerhard. "Aufbau und Entwicklung der kursächsischen
    Kanzleisprache in der Lutherzeit." _BGDSL_ (Halle), 89 (1967),
    121-29.

————————. Rev. of _Die Kanzlei Kaiser Maximilians I.: Graphematik
    eines Schreibusus_, by Hans Moser. _DLZ_, 102 (1981), cols. 723-
    25.

————————. _Die kursächsische Kanzleisprache zwischen 1486 und 1546_.
    Deutsche Akademie der Wissenschaften zu Berlin, Veröffent-
    lichungen des Instituts für deutsche Sprache und Literatur,
    Series B, Vol. 34. Berlin, 1967.

Kittel, Erich. _Siegel_. Braunschweig: Klinkhardt & Biermann, 1970.

Klüpfel, Engelbert. _De Vita et Scriptis Conradi Celtis_. Freiburg i.
    Br.: Libraria Wagneriana, 1827.

Kluge, Friedrich. _Deutsche Sprachgeschichte: Werden und Wachsen
    unserer Muttersprache von ihren Anfängen bis zur Gegenwart_.
    Leipzig: Verlag Quelle & Meyer, 1920.

————————. _Von Luther bis Lessing: Aufsätze und Vorträge zur
    Geschichte unserer Schriftsprache_. 5th ed. Leipzig: Verlag
    von Quelle & Meyer, 1918.

————————. _Von Luther bis Lessing: Sprachgeschichtliche Aufsätze_.
    Strassburg: Verlag von Karl J. Trübner, 1888.

Kobolt, Anton Maria, and Benefiziat Gandershofer. _Ergänzungen und
    Berichtungen zum Baierischen Gelehrten-Lexikon_. 2 vols
    Landshut: Verlag bei Franz Seraph Storno, 1795-1824.

Kohlweg, Christa. "Die Brüder Ziegler im Dienste Kaiser Maximilians."
    Diss. Graz 1978.

Kolroß, Johann. _Enchiridion_. See Johannes Müller.

Krantz, Albert. _Saxonia_. Cologne: Iohannes Soter alias Heil ex
    Bentzheim & Socii, 1520.

Kraus, Victor von. "Itinerarium Maximiliani I. 1508-18: Mit
    einleitenden Bemerkungen über das Kanzleiwesen Maximilians I."
    AÖG, 87 (1899), 229-318.

_____. Maximilians I. vertraulicher Briefwechsel mit Sigmund
    Prüschenk Freiherrn zu Stettenberg. Innsbruck: Verlag der
    Wagner'schen Universitaets-Buchhandlung, 1875.

Krendl, Peter. "Über Hosenbandorden, 'Feder' und andere burgundische
    Kleinodien Karls des Kühnen." ZHVSteierm, 72 (1981), 7-26.

Krones, F. X. Umrisse des Geschichtslebens der deutsch-öster-
    reichischen Ländergruppe in seinen staatlichen Grundlagen vom
    X. bis XVI. Jahrhunderte: Ein Versuch. Innsbruck: Verlag der
    Wagner'schen Universitäts-Buchhandlung, 1863.

Laschitzer, Simon, ed. Der Theuerdank: Facsimile-Reproduction nach
    der ersten Auflage vom Jahre 1517. JbKhS, Vol. 8. Vienna,
    1888.

Leder, Klaus. "Nürnbergs Schulwesen an der Wende vom Mittelalter zur
    Neuzeit." In Albrecht Dürers Umwelt. Nuremberg: Selbstverlag
    des Vereins für Geschichte der Stadt Nürnberg, 1971, pp. 29-34.

Luther, Martin. D. Martin Luthers Werke. Kritische Gesamtausgabe:
    Tischreden. Vols. I, V. Weimar: Hermann Böhlaus Nachfolger,
    1912, 1919.

Maaler, Josua. "Praefatio." Die Teütsch spraach. Zurich:
    Christophorus Froschouerus, 1561.

McGuigan, Dorothy Gies. The Habsburgs. Garden City, N.Y.: Double-
    day & Co., 1966.

Martin, Ernst. Rev. of Das Leben des Heiligen Hieronymus in der
    Übersetzung des Bischofs Johannes VIII. von Olmütz, ed. Anton
    Benedict. ADA, 6 (1880), 313-17.

Maschek, Hermann. "Ladislaus Suntheim." VL, 4 (1953), cols. 345-47.

Mattheier, Klaus J. "Wege und Umwege zur neuhochdeutschen Schrift-
    sprache." ZGL, 9 (1981), 274-307.

Maurer, Friedrich. "Bericht über neuere Arbeiten zur Geschichte der
    deutschen Sprache." DU, 3 (1951), 80-87.

Maurer, Friedrich. "Schriftsprache und Mundarten." DU, 8 (1956),
        5-14.

_____. "Zur Frage nach der Entstehung unserer Schriftsprache."
        GRM, 33 (1952), 108-15.

_____. "Zur vor- und frühdeutschen Sprachgeschichte." DU, 3
        (1951), 5-20.

Mayer, Josef. Geschichte von Wiener Neustadt. 3 vols. Wiener
        Neustadt: Selbstverlag des Magistrats Wiener Neustadt, 1924-27.

Mayer, Theodor. Die Verwaltungsorganisationen Maximilians I.: Ihr
        Ursprung und ihre Bedeutung. Forschungen zur inneren
        Geschichte Österreichs, Vol. 14. Innsbruck, 1920.

Meisner, Heinrich Otto. Urkunden- und Aktenlehre der Neuzeit. 2nd
        ed. Leipzig: Koehler & Amelang, 1952.

Merkel, Felix. Das Aufkommen der deutschen Sprache in den
        städtischen Kanzleien des ausgehenden Mittelalters. Leipzig:
        Verlag von B. G. Teubner, 1930.

_____. Die Epochen der deutschen Schriftsprache. Athens:
        Nationale Kapodistrische Universität Athen, Philosophische
        Fakultät, 1939.

Moser, Hans. Die Kanzlei Kaiser Maximilians I.: Graphematik eines
        Schreibusus. Innsbrucker Beiträge zur Kulturwissenschaft,
        Germanistische Reihe, Vol. 5. Innsbruck, 1977.

_____. "Zur Kanzlei Kaiser Maximilians I.: Graphematik eines
        Schreibusus." BGDSL (Halle), 99 (1978), 32-56.

Moser, Hugo. Deutsche Sprachgeschichte. 6th ed. Tübingen: Max
        Niemeyer Verlag, 1969.

_____. "Die Entstehung der neuhochdeutschen Einheitssprache."
        DU, 3 (1951), 58-74.

_____, and Hugo Stopp. Grammatik des Frühneuhochdeutschen.
        Vol. I in 2 pts. Heidelberg: Carl Winter Universitätsverlag,
        1970-73.

Moser, Virgil. Historisch-grammatische Einführung in die frühneuhoch-
        deutschen Schriftdialekte. Halle a. d. Saale: Verlag der
        Buchhandlung des Waisenhauses, 1909.

Müllenhoff, Karl, and Wilhelm Scherer. "Vorrede zur zweiten Ausgabe."
    Denkmäler deutscher Poesie und Prosa. 3rd ed. Berlin:
    Weidmannsche Buchhandlung, 1892.

Müller, Jan-Dirk. Gedechtnus: Literatur und Hofgesellschaft um Maxi-
    milian I.. Forschungen zur Geschichte der älteren deutschen
    Literatur, Vol. 2. Munich, 1982.

Müller, Johannes, ed. Quellenschriften und Geschichte des deutsch-
    sprachlichen Unterrichtes bis zur Mitte des 16. Jahrhunderts.
    Gotha: Verlag von E. F. Thienemann's Hofbuchhandlung, 1882.

Naumann, Hans. Geschichte der deutschen Literatursprachen. Leipzig:
    Verlag von Quelle & Meyer, 1926.

Newald, Richard. "Probleme der neuhochdeutschen Schriftsprache."
    Zeitschrift für deutsche Bildung, 8 (1932), 177-85.

Noordijk, Dirk Gerardus. Untersuchungen auf dem Gebiete der kaiser-
    lichen Kanzleisprache im XV. Jahrhundert. Diss. Amsterdam 1925.
    Gouda: T. van Tilburg, 1925.

Paul, Hermann. "Gemeindeutsch." BGDSL, 12 (1887), 558-60.

Penzl, Herbert. "Althochdeutsch /f/ und die Methoden der Lautbestim-
    mung." ZMF, 31 (1964), 289-317.

_____. Geschichtliche deutsche Lautlehre. Munich: Max Hueber
    Verlag, 1969.

_____. Lautsystem und Lautwandel in den althochdeutschen
    Dialekten. Munich: Max Hueber Verlag, 1971.

Pietsch, Paul. Martin Luther und die hochdeutsche Schriftsprache.
    Breslau: Verlag von Wilhelm Koebner, 1883.

Piirainen, Ilpo Tapani. Graphematische Untersuchungen zum Frühneuhoch-
    deutschen. Studia Linguistica Germanica, Vol. 1. Berlin,
    1968.

_____, ed. Zur Entstehung des Neuhochdeutschen: Sprach-
    geographische und -soziologische Ansätze. Bern and Frankfurt
    a. M.: Herbert Lang and Peter Lang, 1972.

Polenz, Peter von, and Hans Sperber. Geschichte der deutschen
    Sprache. 7th ed. Berlin: Walter de Gruyter & Co., 1970.

Popelka, Fritz. Geschichte der Stadt Graz. 2 vols. Graz: Verlag Styria, 1959-60.

Posse, Otto, ed. Die Siegel der deutschen Kaiser und Könige. 4 vols. Dresden: Verlag von Wilhelm Baensch, 1909-13.

Ranke, Friedrich. "Ulrich von Pottenstein." VL, 3 (1943), cols. 918-23.

Raumer, Rudolf von. Gesammelte sprachwissenschaftliche Schriften. Frankfurt a. M.: Verlag von Heyder & Zimmer, 1863.

_____. Geschichte der germanischen Philologie vorzugsweise in Deutschland. Munich: R. Oldenbourg, 1870.

Reichard, Elias Caspar. Versuch einer Historie der deutschen Sprachkunst. Hamburg: Johann Adolph Martini, 1747.

Reicke, Emil. Lehrer und Unterrichtswesen in der deutschen Vergangenheit. Leipzig: Eugen Diederichs, 1901.

Roberge, Paul T. Rev. of Die Kanzlei Kaiser Maximilians I.: Graphematik eines Schreibusus, by Hans Moser. MGS, 6 (1980), 153-59.

Rückert, Heinrich. Geschichte der neuhochdeutschen Schriftsprache. 2 vols. Leipzig: T. O. Weigel, 1875.

Rupprich, Hans. Das ausgehende Mittelalter, Humanismus und Renaissance 1370-1520. Vol. IV, Pt. 1 of Geschichte der deutschen Literatur. Ed. Helmut de Boor and Richard Newald. Munich: C. H. Beck'sche Verlagsbuchhandlung, 1970.

Santifaller, Leo. "Bericht über die Regesta Imperii." AAWien, 106 (1969), 299-331.

Scherer, Wilhelm. Zur Geschichte der deutschen Sprache. Berlin: Weidmannsche Buchhandlung, 1868.

Schirokauer, Arno. "Der Anteil des Buchdrucks in der Bildung des Gemeindeutschen." DVLG, 25 (1951), 317-50.

_____. "Frühneuhochdeutsch." In Deutsche Philologie im Aufriß. Ed. Wolfgang Stammler. 2nd ed. Vol. I. Berlin: Erich Schmidt Verlag, 1957, cols. 855-930.

_____. "Zur Bedeutung von 'Gemeindeutsch.'" PMLA, 63 (1948), 717-19.

Schmidt, Wieland. "Florian Waldauf von Waldenstein." VL, 4 (1953), cols. 769-73.

Schmidt, Wilhelm, et al. Geschichte der deutschen Sprache. 2nd ed. Berlin: Volk und Wissen Volkseigener Verlag, 1970.

Schmitt, Ludwig Erich. Die deutsche Urkundensprache in der Kanzlei Kaiser Karls IV. (1346-1378). Halle a. d. Saale: Max Niemeyer Verlag, 1936.

————. Zum Stil der Urkundensprache in der Kanzlei Kaiser Karls IV.. Diss. Leipzig 1936. Gräfenhainchen: A. Heine GmbH., 1936.

————. "Zur Entstehung und Erforschung der neuhochdeutschen Schriftsprache." ZMF, 12 (1936), 193-223.

Schönherr, David. "Der Schreiber des Heldenbuchs in der k. k. Ambraser Sammlung." Archiv für Geschichte und Alterthumskunde Tirols, 1 (1864), 100-06.

————. "Über Marx Treytz-Saurwein, Geheimschreiber K. Maximilians I., dessen Heimath und Familie." AÖG, 48 (1872), 355-74.

Schützeichel, Rudolf. "Zur Entstehung der neuhochdeutschen Schriftsprache." Nassauische Annalen, 87 (1967), 75-92.

Schulte, Christel. "Gibt es eine oberdeutsche Form des Frühneuhochdeutschen?" In Zur Entstehung des Neuhochdeutschen. Ed. Ilpo Tapani Piirainen. Bern and Frankfurt a. M.: Herbert Lang and Peter Lang, 1972, pp. 31-56.

Schultz, Alwin, ed. Der Weißkunig nach den Dictaten und eigenhändigen Aufzeichnungen Kaiser Maximilians I. zusammengestellt von Marx Treitzsaurwein von Ehrentreitz. JbKhS, Vol. 6. Vienna, 1888.

Seeliger, Gerhard. "Die älteste Ordnung der deutschen Reichskanzlei. 1494. Oktober 3. Mecheln." ArchZ, 13 (1888), 1-7.

————. "Die Registerführung am deutschen Königshof bis 1493." MIÖG, Ergänzungsband 3 (1890-94), 223-364.

————. Erzkanzler und Reichskanzleien: Ein Beitrag zur Geschichte des deutschen Reiches. Innsbruck: Verlag der Wagner'schen Universitäts-Buchhandlung, 1889.

Seuffert, Burkhard. Drei Register aus den Jahren 1478-1519: Unter-
        suchungen zu Politik, Verwaltung und Recht des Reiches,
        besonderes des deutschen Südostens. Innsbruck: Universitäts-
        Verlag Wagner, 1934.

Seyler, Gustav A. Geschichte der Siegel. Leipzig: Verlag von
        B. Elischer Nachfolger, 1894.

Skála, Emil. Rev. of Die Kanzlei Kaiser Maximilians I.: Graphematik
        eines Schreibusus, by Hans Moser. Germanistik, 19 (1978), 294.

Socin, Adolf. Schriftsprache und Dialekte im Deutschen nach Zeugnis-
        sen alter und neuer Zeit. Heilbronn: Verlag von Gebr.
        Henninger, 1888.

Spilling, Herrad. "Schreibkünste des späten Mittelalters." Codices
        manuscripti, 4 (1978), 97-119.

Spitz, Lewis W. Conrad Celtis: The German Arch-Humanist. Cambridge:
        Harvard University Press, 1957.

Stammler, Wolfgang, and Karl Langosch, eds. Die deutsche Literatur
        des Mittelalters: Verfasserlexikon 5 vols. Berlin:
        Walter de Gruyter & Co., 1933-55.

Steinberg, S. H. "Medieval Writing-Masters." The Library, 4th ser.,
        22 (1941), 1-24.

Straßner, Erich. Graphemsystem und Wortkonstituenz: Schreibsprach-
        liche Entwicklungstendenzen vom Frühneuhochdeutschen zum
        Neuhochdeutschen untersucht an Nürnberger Chroniktexten.
        Hermaea, Germanistische Forschungen, n.s., Vol. 39. Tübingen,
        1977.

_____. Rev. of Die Kanzlei Kaiser Maximilians I.: Graphematik
        eines Schreibusus, by Hans Moser. BGDSL, 102 (1980), 76-79.

Sutter, Berthold. "Die deutschen Herrschermonogramme nach dem Inter-
        regnum: Ein Beitrag zur Diplomatik des Spätmittelalters."
        In Festschrift Julius Franz Schütz. Ed. Berthold Sutter.
        Graz: Hermann Böhlaus Nachfolger, 1954, pp. 246-314.

Tennant, Elaine C. "An Overdue Revision in the History of Early New
        High German: Niclas Ziegler and the Habsburg Chancery
        Language." DVLG, 55 (1981), 248-77.

Tennant, Elaine C. "The Habsburg Chancery Language (1440-1519)."
     Diss. Harvard 1977.

_____ . "'Vom mangel vnd fähl vnsers A be cees/ im Teutschen
     lesen': On the Practice and Theory of Vocalic Marking in
     Early New High German Texts." Codices manuscripti, 7, No. 3
     (1981).

Der Theuerdank. See Simon Laschitzer.

Thompson, James Westfall. The Literacy of the Laity in the Middle
     Ages. University of California Publications in Education,
     Vol. 9. Berkeley, California, 1939.

Thornton, Thomas P. "Die Schreibgewohnheiten Hans Rieds im Ambraser
     Heldenbuch." Diss. Johns Hopkins 1953.

_____ . "Die Schreibgewohnheiten Hans Rieds im Ambraser Helden-
     buch." ZDP, 81 (1962), 52-82.

Tschirch, Fritz. Geschichte der deutschen Sprache. Vol. II. Berlin:
     Erich Schmidt Verlag, 1969.

Ulmann, Heinrich. Kaiser Maximilian I.: Auf urkundlicher Grundlage
     dargestellt. 2 vols. Stuttgart: Verlag der J. G. Cotta'schen
     Buchhandlung, 1884-91.

Unterkircher, Franz. "Kommentar." Ambraser Heldenbuch. Codices
     selecti, Vol. 43. Graz, 1973.

Verdroß-Droßberg, Ernst. Florian Waldauf von Waldenstein. Schlern-
     Schriften, Vol. 184. Innsbruck, 1958.

Die deutsche Literatur des Mittelalters: Verfasserlexikon. See
     Wolfgang Stammler.

Voigt, Georg. Enea Silvio de' Piccolomini, als Papst Pius der Zweite,
     und sein Zeitalter. 3 vols. Berlin: Verlag von Georg Reimer,
     1856-63.

Volz, Hans. Vom Spätmittelhochdeutschen zum Frühneuhochdeutschen.
     Tübingen: Max Niemeyer Verlag, 1963.

Waas, Glenn Elwood. The Legendary Character of Kaiser Maximilian.
     New York: Columbia University Press, 1941.

Waterman, John T. A History of the German Language. Seattle:
     University of Washington Press, 1966.

Wehmer, Carl. "Die Schreibmeisterblätter des späten Mittelalters."
In Miscellanea Giovanni Mercati, Vol. VI, Studi e Testi 126.
Vatican City, 1946, pp. 147-61.

_____. "Schreibmeister von einst." Archiv für Buchgewerbe und
Gebrauchsgraphik, 76 (1939), 37-58.

Weinacht, Helmut. "Archivalien und Kommentare zu Hans Ried, dem
Schreiber des Ambraser Heldenbuches." In Deutsche Heldenepik
in Tirol. Ed. Egon Kühebacher. Bolzano: Verlagsanstalt
Athesia, 1979, pp. 466-89.

Der Weißkunig. See Alwin Schultz.

Werbow, Stanley N. "Die gemeine Teutsch." ZDP, 82 (1963), 44-63.

Wiedemann, Theodor. Dr. Johann Eck, Professor der Theologie an der
Universität Ingolstadt: Eine Monographie. Regensburg: Verlag
von Friedrich Pustet, 1865.

Wierschin, Martin. "Das Ambraser Heldenbuch Maximilians I." Der
Schlern, 50 (1976), 429-44, 493-507, 557-70.

Wiesflecker, Hermann. Kaiser Maximilian I.: Das Reich, Österreich
und Europa an der Wende zur Neuzeit. Vols. I, II. Vienna:
Verlag für Geschichte und Politik, 1971, 1975.

Wolf, Norbert Richard. Regionale und überregionale Norm im späten
Mittelalter: Graphematische und lexicalische Untersuchungen
zu deutschen und niederländischen Schriftdialekten. Innsbrucker Beiträge zur Kulturwissenschaft, Germanistische Reihe,
Vol. 3. Innsbruck, 1975.

Wülcker, Ernst. "Die Entstehung der kursächsischen Kanzleisprache."
ZVThürG, n.s., 1 (1879), 349-76.

_____. "Lauteigentümlichkeiten des Frankfurter Stadtdialects im
Mittelalter." BGDSL, 4 (1877), 1-47.

_____. "Luthers Stellung zur kursächsischen Kanzleisprache."
Germania, 28 (1883), 191-214.

Index of Names